WITH
BRENDAN
BEHAN

WITH BRENDAN BEHAN

PETER ARTHURS

ST. MARTIN'S PRESS,
NEW YORK

LIBRARY OF CONGRESS CATALOGING IN PUBLICATION DATA

ARTHURS, PETER.
  WITH BRENDAN BEHAN.

  1. BEHAN, BRENDAN—BIOGRAPHY.   2. AUTHORS, IRISH—
20TH CENTURY—BIOGRAPHY.   I. TITLE.
PR6003.E417z56   822'.914   80-28070
ISBN 0-312-88471-0

DESIGN BY MANUELA PAUL
10 9 8 7 6 5 4 3 2 1

FIRST EDITION

This book is primarily dedicated to my friend, mentor, early-morning and late-night listener and wherewithal provider Arthur C. Clarke.

It is also dedicated to my writing godfathers, Norman Mailer, Arthur Miller, and Charles Jackson, and my patient, understanding and sharp-eyed editor, Michael Denneny.

To Paul Hall, the late president of the Seafarers' International Union, Frank Drozak, the current leader of the SIU, James Gannon, *SIU Log* editor, and to all of the gallant men of the SIU who carve their living by serving aboard the back-bending ships that go down to the sea.

To the subjects of loneliness, madness, and alcoholism, and the persistence of dedicated penmen throughout this mad world that we coexist in. With great humility I thank you one and all.

Without your camaraderie, inspiration, encouragement and the lonely solitude which you prevailed upon me, this book could not exist.

I also wish to thank my tireless typist Brenda Repland.

He who knows nothing, loves nothing. He who can do nothing understands nothing. He who understands nothing is worthless. But he who understands also loves, notices, sees. . . . The more knowledge is inherent in a thing the greater the love. . . . Anyone who imagines that all fruits ripen at the same time as the strawberries knows nothing about grapes.

PARACELSUS

Foreword
by.
Arthur C. Clarke

Before we get any further, I had better admit that I never met Brendan Behan in my life, though I still don't understand how I managed to miss him. To make matters worse, my image of him is irrevocably colored by Peter Sellers' "In a Free State" (recorded on EMI PMC 1111, 1959). In this brilliant parody—at least, I *thought* it was a parody before I read this book—the temperamental Irish playwright Brendan Behan eventually strangles his hapless BBC interviewer when he discovers that the studio carafe contains (ugh) water. ("What's this filthy stuff doing here? A man could die o' thirst. . .")

So what am *I* doing here? It's a long story and begins in the mid-1950s, when I first discovered the Hotel Chelsea and its unique fauna. For almost a quarter of a century, the Chelsea was my second home—the base from which I ventured out on lecture tours, flew to Cape Canaveral for moons shots, and even managed to do some work, despite the surrounding distractions. Thus the novel *2001: A Space Odyssey* was written—several times—up on the tenth floor.

One of the many reasons I felt at home in the Chelsea was its totally democratic, easygoing atmosphere; about the only house rule was "Bring out your own dead." As a natural born slob who hates ties even more than socks (I must be the only person ever to attend an IBM banquet wearing a sarong—which I hasten to add in purely *male* attire here in Sri Lanka), I was happy to wander round the lobby and echoing stairway in whatever I grabbed first from the clothes closet. At least that is my recollection; but another resident suggests that my wardrobe must have contained a few conventional items:

> The Chelsea, a seedy, run-down, part residential, part transient, past-its-prime hotel, has long been a home for notorious writers like Thomas Wolfe, Brendan Behan, Dylan Thomas and Clifford Irving. More recently it has become a mecca for way-out British rock-and-roll groups "on the road" in the United States. But though Clarke loved the free and easy atmosphere of the Chelsea, he couldn't quite go along with it all the way. He continued to rise at 7 A.M., don his customary English suit, vest and tie, and, with attaché case in hand, venture into the totally deserted corridors and elevators still pervaded with the stale marijuana smoke of the up-till-dawn Chelsea clientele.

Thus Dr. Jerry Grey, in his lively book about the space shuttle *(Enterprise,* William Morrow, 1979). He must have caught me on my way to the CBS-TV studios, or on my first (but not second) day at the Time-Life Books division. In any event, Jerry's independent assessment of the Chelsea's ambience will prove that I am not exaggerating.

Looking back on those years, it seems to me that most of the friends and acquaintances I made in the United States were first encountered at the Chelsea. Amongst them was an Irish seaman and ex-boxer named Peter Arthurs, who disappeared from time to time into gigantic oil tankers and then emerged, in a crippled condition, to sue the owners for negligence. When he was not hobbling between the Seaman's Union, his lawyer, and the hotel, Peter had plenty of time for conversations and socializing, so it was inevitable that we should meet sooner or later in the lobby or the immediately adjacent bar. And it is typical of the stimulating way in which the Chelsea's social and professional crosscurrents mix people of entirely different interests and walks of life that it was through Peter—and not the other way around—that I got to meet such writers as Arthur Miller, Charles *(Lost Weekend)* Jackson and Norman Mailer. They were already friends of his.

Like most Irishmen, drunk, sober, or half-and-half, Peter was a good talker and was full of stories about his old buddy Brendan. When, by the mid-1960s, I'd heard these for the seventh or eighth time, I finally said in exasperation: "Why don't you write them down?" It was obvious that Peter had a great deal of unique information about Brendan, which might be of interest to a wide public. I also thought (and hoped) that the discipline of writing would a) keep Peter away from the gargle (q.v.) and b) provide the psychotherapy which, as we sane, well-balanced English are much too polite to mention, all refugees from Erin badly need to overcome environmental handicaps.

After a lot of prodding, and sundry emotional and financial crises, Peter bought a stack of paper and started to write down everything he remembered about Brendan. When he could no longer afford to live at

the Chelsea, he holed up in a downtown loft, where his manuscript was
in permanent danger of being eaten by cockroaches. (Peter ran no
small risk himself, if they ever caught him when he couldn't fight
back.) I met him whenever I was in town, made sure that he had at
least one good meal at El Quijote or the Angry Squire, and provided
any other assistance that seemed necessary. This was not always easy to
decide; it is fatal to throw too many life belts to struggling writers.

When, to my pleased surprise, Peter had produced some hundred
thousand words of reminiscences, I sent him to meet Jack Scovil, vice
president of the Scott Meredith Agency, which has represented me for
(good heavens!) more than thirty years. Although Norman Mailer,
Arthur Miller and I all played roles as midwives—or godfathers—of this
book, Jack deserves the credit for finding the brawling infant a home.

Now, having just completed my first reading of the whole manuscript only a few hours ago, I am still slightly punch-drunk. My sense
of syntax is partly paralyzed, and it will take me some time to unscram-
ble my vocabulary. I don't envy Peter's editors (there *must* be more
than one—no single person could stay the course) but I sincerely hope
that there will be the minimum of tampering with the original text.
Much of it reminds me of James Joyce—except that Peter's meaning is
always perfectly clear, however unorthodox his use of words.

I congratulate him on performing an extraordinary feat of literary
reincarnation. His book, unlike many in the marketplace today, deliv-
ers exactly what its title promises. When you turn these pages you will
be, whether you like it or not, With Brendan Behan.

Columbo, Sri Lanka
June 7, 1980

I awoke and put my bare feet down onto the cold damp floor. Forks of bitter cold skittered up my legs and rattled my lower intestines. I got out of bed, walked to the window, and took a deep breath. I felt hopelessly confused.

For seven or eight days I had slept the sleep of the just, intermittently waking up to urinate into a makeshift commode and sip water from a porcelain jug that I had placed on the dresser at the head of my bed before falling off to sleep several days previously.

Before my last tumble into bed I had raised the window to allow a smidgen of air to permeate the small room. In my haste and sweaty confusion, I had raised the window a great deal higher than I had intended. This much, at least, was clear to me. New York was undergoing one of its worst snowstorms in several decades. Layers of the crispy white stuff were piled up on the floor, inside the window frame, and on the furnishings. The air inside the room was raw and biting.

The time, according to my electric clock, was five forty-five. The appearance of the room's semidark interior and the quietude of the street told me that the time was in the A.M. On Union Street a few hurrying footsteps shattered the cold grey dawn. Neighbors were making their way to work and into the jaws of the workaday city.

The month of the year was March. The year was 1961. Brooklyn never seemed so eerie, so lonely. New York City was suddenly the worst place in the universe to fall sick in. I was suffering from bronchial pneumonia, dehydration, a broken nose, and malnutrition. My eyes

1

still smarted from the acid burns they had endured a few months previously aboard Albatross Tanker Corporation's S.T. *Erna Elizabeth.*

I made my way down the dimly lit hall, staggered into the bathroom, stared into the mirror, and gasped at my reflection. I had lost twenty-five or thirty pounds. I hadn't eaten in almost two weeks. My face was swollen out of proportion. My eyes were black and blue and pencil thin.

Questions rattled my brain. Just exactly how sick was I? Would I recover? Should I make a run to the hospital? Would I succeed in making it and if so, was there a guarantee that the doctors would take me in, considering the name-calling circumstances in which I'd left?

I hurried from the bathroom, down the stairs and onto Seventh Avenue, thinking that a good bellyful of grub and a potful of tea would restore me. The very thought revived me. I banged on the door of Gay's Delicatessen. No one answered. Rivulets of sweat dripped down my face. Suddenly it dawned upon me that the store was closed. The streets were comparatively barren save for the mounds of snow that lay against the facades of stores and the wheels and fenders of barely visible automobiles. I shook like a leaf.

Looking down at my underwear-clad body, I realized that in my confusion I had charged down the street seminaked. A thin layer of ice coagulated on my arms, legs, and chest. Icicles hung from my nose. In the distance, a police patrol car approached on Seventh Avenue. I darted back to my rooming house, mounted the steps, fidgeted with a set of keys and a keyhole and charged back into my sweat-saturated bed. Soon I was asleep.

Three days later, Duke, a friend, a former shipmate, and a current employee of New York City, woke me up.

"Listen sweetheart," my well-informed friend said, "yur landsman is in fucked-up shape in the Norwegian Hospital. You pinned a broken jaw on him, not to mention the fact that he's missing half a row of front teeth, top and bottom. Furthermore, he's eatin' his meals through a straw that's inserted between some wiring in his jaw . . . pretty tough when yur suffering from a clatter of broken ribs."

"But who gives a rat's cunt," I retorted. "It was he who started it. I was merely drinking my beer, the next thing I knew, I was down on my knees drinking out of the toilet, not to mention all the other injuries and embarrassments I was forced to endure—"

My protestations were sharply interrupted.

"Listen, Irish—you know I luv you, yur a real sweetheart of a kid— not necessarily the smartest kid on Union Street, nevertheless, a smart kid, a nice boy. But let's face it, you fucked up, you stepped on yur own cock. You came back to the joint all dolled up in a load of fancy rags and a big fuckin' mouthpiece in yur mouth. To make matters worse you had to go and fuck up the entire enchilada by making a big speech about anyone who steps in will get the same treatment, et cetera . . . Yur countryman is in the hospital, yur not . . . Yur out here enjoying life, drinking and balling the broads, he's sucking corn beef and cabbage through a straw . . . So looka here, kiddo," Duke went on with great concern, "why don't you jump down to yur union hall and ship out for a while until the heat is off. I hear the weather in India is gorgeous. If you don't blow the neighborhood for awhile, it's *your* pussy. It's only a matter of time before the fuzz gets wise to yur hangout, then it's a year in the slam guaranteed, sweetheart, you know I luv you, no shit Irish, no shit. Drop me a postcard . . ."

My mentor slammed the door behind him.

The following day, I phoned Thomas Gordon, my attorney.

"Listen Tom, I just got some bad news, a friend who lives out of town just phoned. Apparently he's in bad shape, cancer or leukemia or something. I didn't feel like getting too personal or nosey over the phone, just promised I'd come as soon as possible. I was just wondering how much do you reckon we can get for my eye case against Albatross at this point?"

An exasperated sigh and the sounds of a creaking armchair came over the wire.

"Listen Pete, when we signed we went for a quarter of a million bucks. The papers are still here on my desk. But that was only a few weeks ago. If I get them on the blower at this point in time, we're lucky if we're offered a bag of peanuts. Forget it. Ship out, let it stew for awhile, you got nothing to worry about, you're single and a good-looking stud. Call me in a year or two and like I said, don't get your balls in an uproar, the calendar is not too overly jammed. Have a nice trip."

The phone went dead. I called back immediately.

"Listen Tom, give it all the charm you've got. Go for at least ten big ones, but for fucksake go. My friend is getting sicker by the hour, might even die. Good luck."

I slammed down the receiver and dashed up the steps of my temporary home. A big furry Alaskan cap kept my face warm while shielding my identity from the Park Slope police, who were still fidgeting with the warrant for my arrest.

For thirteen years I had been a merchant seaman. I served aboard ships of eight different flags in all shipboard departments. In December 1960, while hand-hosing a cargo tank on the S.T. *Erna Elizabeth,* my eyes were doused with acid. When the vessel docked on January 6, 1961, the specialists at the Marine Hospital on Staten Island examined me and declared me "not fit for sea duty." They gave me a jar of medicated salve with strict instructions (which I ignored) to apply it generously to my eyes three times a day.

During my weeks of convalescence I did what I usually did when idle and anxious, and went to a local boxing gym and sparred with those who appreciated my services. The Trinity Boxing Club in Brooklyn was my favorite gym. Twice a week I boxed three three-minute rounds with a black power puncher named Jimmy Dupree, who later went on to lay claim to the world's light heavyweight title. The understanding between Dupree, his manager, and me was that he would go easy. I was merely an overstuffed middleweight and a guy fighting for the love of the sport while doing Dupree a favor.

One day along about the middle of February, halfway through the second round, as I was reaching down hard into my lungs for a smidgen of air, coming off the ropes with my left hand down at my side, Dupree cut the ring by sending over a solid straight right hand. My nose absorbed the brunt of the blow. Seconds later, Ricky Fizano, a fight promoter who worked at the Trinity, peeled me off the rosin-splattered canvas. Downstairs in the dressing room I looked painfully hard in a dirt-encrusted mirror. My nose was as flat and almost as wide as my face. No discernible signs of bone or gristle were in evidence. The left and right sides of my nose were pushed up under my well-blackened eyes. My eyes were gradually closing. Water seeped from them and ran down my cheeks.

"Hey man . . . looka here baby, but gee I didn't mean to nail you," a voice was saying while a hand patted me on the shoulder. "I'm sorry but like I didn't expect you to come off those ropes so fast. I was only figuring on feigning the punch."

"Ah, that's okay, Jimmy baby," I muttered into the mirror, "it'll teach me a lesson not to go jerking off in the dressing room prior to doing a work-out with you. Forget it man, next time, shit."

I subwayed home to Park Slope, and applied sockfuls of ice to my busted beak and puffy face.

The following Saturday night, on my way home from a dance at the Danish Athletic Club, I stopped off at Quigley's Bar and Grill on Seventh Avenue and hoisted a final few for the night. Along about 2:30 A.M., a horde of West Coast of Ireland-born sandhogs swarmed into the rustic tavern and became excessively boisterous. Now well into my cups, I advised one of the hogs, the leader of the coterie, that I intended to finish up my imbibing in peace and quietude. Suddenly I found myself in an embarrassing situation. My head was jammed into a porcelain bowl in the rear of the pub. Fists and feet hammered the nape of my neck and back of my head. I blacked out.

Later I came to, lying face up on the filth-strewn floor. A big beefy face hovered above me, and in a typical County Galway accent a voice was calling me a faggot and daring me to "get up like a man and take your medicine."

A hot stinging pain suffused the right side of my back. My rib cage was crushed. Then the memory of my last waking moments came back to me. I was in a kneeling position in the smelly lavatory. My face was in the mucilaginous bowl and in the process of being forced down into the sewer. Frightened, I swallowed hard and wished that I had chosen to choke instead. A huge hand took hold of my back and lifted me into the air. I recalled swinging like a pendulum, experiencing the greatest pain that I had ever experienced, and blacking out. Now the largest human hand that I had ever seen was swaying to and fro in front of my shit- and piss-caked face, and defying me to "stand up."

"Get up get up you dirty blaggard you," my landsman bellowed. "Get up and take what's coming to you." With my thumbs I scraped the waste from my eyes and cautiously got to my feet. My vision started to return. Next, I saw a huge hamlike paw winging towards my face. I ducked, moved half a step to the right, allowed the fist to go over my head, and with all of my speed and limited boxing savvy, I bounced a left hook off the protruding jaw of the hog. The three-hundred-pound white orangutang pitched to the floor, face first. I sighed and fled from the pub, my nose, teeth, and face almost intact.

Minutes later I found myself standing naked in front of my bath-room mirror taking inventory of my accumulation of black and blue welts, contusions and abrasions. A perfect impression of a huge hand was etched in my lower back. My penis was enlarged, my testicles were swollen, one of them was hanging way down. I felt lopsided.

A short while later, wearing my Ace elastic handwraps, mouthpiece, aluminum athletic supporter, and boxing shoes, my face heavily smeared with Vaseline, I was back in the pub finishing up some pre-viously unfinished business. I left the hog draped across an old hissing radiator and went home.

Approximately two hours later, just as the dawn was stealing in through the windows of my room, I looked out and saw a swarm of police patrol cars parked on either side of the street. A clog of irritated-looking officers were yawning, making derogatory remarks about me and my homeland and kicking at the fenders of their radio cars while their eyes scanned the length and breadth of Union Street.

"Yeah, I think I know the guy," a short pugnacious-looking officer shouted, "he's a big chunky guy with a boozer's face." The officer was swinging and twirling his nightstick and slapping it against the leg of his pants each time that the twirl came to a stop. I dressed quickly, dropped into the backyard of the house by way of a rear window, vaulted a wall, and spent the remainder of the night with a friend who lived on South Elliot Place.

Two weeks later I retained Thomas Gordon as my attorney, and brought suit for a quarter of a million dollars against Albatross Tanker Corporation for injuries to my eyes, then checked into the Marine Hospital on Staten Island and underwent surgery to correct the broken nose I'd gotten in the fight with Dupree. Postsurgical complications set in and I discharged myself from the medical facility. My trek from Staten Island to Brooklyn consisted of a bus ride, a boat ride, two subway rides and several collapses onto the snow-blanketed streets. Finally I arrived home and fell into bed.

During my hospitalization, a John Doe warrant for my arrest had been issued by the local fuzz factory. The bulk of the patrons of Quigley's—friends and admirers of the sandhog—had given the police a substantially adequate description of me. The hog was hospitalized at the nearby Lutheran Medical Facility. His complaints: concussion and a broken jaw. Also, he was demanding my arrest and was in the process of filing charges for aggravated assault and battery. Any illusions that I harbored about the Irish having a sense of humor were suddenly dispelled. I arrived at the irrevocable conclusion that a quick change of scenery would do me no harm.

A few days later, I subwayed down to Fulton Street, signed a release form and picked up a check for five hundred dollars from Albatross. The following day, with the residue of pneumonia still in my lungs and the detritus of winter still on the ground, I boarded a turboprop and flew to sunny southern California.

II

I arrived at Los Angeles International Airport and jitneyed down to Wilmington town, a small seaport in the heart of Los Angeles's vast waterway. I checked into the Don Hotel on Avalon Boulevard, then registered at the local dispatch hall of the Seafarers International Union (SIU). I registered in the deck department, in group two, the slot reserved on the rotary hiring board for able-bodied seamen. Jobs of the day are called every hour on the hour. My preference of run and type of ship was aboard a Waterman C-2 cargo vessel running to the Far East: Japan, Korea, China, Formosa, the Philippines and Hawaii. During my seafaring career, I had made that run on a number of occasions.

For the next couple of days, I hung around the hall and reoriented myself with the "West Coast stiffs." I made inquiries regarding shipping and much to my chagrin discovered that shipping was slower than slow. It was at a standstill. In the port of Wilmington, nothing was moving, not even the wind. Since there was no purpose to be served in hanging about there, I decided to take a respite and bus it to Hollywood where I would hopefully find some temporary work and rub elbows with the stars—one in particular, Kim Novak.

I checked into the Hollywood Wilcox Hotel.

Prior to my departure from New York, Phillip Auditore, a Brooklyn resident who in 1951 had signed an affidavit of support and sponsored me to live as a permanent resident of the United States, gave me a letter of introduction to a television writer named David Greggory. Greggory lived in a uniquely designed house which clung to a very precipitous hill overlooking West Hollywood.

At a party in Greggory's house I was introduced to Ron Nyman, an actor, who informed me that he was interested in selling his old Buick sedan. Figures were bandied about and a bargain was reached. I became the owner of a dilapidated powder-blue Buick. Its cost to me—seventy-five dollars. The car was substantially utilizable, save for the fact that there was little or no tread on the front tires and the car's battery was in dire need of being replaced. I was not in possession of a viable driver's license. However I did possess an impressive-looking but outdated British license. For the next two or three days I drove around and familiarized myself with the layout of the town.

At the employment agencies I discovered that jobs—even of a menial nature—were few and far between. I grew lonely and bored. I missed the camaraderie of my seafaring buddies.

Being a lifelong exponent of physical fitness, I went to the local branch of the YMCA, took out a quarterly membership and began a daily routine which consisted of rope jumping, bag punching, calisthenics, and light sparring sessions.

In a few weeks, much of the weight that I had left behind in New York was replaced. I also developed a daily outdoor roadwork routine, bundling up in my heaviest cottons and running two or three miles a day in Wilshire Park and along the famous boulevards.

One Saturday morning, having finished up my routine exercise program, I decided to risk a dip in the chlorinated swimming pool on the ground level. The fabric of my eyes and nose were still tender and vulnerable from the run-ins with the acid and the surgeon's scalpel. Caution was not a thing to be thrown to the wind, but I was eager and anxious. The afternoon was going well. I swam several lengths of the Olympic-sized pool. A welcome sense of relaxation was slowly seeping into my bones, my psyche. It was a sense of healing.

I labored hard at keeping my head above the chemicalized depths, and suffered only a small amount of irritation.

Suddenly it dawned upon me that my aquatic workout was not as propitious an experience as I had thought. A small, roly-poly figure of a man with a battered face and a twisted nose was enjoying himself immensely by diving from the pool's perimeter. On several occasions he landed on my back. I moved to a corner of the pool and draped my arms over the walls of its hip-deep end, then watched in silence.

I observed the rowdy little figure as he scrambled up out of the water and took a standing position on the tiled perimeter of the pool's deep end. He made a series of attention-compelling hand and head gesticulations. Once this was accomplished he blessed a half-submerged cadre of laughing idolators with *In nomine Patri* and sprinkled their heads with improvised holy water that he scooped up from the pool. Then, cupping his genitalia with one hand and pinching his nose with the thumb and index finger of the other, he shouted, in a Dublin accent, "Ah, Oscar, but yew had it both ways," and "Here goes sweet fuck all," dropping his swimming trunks to his ankles. A raucous burst of applause went up from the spectators. I deduced that he was referring to Oscar Wilde. I went back to my swim.

A few minutes later, the fat face with its mop of thick, black glistening hair once again appeared at my end of the pool, at my side. Just as I was about to make my turn to swim back down to the deep end, the rotund figure made a quick splashing motion that prevented me from making my turn. An endless geyser of water from the small mouth shot upwards and splattered my face, shoulders and chest. The mouth itself remained approximately one inch below the water's surface. A fiendish little grin followed. I decided to let the man have it, but just as I finished sucking in my guts in preparation for an assault, the prankish little man swam away as though he were a minnow suddenly endangered.

No excuse-me's or apologies were offered. I reached the other end, tense with annoyance. I saw he was coming my way again. Disgusted, I vacated the pool and repaired to the adjacent sauna room. I found an empty seat and sat for a time, angry and sweating. I picked up a bucket, filled it full of water and splattered a tubful of stones in the corner. A roar of steam spiraled upward, fogging the room. I hurried back to my seat in an arsewise motion. My buttocks banged into what felt like a face. In the thick steam, I found myself sitting in someone's lap. I jumped to my feet with a stream of hurried apologies. They were quickly curtailed when my bleary eyes came in focus. I saw the face of the man who had been splattering water all over me in the pool. The brattish-looking elf with the rotund figure and the Mickey Mouse grin was squatting imperiously on my stool, undaunted and picking his nose.

I decided I'd had it. Before I could unleash a single word, the runt was up and darting out of the room. Disgruntled, I trotted out to the shower room in the hopes of taking a fast shower and making a speedy departure. I soaked my head, face and body in the downpour of water, then hastily lathered my torso. I backed away from the downpour and continued to lather, then again I backed into the cascadence only to discover that I was standing on someone's toes!

Turning, I discovered that the man who had fucked up my workout was again back on the job, bollixing up the remainder of my planned relaxation. The familiar popeye grin was intact. I looked around the empty shower room, then turned and glared at the blubbery figure. "What the fuck do you want from me?" I sputtered as I reached for my towel. My efforts were in vain. The runt had swiftly departed, leaving me perturbed. I made a beeline to the locker room and put on my shoes and socks.

While I was combing my hair in an oblong-shaped mirror, I caught the reflection of the dumpy little character.

He was dressed in a navy blue silk mohair suit. He moved around the room, shuffling, talking, peering around locker corners, and acting like a man in hot pursuit of something out of his immediate reach. I became curious and went back to combing my hair, keeping a scrutinizing set of eyes on him.

In a matter of seconds, the little man with the big mouth was talking to an exceptionally well-built young man. The naked youth, looking puzzled, listened to the fast-gushing monologues of the fatso who was now talking sixteen to the dozen. The youth continued to towel off his damp torso. My curiosity intensified. I moved closer, making my way across several rows of wooden benches. Suddenly the diminutive Irishman let loose with a string of invectives, savagely denigrating the contemporary youths of Ireland.

"The f-fucking, d-dirty rotten pack of c-culshies and s-savages that they are. They think bejayzus that they can come here and to every other country in the world and get everything for nothing as if the fuckin' world owed them a living. Shur the ignorant half of them wouldn't know the difference between rheumatism and communism."

The little man then turned and I saw him watching my reflection in the mirror. Quickly, he switched his verbal assault to another subject.

"I mean to say, I realize that poor aul Jack Paar is a great skin and shur I'm aware that like the rest of us he has to make his bit of a living, but that's neither here nor there. I c-can't change me way of livin' just to be on his fuckin' aul tuppenny talk show for jayzus sake. Isn't it him who sends the telegrams? Here, shur haven't I got one here in my hand at the moment?"

He put his hand into his pocket and extricated a piece of paper. "Shur isn't he always begging me to come on his talk show and talk about this and talk about that, but at the same time scared half out of his ballox that I'll cum up with something that will scare the cunt out of the midnight Yanks out in East jayzus Sascatchacunt or Sascatchawank or whatever they call the fuckin' kip. But let him take his chances like the rest of us. If he gets his balls cut off the air so fuckin' well be it! Up the Republic and fuck the begrudgers."

Curious, I moved a bit closer.

"My attitude in life," the man continued, "is this. If it's in yew to go out and take yur chances, cum what may, yew'll do so, but for jayzus sake worry about the cuntin' consequences later, but—"

"Excuse me, sir," I cut through his monologue, tugging on the sleeve of his sweat-drenched jacket, "I have reason to believe that we are landsmen."

The tiny figure half turned and looked down at my hand on his sleeve. A look of apparent disgust crept into his face.

"Jayzus crucified fuckin' Christ, but yew meet the bastards everywhere, don't yew?" he said as he again turned his attention to the youth. His smirk broadened with delight. His pint-sized pugnacity caught me totally off guard. "Bastards" I took to mean our landsmen.

The Irish. The hell with it. I decided to do a quick return to my locker and finish up my dressing.

"Excuse me, sir," I said, tightening my grip on the man's sleeve, "but before I depart I want you to know that I am in firm agreement with you on your remark about the 'bastards.' Yes, siree," I said, "the bastards seem to be everywhere, don't they? Glad you agree. They're like incest and lice, the unfortunate world seems to be infested with them."

Then turning to make my way back to my locker, I had a hunch that I should be familiar with the identity of the man I was trying hard to insult. Suddenly, I felt guilty as I realized who the little character was. Here I am, I said to myself, standing in the presence of a world-respected Irish man of letters, and I am balls-arse naked and belligerent. Quickly my forearm shot down between my legs.

"Excuse me," I said, "but aren't you Brendan Behan, the Dublin drunk who is usually in trouble with the law?"

He heaved a sigh of exasperated annoyance. A short period of eerie silence elapsed.

"So *don't* answer," I sputtered, "who the fuck gives a good shite!"

I climbed up onto one of the wooden benches. "What the fuck would you expect from a Dublin jackeen anyway?" I barked.

"Well now, I'll fuckinwell tell yew this much avick and I'll tell yew no more," a voice said sharply, momentarily halting my flight. "I've been paying Behan's bills, combing his hair, brushing his teeth, polishing his shoes and juggling his balls and his taxes for the past thirty-eight years. Now yew seem like a moderately intelligent sort of a chap, yew figure out the rest."

I turned and looked down into the beefy face of the man. "Then you *are* the bogman Behan," I said. "But I'm shocked. I always thought you were well in excess of six feet and weighed in the region of several hundred pounds. Why, you're no more than . . ."

He registered another sigh and a look of boredom. 'Nice to meet you, Mr. Behan," I concluded and hurried away.

Minutes later, a hand was placed on my shoulder. A voice crackled over my head. "Listen avick, but there's a luvly lady waiting in the lobby. She wants to see yew. She has a thing or two to talk to yew about. Will yew be a good chap and cum with me?"

Just as I was about to ask who the woman was, the impatient voice inquired, "Where avick may we first find for ourselves a scale to weigh our fat?"

Mr. Behan, at my suggestion, followed me into another facility. A doctor's scale was found. "Get up there, Mr. Behan, if you will," I said while I adjusted the measuring device on top of the scale. "Well, sir, you're a neat one hundred and fifty-two pounds, right on the button," I said as I noticed the indicator come to a stop.

"But how much is that in stones?" the man asked.

"That's ten stone twelve," I said. "You're a few pounds heavier than a welterweight, a few more lighter than a middleweight. With your kind permission sir, I pronounce you here and now fit as a fiddle and twice as twangy."

My words caused the sagging face in front of me to perk up with delight. A quick fusion of amusement came into him.

"Begod avick but shur that's fuckin' great aul gab altogether. Marvelous, what! Yur a brick, cum on, cum on, the other one will be delighted to meet yew. Yur aul guff will put a spark of life into her. She'll go mad altogether, indeed bejayzus she will. Shur that's the best bit of gab that I've heard in ages. Where in the name of jayzus did yew ever get such great aul guff atall atall?"

The little man's big words made me feel I was ten feet tall. I finished dressing rapidly. I nodded and smiled as he patted me on my shoulder, then followed him into the rustic lobby.

"She'll be pleased as punch, and happy as a whore in a confession box who's been granted a bishop's pardon," he stuttered while we made our way to the Y's entrance.

Just inside the door, sitting on a wooden bench, was an attractive auburn-haired, unfashionably dressed, pensive-looking lady, whom Mr. Behan introduced to me as Beatrice.

"He's a great aul skin from the jayzus country like ourselves. He has a great bit of gab on his jib. He'll stir the cockles of yur heart. Talk to him, go on."

The three of us traipsed out into the bright sunlight of that memorable day in the month of May. Beatrice and I developed an immediate rapport as we fell in behind the diminutive man who moved several paces ahead of us, his huge head bobbing and weaving. He moved with short, quick henlike spurts, his right shoulder ahead of himself, his shirt open to the waist, his coat collar crumpled up, his hair matted with sweat, his shoelaces untied, as he shuffled and made scores of pious papal-like waves to any he thought recognized him. At the corner of Wilcox Avenue and Hollywood Boulevard, we crossed and went into the Pickwick Bookstore.

The Pickwick was a double-tiered store thronged with tourists and gape-eyed gawkers. Beatrice and I wandered around and perused the bountiful shelves. Brendan moved away from us and engaged a swarm of youthful book lovers in conversation. He asked and answered questions by the score, stopping here and there to select and autograph paperback books which he took from the shelves and roguishly slipped into the pockets of the giggling youngsters. With great jollity he accepted the accolades of the awestruck youths, who reached out to touch him while he showered them with compliments regarding their youthful bloom, meanwhile uttering derogatory remarks about American priests, politicians and politics.

"A fella once said to me," he began in a barreling-ahead manner, " 'I hear that you envy the young.' 'Yew did,' said I to the dirty little ballox. 'Well now,' says I, 'I'll admit that I envy their livers, but I never heard of it being said that I envy or disliked youths merely because of their age.' Another chap says to me one day, 'Mr. Behan' 'Yew can call me Brendan,' says I, 'since me name is Brendan.' No civilized Christian was ever christened with a name such as 'Mr.' 'Mr.' is for the Protestants. Protestants on horseback. I'm a Catholic, a bad one at that, nevertheless a Catholic. Anyway, says he, 'Brendan, since you're a man of genius, a man of letters, how come you don't get yourself into politics?' "

A look of affected shock quickened across his face.

" 'Politics! Politicians!' says I to the cunt. 'Well,' says I, 'first and foremost, I only have one face and that's not two, and second, me middle name is Francis and not Janus.'

"An aul fella cums up to me one day in Dublin. It was the day of our national elections. Anyway, the poor aul ballox was sweeping the streets for that was his unthankful occupation. Says he, 'Brendan, you're a man of wisdom, who do you think will win?' I looked at the poor aul skin square in his watery eyes and, says I, 'Who will get in? Indeed whoever gets in, you,' says I, 'will go on sweeping the streets, so what difference does it make to us, the fighting people of Dublin, the working stiffs of Ireland? One crowd is as good as another. They're all a shower of two-faced whores.' The aul fella went on sweeping the poxy street. Another time this aul one cums up to me, and, says she, 'Brendan,' says she, 'yur such a luvly darlin' man, I'm wonderin' why a man like yurself ever took to the gargle.' "

Brendan stopped to explain to his burgeoning coterie that when he was growing up in the slums of Dublin, the word "gargle" meant strong drink—whiskey, gin, cognac, and so on.

"To get drunk was a social victory and no disgrace. To get enough to eat was an achievement. 'Well,' says I, 'strange as it may seem, even though I'll admit that I was born in a bottle and grew up in a glass, I never turned to the drink. It was the fuckin' aul drink that turned to me,' says I, and with that the poor aul whore took off down the road.

"I was reared a strict Dubliner and lived in a tenement; the only land we ever owned was the dirt in the dandelion box in me grandmother's windowsill.

"I was a house painter be trade. The only reason why I turned to writin' was because all of the marblin', paintin', grainin' and puttyin' that goes on in the city of Dublin wouldn't keep me in grog through a novena. I'd even paint for royalty. Who cares says I, just as long as they paid the goin' rate.

"B-but I m-must t-tell yew now, in Dublin there is a great aul working man's hangout that's overrun by widows. It's called the Widow's Pub, naturally, what else? Well there are fat widows, skinny widows, and every other class of widow that meets yur fancy. I suppose, in all practicality, yew could call it a boo-hoozer since most of its patrons just sit and whine and wait for the chaps like Peter here who earn their livin' by goin' out to the water, to come home and buy them drinks. Then the cryin' stops and they drink in unison from one end of the crucifixion day or the livelong night to the other.

"One day a fella cums up to me on Grafton Street in Dublin. Says he to me, 'Brendan,' says he, 'shur I remember well, when yew didn't have the price of a glass of malts in your corduroys! When yur arse was hanging out of yur pants!'

" 'Yew do,' says I! 'Well now,' says I, 'indeed bejayzus yew don't remember it half as well as I remember it mesself.'

"P-people are always cumin' up to me, looking me hard in the face and sayin', 'Brendan I hear yur dyin, is it true?' N-now I don't mind telling yew dying as a lark is a thing most unsuitable for such a garrulous man as mesself. But shur then again shur I suppose every good comedienne has a few good Irish wake jokes in her repertwat, what!!

"When tellin' a yarn I love to stop and quote mesself. My quotes have a way of spicing up the conversation. In this respect I'm like Shaw."

Brendan was obviously more of a monologuist than a conversationalist.

The starry-eyed youths were taken aback by the rawness of his gab.

His other topics ranged from man's inhumanity to his fellow man, to cruelty to animals, the disregard of civil rights of the old, the sick, the disenfranchised, the world's victims of exploitation, unjust economic systems, and his own personal concern for those who could not openly profess their faith.

While he rambled on, Beatrice, in her own distinct Dublin accent, talked incessantly about Brendan, his incarcerations, institutionalizations, debacles and illnesses, his fears, phobias, hates and loves. It was now obvious to me that the lady I was deep in one-sided conversation with was very familiar with the eccentricities and the idiosyncracies of the loquacious man.

As we continued on Brendan's heels, I found myself taken aback by the puzzling combination in Beatrice's personality. With cautious, frightened and slightly distrustful eyes she rambled ahead and poured out her all, yet a note of total trust underlined her every twitch and utterance. Throughout our one-sided conversation she remained composed and with a very concerned expression. Her expression never changed.

"You're Brendan's traveling secretary," I said in a confused manner.

"No, I'm his wife," she replied in a voice void of embarrassment or amusement. Then she continued with her descriptions of his achievements and his plans.

Brendan continued to laugh incessantly at his own quick verbal jolts. Beatrice then switched her talk to the major changes that Brendan would have to undertake if he chose to remain amongst the living. His deteriorating state of health was obviously the fear uppermost in her mind. I struggled to listen to them both.

With a familiar, short Latin psalm, Brendan finally dismissed his fans. Then he turned to me and said, "Listen avick, but there is something that I wish yew to do for me." He handed me two soft-covered books. "Now be a good boy, read these two books, but not here in this store," he said wryly, practically pushing the books into my face. I reached out and took hold of them, then took a glance at their titles. One of the books, *Borstal Boy*, was written by Brendan. The other, *Sailor on Horseback*, was a biography of Jack London by Irving Stone. I had never heard of either book.

"Read this one first and read it carefully," Brendan said firmly, as he pointed to *Sailor on Horseback*.

When I first became a professional merchant seaman, a job that provides a burdensome amount of spare time, I developed an avidity for reading. I had read most of the works of London.

"I'll read your book first," I said with a face full of pride.

A look of anger and hysteria suffused his face. "No! No! No!" he bellowed. "I said for yew to read *Sailor on Horseback* first. So go ahead and read the fucking thing like yur told."

"Since Brendan wants you to read the London book first," Beatrice interjected cautiously as we moved to the door, "be a good boy and read that one first, then you can get on with the other. Brendan can then be autographing the first one while you are going through the second one." A strained smile creased her face.

"Yes, yes, of course," I said as I thumbed through Stone's book, while I attempted to understand the meaning behind his insistence on the order of my reading.

"Yew can read the other cuntin' aul thing any time," Brendan said sharply as we followed him out onto Hollywood Boulevard.

We continued on, then made a right on Cahuenga Avenue and entered a dark, maroon-curtained bar called The Comet. It was a gay bar. Dozens of homosexuals sat around in maroon upholstered booths. The bar was deep.

"I hear that yur man Rock Hudson is a queer!" Brendan shouted to an effeminate-looking bartender, while making his way into the rear of the bar. No one answered. Our presence passed unheralded. My intuition forewarned me that we were not welcome. Beatrice and I sat in a booth. Brendan went up to the counter and ordered three bottles of soda water while Beatrice continued her list of Brendan's what-to-do's and what-not-to-do's should he decide to stay with the living and long enough to "finish up his new play, *Richard's Cork Leg*," a play whose story according to Beatrice, took place in Dublin's Glasnevin Cemetery.

Brendan sat down in a booth that was packed with gay men. He rambled on in a non-sequitur manner, but the bulk of his jokes and anecdotes seemed to hold no interest for the gays.

"I just arrived here in Hollycunt or Hollypussy or whatever they call the prick of a place," Brendan began, "and naturally being a professional writer I'm a curious man. I'm only interested in the man's sexuality for this same reason. Good writing is made out of facts and not out of fiction. I realize that this quagmire is a fantasy land, but that's none of my immediate concerns. In regards to one's sex, that is their concern and not the concern of others. That is to say, just as long as a man, an adult, a matured and civilized human being does not inflict himself onto the will of others, the young in particular. I personally regard the stuff as something pure, something moral and decent, a natural body function, something to be done in private and not, as a contemporary of mine once said, something that should not be done on the streets where it might frighten the horses.

"In Dublin, dying is a thing that they take seriously. An aul one who once lived beside us made her living be makin' habits for the dead. She did okay for herself. Do yew know why? Well, one reason was, she didn't have to worry about constantly changing her patterns. The fashion of the dead never changes in Ireland."

A number of the bored homosexuals arose, waved to the bartender, and quickly departed. Outwardly undaunted, Brendan kept up his barrage of staccato comments, jokes, jibes, limericks and opinions. Beatrice, unsmiling, talked on about her own favorite topic: Brendan Behan.

In an attempt to stop the exodus, Brendan was up and doing a surprisingly agile soft-shoe shuffle while playing a harmonica, which he had taken from his coat pocket. Sweat poured from his forehead and saturated his suit, shirt and tie. Finally he finished up with a few verses of his own rendition of "Lady Chatterley's Lover" and a few bars of a song called "The Old Triangle." This was a song, according to Beatrice, that Brendan had written specially for his first play, *The Quare Fellow,* a play (according to Beatrice) that was packed with high tension and Brendan's special wit and genius.

> I'm Lady Chatterley's Lover
> A game-keeper that's me
> I love pheasant and plover
> But mostly I love Lady C.

> A hungry feeling came o'er me stealing
> And the mice were squealing in my prison cell
> And that old triangle
> Went jingle jangle
> Along the banks of the Royal Canal.

> To begin the morning
> The warder bawling
> Get out of bed and clean up your cell
> And that old triangle
> Went jingle jangle
> Along the banks of the Royal Canal.
> And the screw was peeping
> And the lag was weeping

Next he sang what he described as a song that he wrote in protest against the Irish for their banning of his book, *Borstal Boy:*

> O me name is Brendan Behan I'm the latest
>   of the banned.
> Although we're small in numbers we're the
>   best banned in the land.
> We're read at wakes and weddin's and in every
>   parish hall.
> And under library counters sure you'll have
>   no trouble at all.

At the song's conclusion he hollered, "And *I've* banned the censorship board and there's no appeal from my decision. I can tell yew this much," Brendan went on in his heated rhetoric, "I don't have to worry about the price of a pound of rashers or black puddin' but they do. That's their lot.

"Many years ago I stopped looking for the answers to political problems and became a writer, a good one from what I've been told. I must be, I earn three thousand Yankee dollars per week. In New York any time that I want to go on television all I have to do is say the word and I get a fistful of dollars. Not bad for a boy from the bog, eh?" Brendan winked and asked one slightly entertained-looking youth. Then he sat down.

A short while later, he arose and did another little dance. It was a familiar Irish jig, the blackbird. "People keep saying to me, 'Brendan why do yew have to curse and swear so much?' 'Well,' says I, 'shur how the fuck am I supposed to write about Irishmen, mesself included, if I don't use curse words?' The other aul fucker Lawrence got away with it didn't he, so why can't I? After all, isn't the word *fuckin'* part of the Irish national heritage?

"Where I cum from, killing yur wife is considered a natural class of a thing. A sort of pastime. The world is made up of four sexes, men, women, old men, old women, and I can truthfully say in all of me own travels I have never met anything sexually worse than mesself.

"Another aul aunt of mine went to the GPO on Easter Monday, 1916, the day of the Irish Rebellion. She refused to get away and kept insisting to see her husband. He finally came over to a sandbagged window and roared into her face: 'Will yew for jayzussake Maggie go away!' Do yew know what she did? She shouted back: 'But shur I only wanted to know if yew were going out to your work in the morning.' "

Brendan then sat pensively for awhile.

But in a matter of a few minutes, he was again up and on his feet, trotting back and forth from bar to booth and vice versa, recounting his days as a terrorist on the run, a former IRA outlaw in Liverpool with a mission. His mission: "to blow up the brand-new battleship, the pride of the British Navy, his Royal Highness's *King George V*." In graphic detail, he told of his times in a Borstal institution for youthful offenders. In one frothy uninterruptible monologue he relived his Aubrey Street arrest and subsequent conviction. Taking an empty soda bottle in hand, improvising a handgun, he recounted the arrest by "the two cops who had been tipped off" about his Liverpool whereabouts. "Yew two big cabbage-headed fuck faces," he roared. "Yew wouldn't have cum through that shagging door so easily if I had a gun in me hand!"

Next, with the bottle still in his grip and in a more frenzied manner, he told of a big shoot-out that he had been the protagonist of. According to him, the incident took place on Easter Sunday, April 5, 1942, at the Glasnevin Cemetery in Dublin. The gunfire was provoked by officers of the special branch of the Irish police, a contingent that is known to keep a close eye on activities of the IRA. "Had the dirty murdering whores not tried to murder me first, I would not have murdered them," Brendan hotly exclaimed while peeling off his jacket and slamming it to the floor.

When one of the patrons asked Brendan how many of the cops died in the shoot-out, Brendan quickly changed the subject by making a clarion call for the swift passing of a law that would protect "the most innocent and helpless victims of our society from the filthy hands of the most cowardly animals of our society." Then after a lengthy pause, a prevailment of silence, he repeated his call and made it known that he was referring to children and child molesters. During this little speech, he worked himself up to a shattering climax. Then he peeled his jacket from the floor, adjusted his suspenders, and sat down between us. He wiped the sweat from his face and sat for a time with his head lowered, as though he were pondering his future while delving deep into his past. With his chin still dropping to his chest, Brendan muttered to no one in particular, "I'm not a warlike man, I'm an amiable person, admittedly a garrulous man betimes, but a decent sort of a skin, ask Beatrice, there."

The majority of the patrons had now sauntered away. The small exodus continued.

"Don't you get the feeling that our welcome is waning?" I said to Beatrice.

"Yes, yes, I do," she said, her eyes lighting up and her ears piquing.

"Don't you think that we should go now, pet," she said to Brendan in a motherly manner, adjusting his suspenders and straightening out a lock of his hair that hung down over his eyes.

We departed and when we came to Hughes Supermarket, Beatrice selected and purchased several pounds of raw meats and vegetables. "You will come up and have a bit of supper with Brendan and me, won't you, Peter?" she said with enthusiasm.

"Most certainly I will," I said, reaching out and taking the two paper bags full of groceries from her.

Within minutes of our arrival at their apartment, a huge mugful of tea was put into my hand. Then Beatrice handed me a green leather-backed copy of Brendan's most famous play, *The Hostage*.

"Here, Peter," she said exuberantly, "maybe you would like to read Brendan's Broadway play."

I thanked the lady of the house and sat down to read.

For the next hour or so, Brendan and I sat in the living room reading. Beatrice remained in the kitchen readying for supper. I thoroughly enjoyed the play, although I had difficulty decipering its total content. I found it thin of plot, although it was a work full of flash, gusto and verve. What surprised and disturbed me about the play was how its text was so anti-IRA in its attitude. The play was a mockery of that organization and everything it stood for. If indeed Brendan was a genuine rebel, patriot and socialist, surely his writing portrayed no such sentiment.

Amongst Brendan's targets of hypocrisy and fraudulence were religion, sex, politics, the judiciary and the reformatory system. The work was mottled with a host of big name droppings. *The Hostage* left me with the impression that Brendan was a man who sorely desired to stomp the shit out of *all* societies. Leslie, the captured British soldier who is the title character in the play, came off as the most sympathetic character in the cast, even though he is surrounded by a bevy of low-class Dublin doxies, homosexuals, and IRA men on the run.

What charmed me about the dialogue was how Brendan obviously did not believe that dialogue as didactic art has to be moral or instructive. I admired his convictions, and thanked both him and Beatrice for letting me read the manuscript. "Great stuff Brendan, thanks for letting me read your work." I said, gingerly, putting down the manuscript.

"Not at all, avick, shur I knew yew'd be amused," he chuckled, throwing down his paper and beckoning me to join him at the supper table.

During my reading of the play, Brendan had sat uncomfortably in his chair, picking his nostrils and throwing surreptitious little glances at Beatrice as she buzzed about the kitchen rattling her culinary objects. Never once did either of them talk or look at me.

Sitting at the table, I attempted to ask Brendan a question or two about the play.

"Cum on now, avick, and forget about that cuntin' aul thing for now," he said with an irritated wave of his hand. "Here," he said, placing a big plate full of steaming hot food in front of me, "get this lot into your guts while the going is good and plentiful, shur jayzus, avick, shur yew must be lost with the hunger. Beatrice, pour the boy another mug of brown poison like the good girl that yew are," he ordered his spouse.

Brendan attacked his food voraciously, picking up bits and pieces of steaming hot steak, ribs, chops, livers, and kidneys, examining them and placing them on the table beside his plate.

"Brendan's on a strict high-protein diet," Beatrice said as she sat down.

Shards of fading sunlight streamed in through the high-curtained windows of the living room. None of us spoke. The room was in silence, save for the occasional crackle and crunch of a rib bone being munched on then sent crashing to the waste bin. Brendan's culinary antics were a sight to behold. He derived some satisfaction out of pawing over and carefully selecting a juicy morsel, chewing on it, breaking it in two with his mouth and fist, sucking its final substances from its stalk, then slamming it into the bin, his eyes blinking as it came to a final halt. I burst out in a gale of uncontrollable laughter. Then sensing that I had possibly offended them, I thoroughly assured them that my laughter was purely a hangover from the reading of *The Hostage*. The Behans eyed one another.

Brendan swallowed mugful after mugful of scalding hot tea. As soon as he had finished one mugful, Beatrice quickly placed another one in front of him. His method of informing her that he was ready for another was to bang the bottom of the empty mug on the table. Beatrice seemed not to mind.

As the afternoon wore on Brendan continued to pick, break, munch and slam, never once looking up or emitting a single word. He merely sent out little medleys of waves, bangs, grunts, groans and gesticulations whenever he felt that the cups or plates were in need of refueling from the stove or from the tea pot. Much to my astonishment, Beatrice seemed to totally comprehend his meanings. Sporadically, he carefully selected a huge juicy chop, chunk of liver, kidney or steak and placed it in the middle of my plate. "Go on avick, get that into yew," he demanded. Even though my shrunken stomach was more than filled, I elected to follow his demands and attack the contents of the plate, lest I run the risk of offending him. When he felt that a chunk of meat was not adequately cooked, he quickly impaled it upon his fork, muttered something incoherent to me but comprehensible to Beatrice, who in turn took the food from the fork, placed it in the pan, and allowed it to cook some more, prior to putting it back onto my plate.

The soothing warmth of the diminishing southern California sunlight continued to stream in the window and splatter the room with an amber glow. Brendan's small, alert eyes, suspicious and probing, fascinated me as they scanned the girth of the table. Never did he look me square in the eyes. He aimed intermittent little glances to the level of my chin or to my mouth, then quickly shifted his penetrating eyes to Beatrice, and made motions of approval in regard to my capacity to eat. Beatrice beamed, smiled, fidgeted and waffled.

For several years, on board ships, in libraries, in foreign ports of travel, and on the theater marquee at the Cort Theatre in New York, I had heard of and read about and been told of Brendan Behan, the world-famous writer and charismatic character whose dinner table I was supping at. I had read countless stories of his life's history and his achievements. I had heard of his numerous appearances on the Jack Paar nightly talkathon. I had come to regard Brendan as a man of enormous courage, acerbic wit, and cosmic genius, an Irishman of great intellectual prowess. I held him in great awe and was pleased to have been given this opportunity to personally know the man. I looked upon him as a man whose genius transcended many boundaries, a cult figure on more than one continent for reasons that he had stood by his bone marrow convictions in a brave effort to secure a modicum of social justice for all. I envied Brendan Behan. His fabulous, colorful life had been a succession of triumphs. He had brazenly and successfully displayed his scorn for the conventions of Ireland's powerful Catholic Church. He took it upon himself to live his life as freely and as scandalously as he chose to do. He was a lover of life who had succeeded well in prompting world leaders to talk about him. I also regarded him as a maker of mischief and a unique writer who wrote fearlessly and utilized his unique talents to experiment and test the frail boundaries of the theater and explore all of its possibilities.

Brendan had first come to my attention when I read of his infamous TV interview on the Ed Murrow show, "Small World," on CBS. It was a half-hour program on the art of conversation. The show was a montage of film and sound strips from the telephone conversations of Murrow in London, Brendan in Dublin, and Jackie Gleason and literary critic James Brown in New York. Halfway through the show, because of his drunkenness, Brendan's footage was eliminated from the program. Later, Gleason commented, "Brendan came through one hundred proof. It wasn't an Act of God; it was an Act of Guinness." Murrow's comment was, "We have encountered difficulties beyond our control." The *New York Daily News* explained, "If the celebrated playwright wasn't pickled, he gave the best imitation of rambling alcoholism you ever saw." While CBS explained that Behan started out sober as a judge, what happened afterwards was unexpected—and unavoidable. During delays in shooting, Behan excused himself frequently and made trips to another room. His condition became progressively worse each time he returned.

At that time I was in New York, in between engagements as quartermaster on board dredges, operating for the Construction Aggregate Corporation of Chicago. My assigned duties were in the Bay of Maracaibo, Venezuela. I was "in between ships," having been duly discharged from the *Chester Harding*, and en route to join the S.S. *Sand Captain*. Brendan was then imbibing and giggling his way to immortality.

Strangely, here now, I found it difficult to accept the fact that this was the same man. I found it impossible to believe that the man before me was the gut writer whose pen of fire had set the world ablaze with his bent for satire, his reputation for assaulting establishments in his defense of the working class and their rights to life, liberty and a place in the blaze of life. Somehow the man did not seem to fit what I had read and heard.

After we had eaten, Brendan hastily repaired to the depths of a huge chair that sat in the middle of the living room. A heavy blanket of depression and darkness came over him. Here was a heavy, dour, brooding introvert, a troubled hulk, a man who in the quieter moments of his moral aloneness reminisced and sipped with the dead.

However, I appreciated having been invited to sup at his table and temporarily participate in his fire of life, whatever the origins of its embers be.

"Would you like to take a look at today's rags?" Beatrice asked, handing me a pile of local papers. "Brendan refers to all American papers as 'rags.' "

"Yes, thank you," I said, taking the papers from her hand. "But why does Brendan refer to them as 'rags' " I chuckled hoping to lighten the drooping atmosphere.

"Why don't you ask Brendan?" she snapped, in a manner that surprised me.

"What did you mean, Brendan, when you christened the papers the 'rags'?" I asked warily.

Brendan pulled his newspaper further up to his face, snickered and blurted, "Shur the cuntin' aul things are full of advertisements and announcements of fuckin' aul bargains to be had for little or sweet fuckall . . . page after page of typical Yank bullshit," he chortled. Then he slammed the papers on to the floor and stormed into the bathroom. Minutes later he returned, picked up the paper and continued to read, this time in a more sullen manner, occasionally stopping to pull his paper up to his chest and squint as though something of great importance had caught his fancy, but again his probing eyes crept up and around the edges of the paper, and peered at me.

I thought perhaps as a writer he wanted to ask me about my background, my nature. His eyes continued to flutter and blink.

"I'd say that there bees some quare aul goings-on out there on them ships at sea," he suddenly stuttered, ruffling the paper.

"Well, yes, Brendan. Plenty. Loads of action, punch-ups, smugglings, drownings, shootings, sabotage, a bit of everything. It's an exciting life."

He sighed and went even deeper into the misery that I had earlier observed. I went back to reading. In the next few minutes a pall seemed to sweep over him. The corners of his lips curled. His eyes bore the threnode of a loser. The Rabelaisian good humor and high spirits that he displayed in the pool and in the bar were no longer in evidence. A patina of wickedness crept over his beefy countenance.

The stagnant Hollywood air still held the heat of the day. Street noises sounded muffled in the distance.

The worlds of literature, madness and alcoholism were subjects that were always very close to me. Brendan's behavior brought me vivid memories of my seldom sober, always unemployed father—hostile, drunk and malevolent. When I was fourteen years of age I ran away by stowing away in the chain locker of the S.S. *Black Sod.* I was tired of being my drunken father's do-gooder and go-getter, his supplier of the wherewithal essential for the purchase of his daily doses of fantasizing liquid, his "malts," his "gargles." Alcoholics and alcoholism were nothing new to me. Brendan broke into my reverie.

"What would yew say to a swim in the downstairs puddle?" he suddenly asked with a lighthearted chuckle.

"The downstairs puddle?"

"Yes avick," he grinned robustly, taking on a complete change of personality. "If yew look out the window there yew will get a gander at our azure blue puddle in the yard at the arse end of the building."

"Sure Brendan," I said excitedly, "but I don't have trunks to wear."

"Not to worry me aul son," he chirped. "Here, cum over here and try these on for size," he said, trotting into the bathroom and beckoning me to follow him. He reached up and extricated a pair of "togs" from off the curtain rod. Together we donned our togs. Just as I was in the process of zipping up mine and stepping back into the living room, Brendan reached out, grabbed hold of my cock, and began to fondle it. Taken aback by his action, I conveyed to him that I had once read where it is against the advice of the medical profession to indulge in sexual acts directly after eating.

"F-for f-fucksake avick, b-but will yew not be going on with s-s-such shite. Never believe anything that yew read in books. B-books are nothing but a package of f-fuckin aul lies and b-bullshit. Leave the reading to the culshies and the savages . . ."

A look of pure excitement seeped into his eyes as he continued to fondle my cock and watch it rise to tumescence. Then with the aid of his free hand, he reached up and opened the mirrored door of the medicine cabinet, then he jerked me off while gleefully observing our reflections in the mirror. His cherubic countenance was aglow with boyish delight as a reel of masturbatory fantasies seemed to flicker across his mind.

From the time that I was eight or nine years old, attending school at the Christian Brothers National Schools of Ireland, scavenging for salable deckers of coal and ferreting out the price of my father's "malt money," homosexual propositions had been common occurrences in my life. I encouraged these frequently paying propositions. Then I could give the coins to "himself." Life with a wicked sober father was too difficult to endure. Life with a drunken father was comparatively simpler.

My father, who we referred to as "the badger" when he was drunk, was a vicious, demanding blood alcoholic who stooped to low gutteral levels to garnish the price of his "bellyful." Often he sent me out with strict instructions that I was not to return home without "the few bob" to purchase his Guinness. When all else failed, I was compelled to hang around outside waterfront bars or the town hall lavatory and entice drunken sailors, tourists and northern travelers to molest me. My hung-over cantankerous parent was vividly aware of where the money came from and how it was earned. But that was something that he and I never discussed. I merely forked over the "spondulicks" (as we amiably referred to it) and sent him on his merry way to his favorite pub where he quickly anted up his "decoration money." Another day in our household would pass in semilivable peace.

By the time that I had reached the age of twelve, I had grown accustomed to the price of peace with the badger. My mother, a self-proclaimed martyr, claimed that she had no control over the matter. My hatred for my mendicant parents developed faster than my bones. A terminal degree of low self-esteem was woven into the wickerwork of my life. At the age of fourteen, I stowed away to sea.

In 1949 and 1950, when I was fifteen and sixteen, I served as a messboy, deck boy, and junior ordinary seaman aboard the Norwegian flagged cargo and tank ships M.V. *Belinda,* S.T. *Salamis* and M.V. *Marna.* In the fall of 1950 and in the winter of 1951, I sailed as ordinary seaman and able-bodied seaman aboard the Panamanian ships, S.S. *Bulk Trader* and *Bulk Star.* The practice of homosexuality amongst the younger members of the unlicensed personnel was commonplace. Homosexuality was looked upon as an essential emotional outlet. Mutual masturbation and sodomy amongst the teenagers were the two most common acts.

"G-great man avick, g-g-great m-man . . . shur the fuckin' aul w-wank is the only t-today for the b-body . . . the b-best man f-for the c-cuntin' n-nerves . . . yur a great h-horse of a boy, a whale of a lad," Brendan muttered. He had by now reached up, taken hold of my right hand, wrapped it around his tumescent prick, and begun to masturbate himself with my hand held in his hand, while in unison he masturbated me with his other hand. Looking in the mirror at Brendan's penis, I felt a sudden twinge of compassion for Beatrice. Brendan had the biggest prick that I had ever seen.

Brendan became ecstatic and gregarious as the workout went on.

"B-bejayzus, avick, d-do y-yew know w-what it is, y-yur a fuckin' great b-bull of a b-boy, b-better than an ass w-working w-wonders under a load of t-turf. I'll bet that they went mad for yew on them ships."

His eyes and face became an inebriation of ecstasy as his excitement grew, but I was experiencing more than a little difficulty in keeping my cock tumescent. Brendan Behan was not exactly my type of sexual partner, not exactly the type of man who sent electrifying throbs of sexual gratification surging into my veins.

In the heat and ecstasy of our workout, I had totally forgotten about Beatrice. I looked right and suddenly much to my horror discovered that the bathroom door was ajar. Outside, in the kitchen I could hear her buzzing about taking care of her household chores. I reached over gently, took hold of the door knob, turned it half a turn, closed the door and allowed the bar to slip into place, then turned my attention back to Brendan's hand, and hoping I could keep my penis in bloom until such time as he and I reached our sexual climaxes. Each time that I looked down, I realized that the will was there, but the flesh wasn't.

My door-closing action was not taken too kindly by Brendan. With a look of extreme irritation, he reached over and reopened the door.

"But she'll catch us in the act," I whispered.

"Let her catch us. It will do her a world of good," he exclaimed in a loud whisper.

We finished up our reciprocal hand jobs, rinsed, pulled up our togs and headed for the pool.

The perimeter of the pool was mottled with guests. Brendan went into another display of his aquatic exhibitionistics. He started out by dipping his fingertips into the pool, blessing his coterie, mellifluously singing a few bars of a Catholic hymn, then finishing up his short, improvised mock mass with his cherished Latin psalm. Again, grabbing hold of his nose with one hand and his genitalia with the other: "Here goes sweet fuck all," he said as his feet broke water. Brendan remained underwater for a very long time. Concern grew in the faces of the gathering.

A full three minutes later, he broke water, scrambled up over the perimeter, and in a quick little charge did a complete clockwise tour of the pool, stopping at each and every aluminum chair along the way to tell a personal anecdote, a yarn, or a joke. Bursts of laughter greeted his every utterance.

The majority of the guests were ecstatic, as they watched him do his laps in the nude. Somewhere in the chemicalized depths of the pool were Brendan's colorful, flimsy, togs. He talked incessantly in a rambling and discursive manner, never stopping to see if he was interrupting a conversation. The marathon gush revolved around his literary triumphs, his days in Borstal, his bouts with booze, his attitude towards the law and sex, and his brushes with death. He banged away like a woodpecker, fighting for its final peck.

"New York—they can fuckinwell say this and they can fuckinwell say that," he went on, "but at any hour of the day or night yew won't be stuck for a bite to put in yur guts when the hunger or the thirst is on yew, no need to worry about getting bitten by a stray sheep, either, I can tell yew.

"Did I tell yew that the only shower of balloxes that I personally ever knew who were staunch believers and advocates of capital punishment were murderers? The real murderers of our society: the politicians and the priests. Nearly every thief that I ever knew was a Tory. . . .

"God be with the working class. Shur, next to a corkscrew aren't they the only ones who will do yew a good turn without expecting yew to give half of your arse or one of your testicles in return. In Dublin yew can always tell a civil servant by the way he drinks under an assumed name. Acourse yew can't always blame them for that, for bejayzus when I was a boy growing up, many a man's pint was lifted from under him by some aul codger and all because the poor chap hadn't the good sense of mind to hold his nose well in over the rim of his glass while he was taking his sup." A short period of silence ensued while Brendan scratched his scrotum and wiped the sweat from his brow. Then he hammered ahead.

"Well at first they didn't know what to do with me play, *The Hostage,* but as soon as I heard someone shouting blasphemy and hooligan at a performance of it, at the Olympia Theatre in Dublin—Dublin is the city of my birth, well jayzus s-shur I knew I was in the tradition of the great O'Casey.

"When I was asked to comment on Irish folksingers, says I, they should all be takin' out and shot. 'Why?' says the interviewer. 'Well,' says I, 'there has to be better ways to line coffins.'

"Shur if I was to take notice of me critics I'd be in the madhouse, wha!

"S-shur the number of people who purchase books in Ireland wouldn't keep me in drink for the duration of a high holy mass."

Approximately once each fifteen minutes, Brendan arose, scurried over to the edge of the pool, scooped up a handful of water and rinsed the sweat from his face and neck. He talked and rinsed simultaneously.

"When I was staying in Ibiza—that's an island off of Spain that's owned and operated by Spanish fascist louts—I was writing *The Hostage* . . . wrote the play in the Gaelic language the first time around. Gaelic is me national heritage, the first language of Ireland. Well this cuntin' Spanish reporter comes up to me and says he, 'Mr. Behan, what event would you like to witness here in Spain?' " Again he stopped and stared into space. ". . . Did I tell yew that I wrote the cuntin' aul thing in a matter of twelve days? Shur I only write the fuckin' things when I'm skint. 'Well,' says I, 'first of all me name is Brendan and not Mr.

Behan. Now in answer to yur stupid fuckin' questions,' says I, 'what event would I like to witness most during me stay in Spain? That's an easy one,' says I: 'Franco's funeral!' A few days later I got an order of eviction from the local gendarme. I don't know why! Neither do I care!

"Once when I was engaged in doing a painting job for this aul one, do yew see it was of a morning after a big one the night before, know what I mean" (winking to his audience) "and I fell asleep on the job. Next thing yew know I heard a door opening. Cute as the cuntin' Christian that I am, I closed me eyes and pretended that I was asleep. Suddenly a familiar culshie voice says: 'Sleep on Behan, sleep on, for while ye're asleep ye have a job, but byjayzus as soon as ye're awake, avick ye're fuckinwell sacked.' But I'll tell yew this much, in spite of the fuckin' aul foreman's voice, it was the most comfortable and appreciated sleep that I ever had. It was the only sleep that I was *ever* paid for.

"Aul Allen Ginsberg once introduced me to a chap in New York who, like himself, was a poet who told me that he earned a hundred dollars a month from the government for being mad. Says I, in Ireland our poets go mad all the time and get sweet fuck all for their efforts. It just goes to show yew that there is no justice in this world, but shur then again that's show business. Shur amn't I a showman mesself.

"In the Blue Lion, a well-known Dublin pub, aul ones with faces on them as terrible looking as platefuls of mortal sins will sit for hours waiting for me to buy them a pint. They're like a horde of fuckin' aul sows. They stare at me like sows looking into a swill barrel as they wait for me to spring for their morning malts.

"A fellow prisoner who was once about to be hanged for splitting his wife in two with an ax, turned to me and says he, 'Brendan does hanging hurt?' 'I never experienced the hurt of a hanging,' says I, 'nor did I ever talk to anyone who did. I don't think so,' says I, 'but,' says I, 'if I ever meet anyone who did, I'll let you know.'

"The Guinness family have always been good to me, but then again, I have been good to the Guinness family . . . fair field and no favor.

"Me mother always said that she'd like to see Paris before she died. Yew better hurry up, says I, for indeed yur chances of seeing it afterwards are few.

"Shur when me play *The Quare Fellow* was due to open at the East End in London, s-shur didn't I invite f-fuckin' aul Pierrepont the whore of a hangman. Needless to say the c-cunt d-didn't cum. He was too busy working in his Oldham Pub, selling porter to the Irish working class no doubt. An order to shoot me on sight was once put out by a judge in Dublin, me own native city, wha! There's civility for yew! Well do yew know what *I* did?! I sent back a note to say if yew can sentence me in me absentia, yew can fuckinwell shoot me in me absentia. I signed the document 'Long Live the Republic and fuck the begrudgers.'

" 'I hear someone's dead belonging to yew,' a fellow says to me one day in Dublin. 'It's not yourself be any chance,' says he. 'No' says I, 'it's not, but if I hear where there's a good wake going on, where the Guinness and the sandwiches is good and plentiful, I'll be sure to give yew a shout,' says I to the turkey-toed cunt-faced fuck as he took off down the street with a head on his shoulders as big and as hungry-looking as a lodging house cat."

In the course of Brendan's tireless spiel, dozens of guests had come and gone. From the range of expressions on their faces I gathered that there were those who felt that he was too self-aggrandizing, too exhibitionistic. There were also those who did not approve of nudity. Many others regarded him as unique, refreshing and a colorful entertainer.

Finally he culminated his one-man gabfest with an emotion-packed attack against the evils of child molestation and child molesters. Halfway through his frenetic outburst, Brendan became upset and out of breath. He choked, panted, stuttered and stammered, his hands fidgeted and trembled, then suddenly he arose, pointed to the pool and hollered to me, "Cum on now Peter, avick, for fucksake, get in here and soak your ballox before we go up for our tea."

I first declined, then I acquiesced and walked down the three steps of the pool's shallow end and submerged myself. Brendan then dove into the pool.

After a few dives, his composure returned. In a matter of minutes, he again took up his position amongst the cadre, and in a voice that was much more controlled, he finished up his assault against the child molesters while again calling for a swift mandate of law that would put them behind bars "for all eternity." "The dirty man-beasts should have a blowtorch put to their dirty balls for committing such heinous crimes against innocent children," he snapped. Again he went into a deep dark mood.

Suddenly he turned to me and said, "Listen avick, yew can say what yew want about yur aul Cavan mother, but by God she put it into yew when yew were a lad growing up."

His remark took me off guard. My mother did in fact, hail from County Cavan, in the Irish midlands. I had not told Brendan of this! How did he know, I wondered. Brendan and I then took the freight elevator to his floor. Beatrice remained at the pool. In the apartment Brendan followed me into the bathroom and made another grab for my genitalia as I was taking off my togs.

"I'm sorry, Brendan," I said, "but my interests in homosexuality are limited. Homosexual acts without the presence of a female do not ordinarily excite me. I am not a bona fide homosexual." Then at his insistence I followed him into the bedroom, where he lay down on his stomach on top of the bed and begged me to sodomize him. My answer was again a flat no. He became extremely sullen, then arose and darted into the living room.

"L-listen avick, b-but I was w-wondering if yew'd be interested in having an aul g-go at the o-other o-one," he suddenly asked.

For a brief flurry of seconds, I didn't quite understand what he meant, then it dawned upon me that Brendan was asking me if I would consent to fornicating with his wife. I deduced that he would insist on joining the party or at least observing the goings-on.

"Why naturally I would, Brendan," I chuckled with assurance. "Just let me know where and when to begin," I concluded, by no means believing in the genuineness of his question. His eyes blazed with a mischievous delight.

"G-good m-man, I'll have a ch-chat with her w-when she g-gets b-back."

Beatrice returned and inserted some things into the refrigerator. Twilight had fallen. Dusk slowly gathered and crowded the three-room apartment. Brendan arose. "Listen Peter but yew'll have to excuse us but we do have a number of things to do tonight and time is getting on . . . shur we'll see yew another time . . . I mean to say, it's not like me grandmother used to say, 'We'll all be off to America in the morning,' " he said showing me the door.

I was taken aback by his sudden abruptness, nevertheless I thanked him for his hospitality. Then gathering up the books that he had purchased for me, I said, "I would be most grateful to you if you will autograph these books for me, Brendan."

A look of inexplicable anger suffused his face. "Beatrice will tell yew about that," he snapped as he darted into the bathroom. I heard the lid of the commode go down hard on the porcelain rim.

In my quandary I noticed that the bathroom door was left ajar. In my mind's eye I caught a glimpse of Brendan sitting on the commode carefully scrutinizing me with one eye open, the other half-closed surreptitiously.

"Is there anything wrong, Beatrice?" I asked perplexedly.

"Oh, what Brendan means is that *after* you have read the books he will autograph them for you. But don't forget," she said, as she led me to the door, "remember to read the London book first, then *Borstal Boy*."

I bade the lady *slan leat* (Irish for good-bye), then walked down Cherokee Avenue, crossed over Hollywood Boulevard, then down Wilcox Avenue. In the lonely solitude of my room, I wondered what I had said or done to make Brendan so upset. I reached for the phone, then dropping the receiver back onto its cradle, I decided to forgo any attempt to pursue a friendship that would be a waste of time.

I had spent an afternoon in the company of a fellow Irishman. I was baffled, but I was aware that the subject of homosexuality was one with many ramifications and complexities. For the first time in my life I had been befriended by a celebrity. A celebrity of enormous magnitude. I felt ill at ease and prayed that I would one day again find myself in the intimate company of the Behans, but somehow I felt that that would never happen. A pall of sadness crept over me. I dropped off to sleep.

For the next few days I worked out at the Y and did roadwork in the park. My workout hours revolved around the daily plumbing, carpentry and painting jobs that I conjured up here and there. My weight went up to a solid one sixty-eight. Feeling proud, I had a composite of pictures taken of myself. Along about the middle of May I decided to return to Wilmington. I called the SIU and discovered that shipping was like an energized yo-yo and now on the upswing. Also, daily work, toting stacks of bananas on the San Pedro waterfront, was flourishing.

Returning to the semi-fetal-like existence aboard these steel entrapments was a thing that I did not relish. Hand-hosing, chemical spraying and scraping the toxic muck from the intestines of supertankers had taken its toll. My lungs had absorbed a substantial amount of damage. Hyperventilation attacks were becoming more repetitious. My hands were gnarling long before their time. I was twenty-seven years of age. My attitude towards life was becoming one of dismay and disillusionment. I had had a bellyful. I wanted out. However, I had made my bed in life. My small nest egg was quickly depleting.

Early in the morning on the day that I planned to leave, I was awakened by the phone. Light streamed in from the outside street lamp. It was three-seventeen A.M.

"Is that yurself avick?" a familiar guttural voice crackled across the wire. "Listen me aul s-son b-but I was just wonderin' how far into *Sailor* have yew gotten? Or indeed did yew even bother to open it atall says yew, wha?"

"Excuse me Brendan," I said hazily, "but I must make a quick dash to the jax. Be back in two shakes of a cow's diddy."

I dashed into the bathroom, doused my face and the nape of my neck and wondered just what in hell Brendan Behan was up to calling me so early in the morning and asking me such questions. I reflected for a moment. True, the Irish are a very nonreading class of people. True, many of them never cracked open the covers of a book. True, I had not in fact opened either book. But that was only because I had been busy building my run-down body.

I dashed back into the room, picked up the book, and in a frenzy scanned the first few chapters, stopping here and there to underline paragraphs Brendan was bound to be familiar with.

"Sorry, Brendan," I said, "but you know how it is when you just wake up. Had to relieve my brain, among other things. Now in regards to *Sailor,* I'm already into page—"

"Oh never mind, avicko" he interrupted, "that's neither here nor there. I was beginning to wonder if something had happened to yew, thought maybe yew fell into the bowl and got flushed through the sewer. I was just putting on me coat to go down to Sunset Boulevard and dig up a few manholes to see if yew were swimming about down there with the rest of the movie stars." A faint chuckle and an eerie silence followed. Then just as I was about to answer—

"Did yew see any nice lassies in Hollywood recently? Listen son, talking about lassies, there's a very luvly lassie here who wishes to have a word or two with yew, will yew hold on for a wee minute till yur woman cums to the phone?" Then Beatrice's voice was on the wire.

"Oh hello, Peter," she said exuberantly. "I have great news for you. Brendan was up early this morning and did some work on *Richard's Cork Leg.* I'm delighted, must be the smoggy air or something. Brendan says that you're to come over a little later for your breakfast. Then after breakfast, while I'm doing my shopping at Hughes, the two of you can have your swims. Brendan says that you're not to bring your togs. There's an extra pair here that you can wear. You will be a good boy and come, won't you? The men from the press will be here at around nine. Brendan will introduce you to them. *Slan leat agus an ploblacht abu* [good-bye and long live the Republic]."

The phone went dead before I had a chance to utter a word.

Groggy, I scurried back to the bathroom, stepped under the shower and allowed a generous amount of water to hit the nape of my neck. The knowledge that my friendship with Brendan was still alive and flourishing made me feel good. Whatever I had said or done, or didn't do to upset the man was now a thing of the past.

I sat on the edge of my bed reading *Sailor on Horseback.* I would arrive at the Montecito armed and ready. A flood of questions suddenly entered my brain. I hadn't given my last name or the name of my hotel to Brendan. How did he know who and where to call? I wondered awhile, then dismissed the thought and took the elevator to the street.

The avenues and boulevards of Hollywood were barren save for the occasional jaded hooker on her way home after a long night of propositions and calisthenics. The town itself looked like any other big old American country town with its occasional palm tree and garish pinball parlor. I quickened my pace and arrived at the Behan apartment as the light of day dissipated the dark of night.

"Oh, here's Peter," Beatrice exclaimed jubilantly, opening the door. The odor of cooked meats exulted my nostrils.

"Good man," Brendan shouted from the other end of the narrow hallway that divided the living room from the kitchen.

He was dressed in an old, ragged housecoat that was tied around the middle with a piece of string. His genitalia were exposed. His penis was erect and dripping semen. Brendan apparently was always hungry and horny.

"Come on in for jayzus sake, cum in, cum in and sit yurself down on the parliamentary side of yur arse!" he hollered, pulling a chair from under the table and pushing me into it. "Yew'll have yur bit to eat now before the crows fly in the window and steal it all away in their beaks. Give the boy his mug of mud and throw on a steak and a few chops and whatever else yew can find in that cuntin' contraption," he said, pointing to the refrigerator.

Beatrice bustled and followed the orders of her pint-sized paramour. As I sat at the opposite end of the breakfast table looking at Brendan, I suddenly realized that he had at least one physical handicap. All of his teeth on the left side of his mouth were missing, knocked out in a fight with the cops or convicts, I assumed. We ate in silence.

"Will we go for a bit of a ramble on the boulevard?" he suddenly said.

"Do you wish for me to wait here or to come along with you both?" I asked.

"Oh, Brendan is talking to *you*, Peter," Beatrice blurted.

"Certainly, Brendan," I said. "I'd love to."

"If we leave right away we can have the whole cuntin' town to ourselves," he said as he patted me on the shoulder.

"*Slan leat mo bean* [good-bye woman]," I said to Beatrice as we left.

We walked down Cherokee Avenue in total silence, then Brendan suddenly said, "What do yew think of the other one, avick?"

"Well she seems like a very hospitable and charming lady, Brendan, also she seems to think that the sun shines from out of your asshole and your asshole alone," I opined.

My words sent Brendan into a spin. He turned, looked me hard in the face and stared. We continued west on Hollywood Boulevard. Occasionally Brendan stopped to look up at some huge garish billboard or marquee, and make a derogatory remark concerning its announcement. Intermittently he tried to speak to me but underwent hardships in getting his words. Finally he blurted, "I s-suppose when yew ch-chaps are out there on those sh-ships for f-fuckin' weeks on end, sh-shur I mean to say shur yiz are young and healthy and shur why not . . . I mean . . ."

His beefy face was flush-red. He moved several paces ahead of me, his two small hands joined behind him, his fingers twitching nervously. Finally we came upon the courtyard of the famous Grauman's Chinese Theatre where the glamour of Hollywood is "immortalized" in concrete. Impressions by the hundreds are embedded in the cement at the entrance of this pagoda-facaded cinema. The impressions of famous hands, legs, beards, guns, horses' hooves, noses and lips abound.

"Indeed what a load of fuckin' aul shite, typical Hollywood bullshite. The fuckin' aul Yanks, they think of everything, anything that will fetch an extra buck for them." Brendan bellowed as he jotted copiously on a wad of paper that he had extricated from his coat pocket.

"Here, avick, over here son, get a gander at this crock of shite," he said, pointing to an impression of a famous signature. "Indeed bejayzus if the whores had put an impression of her cunt or her asshole in the stuff, they would have been a damn sight more accurate, for bejayzus that was about the sum total of her talents."

Again he attempted to question me regarding the mysteries of man's lonely life at sea and all of its strange ramifications. As before, he experienced embarrassment, stopping halfway through his question. Silence prevailed. We continued to read the inscriptions.

"Brendan, if you're asking me if there is mutual wanks and shipboard buggery going on far out to sea, indeed the answer is an emphatic yes. It most certainly happens. And why not? Shur any man who is not mature or man enough to respect his needs and the needs of his neighbors . . . well, I suppose there has to be a thing or two wrong with such an infirm-minded son of a bitch. On board ships of the U.S. registry, I'd say that the practice of corn-holing and flipping one over the wrist for your fo'c'sle partner is a thing seldom practiced. You see, Brendan, the Yanks are a little behind the times when it comes to such needs in mortal men. My guess is that the great machine is more interested in getting the male populace married off and producing babies to keep the big wheel in crank, but aboard ships of the Scandinavian registries, with particular emphasis on the Norwegians, well Brendan, that's a different story. The Norwegians it appears are much more humane, understanding and to the point in these sensitive matters. However, there are rules of the game, that have to be observed."

"R-rules of the g-game?" he asked in a startled manner.

"Yes, well you know what I mean, Brendan, once you're in, you're in. Once a package deal is made, it's made. What I'm digging at is this—once you get together in a fo'c'sle with a coterie of shipmates and verbally sign up to go through a series of fucks and wanks or whatever else that's goin', you toss a coin or flip a card to see who gets corn-holed first, asshole banditry is in, then the next fellow gets his and so on right down the line. But you don't under any circumstances decide that once you've had yours, you're going to fuck off complaining of a sore asshole and leaving your partner standing with his dick loose. No siree, Brendan, that's the type of stuff that invites trouble, big trouble. Then you really wind up with a hot asshole."

Brendan was totally taken aback with my candor. He charged about the spacious courtyard, turning, twisting, wincing and staring at the impressions as if intoxicated.

"That's a g-great y-yarn y-yew j-just told," he blurted as he moved down the boulevard at a quick pace. Some four or five paces further on, he stopped, turned and shouted, "B-bejayzus s-son, sh-shur it's a great ch-chap that yew are altogether, a g-great and wonderful b-boy. Y-yew can say what yew like but yur p-poor aul d-drunken father, God help him, but he must have done his best to put it into yew when yew were a boy." Then he quickened his pace.

Finally I caught up to him and we both took a sharp left turn down into the Montecito parking lot, around the rear of the hotel and up into the service elevator.

"Open, open, open up for fucksake!" he cried as he pounded on the door. "C-cum on now s-son," he stuttered as Beatrice opened the door and let us in. "Go on Beatrice, put on a panful for the boy, he's famished with the hunger."

Brendan made a quick gallop to his electric typewriter. In a frenzied fit he peeled off his jacket and flung it to the floor. Then he began to pound on the keys. He was an exceptionally fast typist. In a matter of minutes up to a dozen pages were disgorged from the mechanical depths. He beamed cherubically as he took hold of each page, extricated it from the roller and flung it over his shoulder. Quick enigmatic looks and approving winks in my direction followed each little extrication.

Beatrice bubbled with delight as she set the table for our second breakfast. "Your teas will be ready in a minute," she said excitedly.

In a flash Brendan was in the kitchen pawing over and selecting the meats to be cooked for my breakfast. "Cook it well," he barked at Beatrice, "the boy likes his meats well done." Again Brendan was right! I have always cherished the taste and the aromas of well-cooked meat. We ate in typical silence.

On one occasion a small slippery chunk of steak wiggled from his grip and slithered to the floor, ricocheting and rattling against the legs of the table and chairs as it came to a halt alongside the refrigerator. Brendan laboriously bent down, picked up the bone, cursed it, sighed, then handed it to Beatrice who, in turn, rinsed it under the tap, dried it with a towel, and handed it back to him. Another lightning-quick gush of indecipherable invectives were spewed, then the defenseless morsel quickly disappeared down his gullet. A sadistic little chuckle followed.

"The chaps from the UPI will be here shortly," Beatrice said.

"The UPI," I said perplexedly, "what or who is the UPI?"

"Why don't you ask Brendan?"

Brendan continued to munch, then suddenly he stopped. The Behans eyed one another.

"The UPI is a syndicated column that is based here in this dreary quagmire," he ejaculated. "It is sometimes referred to as the United Press International. Its purpose is to record any and all interesting events that take place. That is to say, if in fact any such thing does take place, a thing which I very much doubt, but so be it." Then he went back to his bone. Beatrice fidgeted and gulped.

"We'll go for a dip," he suddenly said, darting into the bathroom.

Uncertainly I followed.

"Here avick, be a good chap and stuff yur ballox into these," he muttered, handing me my togs. He grabbed me. A look of ecstasy suffused his face as our penises grew. His expressions ran a gamut from ecstasy to anticlimax. Another tender of high accolades followed.

He beamed and went into a paroxysm of titters. "Bejayzus avick, but do yew know what it is? I'd be lost without yew. Indeed yew may never have gone to school but yew must have met the scholars on the way home. Shur aren't yew the flower of me flock, the heart of the roll. Indeed the fuckin' aul nuns and the Christian Brothers beyant in the nettle country, they didn't succeed much in destroying yur good God-given brain avick, wha . . ."

Along about eleven A.M. two men from the *Los Angeles News* arrived, and set up their recording equipment.

Brendan was in fine fig. Barefooted and ecstatic he strutted back and forth on the carpeted floor like a royal porcupine in heat. He asked and answered questions by the score, stopping here and there to do a little soft-shoe shuffle, and to launch another verbal assault against the child molesters. "The dirty man-beasts!"

Brendan sat up center and declaimed on a variety of well-selected topics, with great gusto and force, and spoke in orotund tones. He was uninterruptible and unstoppable. On a number of occasions, the interviewer tried to squeeze in a question. The man soon discovered that one did not talk to Brendan. One talked at Brendan, and was talked to by Brendan. Brendan prattled on like a truckful of hungry geese. "Now this has to be off the fucking record," was his quintessential line as he held an uncompromising glare, remained mute and ordered the turning off of the recording device. Seconds later, when his clandestine remarks were culminated, he instructed the man to once again turn the control button to "on." The history-making event continued.

His *mots* for the morning were on homosexuality and pedophilia. In a matter of minutes, he was saturated with sweat. Beatrice sporadically toweled him off, then once again he was on his feet swinging his cup and saucer, and blessing us all while singing Latin psalms. "*Dominus vobiscum et cum spiritu tuo Hosanna in excelsis benedictus qui venit in nomine domine Hosanna in excelsis."* Then reverting to the language of the English: "Holy, holy, holy heaven and earth are full of thy glory. Hosanna in the highest. Blessed is he that cometh in the name of the Lord. Hosanna in the highest." Then swallowing the last dregs from the cup, he wiped his mouth with a clean white handkerchief that Beatrice had handed him. Next he genuflected, thumped his abdomen, arose, spread his venerable hands over his makeshift chalice and improvised host. Then turning to the three of us, with a stoic expression on his face, he muttered, "Take ye and eat ye of this for this is my body and this is my blood." Sometime during the interview or prior to its commencement, he had pocketed a few biscuits in preparation for his mock mass.

His little recital was commendably realistic, but obviously not appreciated by the newsmen. Lightning-quick jokes on the subjects of altar boy–buggery by members of the Church's higher ecclesiastics abounded. He interrupted his proceedings to savagely condemn the so-called strict Christian ethic for its condemnation of the homosexual act between mature adults, regarding it as an intrinsic wrong, an aberration of mankind. "Shur fuckin' aul jayzus shur what of it, so who cares what grown-ups do or don't fuckin' well do. Shur just as long as they don't do it in the meadows where it might frighten the sheep," he roared with great jollity while toasting his cup.

He continued his mock mass, improvising the paten and chalice with his cup and saucer while displaying an enormous avidity for what he was doing. He said the introductory prayers, proved himself well versed with the reading from the Bible, the creed, the intercession prayers, and the entire Roman theology. I deduced that he had at sometime in his life been an altar boy.

Pious words, genuflections, and smatterings of derogatory little chuckles and giggles emitted from his puckered-up mouth, while his eyes darted and rose pseudosanctimoniously towards the ceiling. He prayed, chanted, scratched his scrotum and raised the improvised wine with tea. The bread with bread. He kissed the consecrated altar, and passed the saucer amongst us as though he were taking up the mass collection.

The newsmen sat and snapped picture after picture of him at play.

Finally, elevating the bread and teacup in consecration: "This is my body and this is my blood," The mock mass was over. The men sighed with relief. Beatrice took the cup and saucer from him and placed them in the kitchen sink. The men attempted to question him on world topics, but with an acerbic little grin, Brendan arose and extended his right hand. The interview was obviously over. The men quickly departed.

Brendan ordered Beatrice to "conjure up a bit of grub for us."

Shortly after noon, a man from the UPI arrived and introduced himself as Joe Finnegan. Finnegan remained for lunch, a swim, and an interview. At one point during the interview, he turned to me and asked, "What is *your* name, and what are *you* doing in Hollywood and in what way are *you* connected to Brendan?" He sat poised with pencil and paper in hand.

Brendan became furious and charged around the room like a cuckoo clock suddenly gone haywire. Finnegan quickly returned his attention to his central character. Brendan's sullen face instantly softened. In one lilting monologue he espoused and opined on everything from the senselessness of filters on filter-tip cigarettes to the futility of attempting to convince Irish Catholic females that the "dropping of their knickers at the strategic moment was a thing highly essential to their futures."

Bright and early on the following morning, I was awakened by "Listen avick I'll see yew right away on the corner of Hollycunt and Las Palmas." Brendan's strict instructions were given in a clandestine whisper. Minutes later I arrived clad in a pair of black pants, black shoes, black shirt, and white tie. We met on the southeast corner. Brendan looked east and west of the semibarren boulevard. I looked north and south. We nodded affirmatively. Brendan dashed south on Las Palmas and did a quick scan of the freshly published tabloids. His bulging face turned purple. He fumed and spumed. Finally, he came upon a "rag" that sported a sequence of him in action. Pictures of Brendan with his cup in one hand, his saucer in the other abounded. My name was mentioned in the news-making story.

His composure returned. He chuckled and smiled. "Marvelous, fuckin' jayzus marvelous." The newspaper hawker was handed a ten-dollar bill. "Keep the change, yur blood's worth bottling," Brendan said as he motioned me away.

"We'll stop off at yur house for a bit," he said, bemusedly.

"Certainly Brendan," I said. We continued on down the boulevard.

Upstairs in my room I excused myself to go to the bathroom. When I returned to the room, I found Brendan lying facedown, naked in bed, my pillow tucked under his crotch.

"I'm sorry Brendan," I said, "but you see, in my humble opinion, I consider sodomy to be a most brutal and cowardly act, the most primitive and disgusting of defilations to the body house. What I did when I was a horny youngster at sea on ships has nothing whatsoever to do with what I feel and do now in my adulthood."

He lay motionless for a time. An ominous, guilt-ridden silence pervaded. He turned, avoided my face, dressed and quickly departed. My remarks to Brendan didn't reflect my true climate on the subject. I simply could not sodomize Brendan. Yet, I was vividly aware that in spite of myself I was growing to care about him, but not physically. I felt ashamed at my inadequacy. I knew that I was beginning to genuinely love Brendan Behan. Never before had anyone shown so much concern for me and my well-being. I was now vividly aware of the man's most desperate needs.

In the weeks to come, early each morning I was awakened by my phone. Brendan and I developed a symbiotic relationship. We treated one another with equal deference. Brendan's attitude towards me continued to be one of caution, concern and courteousness. We became a pivotal point and integral part in each other's lives. Beatrice was delighted with our befriendment of each other. She encouraged our friendship.

The final draft of *Richard's Cork Leg* was now well underway. He shared its progress with me.

Brendan's exultations bolstered my spirits. My physical presence, our after-breakfast wanks and my stories about shipboard buggery became a cathartic force in his writing. He said I was a bright and shiny Apollo. His occasional naiveté amazed and amused me. His acolyte innocence sometimes stultified me. I was made privy to the secrets of his soul and the innermost nucleus of the man. When I told him I loved the razzmatazz of his pizazz, he chortled.

I was now getting to know the man, who was a far cry from the myth. I felt mesmerized. No sooner would Beatrice have started her daily run to Hughes Supermarket, Brendan would pick up on the very syllable where we left off the day before, and beg me to go into the retelling of the same boy-buggery story. He took to these stories as voraciously as a vampire attacking a network of varicose veins. They relieved his early morning doldrums and dyspeptic humor. Brendan was much more a sensualist than a romanticist. Shipboard homosexuality, and every other aspect of the entire homosexual catalog, sent his ears aflutter. Yet I felt that, deep down, he was a desperately tortured creature. His tension was palpable, but our relationship seemed to afford him a soothing effect. After breakfast, a bouncy, nervous energy flooded into his every nerve and fiber.

Brendan's main problem was a kind of sexual hysteria that hung over him like a wet overcoat on a small hook. It dominated his every twitch and tremor. The void of sexual satiety in him was causing problems of major proportion. It stymied his discipline, stunting his growth as a productive writer. Now, my thoughts and easy candid opinions seemed to afford him placebo-affective nourishment that he needed. New waves of fresh ideas flowed for him.

My message to him was short and simple. "We are all, each and every one of us, independent individuals going our own way in life and entitled to fulfill our personal needs, including sexual satisfaction." I opined that Christianity had no right to deny a sexual animal his civil rights. He told me my appraisals of life brought his soul a renaissance. His creative juices flowed profusely. He said he loved being with me. The man beneath the facade became a part and parcel of my psyche.

Brendan was not by habit especially friendly with others. He was too egocentric and violent. But his violence was verbal. He joked a lot, but laughed little. He never ceased coaxing for sexy anecdotes.

If I told him something of an exceptionally titillating nature such as a sodomistic attack on a very young, gullible and easily conned merchant seaman, his eyes lit up and shone like a pair of collection plates at a Catholic high holy mass. He'd demand that I retell the story. Stories of mutual locker room wanks and sodomy between professional boxers who had, minutes before, punched each other faceless excited him enormously. He had great difficulty in equating strength, force and masculinity with homosexuality. But shipboard stories were his preference.

"And what would the captain say or do when he found out what was going on on his ship?" he once sputtered.

"Very often it's the captain himself who does the conning," I explained.

"Sweet mother of merciful jayzus, shur isn't that great," he sputtered. "The best yarn I've heard in years. I'll stick it in me play, wha!"

In the Behan household, pandemonium was a thing that was never more than a few frayed threads away. He'd always call for more. I became an avid liar. I recounted dozens of stories concerning sinkings, drownings, tanker explosions, shark attacks on fellow seafarers who had fallen while working over the side and beatings at the hands of rival union goons and the police. Brendan waved these stories away as if they were the most boring stories of the century being told by some arthritic old lady in a confession box on a late Saturday night. Brendan had a one-track mind. He was also the most paranoid person that I have ever known. To catch someone in even the smallest of lies was to him a monumental achievement. One morning as I was emotion-deep in a yarn he quickly interjected, "Listen avick but I meant to ask yew, what was the name of that ship and where was she headin' for at the time that yur man buggered the boy?" I was annoyed.

"The name of the ship was the *Perfugistania,*" I retorted sharply. "She was owned and operated by Spielbugle Tanker Corporation of Liberia. The captain's name was Diakakis but we usually referred to him as Diddles Diakakis by virtue of the fact that he never let up with his diddling and cackling when he was amongst the younger lads in the crew."

Brendan looked at me as though I were a man who came to rob him of his soul. He dashed out of the kitchen and into the bedroom, slamming the door behind him.

But Brendan was a multifaceted, multidimensional man who never ceased to entertain me. His dependence upon me afforded me the fulfillment of a dire, inherent need in me.

In the Behan apartment Brendan seldom spoke, much less held conversations. Beatrice spoke only when spoken to, which was something that seldom happened. Yet, Beatrice sorely loved her husband. In her

eyes he could do no wrong. He was a major celebrity. A world fig-
urehead. A celebrated author, playwright and artist. She relished her
station in life. His bacchanalian swings did not seem to vex her. However, he and Beatrice lived in no easy alliance. They got along in their
own different spheres.

Irishmen are men who very often measure their women's worth in
terms of their docility and bovinity. Since Brendan showed no compul-
sion to provide for her, Beatrice had no legitimate claim to personal
independence, personhood or assertiveness. She now depended a great
deal upon me. This was something else that I was inordinately proud
of. The delicate subject of family life, its tender tendrils and ramifications, was of no gut interest to Brendan. Rarely did he display a morsel
of sensitivity or outward solicitude towards Beatrice. Rather than being
his wife, she was his nurse and watchdog in war.

She was always indelibly there, crisp and capable, a bedazzled,
slightly bovine figure wandering in his wake, in the steamy jungles of
his raw rhetoric and attention-grabbing shenanigans. She basked in his
celebrity but was embarrassed over her inability to curb his antics.

In her immediate presence he exuded great concern for my health
and well-being, while complimenting me and punching my chest,
shoulders and arms, in a praiseworthy manner, but never complimenting her.

When he was not listening, in sotto voce she told me of her studies at
an art college in Dublin and how she had gained a small measure of
success as a painter prior to her marriage to Brendan in 1955. Subsequently, the exigencies of her marriage cut deeply into her time. Her
painting and sketching were quickly curtailed. She told me that she
once worked as a botanist at the Museum of Natural History in Dublin. I deduced from her conversation snatches that she was thoroughly
convinced that Brendan was a literary genius and possibly the greatest
Irish dramatist who ever put pen to paper. It was for this reason she
waylaid all her dreams and desires to conduct her wifely responsibilities. Brendan gladly let her. From the beginning of their marriage, she
put him on a pedestal and worshipped at his shrine. She took care of
everything that she felt might impinge upon his time. Anything that
was conducive to his needs was A-O.K. with her. Somehow she always
seemed to survive his caperings and cosmic panics.

Although Beatrice represented the perennial mother figure to him,
Brendan loathed the infirmities of females. This attitude endeared him
to me even more. The painful barren solitude that he imposed upon
her without the leaven of concern somewhat distressed me, for the
reason that her countenance constantly bore the mask of the betrayed.
I admired this compassionate, patient, commonsensical woman who
was totally void of grudge and incapable of rage or emotional outburst.
Brendan was her manchild. I was her adopted. For the first time in my
life, I felt needed, wanted and important. Beatrice was the ideal spouse

for Brendan, always on the go, a servile figure, washing, cooking, desperately avoiding eye-to-eye encounters as she hurried from room to room, avoiding his path and never venturing an opinion. When he needed to know something, with great cordiality he asked me his questions. When he felt the need to address his wife he always spoke to her in full octave range and from another room. He referred to her as Beaaatrice, putting his consonance on the *a*. She always reponded to his call with instant fervor.

During our many walks, Brendan complained bitterly over Beatrice's inability to produce for him a son. He whined and lamented and gave a strong indication that the barrenness of a childless home had caused him an additional welter of mental anguish. I arrived at a conclusion that Beatrice felt inadequate and somewhat guilty. Perhaps it was for this reason that she behaved so obsequiously and kept quiescent and caged her true physical radiance.

The Irish, by virtue of their strict macho, Catholic upbringing, have great difficulties in showing their emotions or expressing their feelings. I had observed this lifelong inadequacy in my father. In spite of his protestations and behavior I felt that Brendan was very fond of Beatrice.

"Do we have children?" he liked to chirp in public. "Certainly we have children, one child! *Me*. Ask me wife over there, she'll verify me statement," he vociferously concluded.

"Genius" was the specific encomium that titillated Brendan most of all. "I'm a genius, I must be, didn't yew read today's rags?" he often said, interrupting his one-man gabfests, "If yew don't believe me, ask Peter or Beatrice there, go ahead." We both nodded affirmatively.

In public, the kaleidoscopic-faced showman displayed a totally different side to his nature. In the hotel's waiting room, at the poolside and along the illustrious boulevards, when expounding, Brendan's face took on a scintillating mixture of innocence and shyness that is characteristic of the Celtic people. It is a sophistication that is often indefinable to the eye of the stranger. Yet Brendan was supremely ugly and physically unattractive. His mind was not in the true sense of the word analytical or clinically objective. He lived a less than serious sort of existence, always on the go, playing little get-even games and acting out bizarre sexual fantasies; setting someone up for quick emotional and verbal KO's was a pathological part of his master plan. He exuded a bantamweight spontaneous agility, a jungle electricity and a pseudo-venomous squint that always fascinated and compromised me.

In bars, restaurants and other public places, he belabored and shocked the famous and the fatuous. He became increasingly bold and assertive as he told and retold bawdy, scatalogical stories, while with straight-faced obscenities he answered questions about his works and the well-publicized state of his declining health. Scholars and critics were his favorite victims. This was the phenomenon of the recalcitrant

Brendan Behan, the most famous contemporary Irish man of letters. He expounded opulently on political trends and plentiously alluded to his own left-wing leanings. He claimed to have a promiscuous affection for people of every stratum and an emotional identification with those from the lowest levels of society. Somehow I felt it difficult to accept these statements for reasons that his political naiveté never ceased to amaze me. His so-called far left leanings and his unsupported knowledge were in constant conflict with his own emotional and sexual upheavals. In this totalitarian town of plastic people he desperately wanted to be heralded as the romantic liberator.

Brendan's supersensitivity to every human nuance, along with his self-deprecating gab and his enormous good nature, both exhausted and exasperated me and endeared me to him. In a few short days, I became determined to solidify our friendship and become a centripetal force for his erratic behavior and abnormal life.

In my company, Brendan was usually in ruminative good humor. We drove around and did a great deal of sightseeing. He was a model of deportment and the wittiest and most charming entertainer that I had ever known. He accepted my comments, opinions and suggestions with grace and accolades. He constantly worried about my health, comfort and immediate needs and insisted that we stop at every steak house that we drove by. In my immediate company he was remarkably whole and in command, as he lived up to the shocking things that his public expected of him.

He criticized American females for their rudeness and their non-femininity while he ridiculed the American male for his nonmasculinity and his constant use of cologne. In his own unique way he promoted great excitement, hilarity and joy as though it were the last remaining virtue left to mankind. He exposed a great human compassion and special consideration for those he had just met and liked. Handouts abounded as he strolled the avenues where the down-and-outs gathered. He was forever cashing pocketfuls of travelers checks.

Brendan's impressions of people were lightning-quick, accurate and irrevocable. On the occasions when he was verbally assaulted for the provocativeness and the salty language in his plays, Brendan assumed a pouting awestruck wounded look and looked to me for immediate assistance, which I gladly undertook to administer in the form of threatening words or punches. For this he was grateful and proceeded to tender me with warm invectives.

Brendan reveled in making lascivious remarks and pinching voluptuous females on their ample derrieres. When these advances were rebuffed he ended up sulking, pouting and making remarks about his ugliness and the real nitty-gritty wickedness of the female species. Next he proceeded to mumble in monosyllables and threaten to get recklessly drunk. These little episodes usually ended up with Brendan and me wending our way to my hotel room in benumbed silence while we mutually agreed that all sex fiends deserved to be shot on the spot.

In the solace of my tiny room, Brendan made no bones about the fact that he saw himself as an impostor and a literary fraud. These momentary, self-pitying outbursts sent him reeling into fits of unshakable depression. I felt honored to be the one Brendan had selected to whom to make privy such soul-purging confessions.

Doors were beginning to open for me that were never before opened. I was meeting people whom I had fantasized about meeting for an eternity, but had not even in my most vainglorious moments expected to meet. I felt reborn.

IV

Brendan had an irritating habit of keeping secret his immediate plans.

One morning directly after we had eaten, he turned to me and said crisply, "Cum on avick, let's go for a ride."

"Where are we going, Brendan?" I asked with great surprise.

"Don't concern yourself avick, follow me. Beatrice too!"

The three of us piled into my car and drove off. Finally we came to a pair of very tall wrought-iron gates. They were the gates to Forest Lawn Memorial Cemetery. "Park the car there," he demanded, pointing to a spot inside the gates.

"But that's obviously against the cemetery rules," I retorted.

"Park the cuntin' thing over there," he said peremptorily. Brendan was in a strange sullen mood.

The cemetery is the final resting place for many of Hollywood's screen stars: Theda Bara, Humphrey Bogart, Francis X. Bushman, W. C. Fields, Errol Flynn, Jean Harlow and many more. It is a vast expanse of green rolling hills, towering trees, splashing fountains, sweeping lawns, singing birds and a colorful array of uncanny inscriptions carved in fancy headstones.

Brendan picked up a batch of pictorial guide maps. "Follow me," he said exuberantly. Suddenly he was as bouncy and as bubbly as a boy at Christmastime. With pencil and paper in hand he copiously copied notes from the wittiest of the inscriptions.

Other visitors who momentarily crossed his path were rewarded with a few of his witticisms. He was nonstop.

"In Dublin it is said that I have a sense of humor that would cause me to laugh at a funeral. That is of course providin' it isn't me own funeral. But I must say dyin' as a lark is a thing that doesn't suit my temperament. It's too permanent. I'm a garrulous man be nature.

"A colleague of mine says to me one day, 'Brendan,' says he, 'my plays will be remembered long after you're dead and rotten in your grave.' 'They will,' says I to the cunt. 'Well' says I, 'but *yew* won't remember them after *yew're* dead and rotten in *yur* grave. Fuck off says I!'

"Me uncle Peadair Kearney wrote the limericks to the, er, excuse me, I mean the lyrics to the Irish national anthem. The Irish government, the good-natured shower of hypocrites that they are, on the day of his funeral didn't they have all of Dublin's traffic lights synchronized the color of green to enable the cortege to get to the cemetery on time— on time for the priest to get on with his funereal obligation, then stock up on his evening malts before the pubs closed!

"A reporter once described me as a methylated martyr. I'm a bad Catholic by nature. Bad Catholicism is the religion of all great artists. Rabelais and Michelangelo in particular. But this is me religion only when I'm dying. In such instances I'm God-fearing and very religious.

"Country people put years on me. They're as talkative as a tomb. Talking about tombs, that reminds me, I must say me prayers." Brendan blessed himself, then charged over to the side of a freshly dug grave.

"Cunt over here Peter, avick," he shouted from the gravesite. "And get a gander at what yur man whispered to yur woman seconds before he split her in two with the family hatchet.

"Here, me aul son, did yew see what the other greasy ballox shouted to the sheriff just before he slipped from the bridge," he shouted from another site.

At another burial site he laughed hysterically. "No, no, no, no bejayzus yew won't me darlin' daughter, no indeed yew will not, now, not even in the highest hole of yur arse."

I rushed over to get a closer look at what was amusing him.

The inscription read: "Good night, my sweet, see you in the morning."

"That will teach the cunt a lesson not to go upping the poor aul ballox with a fatal kick in the nuts just because he arrived home roaring drunk after a hard day's work in some pig-packing factory," he concluded.

Brendan appeared happier than ever before. He was charming, wild, witty and gracious. His face was cherubic and glistened with a rare youthfulness. Unquestionably, he felt at ease here amongst the monoliths and the floral wreaths. The elegance of his talk, the lightning-quick acerbity of his wit and the spontaneousness of his spirit exhilarated me. He continued to behave like a kid in a candy store as he meandered around the grassy knolls and grey headstones, crouching, blinking, wincing, snickering and commenting and jotting.

"Listen avick," Brendan said to a high-braided attendant who had crossed his path, "The only reason why I've been staying alive is to save funeral expenses, b-but I'll tell yew this much, now that I've heard of yur low bargain rates, and yur policy of accepting American Express travelers cards, I promise yew I'll think twice about the immediate future."

Brendan gave the perplexed youngster a reassuring tap in the left kidney and moved on, then stopped short, turned and said, "But don't misunderstand me now, I don't mean to say that I want to spend me better days as a box of snuff in the vest pocket of some upper-middle-class cunt who considers himself too grand to appreciate the working class amongst us." At his instruction we moved off. Brendan was suddenly confronted by a tearful little old lady who was nervously fondling a pair of rosary beads. The old woman smiled wanly, interrupted her prayers and arose to greet him.

"Oh, Mr. Beean," she exclaimed excitedly, "I'm so thrilled to meet you, and above all places, here in Forest Lawn. I was in New York last fall and had the great fortune of being able to see your wonderful play *The Hostage*. I was wondering Mr. Beean, is there a message in your play? And if so, what is it?" The woman dabbed her cheeks, smiled and waited.

"Message! Message! Message! What am I now, some sort of a fuckin' messenger boy from the local post office is it?" he snapped.

Shocked, the old woman blessed herself and scurried back to the grave. "I'll pray for you, Mr. Beean," she said dolefully, bowing her head.

"Pray for me! Pray for me! Why? Am I scheduled to be executed?"

Here and there, gravediggers were bending their backs, digging holes and building perpendicular walls to separate the living from the lifeless. Traipsing amongst the crypts and fountains, Beatrice intermittently brought me up to date on Brendan's European debacles with the law. I listened attentively, then ambled off on my own. The sun shone brightly.

Suddenly I heard a paroxysm of shrieks and screams. I ran up to the top of a nearby hill and saw Beatrice jumping up and down like a yo-yo. "Quick! Peter, it's Brendan. He's in trouble. Hurry, something is the matter with him."

I dashed over to where Brendan was standing with his two hands to his face. He seemed to be in pain. "What's up, Brendan?" I said placing a hand on his shoulder.

"It's the other dirty fuck face," he lamented still holding his hands to his eyes. "He tried to blind me, the whore." He pointed to an urn.

"Who, Brendan, who?" I asked excitedly as I scanned the vast acreage.

"The poxy-faced ballox doused me eyes with red-hot ashes," he roared as he kicked a marbled wall that contained several rows of urns. An attendant approached on foot.

"Listen, Brendan," I said, "but I think it's time for us to go."

Brendan continued to thump and kick the wall. "Let me at the cunt!" he roared as he attempted to pull a tiny glass door from the vault where an urn was placed.

Finally we started back to where the ashen-faced Beatrice stood waiting.

"Did yew ever fuck a boy in a cemetery?" he suddenly asked.

"Naturally I fucked a boy in a cemetery," I assured him. "Isn't that what cool marble stones are for? For keeping your balls cool while doing what comes naturally."

Brendan chirruped with glee.

We made our way up a precipitous knoll. Before reaching its top Brendan stopped short, blinked and asked, "D-did yew give any more thought to what I asked yew the other day?"

"What did you ask me the other day, Brendan?"

"The t-thing about doing the threesome with the other aul cow above," he said nodding towards Beatrice.

"I'm glad you asked, Brendan," I said with affected excitement. "As a matter of fact that is the one thing that has been uppermost in my mind. I think the time for doing is here and now. What say, Brendan, shall we get on with it and quit the gab?"

"W-we'll t-talk about it l-later," he sputtered as we quickened our pace.

"Blazes," Beatrice chuckled, "you two seem to be enjoying your-selves."

"We are indeed, Beatrice," I said emphatically. Brendan sauntered away. Beatrice once again picked up the threads of her favorite topic. She continued her litany and told me of a doctor in Canada who wanted Brendan to undergo neurological tests and head X-rays. The doctor believed that something was pressing on Brendan's brain. Bren-dan wouldn't hear tell of it. He claimed that the whirr of the camera would make him dizzy. She also told me of various psychiatrists who recommended deep psychoanalysis for Brendan. But he wouldn't hear tell of submitting himself to such counterproductive nonsense. "Shur if they ever removed me neuroses, it's back to the paint pot and the brush it would be for me. Shur isn't me neurosis the pick and the shovel of me trade," he had said.

Brendan suddenly reappeared, grabbed hold of my sleeve and whis-pered into my ear, "D-did I ever tell yew avick, b-but I know a chap in Dublin who works in a morgue, luvs to ride the corpses. Says it's a great gas. Did yew ever fuck a corpse?"

"No, it's not my style, Brendan."

He snickered and scurried away. A short while later he rejoined us. He was agog with glee as he read his latest notes to us. Then he stuffed them into Beatrice's handbag. Brendan was an inveterate gatherer of brochures and colorful pamphlets. Later I came upon him as he was standing gaping with gawk-eyed wonder at a statue of two toga-clad Roman gladiators. One of the gladiators was standing over his fallen foe.

"Peadar a cara" [Peter my friend] Brendan said, his hands twitching behind his back, "what do yew think that the chap standing up is about to do to the bugger on the grass?"

"Bugger him up the arse," I said. "Isn't that what you would do if you were in his sandals?"

"Good man, avick." Brendan chuckled and darted away.

Prior to winding up our day at the cemetery, we visited the Wee Kirk of the Heather, the Little Church of the Flowers, God's Garden, the Memorial Court of Honor, and the Last Supper Window, which is a magnificent stained glass re-creation of Leonardo da Vinci's master-piece. We also sat through a late evening screening of Jan Styka's painting of the Crucifixion. Other spiritual experiences that we savored were the unveiling of the Resurrection, the Paradise Doors, and the multimillion pieces of Venetian glass mosaics.

A short while later, after Beatrice and I had returned from making a call to nature, we discovered that Brendan was nowhere in sight. We called his name and heard the echo of our voices reverberate through the high walls of the mortuaries and mausoleums.

"I have a hunch that he might be in the car waiting for us," I said, beckoning her to follow me.

We hurried to where the car was parked, but Brendan was still no-where in sight. Suddenly I caught a glimpse of a familar intractable looking mop of hair bobbing up and down in the front seat. I rushed over and found Brendan crouched on the floor. His eyes glistened with mischief and malice. I banged on the rolled-up window, "Open up, Brendan, open up!"

Brendan bared his half a mouthful of rotten teeth and snickered.

"Open up, Open the fucking door!" I yelled.

He fidgeted with the button control panels on the insides of the doors. The windows charged up and down. The radio played, my bat-tery lay dying under the hood.

For a considerable period of time Brendan had displayed a great love for toying with my car radio. En route to the cemetery I had in graphic detail explained to him that the life of the battery was long past extinction. To play the radio or to meddle with the window control buttons prior to turning over the engine would prove disastrous. "The baldness of the front tires is also a danger to the life of all of us," I explained.

Brendan had listened attentively to my warnings. He seemed keenly interested. A look of fear had crept into his face.

I placed my hands on top of the car and shook it violently, then dashed from one side to the other, demanding that he open up.

A frenzied little sneer froze in his porcine puss. The windows continued to jump up and down. I shot my fingers in over the rising glass and tried to stop the elevation of a window. My intentions were to reach down and lift the lock button on the inside of the door.

The tips of my fingers became bruised and discolored.

He grinned with devilish delight.

Finally I was able to slip off a shoe and jam it hard between the rising glass and the top of the door. I worked frantically and finally succeeded in getting the window lowered enough for me to get my other hand in and raise the button. Infuriated, I opened the door, grabbed Brendan by the collar of his coat, extricated him from the seat and slammed him onto a well-manicured lawn.

"What the fuck do you think you're doing?" I yelled.

"Just trying to get the bit of news on the radio," he reciprocated with an affected innocence.

I jumped in behind the wheel, inserted the key and turned it. My heart pounded. The engine whirred, sputtered, and croaked. My face fell into the palms of my sweaty hands. The battery was as dead as the citizens that lay planted in the hills around us.

Hysterically, I ordered Beatrice to sit behind the wheel, then ordered Brendan to assist me in pushing from the rear. Beatrice refused to sit. Brendan wouldn't push. A bargain was reached. Beatrice pushed from the rear. I pushed from the side with one hand on the steering wheel. Brendan sat in the front seat, picking his nose and complaining profusely "B-bejayzus but we'll never get back to Hollypussy at this fuckin' rate of going."

Sweating and exhausted, I finally reached the outside of the cemetery and onto the highway. I started to run and minutes later came upon a gas station where I hired the services of an attendant with a set of battery-boosting jump cables. When it came time to ante up for the services rendered, Brendan refused to dig into his pockets. His contention was that since the car belonged to me, the maintenance of its internal organs was *my* dilemma.

"But we came here on your account," I demanded.

Brendan stood by his convictions and picked his nostrils. I remained adamant. The attendant departed in a huff, unpaid. We drove off.

On our way back to the hotel I reached under the dashboard and with one hard jerk destroyed all of the wires leading to the radio. With a spare screwdriver I destroyed the mechanics of the window-control boxes. Brendan tittered and juggled his lapful of notes.

"Marvelous, fuckin' jayzus marvelous, indeed the poor aul Yanks, they do have a sense of humor after all," he chirped. "Too bad they have to wait until their death to say what's on their minds."

His face was aflutter with impish delight as he studied and organized his precious possessions.

The evening air held the heat of the red-hot day. Cars were piled up in front of my dust-laden windscreen as I stopped for a red light. To the right of me was a twin-entranced gas station. One entrance facing north and south, the other leading into a side street.

Brendan grinned. My blood boiled. The light turned green. My foot went down hard on the brake. I turned the wheel hard to the right. Brendan's feet flew up against my chest. His plethora of notes scattered like confetti. Beatrice came flying over the backseat of the car. Brendan roared and savagely denigrated the contemporary youths of Ireland. "The miserable fuckin' savages."

"I wholeheartedly agree, Brendan," I said. "It's a sad state of affairs. Indeed! Indeed!" I hit the gas pedal.

Brendan's face was suddenly splattered up against the windscreen. His hands and legs were entwined around the instruments on the dashboard. Beatrice worked frantically to free him. I pushed down harder on the accelerator. The hand on the speedometer registered ninety miles per hour.

Brendan slid to the floor and gathered up his notes. I brought the car up to its maximum speed, hit the brakes, then the gas pedal, again the brakes, and made a series of sharp right and left turns. Brendan was experiencing great difficulty organizing his papers. "We'll soon be home Brendan," I said joyfully as I continued my top-speed, zigzag course.

"Not if yew keep this fuckin' lot up," he moaned. "In the name of the holy vinegar fuckin' jayzus," he sputtered, "is it trying to murder the lot of us yew are?"

In the rearview mirror Beatrice looked the picture of death. *"Blazes, blazes,"* she moaned. A hand totally drained of blood crept up over the back of my seat and pointed to the speedometer.

"Since you're a man of wisdom and rare words, Brendan, I'll slow down a bit," I said, "but I hope you realize that my slowing down will put us home a little late, too late for the evening news perhaps!"

In the apartment we ate in silence.

"If you'll be kind enough to excuse me, B.B. and B.B.," I said, "I must be off. Thanks for a perfect day."

Brendan followed me to the elevator. Just as the door was about to shut in his face, he stuck his head in and whispered seriously, "Listen avick, but I've been doin' some careful thinkin'. I think maybe yur right, tomorrow morning we'll go down to the grease monkey's and get a set of tires, ones with a few pubic hairs on them at least, what?"

"I know what you mean Brendan," I said. *"Slan leat anois a cara* [Good-bye now, my friend]."

For some time, I had been vividly aware of Brendan's unique set of delicate emotions. I also discovered that the best way for me to handle these impromptu upsets was to retaliate with little shows of violence and self-fortitude.

The following day he purchased a small secondhand portable radio. Nothing else.

Some of southern California's vast network of highways and freeways were then made up of four different lanes, two lanes on the northbound side, two on the southbound. The outside lanes are designated by the Traffic Control Bureau for the slower-moving cars, the inside ones for the faster cars. Drivers who drive slow on the fast lane, just as the drivers who drive fast on the slow lane, can be ticketed by the disgustingly patronizing spit-and-polish Highway Patrol Police.

Brendan Behan was sometimes an extremely difficult man to chauffeur. He was always in a hurry getting to his destination. One morning I again reminded him of the condition of the tires and the battery and the stark necessity to replace them.

"Certainly, acourse me aul son, shur we'll get new ones first thing in the mornin'," was his reply.

To keep my tires from overheating and bursting, I was forced to drive a zigzag course on these lanes while I kept a sharp eye out for the Highway Patrol. A front wheel blowout became my greatest fear.

Brendan had suddenly become an extremely parsimonious fellow. Every nickel and dime spent by Beatrice and me on groceries and gas and oil had to be meticulously accounted for. Attempting to get Brendan to ante up for these daily lay outs was as difficult as extracting wisdom teeth from a pregnant sow. This dramatic change in his nature was inexplicable to me.

One morning as we were about to begin a car ride, I said to Beatrice, "I'm sorry, Beatrice, but from here on out I am going to have to rely on you for the finances to keep the car on the road."

"That won't do you any good, Peter," she lamented, "you'll have to see Brendan about that. I have no money. I never have. Brendan keeps the strings on the family purse. But be careful like a good boy, won't you, Peter! You know how he is!"

By then, Brendan's friendship was a thing that I dearly cherished. He treated me as though I were the quintessential partner that he had searched for all of his life. "Bejayzus avick, but do yew know what it is that I am about to say to yew? B-b-but so far, everything that yew have said or done has been a hundred percent *ceart* [right]," was a constant comment.

He was now into his tenth day of sobriety. A minor miracle was at hand, a record was in the making. Prior to this he had, according to Beatrice, never gone into a fifth day without a glass in hand. The "fifth day crisis" she had dubbed that all-important day. Beatrice watched him like a hawk and waited patiently. "Oh, you will be a good boy and keep a close eye on him for me," was her quintessential line. I constantly assured the fretting lady that "all will be well, just leave Brendan to me."

According to Beatrice the last time that Brendan had taken up a drink was in San Francisco. That drinking spree ended in a major breakdown and hospitalization for him.

But Brendan had taken an incomprehensible dive into sullen fits and anxious outbursts. He repeatedly engaged her in one-sided heated arguments. He appeared on the verge of an emotional breakdown. I found myself entwining my arms around him more often and doubly reassuring him that our future was bright. Beatrice kept up her taut, stalwart exterior and left his well-being to me.

In their household a beguiling aura of mystery, confusion, hysteria, betrayal and domestic menace now steadily prevailed. Betimes I felt like a pawn in a human chess game. On other occasions I felt like the brave rat who came in out of the weather to courageously challenge the keeper of the house. Typical, quick little flurries of eye-to-eye encounters between the Behans were common. Often in discombobulating and embarrassing moments I excused myself and prepared to leave, only to have my exits quickly curtailed by Beatrice's dash to the kitchen and her putting the kettle on the stove. "Oh you must stay a while longer, sure Brendan and I were about to have a cup of tea and you might as well join us," became her standard suggestion.

Brendan's nerves were now in tatters.

My friendship with the Behans was still in its incipient stages and undergoing some sticky vicissitudes. Brendan's true sexual predilections were beginning to astound me. They forced me to take a fair measure of personal inventory.

During the late fifties and the early sixties the vast expanses of highways and freeways that linked California with the rest of America were thronged with thousands of young boys and girls. These children were the runaways of the American society. Children trapped in the cold tar of their circumstances. Products of busted homes, battered by their uncaring fathers and mothers, but by dint of courage and of necessity they utilized their innate cunning and street smarts to garner their freedom.

Brendan Behan loved these children. However, his love for them was a love very different from the love that most other mortal men display for children of that legion.

When driving around on these highways, Brendan made it a habit of keeping a keen eye out for these gaggles of youngsters. He demanded that I pull over when we came upon them.

For purposes of keeping a modicum of peace, I adhered to his demands. No sooner would I have made the pullover, Brendan would be bubbling with excitement and guffawing. "P-pull up avick, pull up and let's give the poor little cunts a lift." He would have already opened the front door and be in the precarious process of stepping onto the shoulder of the highway.

If the majority of the youths appeared to be female or if they were boys that looked wise or pugnacious, Brendan would take on a quick change of venue and sputter "let's drive on avick, shur fuck it all, we'll let some other whore pick them up—we can't be Santa Claus to everyone."

On the occasion that the boys were few in number, clean-limbed and gentle-looking, Brendan was out of the door in a flash, packing the boys into the rear seat, and ordering his spouse to change seats with him while telling me to "drive off."

After I had pulled away from the curbstone a series of familiar questions were put to the boys. "What's yur name avick? How old are yew? Where do yew come from? Where are yew headed for? Where does yur daddy and mammy live? Do yew know me? What's my name?" A series of teasing words followed as he pinched the boys' biceps and shoulders. "Be God avick do yew know what it is, b-but wouldn't I rather get a box of candies from yew than a box in the lip. I'll bet yew like to box!"

In the rearview mirror I watched him flatter the youths and slip his arm around their shoulders and caress them. "Will we move over avick and make a wee bit more room for yur traveling companion what?" he would conclude. Brendan's eyes were bug-eyed. His face flushed. His mouth afroth. Then in a sudden move, he'd make a grab for their genitalia. On a number of occasions directly after he had made this final move one or more of the boys tapped me on the shoulder and demanded that I pull over and let them out.

"Bloody unthankful little scuts," he whined as I pulled away.

I decided to put an end to these nasty actions.

Having carefully constructed a host of viable excuses, I eagerly awaited an opportune moment. One afternoon while we were out driving, Brendan spotted a huge donut-and-coffee sign. "Let's cunt over and have a kaffee for ourselves," he said. Beatrice went to the bathroom. In a carefully selected moment, just as Brendan was in the process of turning to indicate his famous presence, I caught him in an off-guard eye-to-eye encounter. Then in a cool, controlled voice, I said, "Brendan, there is something that I have wanted to talk to you about for some time. What I'm getting at, Brendan, is this. Unfortunately that fuckin' old contraption of mine is on its last legs and just about to drop stone dead." Brendan eyed me with cold anxiety. "Well my dilemma is this, Brendan . . . you know that I am not in possession of a valid American driver's license nor tuppence worth of insurance . . . that needless to say puts me in a bloody bind." I felt nervous.

Brendan's face twitched. His hands flailed. "What in the name of the dilapidated jayzus are yew goin' on about? For the love and honor of God, speak your bit and get on with it."

I swallowed hard. The recess afforded me the exact out.

"Well that's it, Brendan," I blurted, "I can't pick up any more of those fuckin' little highway stragglers. Some other cunt will have to do it in the future."

Beatrice returned. Brendan looked at me with wicked eyes and sagging jowls. I excused myself and darted to the gents'. I put my thumb and index finger down my throat, vomited and pissed a piss of relief. Then returned to the coffee shop. Brendan and Beatrice had already departed. Beatrice sat in the rear seat. Brendan was standing by the hood pounding on it with his fists while kicking the front tires with both feet. We drove off. The remainder of the ride home was spent in silence.

Brendan sat sullenly spitting through his teeth like a demented cat. His face twitched. His brows and his forehead furrowed. Sporadically he turned half a turn in my direction, held his pose, sighed, then he turned back to the window and continued spitting.

Brendan was not a man who forgot or forgave easily. I braced myself for the days ahead. His extreme wickedness sometimes repelled me. It was a thing that also titillated me. When I was a boy growing up in Dundalk, I had played wicked little games with my drunken father and dependent mother.

My car was a two-door model. As its driver and owner I felt certain obligations to my passengers. When readying to make a trip it became my policy to open the door on the passenger's side, push the seat forward and allow Beatrice to take her seat in the back. Brendan always sat up front. Then I pushed the seat back into position and allowed Brendan to take his seat. I closed the door, walked around to the other side, got into my seat and drove away.

At Brendan's silent insistence this routine was quickly abolished, at least for a period of two to three days. The new procedure went as follows: directly after exiting from a bar, restaurant, marketplace or public bathroom, Brendan hastily ran to the car's passenger side, then remained there staring off into space while his elbow was jammed deep into the door's handle. He remained sullen and mute while he kicked at the variegated pebbles or debris that lay at his feet. Brendan always referred to me as "a very bright boy! A boy who was intuitive enough to catch any drift." There was a drift in his pose. A message. The message was that I was expected to walk around to the other side of the car to get in and start up the engine, while he would purportedly open the door for Beatrice. Brendan then did the honors of opening the passenger door to permit his wife to enter. However, just as she was about to get in, he slammed the door shut in her face. Next, he sat picking and snickering.

My next move was to walk back around to her, take her bagfuls of groceries, lead her to the other side, push the driver's seat forward, permit her to get in, then get into my seat and speed off.

During this period of time, Brendan found every viable excuse to get me to "pull over and stop for a while." My patience was thinning. I let this be known to Beatrice. But my protestations were always sharply interrupted.

"Oh, whatever you do, Peter, for God's sake go easy, be careful with him, he's ready to explode," she rejoined.

Brendan developed a routine of sitting sulking, picking his nose, rolling the cretinous matter between his thumb and index finger and flicking it at the distressed lady as she moved from one side of the car to the other.

The easily infuriated little man subsequently kept an even tighter rein on his money purse. Beatrice was virtually penniless. She designated me the sole purchaser of all family needs and warned me to keep safe the Hughes Supermarket checkout slips. She also begged me not to be too hasty in asking him to reimburse me. "He'll pay you back when he gets around to it," she said. "Just hold on to the receipts like a good boy."

My nest egg was next to depleted. To add to my dilemma, Brendan flatly refused to shell out for the gas and oil. The car was a heavy old model. A "burner" of oil and gasoline.

I thought, the hell with it! One afternoon I tapped him on the shoulder and said, "I'm sorry Brendan, I hate to be so demanding, but you see I'm broke, skint, flummoxed numismatically. My roll of green aphrodisiacs is out to lunch, which means that I'm incapable of being further able to buy the essential energy to operate the wheels. The car, I can assure you, will not run on piss, bullshit, or sunshine, not even southern Californian sunshine! How do I know, you might ask? *Simple.* That's primarily what I've been trying to run it on for the last couple of days. Maybe you should phone the *limo* service Brendan! Maybe I should *ship out!* Bye." I walked away. This was the first time that I had spoken to him in such a curt manner.

"Hold on avick, no need to get yur balls in a corkscrew," he shouted running after me in the Montecito lot. "We'll get all the gas yew need, here, take this," he said handing me a sweaty wad.

At a nearby gas station, I purchased two dollars' worth of fuel and a quart of oil. Enough to keep the pile of junk running to get me halfway to where we were going on that afternoon.

"Listen, Brendan," I said peremptorily as the car chugged, sputtered and came to a halt, "if there is anything that I don't need, it's all this fuckin' roadwork on these California highways and freeways. I'm in good enough shape as it is. From here on out you do the jogging for the gas. The exercise will do you good."

The following morning Brendan phoned in early and suggested, "Listen avick, but I have a marvelous idea. Why don't we all cunt off down to Marineland for the day, wha?"

"Get yourself a helicopter, Brendan," I said and went back to sleep.

Minutes later a familiar knock came at the door. I opened up and let Brendan in. A crisp piece of paper was squeezed into my hand. It was a fifty-dollar bill.

"Here me aul scholeara, now I know that I don't have to tell yew, but bejayzus there's plenty more where that fucker cum from, just say the word when yur readies are low." Brendan pushed past me, entered the bathroom, opened the medicine cabinet mirror, adjusted it to where he could view my reflection, stood over the commode with his tumescent penis in hand and watched me examining the bill to see if it was genuine. Then nodding at the money he sputtered "Now whatever yew do avick, for jayzus sake don't let that lolly blow away and slip into some fuckin' aul St. Vincent de Paul box." He laughed hysterically at his wit.

"O.K. Brendan, O.K. You don't have to say high mass, besides it's only Tuesday. Not Sunday."

A few hours later we arrived at Marineland, the renowned tourist mecca.

Brendan was rushed by cadres of camera-wielding tourists. "They'd give you the fucking head-staggers," he moaned as he signed autographs by the score.

Spectacular aquariums displayed highly trained porpoises, seals, dolphins, whales and other former predators of the deep as they obediently jumped through hoops and over hurdles to earn their daily fish.

After the exhibition Brendan went over to a group of people who were dining at a table, and barreled into another of his rodomontades. "B-but in spite of what yew've heard and read of me, at heart I'm basically an amiable sort of chap, not at all the warmonger that yew've imagined, I assure yew. By the same token now I don't mean to say that I'd step out of the shower just to take a leak. Me mother always said, anything that'd shock Brendan Behan wud turn marble to ashes. Me mother, the same mother of course, named me after a boy who crossed the big pond in a leather boat. The boat's carapace, I might add, was made from the tanned hides of Kerry culshies. I always knew that the savages would cum in handy one day.

"We Irish are a marvelous lot of people. Shur it's our national heritage to stand around talking about one another. Today in Dublin, most of the talk yew will hear will be about Brendan Behan!

"Now I must give the IRA its due. Shur didn't they have the good military sense not to promote me above the rank of a courier. As a writer I feel that it is me duty to mesself to let me fatherland down first. I ask yew, how in the name of jayzus can any writer attack another man's fatherland if he doesn't attack his own first!"

The cadre eyed one another, slung their cameras over their shoulders, dumped the remainder of their lunches into rubbish receptacles and departed.

"Huh! typical fuckin' aul Yanks. The bit of humor puts the heart crosswise in them," he spewed in their wake as he sat glumly on a bench.

"They look more like North Europeans to me, Brendan," I said emphatically. "Probably Dutchlanders, chances are they don't speak English."

"Must be a grand thing in life to have traveled the length and breadth of this universe, like yew," he snapped and moved to another gaggle of pursuers.

"Did yew know that me half brother, Rory, was named after the famous Irish homosexual, the one who was hung in the Tower of London, Roger Casement. Me grandmother, a great aul woman, she must have been, she taught me to take a sup at the age of six. Well she always said never trust a man who minds sheep for a livin'. Gets bloody lonely out there on them cold misty hills if yew get me meaning." Brendan stopped and waited, like a seismologist might await another shudder from far below the earth. The coterie giggled and moved on. Brendan muttered in their direction and sauntered over to the side of a huge pool where something of a different nature caught his eye. His eyes quickly fastened on a beautiful, well-constructed, copper-colored, blond-haired little boy who was charging around the perimeter of a big pool. Brendan's eyes were glazed with delight as he watched the boy's every move. "Cum on," he ordered Beatrice and me. We followed our leader and took up a sitting position on a bleacher closer to the pool's edge. The boy's sweet physiognomy and anatomical attributes immobilized Brendan. His searing gaze remained fastened to the boy. Then the boy ran off and joined his parents. His eyes suddenly became watery and sad like peat in the land of arable. Horror seeped into his every fiber. I excused myself and went to the bathroom. Seconds later Brendan came bursting in, grabbed hold of my penis. "Cum on, cum on avick I've something to show yew," he said excitedly. My hot piss splattered all over his hands and sleeves.

"How cum you're so horny all of a sudden?" I asked.

"Just follow me, avick," he demanded.

The shark-filled, huge, round glass tank is the greatest attraction at the aquarium. The major event of the day is when two rubber-suited divers descend into its depths and hand-feed the fish.

"Over here avick, over here," Brendan said excitedly as he pointed into the tank.

His bated breath blurred the glass. "Now watch son, just keep yur eye on the big cunt over there, here now avick, here he is, watch him as he cums by, he's after the other little cunt . . ."

"All I see is a couple of eegits with some sort of an obvious death wish," I said confusedly peering into the tank.

"No no no for jayzus sake avick, get yur eyes in focus will yew, there he goes. Do yew see him now?"

I looked hard in the direction of where Brendan was pointing. Suddenly I realized what it was that caught his eye. A huge grey shark was swimming around, ignoring the divers and their bucketfuls of fish. Directly in front of the big shark was a smaller shark. The two giant fish were traveling at an even speed.

"I'll bet yew a kick up in the ballox that the big snub-nosed cunt is up to a bit of trickery that includes the punier-looking fuck," he blurted. "I'll bet the smaller shark is a boy shark!"

The giant species passed within inches of our faces.

"I'd say *he's* in for it," he said as the small shark cruised by.

"I'd say *he's* about to get his hole," I said as the big fish went by. We watched for a while then moved away.

Brendan copied the graffiti from bathroom walls, scooped up handfuls of brochures and said "Cum on, let's cunt off home where we can have a decent cup of tea and a bit of peace: this fuckin' kip is beginning to give me a case of the galloping crud."

Later that evening we were invited to dinner "at the home of a Dublin friend," whose name I wondered about but dared not ask. Brendan was now as lysergic as a Dublin slumlord. He had been on the water wagon for approximately fourteen days.

As I sat at the table, awaiting a sumptuous meal, the identity of the man at the table's end suddenly came to mind. I had seen him in John Ford's classic *The Quiet Man*. Brendan prattled ahead and jumped from one topic to another. I interrupted.

"You're Barry Fitzgerald," I said excitedly to the man.

"This is Arthur Shields, Barry Fitzgerald's brother, and I'm Laurie, his wife," the lady who was sitting adjacent to the man said.

A bolt of embarrassment shot through me.

Brendan ran to the bathroom and minutes later returned, barefooted, then barreled ahead. A short while later Shields excused himself and went to the bathroom. Minutes later he returned to the dining room. "Here Brendan, I believe you left these behind," he said handing Brendan a pair of thick hand-knitted woollen socks. Brendan pocketed the socks and raced on with his conversation with himself.

Later I asked Brendan why he had taken the socks off.

"Anytime that I'm in the company of fuckin' aul Abbey actors, a fit of claustrophobia cums over me. Me only relief is to take off me socks and dip me feet into a toilet bowl then flush the cuntin' things."

Brendan's brand of revelry and jocularity did not regale all of his viewers.

Just as the three of us were about to bid our hosts good night, Laurie turned to me and in full view of Brendan, said aloud, while shaking my hand, "Oh Mr. Arthurs, it was so nice meeting you. You seem like a very interesting young man, too bad we didn't have the opportunity to talk and find out who *you* are and what *you* are doing in Hollywood, but perhaps some other time. Feel free to call. You are welcome to come here anytime, with or without your friend, *Mr. Behan.*"

During her little speech Mrs. Shields never once looked Brendan in the eye.

She opened the door and we swiftly departed.

All in all, life with the Behans had become so unusual that I had kept an intimate day-by-day journal of monologues, places where we visited, people whom we met, and snatches of conversations.

Also, at Brendan's request, I kept a separate journal of the sexy jokes, whorehouse anecdotes and shipboard jargon that I recalled. Then I passed it on to him at various intervals. Brendan would then pick through the notes and insert what he felt was apropos or recyclable into his current work in progress. *Cork* quickly bloomed.

Brendan was an absolute master at absorbing a story in its original verbatim form, tearing it to shreds, reconstructing it and then using it in his storytelling while putting it across as though it were something that had happened to him personally. Since many of these kudo-getting incidents had happened to me, I sometimes experienced a twinge of resentment. However Brendan was an extremely colorful raconteur. The very fact that he could, with a straight face and a serious expression, pull off such a farce, made my resentments quickly disappear.

On the occasions when he felt that his yarn was not being swallowed by the listener, warily he turned half a turn towards me and said, ". . . and that's a fact, here's Peter here, he'll tell yew, go ahead ask him."

"Brendan's a hundred percent right and a born perfectionist," I blurted before anyone had a chance to compose and pose their questions.

I reveled in the knowledge that I was such a central force in an important daily news-making duo.

For thirteen years prior to our meeting I had basically been a loner. An introvert. A man searching for an identity. Another train of thought was now permeating my brain. The thought of becoming a movie actor. I let my decision be known to Brendan and asked him to drop a few hints when we made our rounds of the parties where directors and producers were present.

Brendan adhered to my request and introduced me thus: "This is my very great friend, Peter Arthurs. He's a tank cleaner and a boxer who does the occasional stint at acting when he gets the chance. I'm thinking of writing a part into me new play for him."

The news of Brendan's decision seemed to go over like a lead balloon. One day I pulled Brendan aside and said, "Listen Brendan, I appreciate your efforts but for fucksake, edit your dialogue. Tell them that I'm an actor who cleans tanks and boxes when his ham-and-egg money is low."

Brendan weighed my words, mumbled and shook his head as though my request was something horrendous.

He continued to introduce me as a tank cleaner and a boxer who did an occasional stint at acting when given the chance. His line about writing a part for me into his new play was now and forever deleted from all introductions.

Brendan, I deduced, did not take appreciatively to being told what to do or what not to do.

In private he was capable of instantly undergoing all of the changes and quirks of a modern-day Jekyll and Hyde. Yet his public showmanship frills and facades never faltered. The short time that it took for the elevator to travel from the lobby to his floor was all that it took for him to undergo one of his incredible transformations. Whenever other guests tenanted the elevator on the way up, Brendan's pomp, dash and bravura remained intact until he stepped from the elevator and watched it snap closed. His face instantly assumed the look of an ostracized bassett hound.

As the days passed, Brendan's nerves seemed to become frayed beyond repair. His indoor humor was of a low gallows type. One day I asked Beatrice, "What is suddenly wrong with Brendan? Why has his personality changed so drastically?" She didn't comment. She merely dropped her head in despair and hurried away from me.

Brendan's fits of utter hysteria and terror were appalling to observe. His implacable loneliness was contagious.

Out of compassion and sympathy for him, I now was in the habit of periodically fucking Brendan between the legs, back and front.

One afternoon, after Beatrice had made an emergency dash to Hughes to pick up a carton of milk and a loaf of bread, Brendan and I climbed into bed. I was getting ready to fuck him when I heard a door open and close. A familiar set of footsteps hurried up the oblong hallway. I jumped out of bed and slammed both doors to the bedroom. I caught a faint glimpse of Beatrice hurrying into the kitchen! Did she see us in bed? I wondered. Quickly I put on my slacks.

"And where the fuck do yew think yur goin'?" Brendan barked.

"She's home, she saw us!" I whispered.

"And shur what of it!" Brendan shouted as he charged out of bed and tried to prevent me from putting on the remainder of my clothes. "Who gives a shite."

"I do," I said emphatically. I continued to dress.

Brendan threw back his head, pulled at his hair and appeared to be on the verge of letting loose a Tarzanlike bawl. I put my hand over his mouth and clamped it shut. His teeth sunk hard into my palm.

"What the fuck did you do that for?" I yelled as I pushed him to the floor and charged into the kitchen. Beatrice was stuffing her purchases into the refrigerator. I bade her good afternoon, but she didn't answer. Neither did she look at me. She possessed a taut exterior. To delve deep into the core of her immediate thinking process and to arrive at a positive conclusion was next to impossible.

V

Wednesday May 31. Very early in the morning I was awakened by an unusually desperate call. "P-Peter will you be a good lad and hurry over at once, it's very urgent."

"Be right over, Beatrice," I said. I was about to put down the phone when I heard a second voice, raspy and mordant.

"Listen s-son, c-can yew cum right away? H-how long will it t-take yew to get here? D-do yew have yur car h-handy? Where are yew?"

Brendan's last question left me in a state of perplexity.

"Be right over Brendan," I said and hurried to the Montecito. For reasons that my car would not always start up, I traveled by foot.

Beatrice looked excessively drawn, and out of it. Brendan was in a severe emotional swivet, dashing from room to room. Finally he sat down at the table. Eye-to-eye glances were exchanged. We ate ravenously and in the usual silence. Beatrice excused herself and hurried from the apartment. "Stay with Brendan, won't you Peter, like a good child," she pleaded as she closed the door behind her.

"How old was the c-chap, the c-chap on the t-tanker, the N-Norwegian s-ship," Brendan asked laboriously. His eyes were bulging with hysteria. "How old? How old?" he reiterated. He began circling the room as though it were a cage.

"D-did yew ever fuck a twelve-year-old boy in a boxing club, avick?" he blurted. I sat staring at him. Brendan became hysterical. I burst out laughing in his face. He eyed me with cool malevolence. Suddenly the erotic deviate of moments before was nowhere in evidence. Brendan was gaunt. He looked like a man who was suffering from a number of intestinal disorders. "What in the name of uncivilized jayzus are yew laughing at?" he roared.

A period of hysterical silence prevailed as Brendan paced the floor, a look of madness growing in his beet-red countenance. He picked up sheafs of manuscript, glanced at them and flung them to the floor. Then he peeled off his housecoat and threw it on top of the papers. "Did yew ever fuck an eleven-year-old boy in a boxing club?" he asked, with terror creeping into his voice.

"Well now, B., let me see," I started slowly. "I stowed away from Dundalk on the S.S. *Black Sod* in 1948 when I was fourteen years of age. I left the Dealgan boxing club the year before . . . of course I didn't become a full-fledged professional seaman until 1950 when I served aboard the Norwegian tanker M.V. *Salamis* . . . hmmm . . ."

Brendan continued to pace, knock over furniture and throw things to the floor. I was vividly aware that our frienship teetered on the outcome of my answer. I pondered my conclusive remark.

"Listen avick," Brendan roared into my mouth, "I'm not cuntinwell concerned with how or when yew became the captain of yur own fuckinjayzus ship or how old yew were when yew won the heavyweight championship of this mad fuckin' world. I only want to know did yew or did yew not ever fuck a ten-year-old boy in a boxing club?" He was leaning over the back of my chair. Our faces were inches apart.

We held our stare for an interminable period. He wiped a driblet of saliva from his mouth. His hysteria burgeoned. His eyes darted while his face trembled.

"Yes, yes, yes indeed I did, Brendan," I shouted. "Of course I did and why not, sure isn't that the natural thing to do? Isn't that what boxing clubs are for, for wisening youngsters up to go their way in this mad fuckin' world that we live in! why, is there something wrong with it?" I asked with a look of affected surprise in my face, arising from the chair.

His face softened. His distraction disappeared. But moments later a flicker of familiar suspicion seeped into his eyes. Again he was on top of me. "Did yew ever fuck a *nine*-year-old boy?" he roared into my face.

"*Nine, ten, eleven, twelve, thirteen, fourteen,* who remembers, who gives a good shite; boys are boys; boys will always be boys," I shouted, "boys are no different than girls, they love to play around and seduce grown-ups. Why do you think so many priests, brothers and scout masters hang around boxing clubs? Who do *you* think seduces whom?!"

His face was suddenly suffused with delight. His hands dropped to his sides. His composure returned. I felt relieved and victorious. He collapsed into the folds of his chair and sighed. "Good man avick, marvelous. When the other one cums back we'll have our tea and our dip," he muttered in exasperated relief.

My answers had gone over like a pope's pardon. Tranquillity prevailed. I felt exhaused, but free. Our vertiginous discussion was over. I had not only given the right answer, I had given it with the right amount of shade and verve. Brendan continued to twitch and groan like an ancient dog that had suddenly found its hearth.

However, his boy-intoxication was taking its toll on my nerves. Depleted after our "dip," I made a feeble excuse and returned to the Wilcox Hotel. More than anything in the world I wanted to be alone. I had spent a great deal of time in the company of Brendan Behan and had lost almost half of the body weight that I had put on since my arrival in Hollywood. I undressed and lay down on my bed and cracked open the covers of *Borstal Boy*.

Along about ten A.M. a recognizable knock came to the door. I ignored the knock. I was now into the fourth chapter of the book. The knock continued. The phone rang. John, the desk attendant informed me that there were complaints about the noise outside my room. I assured him that it would cease immediately. I opened the door.

"D-did yew ever f-fuck a s-small boy in a boxing club?" Brendan asked, saliva dripping from his mouth. "I mean d-d-did yew ever f-f-fuck a very s-small one . . . a wee l-lad, a v-very y-young one, wha?"

Being fully aware of his homo-hysteria, I pulled him into the room. We undressed and masturbated each other.

"H-h-how old was the smallest boy that yew ever fucked?" he mumbled as he salivated, trembled and probed the side of my face in the mirror.

"Sweet mother of palavering jayzus, Brendan, at a time like this how the hell can you think of such things as boxing with little boys in boxing clubs?" I said laughing, my hot seeds of misery splattered all over his ample stomach.

"No, no, no, why, why, why, how, how, how," he roared as he picked up his clothes and darted naked into the hall.

Barbara Harris, an actress who was appearing in *From the Second City* was my next-door neighbor. I had developed a mild crush on her. I feared that Barbara might suddenly alight and get the wrong impression of my sexuality. I was happy to see Brendan go.

Along about the hour of three, I received a call from Beatrice. "Oh Peter, I'm so glad you're in. I'm terribly worried about Brendan. He's been in and out all day, he hasn't eaten lunch or opened the typewriter. I think something is going to happen to him today. Do be a good child and look for him in the bars around the boulevards will you, call me like a good boy. *Slan leat anois* [Good-bye now]."

"Leave it to me, Beatrice."

I continued to read and scribbled into my journal a few impressions. I found *Borstal Boy* to be a very charming, engaging memoir, full of scenery and prison poetry. The book was lively, witty and loaded with spirit. Brendan was a facile story weaver. His stark, gritty dialogue was my type of talk. I also found it to be in spots pushy and pretentious.

Could the life-sized manchild I knew, who was so easily intimidated, possibly be derived from the brash pugnacious, worldly, braggardly youth in the memoir? In the story Brendan was overly concerned and chatty about his hero—Brendan Behan. The underlying thread of the book bore a tone of "Here—look at me now! Wha? Aren't I the great broth of a boy-ho. Shur don't I luv life, isn't it obvious that I don't give a halfpenny worth of shite about the cruel games that life endows us with. Shur don't I revel in them like a good terrorist is supposed to do!"

Brendan also showed a major lack of sympathy and compassion for his fellow Borstal inmates. He treated them as though they were pieces of chess, pawns, sounding boards and extensions of his ego. His perpetual braggadocio robbed the memoir for me of its full and final poetic impact. However the colorful array of anecdotes and vignettes—slightly frothy and heroic—were dazzling, hearty and compelling. The book's protagonist had little or no similarity to the adult Brendan, the creator of the story. I felt that if Brendan the writer had worked a little less on Brendan, the book's thematic boy, and a little more on his counterparts, had he self-indulged less frequently, shone less repetitiously, the book might have become a modern-day literary marvel.

As I waded deep into the final chapters, a favorite "in private" line of Brendan's and a repetitious word of caution from Beatrice came to mind.

On a number of occasions I had tried to question either one of them about the book. Brendan made *his* point clear. "I mean it's all a pack of lies and bullshite," he had said and dropped the subject.

"Be very careful about how you refer to *Borstal Boy*, won't you Peter, when the other fella is around," Beatrice had often warned.

"Very well Beatrice," I said, "but what will I call it?"

"Brendan likes the book to be referred to as a novel and not as an autobiography," she confided.

"Isn't that primarily because he wishes to be accepted as a novelist besides being a renowned playwright?" I asked.

She refused to answer or to talk further on the subject out of fear that Brendan might suddenly appear. Darting out of the blue and suddenly appearing was a favorite sport of the ubiquitous man.

Within the next two or three hours a number of desperate calls from her came in over the wire.

"Did you have any luck, Peter? Did you get a clue?"

"No, Beatrice, but I'll keep up the search, he can't be far away!" I finished up the book. More phone calls came in from the distraught

Beatrice. I reassured her that I intended to keep up the search. I dozed off to sleep.

Along about seven o'clock I received a final desperate call. "Don't worry Beatrice, I think I know where he is, I'll go down to Cahuenga and grab him right away, hold on, he'll be home in a jiffy."

"Oh no, no no P-Peter, don't touch him whatever you do. You know how he is. If you have to put your hands on him, make sure to touch him above the elbow only and for God's sake don't touch him on his right side under any circumstances. You know how he is. All I want you to do is spot him for me and call me as soon as you do, but you will be a good boy now and promise that you'll be careful where you touch him. If you don't the cops will take you too, you know how they work, Peter, you've lived in New York. Call me as soon as you spot him. *Slan leat a buacaill* [Good-bye, my boy]." Beatrice's remarks and instructions left me in a state of quandary. I decided to take another nap. Half an hour later the phone rang again. I was about to assure her that I was just leaving when she chimed in, "It's too late, Peter, they've got him, he's in jail. The news is already on the radio, he's in the twenty-seventh precinct. They got him in McGoo's. The barman called the cops. Come right away, maybe you can get someone to bail him out."

In the lobby of the hotel the radio was blaring out the big news of the day, the arrest of Brendan Behan. Several of the hotel's personnel sat drinking up the news. According to the announcer, Brendan had leveled a substantial amount of profane and abusive language at the bartender in the popular pizza parlor on Hollywood Boulevard. The manager, Mr. Jerry Brentori, called the cops and demanded a citizen's arrest. For the remainder of the day radio shows were momentarily interrupted to keep the local citizens abreast of the news.

Beatrice gave me a substantially different account of the events that took place. Brendan had merely said to the barman "Give me a fuckin' drink." The publicity-hungry barman rushed to the phone. The cops arrived promptly, she lamented. "O.K., Brendan," one of them said, "get into the back of the car that's out front." Brendan jumped and said "Yes, sir," then pushed on past the cops and sat in the car. "Shur they were all smiling their eyes out, " Beatrice went on dolefully.

"You mean the cops?" I inquired.

"And Brendan too," she sighed.

For the next two hours the phone literally jumped out of its cradle. Well-wishers, free-lance writers, religious organizations and cranks called in to offer their prayers. Questions were asked, "Will Brendan write a play about the incident? Is this how the great man gets his material? Is he dying?" Words of caution came over the wire. "Tell Brendan to be careful! Get him out of the pokey quick! This is California; the cops here are a bunch of fascists!"

Offers were made by screen and feature story writers who desperately desired to come to the apartment, to get the "real inside facts," and do "a big money-making story." Percentages were offered.

"I'll leave the phone off the hook for a while," I suggested.

"Please do," the jaded lady said.

Just as I was about to tell the operator no more calls, Martin Bryman, the owner of McGoo's, called in to say, "I consider Brendan a friend and a great man. A friend of the working people of the world. I'd be more than happy to go his bail."

"Please do," I said and hung up.

For a respite I took Beatrice to the International House of Pancakes on Sunset Boulevard. Beatrice brought me up to date on the final events of the arrest. Brendan took it all routinely. He was fingerprinted, booked and put in the pokey. All we had to do now was to await the arrival of Bryman.

I went to the phone and called Arthur Shields. "Brendan's in a jam, Arthur, they got him locked up in the twenty-seventh precinct. Do you have any suggestions? Any connections?"

"Ah, now my boy shur I wouldn't worry mesself too much about Brendan's state of affairs, if I were you," he said in his soft, lilting brogue. "Brendan is a wise and capable man who understands the ways of the world. You will stay in touch won't you, and like Laurie said to you the other day, do come over for dinner. You seem like a nice boy, an interesting lad, call us any time." The phone went down gently.

We drove to the police lockup.

"Looka here, champ," a seasoned newsman barked into my face, "I know you been tru this scene dozens a times in the past but if ya wanna get inta the action ya better get yar arse in gear and get on over to the lobby. Yar buddy is gonna be sprung in a short while."

Next a police officer came to the door of the station house and held up three fingers to indicate that it was three minutes to countdown. The media men rushed forward. Flashbulbs were screwed into place. Tape recorders were tested, "Testing one two three."

Joe Finnegan rushed over and informed me that he had gone to the big baseball game to do the coverage but the UPI ordered him back to Hollywood to do the sketch on Brendan's latest debacle.

A young, intense-looking fellow sidled up to me and said, "Listen mister, I don't know who you are, but it is obvious that you have something to do with the Behans. Why do you allow this bullshit, these farces to go on? Why will you not do something to stop them? Didn't you get enough? Doesn't his wife have any control over him? Why doesn't she grab hold of him and beat the shit out of him? She seems big enough to be able to do the job!"

"Why don't you fuck off and mind yur own small fuckin' business! Who the fuck are you anyway?" I asked, perturbed.

"I'm from the press," the man said calmly as he scribbled into a pad.

Martin Bryman ambled over to me and said "Ready kiddo. You on one side, me on the other, O.K." We eagerly awaited Brendan's emergence.

Like a little bull, he was suddenly on the scene, resplendent in shabby attire. His eyes were crystal clear, darting and mischievous. His hair disheveled, cascading down over his forehead. The zipper of his fly was open all the way down. On his nose he wore two wide conspicuous Band-Aids. The Band-Aids looked more like bunion plasters.

The media moved in. Brendan reacted like a truckload of geese turned upside down. He asked and answered questions by the dozens, sometimes giving the answer to the question before it was asked. He was in full cry as he moved briskly into the outer lobby and into the forest of microphone booms and the blaze of popping bulbs. He condemned the infamous Hollywood smog and praised his captors. "I was treated fair," he said. "Fairer than most other places that I temporarily lodged at." He chuckled at his wit and strutted like a defiant banty rooster. Photographers leaped over one another and crouched in his oncoming path. His beefy face was a constant illumination as it was carefully scrutinized, studied and bombarded with questions concerning recent flare-ups in the Middle East, China's war threats, the preponderance of Russia's sea and air power, Khrushchev's cantankerousness, Kennedy's Catholicism, and the mystique that was growing concerning the condition of his kidneys.

Brendan careened, dodged, feigned, did a variety of U-turns and again and again came into the full glare of the pirouetting cameras, a suggestion of histrionic slouch in his rotund figure.

Finally he shook hands with the desk sergeant, apologized, posed one final pose for the photographers, turned to me and said, "Cum on avick, let's cunt off out of here before these fuckin' eegits drive me to drink. The cunts are never satisfied."

En route to the Montecito, Brendan asked me to drive around town for a spell. "There's a thing or two I want to see," he said mysteriously. Finally, two hours later, at his command we parked the car in the hotel's parking lot and bolted down the hill to Hughes Supermarket. Brendan charged through the stile and devoured everything that lay at his fingertips: vegetables, fruits, bread and raw meats. Their cellophane wraps and all were voraciously gorged. He plunked a dozen eggs into his mouth, crunching them, ingesting their albuminous matter, then dispelling the cracked shells.

"Will you be a good boy and keep a close eye on him for me?" a very tired Beatrice asked, laying her shoulder against a wall, her head dropping in resignation.

"Certainly Beatrice, but look at him, obviously he is enjoying himself."

"Shur I know, he always does. It's his life, he loves it."

Brendan slurped up containers of milk and juices. He ate raw potatoes and stalks of celery by the handfuls, intermittently stopping here and there to register a complaint to one of the attendants in regards to the quality of the foodstuffs on display. Along the route he stopped and chatted up everyone who gave the impression that they might have a thin ear. ". . . b-but in spite of what yew have heard, I'm basically a very shy man. At one point in me life I even entertained the thought of joining the priesthood. Recently I met Louis Armstrong at a party. 'What do yew think of Dublin?' says I. 'Dublin' says he! 'What's that? Is it something I can play?' However, Dublin is a city that doesn't like me. But fair field and no favor. I don't like Dublin.

"Shur the fuckin' Irish, shur the shower of cunts and hypocrites that they are, don't they only call me when they hear that I'm in a hospital, in some jail or if they think that I'm about to die," Brendan complained with an affected pugnacious grin.

At the checkout counter he swallowed handfuls of chocolates and candies, then complained to the bespectacled checkout clerk about the barrenness of the shelves. "Couldn't find a fucking thing that I wanted, a fellow would starve to death in this jayzus joint. Shur didn't I eat better when I was in jail bejayzus."

The bewildered youth profusely apologized and assured the loquacious man that the next time he returned he would very definitely find what it was he was looking for.

"I hope so, I fuckinwell hope so," Brendan moaned.

"He's really having a lark for himself," I said to Beatrice.

"Yes, but wait. He won't go back on the dry now for at least a week. Blazes, blazes, blazes," she moaned lugubriously.

Back in the apartment we attacked huge platefuls of steaming hot food and drank kettlefuls of tea. Then we went down for a dip. We jumped, dived and swam in the nude.

Darkness slowly dissipated. Watching Brendan surface and scramble up out of the pool, I sensed that something was missing! What? Finally it dawned on me. The missing link was his two Band-Aids. They were floating on top of the pool, torn away by the force of a dive. I charged over and scrutinized his face. The bridge of his nose and the parts of his cheeks that the Band-Aids had originally covered were as clear as fresh buttermilk. No contusions or abrasions marred his lily-white countenance. I laughed hysterically.

I recalled my fights with Jimmy Dupree and the Galway Sandman. I thanked them both. At that specific point in time, radio messages were being bleeped across several continents. Typesetters were frantically at work. In a matter of minutes, newspapers, printed in dozens of languages would tell of the event of the night before. Soon, I would become part of history. A small part. Nevertheless a part. I threw myself down onto the dewy concrete and laughed myself into a paroxysm. Brendan threw me sporadic little laser-eyed glances as he grunted, dived, and swam. I was now part of the great man's grapple and grope.

"Night is the time of day when life comes to life and flourishes," Brendan had often said. How right he was.

Along about seven A.M. a gaggle of twittering little girls gathered by the wooden fence that separated the pool from the upper parking lot. Each time that Brendan surfaced the little girls raised their heads over the fence and burst into a medley of twitters and giggles.

Brendan became extremely upset and spewed volleys of wicked invectives. The children crouched and hid. He dove into the pool. He remained underwater for an interminable period of time. Concern grew in the faces of the innocent. Perplexed and frightened, they charged down onto the perimeter of the pool, then looked into its depths with anxiety graven in their faces. One of them quivered. "Oh it's O.K.," I said. "Mr. Behan is only playing hide and seek. I'll bet *you* play hide and seek once in a while?"

Suddenly Brendan was up out of the pool and charging around its perimeter. His face was aglow with malice. His cock was erect. In a fit of fury he charged over to the girls who were cowering behind me.

I grabbed hold of him and dragged him to the edge of the pool. "Stop it, Brendan, they're only little children," I said as he was about to strike the tiniest one. He looked at the children fiercely. His eyes were radiant with pain and hatred. "A couple of ill-mannered little whelps is what they are," he snorted, then heaved himself into the pool.

When we went upstairs Brendan began a series of charges around the rooms. His modes of travel varied. Sometimes he ran sideways, other times he ran backwards. Sometimes he ran face-first. Beatrice sat in the kitchen, shaking. "You will stay, won't you, Peter?" she pleaded.

"Certainly I will." I assured her.

Periodically Brendan would disappear into his bedroom. Minutes later he emerged. The condition of creeping intoxication was evident. Suddenly he stopped running and threw himself down onto the settee. Then he picked his nose, rolled the fruits of his pickings, flicked it at imaginary objects and cursed, "I'll see yew in hell yew rat-faced cunt yew." Next he jumped up off the settee, charged into a corner, crossed one leg over the other, blessed himself, sang a hymn in a puny feminine voice, spread his arms, hands and head drooping downwards while he gave a passable imitation of Christ on the cross. Next he charged into the bathroom, sat down on the commode and made a variety of extraneous little sounds while he observed me with one half-opened eye, through the jar of the door.

In an instant he was back in the living room, picking up and slamming down his rewrite of *Cork*. Then he ran to a window, opened it and tried to jump out. Beatrice let loose an agonized yell. "Peter, quick, quick." I pulled him back into the room. Bleeps of agony seeped from Beatrice's mouth. Her outbursts were met with a series of slaps across the face.

"Take that yew fuckin' aul cunt, yew, yew fuckin' Tibetan whore yew, yew mongolian tramp yew," Brendan yelled. "Yew forgot to get the bottle of milk, yew'd forget yur face if it wasn't screwed to yur cuntin' head." Then he ran into the bedroom and smashed furniture. "Even the fuckin' Dalai Lama couldn't get rid of yew fast enough," he bellowed hysterically.

"Beatrice, I'm very confused and my confusion is growing." I asked, "what's all this talk about the Dalai Lama, and the bottle of milk?"

She sat numb, ashen-faced, crying and incapable of answering. "Oh that's O.K., Peter," she finally said. "In New York it was his coat, in Hollywood it's his milk. When we get back to Dublin it will be something else. For God's sake, be careful, don't say or do anything to antagonize him, let him have his way or he'll go mad."

It now dawned upon me that Brendan looked at himself as being totally depraved. He lived in a vicious comic cartoon fantasy world, a world that had little or nothing to do with reality. He was trapped in a sadomasochistic cul-de-sac from which there was no redemption, neither misery nor malice. He was a living breathing cesspool of sexual perversion hopelessly searching for an individual sexual identity. He was a pedophile who had to blame even the innocent for his intolerable aberration.

"Go on, go on yew dirty aul slut yew, yur as useless as a pair of diddies on a fuckin' nun," he roared into her face as he finally sat down naked at the table. "Yew couldn't remember to add the bottle of milk to yur list when yew cunted down to the market." Then turning to me, "*Yew* always remember to include the milk when *yew* go shopping, don't yew avick," he said with a strained smile. "And what may I ask is any civilized man supposed to do with his tea if he doesn't have the drop of milk to color it with? Did I not earn the right to a bottle of fuckin' milk?" he roared at the ceiling. Turning back to me, "Do yew know what I did avick," he asked. "Well I'll tell yew what I did," he said proudly, his face breaking into a malevolent grin. "I decided that since I am married to a woman—that is, if yew could call her that—who can't remember to include the purchase of a fuckin' aul bottle of milk on her grocery list, well fuck it all, says I to mesself, I'll just fuck off down to the liquor store and get mesself a bottle of whiskey. What say yew me aul son? Wasn't that the wise thing to do?" he asked, putting his chin on the table.

"You did the right thing, Brendan," I said emphatically, winking at Beatrice. "The only intelligent thing to do! You did what any smart man would have done under the circumstances."

Brendan's head was up like a shot. His eyes were as wide as saucers and searching my face. He extended his hand. I shook it robustly, "Good man avick, good man," he said. "At least someone around here has a bit of common sense. Fuck yew, yew begrudger yew," he yelled into Beatrice's face as he again dropped his head to the table.

He snored softly and appeared to be asleep. But in a split second his head was up, his eyes darting. "What time is it?" he whispered to me, "are the papers out yet?"

"It's early yet, pet," Beatrice cut in, in a whisper as she ran her fingers through his unruly hair, scratching the nape of his neck with the other hand and cooing him back to sleep. Again his head went down.

He snored heavily. Then in a full fiery orbit he was up and lashing out with a volley of lightning quick, short left hooks and right upper cuts that sent her flying up against the stove. She shrieked in horror as Brendan kicked her. I grabbed hold of him, put my left arm around his throat and forced his chin upwards. He grimaced in pain.

Beatrice pulled herself together, got up off the floor and grabbed hold of my wrist. "No, no, no, don't hurt Brendan, don't do that to him," she yelled while she pulled at my wrist. I loosened my grip. Brendan bit deep into my forearm then darted down the oblong hall snickering and laughing and referring to the Irish as "culshies and savages." Saliva and blood dripped from his mouth. A trickle of blood oozed from my forearm. I rinsed the blood from my forearm and sat down at the table with Beatrice.

A short while later Brendan and I dressed and went over to the twenty-four-hour newsstand on the corner of Hollywood and Las Palmas. A frantic thumbing through freshly published papers followed, and the object of his search was over. A boyish grin ensued. The hawker was handed a crisp twenty-dollar bill and told to "keep the balance."

Back in my room at the Wilcox, we read extensively: "BEHAN JAILED FOR BAR RUMPUS"; "IRISH PLAYWRIGHT JAILED"; "BEHAN PREMIERES IN HOLLYWOOD JAIL. HE SAW STARS."

The Los Angeles rags described him as a brawler, a sulphuric poet and a police fighter. The *Los Angeles Examiner* described his name-calling as lurid, eloquent and derisive, and stated that he refused to identify himself. Finally one of the police officers went into his personal papers and discovered his identity.

"M-marvelous, fuckin' jayzus marvelous," Brendan muttered as he undressed. Then he sat naked on the edge of my bed, complaining painfully about the ineptness and the lack of business acumen of his wife. He twitched, grinned and groaned "I mean to say, all in all, she's a great aul skin. She's helped me a lot but I'd be suited better if she'd just go and get herself another man. She'd do anything to please me I know, but shur all she fuckin' well *wants* to do is sit beyant in the thistle and the nettle country sippin' tea with the aul ones. They'd put years on yew, talking about the condition of the weather and who's pregnant by who and who's suspected of havin' the pox. I keep telling her that she better wise up. She'll be on her own before she knows it. She better learn to pick up the ball while it's still at her feet. The bubble will soon burst. They're gonna get wise sooner or later!"

Brendan sat and glared at me with a familiar hue and intensity in his eyes, a strange but purposeful look on his face. He rolled over on his stomach and once more asked me to sodomize him.

"I'm sorry B., but the act is to me too vile, too scatological," I explained. A short while later we returned to the Montecito.

Brendan was now off on a ten-day drunk.

His two favorite bars were the Comet and the Nest. His drink was "two J.D.'s and two T.B.'s": two shots of Jack Daniel's and two bottles of Tuborg beer. He devoured each setup of drinks in single stupendous draughts.

His personality underwent a major change. He pursued whimsy with a purple vengeance. He became more childish, demanding, abrasive and cantankerous, his need to run around "in the raw" more obvious. He feigned anger and huff. He behaved as though he was the target of everyone in lotusland. He denigrated movie moguls. His eating and sleeping habits went completely out of sync. He slept no more than half an hour at a time.

Brendan was more player than playwright, a frustrated movie star. He claimed that he detested actors and actresses. "I mean to say shur the half of them is like insects, they have no heart, no soul, no core to their apple. They have no real understanding or grip on life," he liked to spout when sharply interrupting one of his own little outpours. "But shur then again, shur I suppose the poor aul whores are entitled to their bit of a livin' just like the rest of us, shur aren't they children of God, what!"

It seemed to me that Brendan had the emotions of a child in a man's body, that the level of his stability was no more than the age of eight. To determine specifically where and when his true hurt and anger started and stopped as opposed to when his histrionics came into play was no small chore.

Like a seasoned actor he was a master of feigning hurt, humiliation, and hysteria. His childish tantrums were usually theatrical. When Brendan was publicly "on" he possessed all of the combined trappings of a pompous pope. He would become an antisocial maniac who worked arduously to plant the belief that he was an amiable socialist who in his unique puckishness was a pixielike destroyer of the rich and the powerful.

Brendan's frothy attacks against the world's pedophiles and his calls for their swift imprisonment were beefed up considerably.

I also discovered that Brendan was equally as adept at playing the role of the drunk as he was at getting drunk.

One thing was now crystal clear to me. Brendan Behan, the writer, talker, character, performer and showman, had very much arrived. He was at the zenith of his fame. His halcyon days were here and now. Offers of scriptwriting, personal appearances, dinner engagements and requests to do lectures poured in. The more publicly cantankerous, abusive and insulting he became, the greater was the demand for his presence, the more money he was offered. The daily rags carried countless colorful stories of him and his stay in Hollywood. Much to my delight I was often mentioned in these articles.

Prior to his induction into the annals of creative literature, Brendan had earned his "malts money" by working as a columnist for the *Irish Press* and had written stories under the pseudonym Emmet Street. He had good insight into the brand of antics that the media craved. He did not like to have this period of his past be publicly known. When asked to comment on it, "Yes I stayed there until the day that I became famous," he snapped and quickly changed the subject.

The more Brendan talked the more I discovered how many of my boyhood friends and relatives were members of the IRA and had been jailed for their convictions in life.

Brendan subsequently averaged three drunken bouts per day and kept on the move like a lawn mower out of control. In a matter of days, the totalitarian town was at his feet and begging him to perform.

Over one million dollars worth of screen and television offers were eventually made to him.

"B-but shur I have no talents in that area," he complained to a studio representative.

"This is of no consequence," he was emphatically assured.

He was also informed that dozens of screenwriters were available and ready to go to work on his approval. Brendan's mere signature would suffice. His well-aimed and precision-timed push and penny patch was bringing him resounding success and on a grandiose scale. Calls were coming in from as far away as England, France, Holland, Germany and New York. Local and national news magazines implored him to do feature stories for them.

But Brendan both loathed and loved the legend that he had so carefully constructed. "Shur the fuckers wud rub butter on a fat pig's arse. The only reason why they even bother to call me at all is because I happen to have a bit of a name for mesself. If I was the local milkman or some poor cunt flogging turf from the back of a donkey's cart, the whores wouldn't even stop to give me a light," he complained.

Brendan had a multitude of identities and irreconcilable forces in him. It was difficult to envision so many moods in a single psyche. "I mean to say the fuckin' aul Dublin cabdrivers, chancers, horse thieves, whores, chiselers, bookies, con merchants and even the craw-thumpers; shur aren't these my real people, the meat and potatoes of me work. Isn't it from them that I draw me raw material. Shur don't I immortalize them in me plays," he moaned to a cadre of saucer-eyed idolaters who gathered in the lobby for his autograph.

But his greatest moments of reverie derived from his constant conjuring up of small mischief, then elevating it to the high level of his own unique brand of combustibility. He was a living breathing pressure cooker, always on the threshold of boiling over. His well-thought-out and carefully plotted publicity caper whipped him right into the froth on top of this town of stagnant air and wandering souls, this Jericho where dreams and fantasies plummet into nosedives of despair, sometimes even death.

Brendan possessed all of the true rib and gristle appendages of the instant clownsman—a gnome with a multifunctional face. In his unique vaudevillian way he succeeded in transmogrifying his fears and phobias into lucrative high art and entertainment.

When the need to purge himself of his myriad of inhibitions was on him, he was like a suddenly derailed freight train. But these purges were always of a very short-lived nature. He was a protean performer, yet the most inhibited and predictable individual that I had ever known. Buoyed by the shifting winds of his self-indulgence and desperate need to sustain a semblance of emotional stability, he played his part to the hilt and presented himself as the new literary and theatrical critic on the boulevard, the entrepreneur and patron saint of the fifties and sixties freedom of speech movement. He was the self-proclaimed impresario and the maitre d' of the new European and American avant-garde theater and cinema. He talked of his impending death as though it would take on heroic proportions that could not be achieved in fifteen lifetimes. In public he displayed a keen sense of showmanship and was peerless in the craft of ducking riveting verbal darts, particularly when these questions pertained to his legendary background. Brendan's signature mannerisms, his sarin tongue and sententious dialogue continued to shock and startle. He proved himself a master craftsman at interrupting his own monologues at the strategic point and the idiosyncratic second, just where and when the interjection afforded him the maximum measure of impact and safety. He displayed a unique talent for getting embroiled in debates and rebuttals while he put himself across as a soldier of fortune who was jailed for his perverse beliefs in the efficacy of the "old cause," the Irish "political ructions."

Brendan was inordinately proud of his invitation to the John F. Kennedy inauguration ball. He bragged incessantly about it. "B-but I didn't go did I, wha! Why, yew might wonder? Well, the answer is plain and simple! Why, I ask yew, should I lend my good name to that shower of hypocrites and blatherskites, huh! Did they ever do anything for the working class people of Ireland? Shur they're not my class of people atall atall!!" In actuality Brendan was an effete snob, a strategist who always looked ahead with shrewd vision.

The Kennedys were of pure Irish stock. They were big family Catholics, fun-loving and entertaining. Brendan loved parties. Parties where the presence of youth was bountiful. The temptation of resisting the bottle would be too great. The attention of the world was on the new, young, dashing President and his Camelot. Reporters covered every Kennedy move. The risk was too great. Wisely, he elected to remain at home. Brendan was vividly aware of his weaknesses, his impulses. Drunk, he simply could not keep his hands away from children.

This particular little speech was always followed by a catalogue of carefully selected bits and pieces of contemporary Celtic prose reminiscences, added with a pinch or two of punchy poetry, a bit of profanity, a jig, a reel and a yarn that gladdened the ears and glistened the eyes of the listeners.

Next came his mantra, his call for the incarceration of all pedophiles.

Desecrating the American media and its stewardship became his bane. Those who interjected a remark that was contrary to his purported feelings instantly became a human sounding board for his murderous rhetoric.

"My God! Does he talk like this all the time? Who the fuck does he think he is? He's such a little shit, whew!! He's cute. He's a cunt. I love him. He's brilliant. He's a big fuckin' put-on. He's a genius, my genius. He's so brilliant, I could listen to him forever."

These were the type of utterances that could be overheard when Brendan was knee-deep in one of his alcohol-induced fiery orations.

"Under the influence" of his amber-colored lava, in these most vainglorious moments, he saw himself through the eyes of others as one of the finest equipages of the times, a hundred and fifty-two pounds of insouciant charm. A titillating force in international affairs. A champion of literature and life. A brilliant orator, in whose veins the heady wine of Celtic intellectual and literary elitism gushed. The true alumnus of the new Irish literary college.

Brendan saw *himself* as a rogue, a rascal, a brilliant talker, a roaring conundrum, a supple-fleshed pugnacious brawler who was both world-loved and -despised. He saw himself as a blockbuster who effected cultural and subcultural changes that most societies feared and shied away from. And, of course, as an important lion of literature.

Brendan became a flashy, fleshy little bundle of hysteria perpetually on the verbal warpath, asking me questions by the score: "Did yew ever fuck a boy in a boxing club? Was it an Irish boxing club? How old was the boy? How old were yew? Did a priest ever try to bugger yew? Did yew let him? Where? When? Did yew ever get it off with two boys simultaneously? How many captains do yew know who buggered boys?"

He lived in the twilight of the ancient Irish Catholic morality. He staunchly believed in its tenets. He loathed himself for what he was. He was a fast mover and a steady pacer who carefully selected his objectives. Never did he publicly allow his rubbery mask to slip. Seldom did he reveal his true subtleties. Never did he blow a laugh-getting line on anyone who could not further his fame, or help him tighten his grip on the illusion called immortality.

Brendan had a very adroit way of steering all conversations to the private central topic of his personal interest. Sex. Never did he allow his listeners to opine on this sacred topic. He told me I was a substantially talented wit and storyteller. His strict orders to his spouse were that she keep pencil and paper at the ready. I utilized this extra point in my favor, sometimes to drive a wedge between them by starting a story then chopping it off just at the punch line.

His pattings, adulations and exultations, his treatment of me as a living marvel of ultracontrolled empathy, sometimes irritated me.

Brendan's brand of accolades were not exactly novel to my ears.

In the early summer of 1946 when I was still a few months shy of my thirteenth birthday, my father came to my school and made the emphatic announcement that he was taking me out of school permanently. His decision was irrevocable. "He's a big strong broth of a boy who will be of better help to his mother at home. By staying on at school, nothing of any value will be gained," he assured the Christian Brothers. "The boy is not too bright to begin with."

My drunken parent then instructed me to clear out my desk and follow him home. For the next two years I turned my hands to robbing coal from ships and wagons, fish and vegetables from hawkers' carts, blessed candles and holy water from cathedrals, pots, pans, kettles, coats and umbrellas from local tinkers and tailors. Everything and anything that was of redeemable value. At the age of thirteen I was officially run off the Dundalk quays for pimping whores to drunken seamen. The harbormaster subsequently barred me from boarding ships for reasons that I had been discovered robbing sailors' lockers, all for the purpose of keeping "the badger" in his grog money.

My rewards were something less than bountiful, but music to my ears.

"Ah, me aul son Peter, me aul scholeara, is it yurself avick, indeed it is. Did you bring home the bacon, indeed shur don't I know that I can always depend on you. You're the true flower of me flock. Bejayzus avick but do you know what it is, but as soon as the other savages (my brothers and sisters) are all away and gone it's out to America for you and for me. Out, to the land of opportunity where we will pick gold off the curbstones."

The profusion of mellifluous words from my drunken father bolstered my boyhood spirits. These words became the forks of fire of my youth as I carried the little man up the stairs, undressed him, scraped the congealing shit, piss and puke from his thighs and the loins that bore me to this earth.

On March 20, 1950, by virtue of a fire in the forepeak of the Norwegian-flagged loader tanker M.V. *Belinda,* I arrived at the Port of New York and was put under strict medical supervision.

My complaint was a dislocated shoulder. I sent an immediate cablegram to my father: "Dear Daddy Arthurs. Have arrived safely in America. Will write soon."

An instant reply came over the wire: "Dear Son Peter. Please forward a few Yankee suits and a lock of aul quids. Love your old pal Daddy Arthurs."

For Brendan, putting himself across as a brave boy-ho, a gun- and bomb-toting terrorist who defied all odds and conventions and survived international street battles, shoot-outs, bombings, incarcerations, Ireland's worst depression era, and the hobo jungles of Dublin was his forte.

In the days to come Brendan was the protagonist and creator of scores of interesting-to-watch indoor plays and playlets. By early morning, reeling under his first load of "malts" of the day, suffering from fatigue, exhaustion, vertigo and claustrophobia, petrified of daylight and terrified of nightfall, Brendan threw himself down onto the floor of his living room and harangued the ghosts of the past and the alcoholic demons of the present. Smiting down the enemy became the heady wine of his existence, but Brendan's enemies existed basically in his alcohol-soaked brain.

A series of one-man playlets got under way. These little sideshows were a charm to behold. He performed them in an amalgam of languages and always in the same position: lying on his back, with his left leg crossing his flexed right knee, and picking his nose. He rolled and flicked the cretinous waste at his bountiful array of ghosts as they flickered across his mind.

Brendan's stomach, face and neck were swollen out of proportion. His ankles were elephantine in size and discolored. Sweat exuded from his every pore and saturated the carpet.

I watched with curiosity and enthusiasm. The subjects of execution and executioners were clearly uppermost in his mind. A playlet begins: Brendan is in a heated argument with the officer who is in charge of his executioners. The execution ceremony is taking place somewhere in France. The argument is over the quality and the quantity of cognac and cigarettes he is being allotted, just before his execution. He takes a puff, coughs and curses the maker of the "inferior fags." A quick mouthful of cognac is taken into his mouth, rolled backwards on his tongue, then swallowed. He goes into another paroxysm of coughs and salivations. A string of French invective follows. Suddenly he is quiet. His body vibrates, writhes and comes to a peaceful stillness. A serene look enshrouds his beefy countenance. Beatrice sips her tea, nibbles on a piece of meat and looks out the back window. A forlorn look creases her pretty face. Another show gets under way.

Brendan is up on his elbows, his slitty eyes are moving at a rapid pace, following an invisible object as it moves from one end of the room to the other. He emits a profusion of spits and accusations.

"Yew fuckin' culshie bogman yew, yew couldn't earn the price of yur evening porter at home cud yew? Yew had to cum over here and with enough cowshit on yur boots to plant enough cabbage and potatoes to keep an army of yiz in grub for a winter. G'wan yew savage yew, if it wasn't fur the wind and the rain lashin' on yur face and yur neck, we still wudn't know how far the tide cum up last night. I'll bet the aul mother and the father who begrudgingly reared yew never heard of hot water and soap." He raises himself up off the floor and spits into the face of his landsman and imminent executioner, "Take that yew whore's melt, yew. Roger Casement will be remembered long after the likes of yew are dead and rotten in yur grave." The playlet is over. Brendan lies still.

As the morning wore on, Brendan continued to be executed. On another occasion the execution is taking place in Mexico. Brendan is speaking in Spanish. His captors have informed him that he has the option of being shot in the belly or making a run for it to an adobe wall which he must cross before the signal to shoot is given. The shootists, he is advised, are marksmen. Brendan gets up off the floor.

"Shoot me in the heart like a man, yew cowardly swine." His wishes are granted. He puts his hand over his heart, winces in pain, crumbles and falls. But seconds later he surprises "the fascist louts" by jumping up off the floor and doing a little barefooted shuffle. He sings a few verses of his favorite song, "Lady Chatterley's Lover."

Again he is down on all fours. He twitches, winces and snores, then raises his head and puts an ear to an improvised keyhole, "Cum on yew mongoloid fuck yew, cum on I hear yew, I'm here, I'm ready fur yew." He glances in my direction, a look of hysteria on his face. He lowers his head onto the rug and snores.

Suddenly he is up like a shot and into the kitchen. He kneels on the floor and pounds on the table with his hands. He doesn't speak, but it is obvious that he is in need of food. Beatrice runs her fingers through his hair, and massages the lids of his eyes with her thumbs. "Soon, in a minute, pet, be a good boy and stay over there with Peter till it's ready," she says to him in a soft lilting voice. Brendan puts the palms of his hands together and mutters as if he is praying, then he nods to Beatrice who is now placing several eggs in the bottom of the pot, then she puts the pot on the stove.

With a cherubic smile on his face he crawls over to me on his knees and mumbles something in French. "I'm sorry, Brendan, but that is one of the languages I don't speak. How about a little Norwegian?" Brendan doesn't answer. He crawls on his knees to Beatrice who cracks open the eggs, spills their contents into a cup and spoon feeds him. After each spoonful he nods his head affirmatively, then begs for more. When the eggs are eaten he goes back to the floor. The festival of seriocomic drama continues. He crawls around on his hands and knees like a dog in search of a fire hydrant. Finally he comes upon the object of his frustration. He raises his leg and urinates against the leg of my chair, then sniffs the fresh urine.

Lying flat on the floor he periodically punctures the silence with a kick, a laugh, a snicker or a full-scale outburst of vengeance, in a composition of his five favorite languages: Irish, English, French, Spanish and Latin.

Brendan had a seismographic mind capable of recording every tremor. He reveled in bragging that he could hear a mouse pissing on cotton. His superawareness of time was awesome. As the fading sun shone through the front window I checked my watch to see the time, but my watch had stopped from lack of winding. "I'll check downstairs for the correct time," I said to Beatrice, while I reached for the phone.

Brendan raised his back up off the floor, looked at the window, then around the room and said, "It's between a quarter past and half past three."

"What time is it?" I asked the operator.

"Twenty-three minutes past three," she replied. I put down the phone.

Brendan smiled, snickered and lay down.

"Brendan is never wrong about the time," Beatrice said with a look of pride on her face.

Brendan's incursions of the mind went on. In the language of his ancestors he is calling for a priest, kicking and flailing his arms and feet and demanding his inherent right to the last rites of the Roman Catholic Church. He wins his argument. A priest arrives and administers to him extreme unction. Brendan snickers and flicks a wad of nose pickings at the warden. "Yur a disgrace to the culshie Kerry mother that reared yew, yew tulip-shaped fuck, yew."

Brendan apologizes to the priest for his foul language. "Excuse me father, no offense to yew." Then he recites his favorite poems, sings a few of his favorite Irish street ballads and blesses the priest. *"In nomine patris.* Not *yew, yew* poxy-looking cunt yew," he shouts at the warden as he lets him have another wad of snot between his eyes. Then in a violent outburst he savagely condemns the British jurisprudence system for their history of "murdering" and "harassing" Irish homosexuals. "The only crime that Oscar Wilde ever committed was to have three plays running simultaneously in the West End. Yew murdered poor aul Casement because he was a homosexual," he roars at a lamp. Next he bursts into a cadenza of laughter. His face becomes a frieze of contradictory impulses as though he is questioning the merits of his own lightheartedness. His actions are the actions of a man who is updating his memories of the past with the great moment of his present. "And yew and yew," he roars at two more fiends who suddenly creep into his extraordinary field of vision. "Begone yew dirty Judas Iscariots, begone before I stomp yur dirty fuck faces into a cornucopia of twisted shite. And yew, yew pimply-faced runt yew," he tells a painting on the wall, "get away before I get up off the floor, purgatory is no more than an ass's bawl away, I'll see yew there on me way to hell."

Brendan was a man for detail to the nth degree. He was also an epicurean and a connoisseur of the finest wines and liquors. Drinks all around are suddenly ordered. *"Slainte. Skol. L'chaim,"* he says, as he toasts his friends and foes alike.

"This is how it is, this is why I have to keep in with them all!"

"You will be a good lad and stay, won't you," Beatrice moans. "I just want to get him to Dublin to finish *Cork.*"

"Look will yew for cunt's sake not be goin' on like a gaggle of aul ones cryin at a country wake, where did yew think the boy was goin'! Off to jayzus America in the mornin', is it, or what? Leave the lad alone now," he roared at Beatrice. He lies down again. "How far into *Sailor* did yew get avick?" he suddenly asks.

"I finished it, Brendan."

"Yew did! Great man, great. Be god yur a brick! P-poor aul Jack [London] shur the poor lad killed himself with the bloody drink!" he muttered in a tone of despair.

"Oh no, Brendan, that's not the way it happened. Yes indeed he tried to kill himself with the malts, but obviously he didn't succeed. According to Irving Stone, he finally did the job by swallowing a load of morphine just before his forty-first birthday. London died by his own hand."

In a flash Brendan was up and charging around the room like a bull in a barn on fire. "No, no, no, h-how cud yew, h-how cud yew say s-such a thing. I'm surrounded by madmen and m-murderers. *Jaysuz-mercifulfuckinchrist . . .*"

"Quick, quick Peter, the window, the window," Beatrice shouted.

Brendan and I made it to the rear window in unison. Brendan got a slight head start on me. Just as his head and shoulders had made it past the window frame, I managed to grab him by the thighs. He roared and kicked at my groin. Finally I managed to get him back into the room and down onto the floor. He reached down, took hold of my testicles and squeezed them, then he dug his teeth deep into my upper back. He broke loose from my grip, charged around the apartment like a load of rubber bands shot from a cannon, and finally finished up sitting on the commode.

Later in the week, still well into his cups, Brendan insisted on spending much of the wee hours of the A.M. with me in the Wilcox.

Night after night phone calls came in from the beleaguered Beatrice. "Peter, do you know where he is? Have you seen him? Will you look for him like a good boy? Will you call me as soon as you find him?"

Each time that the phone rang Brendan went into hysterics. "Listen avick, if that's yur woman, tell her I'm not here. Better yet, tell her you're not here, tell her you've already gone down to the boulevard to look for me. She'd give a headache to a fuckin' aspirin . . . jayzusjayzusjayzus."

Sleeping with Brendan was harrowing and dangerous. He dreamed and twitched a lot when sleeping. I found it necessary to keep both hands on his wrists while he slept. Then, when I felt thoroughly sure that he was fast asleep, I gently unshackled his hands from my genitalia, slipped to the floor and went off to sleep. Usually within minutes I was awakened by Brendan who was lying beside me and tugging on my penis while he snored.

One night I awoke to a medley of screams and shrieks. I found myself covered from head to toe with blood, tears, sweat, saliva, snot, phlegm, urine and excrement. "Peter Arthurs, Peter Arthurs, I love yew, I love yew, kill me, kill me," he shouted. I wrapped my arms tightly around him and held him until he went back to sleep. Minutes later I was again awakened. This time Brendan was working frantically trying to bite my tongue and my eyes out, while he tried to rip my ears off with his hands. I rolled him over onto his back and pushed a pillow down onto his face. He twitched, kicked and screamed. Then he lay still.

Another night I awoke and found Brendan biting on my cock. Blood trickled from its stem. I begged him to let go. He continued to snore. I tried to choke him but my actions only caused him to bite harder. Suddenly I remembered something that Beatrice had told me on the afternoon of our first meeting. Brendan was a diabetic. Often he went into epileptiform fits and diabetic comas. More than once, she was forced to insert hard objects into his mouth to keep him from biting his tongue off. I concluded that Brendan was then either entering a coma or undergoing a fit.

Slowly, cautiously I raised my back up off the floor, opened the bottom drawer of my chest of drawers, took hold of my shipboard wooden splicing fid and gently inserted its tip into the left side of his salivating mouth. Then with the heel of my hand I smashed the fid deep into his mouth.

I pulled out the fid and clamped the pillow down onto his tear-streaked yellow and blue face. He lay still. I picked him up, put him into bed and observed his coloring return. He slept uneasily and prattled on in his typical semisonorous manner. Then I went in search of his passport. Brendan never carried big bills in his wallet. Between two pages of his passport I found a clatter of Irish and English ten-pound notes. Between two more I discovered some Canadian and American notes. In between others I found a bundle of Band-Aids. They were the same type that he was wearing on the bridge of his nose in the police station.

I took an Irish ten-pound note, a twenty-dollar Canadian note and two American twenty-dollar bills and hid them between the mattress and the box spring of the bed where he lay snoring.

The following day I went to the nearest bank and exchanged the foreign money for American dollars. Then I paid two weeks' hotel rent, went to the nearest gas station and ordered an oil change and a full tankful of fuel. I also purchased several cans of sardines and other delectables to keep body and soul together in case of an extreme crisis.

Since Brendan refused to answer the phone, Beatrice put me in charge of all incoming calls.

"Do yew see these small little hands, well these are not the hands of a real man," he said to me one night at the dining room table as he pulled his shirt sleeves down over his fingertips. The three of us sat and glared at one another. "I'm not a man, I'm a coward, a dirty, filthy nobody," he went on. "It's all lies, dirty rotten lies, a package of fuckin' shite," he cried, tears rolling down his alcohol-stained, unshaven face.

"P-Peter . . . for God's sake, say something," Beatrice implored.

Brendan kept crossing his legs under the chair. It was as though he were trying hopelessly to hide his exceptionally tiny feet, feet that he was ashamed of.

Brendan once confided in me that his shoes were specially hand-made for him by a Dublin shoemaker. They were size four. His woolen socks were hand-knitted by his mother. They were of a heavy supportive nature. Brendan's feet were delicate and unpredictable. Sometimes keeping a semblance of balance was difficult.

During this attempt to purge himself of some bitter bile, the phone rang. I ran to pick it up.

"I'll take the cuntin' thing," Brendan surprised me as he grabbed the receiver from my hand while moving with surprising agility.

"L-listen yew I don't know who yew are, how big yur tits are, how rusticated or slippery yur cunt is, but I'll tell yew this much, I d-don't need yur fuckin' aul three thousand dollars or yur f-fifty t-thousand dollars or yur t-two hundred t-thousand d-dollars," he barked into the receiver. "When I c-cum to yur c-cuntin' c-country I cum with a shirt on me back, a pair of shoes on me f-feet and a pair of p-pants to cover me b-ballox, so with that I'll thank yew for yur offer and yur concern. Good fuckin' day." He hung up and ran back to the table. I deduced that the caller was a female, but then again I couldn't be sure.

Again. The phone rang. The three of us looked at it. No one moved.

"Will you be a good boy and answer it Peter," Beatrice said. I refused to budge. It continued to ring.

"Well, are yew or are yew not goin' to get it?" Brendan roared at me.

I arose and slowly ambled over to the phone. "Yes this is B-Brendan B-Behan," I said in a low guttural voice and in a Dublin accent. "What can I c-cuntin' jayzus d-do for yew," I said, as I imitated Brendan's every inflection, nuance and irascibility. Brendan was mortified.

"Here, g-give me t-that fuckin' thing," he snapped, charging over and jerking the receiver from my grip.

"Sorry B.," I said impatiently, "I was just trying to help, next time I'll know better."

A short while later I again answered the phone.

"Which shower of beggars are on the wire this time?" Brendan snapped.

"They want you to do a speech for a charitable cause, Brendan."

"Find out from the charitables how much they're paying!"

"They say that they would consider it an honor to meet you, but they have no lolly."

"Tell them that I'm not a statue yet, neither am I datty, batty or dotty, but before yew hang up, find out if they have a swimming pool in their backyard . . ."

"Yes, yes they do, Brendan!!"

"Have they got a diving board?"

"No, no board, Brendan!"

"Tell them to fuck off. Tell them to get some other mucker to conjure up their publicity for them. While yur at it, tell the whores that when I cum to Hollywood, I cum with a shirt on me back, a pair o' pants on me arse and a pair o' shoes on me feet."

"Mister Behan wants you to know that when he cum to Hollycrud, he cum with a shirt on his arse, a pair of shoes on his ballox, and a tie on his chin, furthermore I feel morally obliged to tell you that when he leaves this cuntin' quagmire of yours, he will leave with his pants on his—"

"G-give me that cuntin' thing," he roared pulling the phone from me.

"L-listen I don't know who yew are or where yew cum from, but I'll tell yew this much, I'm not runnin' some sort of a Brendan Behan benevolent association for broken-down actors, whores, drunks or the likes. I'll thank yew to cunt off and don't call back."

One afternoon I arrived at Behan's apartment and found Brendan sitting naked in the middle of the living room floor. He was talking up a storm. Beatrice was nowhere in sight. At first I thought that Brendan was talking to himself but seconds later I found the chambermaid wiping down the walls of the bath.

Brendan motioned me away but I decided to stay in the vestibule and listen to his tall tales.

"Did I ever tell yew that I was once an aspiring pugilist, a coming champion of the ring wha!?" he said to the chambermaid.

"Here, sit yurself down on the velvety side of yur arse and I'll tell yew all about it. Well, first of all I must tell yew there were those who did not feel too kindly disposed about me winnin' the title, they set out to destroy me chances, and all was lost by the consequence of a big dose of crabs that I was infected with the night before the contest. Yew see I believe in therapy, and my therapeutic outlet after me months of hard trainin' was a roll in the kip with one of the local doxies. Little did I know at the time that the lady of ill repute also worked for the Irish mafia, the gentlemen who did not wish for me to win. No doubt it was they who infected the girl. When the bell sounded, as per my usual standards I proceeded to throw volley after volley of punches. The other chap thought bejayzus that he was workin in some leather factory. However along about halfway through the ruckus, just when yur man was due to sniff the rosin, didn't I discover that for reasons of me comfort I was compelled to keep reaching down to me crotch and scratching away for all I was worth. The other Dubliner catching on to me jingoistic action took full advantage and bopped me profusely. What cud I do? I know I don't have to tell yew the rest, dear girl. The rest of the yarn is a matter of history. A split decision was rendered—in the other cunt's favor."

"I'll make a deal with you, Mr. Behan," the maid said, laughing. "If you promise to think about it, the next time that I see you, if you can still look me square in the eye and tell me you believe your own nonsense, then *I'll* believe you." The lady departed and left Brendan sitting thinking and picking.

Unfortunately for those who genuinely loved him and depended upon him, Brendan had a great interest in creating minor tempests and subsequently getting those same personages to apologize and placate him with gentle words and for reasons that were totally unbeknownst to them.

He reveled in playing the role of the self-made, good-hearted literary genius who was destroying his health and his talent with gallons of "hard tac."

"Shur me fuckin' bit of success is damn near killing me, wha!" As the days passed he became the newest literary star in the celluloid firmament. No other Irish writer in history so monopolized the attention of the film industry.

Every motion picture studio in the land of awe phoned in and begged him to do cameo performances. Columbia Pictures was the most insistent. That studio was then shooting two motion pictures back to back.

One, *The Notorious Landlady,* starring Kim Novak. The other, *Walk on the Wild Side,* starred Jane Fonda, Capucine and Laurence Harvey. Through the grapevine I had heard that *Walk* was shaping up as a lemon in the daily rushes. This was the film that the studio wanted Brendan to appear in. I also learned that *Landlady* was moving on to London. Brendan instructed me to inform all callers that "I'm a writer and not an actor or anything else that's connected to that bird-brained ilk that is incapable of earning an honest living. Tell them to fuck off."

"Suit yourself Brendan, it's your prerogative."

But the studio's big brass was adamant. Finally I informed them that the man was sick, "very sick and indisposed."

"Oh, that's O.K.," the secretary to the Columbia producer said, "We understand how it is, that's why we have plenty of black coffee waiting. Just bring him along, we'll take good care of him."

I promised the lady that I would do what I could. "Call me later," I warmly suggested.

Columbia called again. "I'm terribly sorry," I said, "Brendan is on a big drunk, he may never sober up again. When he's like this, he's impossible to deal with."

"Oh don't worry," the lady emphatically assured me, "we'll know how to handle him. Just get him into the studio."

"But you have a lot of very fragile equipment on hand. What if he decides to smash a set of sensitive lenses or knock over a camera?"

"Bring him along," the lady said in a tone of resignation.

"I'll do my damndest; be sure to give my love to Kim."

At the Montecito poolside, he informed a gaggle, "I have me own work to do! The perverts and embalmers can take their fuckology and trickology somewhere else, always looking for something for sweet fuck all, I know their game."

Ever since I could remember I have had an extreme infatuation with the incredible physical beauty, the mystical eyes and the unique acting style of Kim Novak. I had seen almost all of her films in ports around the world. My need to see her in the flesh, to touch her, to talk to her and to get even a single word of response, was desperate. Through the industry grapevine, I had heard that Kovacs was a big favorite with Columbia. Novak was their most illustrious female star. Ernie Kovacs, I was informed, threw big star-studded parties. The chances of Novak attending were ten to one in favor. I realized my life's dream would soon become a reality. Novak, I was also assured, was a down-to-earth, easy-to-talk-to woman.

Brendan had told me that *the big Kovacs* party was set for Thursday the fifteenth. He assured me that he had spoken to Kovacs and that my invitation was confirmed. With boyish ebullience, I looked forward to the great event.

One morning directly after Brendan had followed me into the bathroom I closed the door behind us, then stood between him and the door. I screwed up my face, stared hard at him, then said, "Now listen B., you're amply aware of the fact that the big brass at Columbia is going bananas to get you to do the cameo in their lemon of the year *Walk on the Wild Side*. I phoned up and found out that Kim Novak is working on a flick called *The Notorious Landlady* which is being shot on an adjacent lot.

"Now you have readily admitted that at this point in our friendship I am entitled to a thing or two. I promised Columbia that come hell or high water I would usher you over, so what say we quit the grab-arse for a while and skitter off over. If we're lucky I might even be asked to do a small bit as your sidekick in the whorehouse, no doubt that is the scene where they will want to cast you. Also I'm really looking forward to the big blowout in Kovacs' house."

"C-certainly, o'course o'course, s-shur didn't I c-call this morning and tell him I was takin yew, me s-son."

"Good man, Brendan, good man. You're my class of china."

I opened the door, led him to the bedroom, dressed him, made him guzzle several cups of tea, then took him to the parking lot.

Much to my horror, Beatrice returned from Hughes and asked where I was taking him. "To Columbia Studios," I said.

"Oh no, no, no, Peter. I told you before. Brendan is not an actor, Brendan is a writer. I don't want him going over there. Actors make Brendan nervous . . ."

The three of us went back up on the freight elevator.

Now for the first time I realized that, contrary to my beliefs, Beatrice did in fact hold some power over Brendan. However, I did not feel totally deterred, for I too had an arsenal at my disposal.

Hollywood's gay bars were fast becoming "off-limits" for Brendan. He was persona non grata. His late-night outbursts and his denigrations of his wife for "her inability" to bear him a son were too calamitous. He bragged of having his spermatozoa tested for its viability. He raved and told stories of his terrorist days, his days in jail and his personal friendship with convicts who had chopped the heads and hands off members of their families. He told of dissectings by butchers who subsequently filleted the human flesh, then sold it to some local monks as sausage meat. He told tall tales of his personal involvement in incidents where fellow prisoners were ordered to jump on the wiggling figures of other convicts, who moments before had had the hangman's trapdoor sprung from under them.

Then in graphic detail he explained the reasons for the hangman's calculations in regards to the length and circumference of the rope used and the probable error for the unsuccessful drops, his eyes glistening and dancing as he relived the titillating moments of the past.

Revised renditions of my shipboard buggery stories, stories about funeral dirges, hangings, garrotings, bodies rising up out of their coffins as the lids were being screwed into place, became a specialty.

What Brendan never knew was that in the world of psychology and in the eyes of the law, the aberration of pedophilia is regarded as being of a heterosexual nature. Brendan had become such a profuse conjurer of small talk and a mitigator of his own guilts and fears that he never took time to truly measure his own shadow, or to observe the feelings of others. Brendan had conquered and achieved, but in the dark nights of his soul he could not genuinely enjoy his success.

The fact that there was never anything overt or sexually betraying in his speech pattern or in his manner gladdened me. In his outbursts,

Brendan displayed a great envy of Oscar Wilde. He detested the former giant of Irish letters for his brash spirit, and his brazenness to have publicly challenged the powerful Marquis of Queensberry.

Like a ticking explosive device, setting off its detonators at precisely timed intervals, he continuously called for the passing of law that would rid the land of pedophiles. In these late-night settings he came across as a haggard, bone-weary war horse who was coming to the nadir of his days but was on the threshold of finishing up his magnum opus: a work that would deservedly put him into the Valhalla of the greats of Irish literature and alongside of those to whose names his own name was now equal; a piece that would open a declaration of holy mayhem on all who would derive pleasure from indulging in such an insidious crime.

His pedophilia was the key to his emotional cancer. The one major thing that Brendan lived in mortal fear of was the prospect of one day being deported to his native land for committing the crime of child molestation. He bragged incessantly of his socialistic leanings and boasted that one day his political beliefs and public espousing, "will be the undoing of me." He deliberately denigrated those in high pretentious stations. Brendan was a poser and a posturer who was merely playing it close to the vest; thus affording himself a sweet margin of maneuverability in the event of a minor holocaust.

The Immigration and Naturalization Service excludes and deports homosexual aliens under sections 1182 and 1251 of the Title 8 of the U.S. Code, which permits the exclusion of those afflicted with psychopathic personality or sexual deviation or mental defect.

Since Brendan believed that it was essential to his image to keep up a steady bombardment of insults on his "foes," this code was uppermost in his mind.

The phenomenon of machismo was another of Brendan's greatest social problems. He felt essentially miserable with it. But he was brusque and cute. He knew that he was obligated to put on a show and put himself across as the stereotypical Irish self-made genius—the hard-drinking, womanizing, two-fisted brawler. Brendan worked his talents to the bone to come across as a little thumper who regarded the imperceptibilities and the irreversibilities of the life hereafter as some sort of celestial joke; a man who regarded death as life's final quicksilvery laugh and a thing not to be taken too seriously.

One morning a tall dapper gentleman appeared at the apartment.

"Who the fuck are *yew?*" Brendan asked, opening the door.

"I'm Kenneth Vils," the man said with a warm smile. "I'm from the Los Angeles Police Department," the man said, producing his credentials. "Most people around here just call me 'Kenny' or 'the chief.' "

"Cum in, cum in, cum in avick," Brendan coughed, a twinge of fear in his voice. "Here sit yurself down and have a c-c-coffee or a tea for yurself."

The two men talked for awhile. Brendan nodded his head as if in total agreement to everything that the man said. A handshake ensued. Vils departed. The public nuisance charges against Brendan would be lessened, I was informed.

Later that evening, Joe Finnegan phoned in and requested that Brendan be the principal speaker at the annual dinner meet for the Greater Los Angeles Press Club. Brendan liked Finnegan but turned him down flat. Finnegan implored him. A bargain was reached. Brendan stated that if "Kenny" would promise to be there, *he* would come and "do the honors." But his message was emphatic. No Vils, no Brendan. Another flurry of phone calls was made.

Vils, it was learned, had other plans for the evening—obligations to his department. However, Finnegan who was then president of the club, succeeded in making a deal with "the chief." Vils would come later in the evening if the previously designated hour for the dinner could be pushed ahead.

Finnegan subsequently picked up Brendan at the hotel and drove him to the club. Vils arrived and found Brendan drunk as Pontius Pilate, in the process of puking into a bowl that a reporter was eating soup from. He raised his head and saw Vils then jumped to his feet, put his arms around him and muttered, "You're here." He insisted that the lawman sit in *his* chair.

"But where will you sit?" Vils asked.

"Don't worry about me avick," Brendan said smilingly.

Brendan sat on the floor adjacent to Vils. The dinner commenced. Finnegan introduced Brendan to the gathering. A wild burst of applause and bravos went up. Brendan waved, genuflected, thumped his abdomen and mounted the podium.

"L-listen youse guys," he stuttered taking the microphone in hand. "B-but there is only two writers in this t-town that's worth the wearing of their knickers, t-two great aul w-whores . . . H-Hedda H-Hoop . . . H-Hoop . . ." he turned to Vils for confirmation. Vils was now adjacent to the podium.

"It's Hedda Hopper and Louella Parsons," Vils whispered.

"The other aul c-cunt is L-Louella Parsons," Brendan confirmed.

The plug to the amplifier was suddenly pulled. Tex Williams, the renowned cowboy singer and guitarist, hastily mounted the podium. The electricity was turned back on. Williams sang and strummed. The crowd clapped. Brendan became enraged. He charged back up onto the stage, knocking over chairs and tables as he went. "P-play a f-fuckin' Irish jig for jayzus sake," he roared into the cowboy's face. The cowboy ordered his troupe to play a medley of Irish tunes. Brendan danced, clapped and careened, then ordered the musicians to stop. Silence prevailed. Brendan started up again.

"Oh the Duke of Kent is fuckin' the Duchess of York . . . oh the cunt of Kent . . . sorry ladies and jellyfish . . . er I mean the c-cunt of Y-York." Again the juice was disconnected. Brendan was now sweating, ripping off his clothes and pounding his fists on the head of the dead microphone. He fumed with hysteria and anger. "Get this cuntin' thing back on," he demanded.

Finnegan was now down on all fours, crawling towards the podium.

"Get that goddam drunken Irish bastard down off the podium," he roared at Vils, "he'll ruin the party. Quick get the son of a bitch *down.*" Finnegan was livid. Vils smiled, looked down into Finnegan's face and whispered, "But he's here as your guest of honor. It was you who insisted, I'm just an innocent bystander! Also, when we made the deal, wasn't it part of the bargain that Brendan wouldn't be given any booze until I got here?"

Finnegan salivated and muttered. Rage was in his eyes. Brendan continued to do his strip. Finally Vils rushed up to the podium, grabbed hold of Brendan, picked up his tie and jacket and carried him to his station wagon. On the way to the hotel, Brendan insisted on stopping off at an Irish bar for a "cup of coffee." Vils agreed, "But no more booze, Brendan," he demanded, shaking his index finger in Brendan's face.

With his drunken penguin gait and typical aggressiveness, Brendan charged into the pub and hollered to the barman, "Give me a c-c-coffee, and Irish c-c-coffee."

"No booze," "the chief" said to the barman, flashing his shield.

"A shot of Hennessey," Brendan pleaded.

"Coffee," Vils insisted.

"Hennessey."

"Coffee."

"Coffee . . . fuck it, if the queen had a cock instead of a cunt she'd be the king . . ."

Brendan ran over to the jukebox, inserted a handful of quarters and played a medley of Irish jigs, then he careened around the bar and fell in a heap upon the floor. Vils picked him up, sat him down, then ordered several cups of coffee and force-fed them into Brendan's mouth, then he took a respite. A short while later a scuffle broke out. Brendan was up to his gall in a fisticuff with a well-known Hollywood cameraman named Willie Geiger.

He punched Geiger in the nose. Geiger insisted on pressing charges.

"I'll handle it, Willie," Vils said.

Geiger was adamant. He wanted him arrested.

"He won't bother you again," Vils said.

Geiger reluctantly acquiesced. Vils picked Brendan up, slung him over his shoulder and carried him to the car, then drove to the hotel.

"Put him to bed immediately," Vils instructed Beatrice.

Beatrice undressed Brendan and put him to bed. Vils departed via the elevator. However, when he reached the lobby, much to his horror he found Brendan insulting and abusing the effeminate hotel desk clerk. Brendan had charged downstairs ahead of Vils via the stairway. The clerk insisted on an immediate arrest.

"I'll handle it," the big cop assured the clerk, then Vils carried him into the elevator and brought him back up to the apartment.

"I'll put him to bed this time," Vils said in an authoritative voice as he undressed him and put him to bed.

Brendan snored and slept like a bear in hibernation.

"I assure you he won't bother you again tonight," Vils said to the clerk on the way out.

(Today in the famous "32" bar in Los Angeles City, Brendan's alcohol-stained tie is pinned high up on the wall behind the bar. The tie is a hallowed shrine to the memory of Brendan Behan. It was donated by Kenny Vils.)

Approximately one hour later I was awakened.

"Stop whatever yur doing and cunt over here right away."

I charged down to the lobby of the Wilcox, hopped into my car and drove. Suddenly it dawned upon me that I had forgotten to ask Brendan which bar he was in! I parked the Buick on Santa Monica and Vine then began a frantic search of the bars. I found him in the Nest, a leathery type of gay bar. He looked drawn, intimidated and frightened. Two burly men had him bottled up in a booth in the rear of the bar. "Sit yurself down avick," he said as I approached the booth. I pulled the collar of my leather jacket up around my neck, swallowed hard, affected a pugnacious look and sat down.

The two men were assuring Brendan that Boston's bishop had every moral right to condemn *The Hostage* as being "vile and a disgrace to the Catholic Church."

"Fuck the bishop of Boston," Brendan snapped. "In regards to me sentiments concerning the town of Boston itself, well I suppose it's O.K. if yew have an affinity for codfish or clam chowder, but personally I'd rather have me twin sisters working in a whorehouse in Dublin than have me twin brothers servin' as monks in a monastery in Boston."

The men became enraged. "Easy, Brendan," one of them said threateningly.

"I have a better idea," I interjected. "Why don't we adjourn to the parking lot around the corner, the air out there is more conducive to settling arguments."

The four of us adjourned to the lot. Violent words were exchanged. Fists flew. The two men lay adjacent to one another in the lot. Brendan kicked one of them in the groin. "Yur blood's in yur knuckles yew dirty louser yew," he crackled. "See youse at the knicker counter in Woolworth's," he chuckled as we walked away. Brendan charged ahead of me.

At his insistence we repaired to the Comet. I soaked my swollen hands in the sinkful of hot water, then washed some blood from my face. Brendan was unmarked. It was I who had done the fighting.

"In Ringsend, that's a proletarian neighborhood in Dublin, we call a kick up in the ballox a Ringsend uppercut," Brendan said, taking hold of a very delicate looking boy by his lapels and giving him a gentle knee in the groin while banging him on the bridge of his nose with his forehead. A look of affected menace inebriated his face. "Know what I mean?"

"Oh, you must have been a real bitch in your young days!" the boy chuckled in a seductive voice. His remark caught Brendan by surprise. A look of terror crept into his face. He suggested that we leave.

Outside Brendan asked, "What d-did he m-mean by t-that avick?"

"By what, B.?"

"Bitch, avick."

"Bitch, Brendan? . . . oh that. Oh it means great things, bitch in that context means a two-fisted brawler, a tough hombre. It's a typical Yank word." Brendan beamed triumphantly and spirited ahead of me.

Brendan's drinking reached uncontrollable proportions. He continued to be lionized by the greats of Hollywood. The pint-sized Goliath spirited ahead, walloped the sacred cows and shattered the shibboleths of Celluloid City. I became his publicity planner, personal advisor and part-time business manager. An avalanche of invitations and urgent messages adorned every stick of furniture in the oblong living room.

VI

Now into his second big week "on the batter," Brendan's behavior became intolerable. Living with him was untenable. He was an emotional vampire, a sycophantic cretin. He was a destroyer who reveled in killing what he loved most of all. He had a natural propensity for annihilating those whose friendship he cherished best. Those who became consumed in his conscious and unconscious demands lost all sense of their own self and existence.

Brendan drank for effect as opposed to for taste. Drink was his sexual armature, his catalyst, his catharsis, his barrier that separated him from the legend that he had created. His intoxication was his passport to participate in any chosen situation at a given moment while at the same time it served to keep him far removed from situations that he could not emotionally or intellectually deal with.

His sporadic fits of outright wickedness were awesome. He cuffed Beatrice about the face for no rhyme or reason save for the fact that she merely crossed his line of walk at the idiosyncratic moment. Often, I challenged his right to abuse her, but on each occasion she demanded that I leave him alone.

One morning when Brendan was in the process of savagely abusing her, I turned to him and said, "We're goin' for a ride Brendan."

"F-for a ride avick?"

"For a ride, Brendan."

"W-where to s-son?"

"To a boulevard."

"Which boulevard??"

I took him on a thirty-five-mile ride. We sat sipping and talking in the Tradewinds bar on Avalon Boulevard in Wilmington. At my insistence we both drank soda water.

"Brendan, I consider you a good friend and a great writer. I'd like to tell you a yarn about mesself when I was a boy in Dundalk."

I told Brendan of an incident in my young life in Dundalk when I was forced to stoop to a very low level to cadge the price of my father's grog when I was about eleven.

I was standing outside the Town Hall lavatory. A burly soldier in the Irish Army approached and offered me sixpence if I let him suck my cock.

"Certainly," I said and lowered my pants. After he had finished I pulled up my pants and put out my hand.

"Fuck off, you dirty little cunt, you," the soldier said as he prepared to depart.

"You better fork over my sixpence," I said threateningly.

"Fuck off before I call the bobbies and have you put in jail where you belong," he shot back. As the soldier turned to leave, I reached out, took hold of his military cane and cracked him hard across the back of his skull.

He slumped to the shit-infested floor. I reached down into a smelly gaping hole in the concrete floor, scooped up an armful of shit and slammed it into the crack in his skull. A profusion of shit, blood, brains and other vomitous matter bubbled out of his head. Shit seeped from the legs of his pants. I darted out of the public facility, charged down Market Street and into the public clinic where I had five stitches put into my upper lip. My nose had to be reset. In the battle for the sixpence, the soldier had somehow managed to turn and fire off a power-laden uppercut. For the remainder of my life I would have a piece of overlapping lip.

"Here's where the stitches were inserted, Brendan," I said, touching my upper lip.

"T-the d-d-dirty b-ballox," he stuttered, "s-served him right, and yew only a b-boy struggling to earn the price of your poor father's keep!" Brendan was suddenly pale, drawn and filled with fright.

"I think of that incident once in a while," I said, "particularly when I'm in the company of someone who is trying to take advantage of my boyish nature." We stared at one another.

"C-c-certainly," Brendan mumbled, "why wouldn't yew?"

I held an uncompromising stare. Brendan looked horror-stricken.

"W-will we c-c-cunt off back to H-Hollywood avick."

We drove home in ominous silence.

One day, when he was in the wicked process of savagely denigrating

Kim Novak for her acting ability, I turned to him and said, "Ease up there, Brendan, I doubt very seriously if Kim is sitting around talking derogatorily about *you* or *your* writing."

At the time I was holding the car's iron in my hand. I opened both doors of the car, got out and took several whacks at the car's fenders while holding a gaze on Brendan, then threw the iron down onto the floor of the car and drove off.

Our telepathic communication system was beginning to crumble.

Questions pertaining to my personal sexual tastes and former indulgences were becoming overly burdensome. I was now beginning to believe that Brendan was everything in the sexual catalogue with the exception of being a lesbian. But at that, I even wondered.

One afternoon a lady named Madelaine Cole invited us to lunch and a swim at the home of a friend who was the host of a big Hollywood talk show. I suggested to Brendan to "hire a taxi."

Brendan insisted that I drive him to the house.

At the poolside, a man with a very effeminate voice asked Brendan if the known Irish Catholic sexual repression was primarily responsible for the fact that there were more writers, fighters, homosexuals and guerrillas, per capita, in Ireland than in any other country in the world.

Brendan became enraged and tried to throw the man into the pool, then proceeded to the living room and overturned a display cabinet full of trinkets and objets d'art. Later he cooled off by diving and swimming in the pool.

Another afternoon, at his insistence, when I was dragging him home to the Montecito, we began to cross against a red light. Out of nowhere a spit-and-polish officer emerged on a motorcycle.

"But he only put one foot down onto the street," I said to the officer pleadingly as he prepared to write out a summons.

"That's all it takes to violate our traffic laws out here," the glittering man said.

Brendan remained mute, his chin dropping to his chest. I became entangled in a verbal brouhaha with the man of the law.

"Let me see your credentials," the officer suddenly snapped.

More heated words were exchanged. The officer, who looked more like a barracuda on a weekend pass, wrote up a summons, handed it to Brendan—informed him where it could be paid—and sped away. Brendan read the document. "Here avick, it's for you," he said with a smirk and handed it to me. He was right. The summons was made out in my name.

Michael Carr, a songwriter, was one of Brendan's "chinas" (pals) who popped in and out. Carr's name periodically appeared in the daily newspaper and magazine articles about Brendan. One day Carr showed up in a huff and demanded that Brendan not mention his name again when giving an interview. His reasons he explained, were that his family, his friends, and his business associates might regard *him* as "another drunk." Brendan assured his fellow Dubliner that he would "most ardently adhere to his wishes and that no further harm will come to your career, I assure you."

Later that evening Carr came by and asked me to drive him to "his friend's house." His friend was Maureen O'Hara.

Brendan followed me into the parking lot, a scowl on his face. "Where do *yew* think *yur* goin'?" he snarled.

"But I'm only doin' it to get a look at the luvly lady, B."

"Let the cunt get a c-car. Since when are we running a limousine service for every Micky, Dick and Harry who staggers by?"

"Maybe you're right, B. I'll tell Carr to fuck off."

Brendan watched me like a beady-eyed gannet as I shut the gate behind me and walked out to the lower lot, where Carr and my Buick were parked. I exchanged a few hasty words with Carr and quickly returned. Brendan beamed triumphantly. "Good man, avick," he chirped.

He was now the darlin' boy-ho and the pet of the Montecito pool. The pool was his second bed, bidet and bath. The success of his publicity continued to bring a colorful influx of personages, many of whom were as famous as he was. His panache, elfin grin, purblind audacity, his mordant witticisms, his tall tales of barroom brawls and sexual conquests that took place nowhere but in his dervish mind, his famous-man's distinctive distrusts, his cracker-barrel philosophies and pyrotechnic gushes were as welcome as a public flogging.

Burgess Meredith, Mike Kellin, Juanita Hall, Michael O'Herlihy and many more became his communicants. The multidimensional man wallowed in his adulatory success.

"Shur any man who would sit in a tubful of water for hours has to be some class of an eegit. Stewing in me own mud is not my idea of a good wash," became his early morning opening line. However, he did confide that the art of showering was another cleansing process that did not appeal to him.

On the occasions that the poolside was barren of vassals, we spirited down to the Y to view the pulchritude on display. Brendan displayed a very unique way of showering. First and foremost, he waited until three shower stalls in a row were not in use. Then he staggered over, stood directly under the center shower and adjusted the head to an outward perpendicular position. Next, he tipped the first and third heads to forty-five degree inverted angles, then turned on the water. The upshot was that the two outside downpours clashed with the center cascade and created a major blur.

Intermittently, he turned up the hot spigots to send up a steamy vapor. Brendan was thus virtually hidden behind the triple downpours. Whenever he spotted a well-muscled or dimpled derriere he reacted as though he had been shot with one of Hemingway's stupefying jungle darts.

Minutes later he stepped sprightly from the shower, his hair and torso undampened, save for a few droplets of sweat. The purpose of the dry shower was to enable him to get a more thorough view of the youthful bodies as they paraded in and out of the globuliferous room.

When something exceptionally titillating passed, he followed him into the locker room and struck up a non sequitur conversation. My presence alleviated his natural shyness, fear and sexual hysteria.

One hot afternoon, Brendan and I sat cross-legged on the edge of the pool. The unmerciful sun shone through the vistas of smog and assaulted our limbs. A gentle breeze rustled the leaves of the surrounding trees and foliage. Clusters of little birds chirped and sang. Brendan and I spat into the pool in unison. His spits sent up concentric rings in the deep end, my spit caused rings to mature at the shallow end. The two rings spawned and suffused into a single circle then dissipated at the edge of the pool. No one spoke.

A lengthy period of silence prevailed. It was the old familiar silence that italicized the drunken malice in his soul.

"Do yew know a savage in this town called Wald?" he suddenly asked.

"Wald . . . Wald . . . Wald . . . hmmm . . . a man called Wald?"

"Jerry Wald."

"Jerry Wald! Of course, he's a famous producer-director; he made *Key Largo*. Of course, of course."

"I didn't ask yew what the cunt made, I only asked yew if yew knew him. Don't write the fuck-pig's biography for me."

"No Brendan, no . . . can't say that I've had the pleasure of meeting the poor man, why?"

"Wud yew do me a favor son!"

"Don't I usually? What is it?"

"The next time that the cunt calls, tell him to fuck off."

"He's been bothering you, Brendan?! I'll tell him to cunt off B. I'll tell him to write you a letter. Shall I tell him to wait until he sees your picture on the front of the stamp?" A short silence ensued.

"He called this morning. He asked me to write some dialogue for him. For *Ulysses*. He wants to shoot the film in Dublin in the fall."

"I'll tell him to fuck off, Brendan. You can count on me. However, as a word from the wise, don't worry about these Hollywood savages, worry about yourself. Worry about B.B. and B.B. Worry about me. Don't forget *Cork*. You mustn't let *Cork* die on the vine, B., fuck *Ulysses*. Up sodomy. Up your arse." Silence prevailed.

The somnambulistic rays of the sun beat down mercilessly.

"Do yew know a chap in this cesspool called Mineo? Sal Mineo."

"I know *of* him Brendan. Is he bothering you?"

Another paroxysm of spitting and nose-picking ensued.

"I-I-I m-mean to say w-what sort of a b-boy is he?" he continued. "Is he married, is he s-strange or what says yew? Is he an actor, or what is his game? I mean, he has to earn his lolly . . ."

"Strange! Married! Hmmm, I don't know, I don't think so, I'll inquire. He's a movie star, an Academy Award winner. He excels in playing the roles of terrorists, rebels, street fighters. I hear he goes out with fellas."

"G-goes out with f-fellas!" Brendan snorted perplexedly.

"Yes, Brendan, I hear he has no interest in the fair sex."

"Hmmm, terrorists, rebels . . . he called this morning, him and a chap called Todd. Mike Todd, Jr. Do yew know him?"

"Yes indeed, I know him very well. Didn't he used to be Elizabeth Taylor's son? The lucky son of a bitch, he invented Smell-o-Rama or Todd-o-Rama or something about Rama."

"Him and Sal are forming a film company. They want to film *Borstal Boy*. I promised them this morning that I'd write a sequel to the book. What do yew think avick, should I give the chap a chance?"

"Well Brendan, let's see, hmmm, shur, I suppose it's O.K. Fuck it. Why not? Give the boy a break. He needs the work. Maybe some day he will do a thing or two for you. He's a handsome lad . . ."

Brendan's big-name-dropping was awesome. He dropped the names of the illustrious with a superlative ease and a nonchalance that was unparalleled. Sal's name became his pet. One afternoon when Brendan was holding court, a well-known lesbian cut right through his gabfest, and informed him that Sal was "queer."

"Him and Yul Brynner are having a gay old time of it," the lady said smilingly.

Brendan was horrified. Where the subject of homosexuality was concerned he was a hypocrite. Instantly he switched the conversation to another topic. But Brendan was insatiable. He couldn't resist his big-name-dropping. In minutes he returned to his cherished topic. "Oh jayzus Peter avick," he stuttered, interrupting himself, "did I fuckinwell forget again! Remind me to call Sal. The poor boy is dependin' on me. I promised him that I'd write the other fuckin' aul thing for him." Then in a sudden switch, "Oh jayzus b-but I don't know . . . I mean I know the chap is a c-competent actor, but then again he may be a little too olive-oily looking to play the part of an Irish terrorist."

Mike Mineo, Sal's brother and part-time manager, continued to call and inquire about the project. One day over lunch Mike informed us that Papa Mineo lived in the Bronx and was a coffin builder by trade. This piece of news afforded Brendan another quick exit when name-dropping and using Sal's name.

"I-I'm sure the chap is the best man in this quagmire to play the part of Brendan Behan on film, b-but me grandmother always said, 'Never trust the offspring of a coffin maker.' "

Another of Brendan's greatest fears was to come off at the losing end of a big verbal shoot-out. These types of shoot-outs were commonplace at late-hour Hollywood parties.

"I g-got a call this morning from a chap called K-Kovacs, Ernie Kovacs," Brendan said to another sun worshipper. "He's throwin' a party in me honor. Who is he and what does he do for his livin' atall?" he asked a poolside gathering.

"He's a lightning wit, Brendan, sharp as a razor," a resident said.

Brendan shuddered at the vision, dropped the subject, then moved on to a host of other big-name-droppings. "Ah, *Richard,* a great aul skin, a great friend of ours, do we know him, certainly we do, shur didn't we go to see him recently in *Camelot.* He invited us backstage after the performance, didn't he, Peter," he said turning to me. "He wanted to have a few pictures taken with me, and shur why not, shur isn't that the cabbage and spuds of the chap's trade. A damn sight better than heavin' coal in some fuckin' aul Welsh coal mine, I might add."

Brendan was as chock-full of chat as an Irish country pub at closing time. He rambled on incessantly.

"An aul one says to me one day, 'What sort of a lassie is Sean O'Casey's daughter?' 'She's O.K.,' says I, 'and why shouldn't she be, isn't she the daughter of an Irish dramatist who is a card-carrying member of the British Communist Party.' Now in regards to O'Flaherty and his ilk, I'll admit that there is violence in *my* writing just as there is in *his,* but I'll tell yew this much and I'll tell yew no more, I'm not so fuckin' childish about it as he is, but so be it.

"People keep cummin' up to me and asking me about Samuel Beckett, what are his plays about and how much influence did James Joyce have on *his* writing? Well, first and foremost I think that Joyce, besides being a colorless unimaginative writer and an obvious degenerate, he should have been hanged, drawn and quartered, for soiling good paper with the likes of such muck. As for aul Sam himself, he's a great aul skin, a great friend of me own, shur didn't he keep me goin with the occasional handout when I was in Paris, when me readies were low. In regards to his plays, I've seen them performed yes, indeed I have. But to tell yew the truth, I don't understand them! But so what? I like to go for swims in the ocean even though I don't understand the ocean.

"In Ireland and in England, yew can look in the windows of the Blue Train and get a squint at the Tories in the Pullman as they're settling down to their banquets of the finest of wines and, I have no doubt, to anything from a live trout to a young child or whatever else strikes their fuckin' fancies. Shur the only thieves that I ever met were Tories.

"I'll admit that I'm a very ordinary sort of a chap, even though it is true that I have a fair measure of fame. Me mother always referred to me as a 'hard chaw,' a 'proper divil.' As a child growin' up in the Dublin slums it was a common knowledge that my brand of divilment wud hang a parish.

"One night Thornton Wilder, who was at the time in the company of the great man James Thurber, turned to me and says he, 'Brendan, I don't understand yew. Why,' says he, 'will yew not stay on in America!'

" 'Dublin is me home,' says I.

" 'B-b-but shur they'll only give to yew what they have always given to their other great writers and artists!'

" 'What's that,' says I, 'Thornton?'

" 'A swift kick up in the ballox,' says he.

"Robert Morley is another great aul skin and a confidant of mesself. He has the indifference to criticism that comes of rare success.

"Shakespeare, like Shaw, said pretty much of everything. What those two colleagues of mine left out, Joyce, O'Casey, and Wilde with a nudge from mesself, put in.

"In the words of Proust, all that a writer needs is chastity and water! I'm afraid that neither one would suit the likes of mesself. Water is for washing and sailing ships in. B-but the real reason why I drink b-beer is b-because the price of a b-bottle of orange juice or lemon-lime c-costs t-twice as much as a b-bottle of Guinness.

"The only aul b-ballox that I ever knew who admitted to b-being in the Black and Tans was a c-cunt from L-Liverpuddin'—excuse me I mean L-Liverpool! 'Why did yew join?' says I. 'Well' says he, 'I suppose it was because I didn't have the price of the fare to go and join the foreign legion.'

"The Irish who fought for the fascist cunt F-Franco had the g-good common sense to come home with more men than they went out with." Then in a voice fraught with rage, as though the memory of the battles, of the fire on wood and blood on stones, was still fresh in his mind, he continued.

"I'll tell yew this much, if *my* books are to be worth the paper that they're printed on, I can assure yew of this much, yew will never see the names of the l-likes of the Mr. Oliver Cromwell mentioned in them, no by jayzus yew won't, that dirty rotten murderin' c-coward, t-the m-murderer of tens of thousands of children and women in the t-town of D-Drogheda. B-but I'll say this m-much for the l-lout, he d-did in fact d-do one decent t-thing before he died from the pox and that was this, he cut off the head of the other d-dirty lout, the fuckin' aul king, and t-that in my opinion, for, I too, have an opinion, and rightly so, he proved that even a k-king's noggin will cum off when it is properly lopped. Be the same token now, do not misunderstand me, it is commonly well known that I do not have any great love for the c-cunt, or for any other cunt who would murder and massacre tens of thousands of holy children who were g-grouped around a cross of the Redeemer while he delighted in the slow process of his individual murders, sticking and killin' them one at a time. In between psalms he had his murderers shout 'Kill the nits and there will be no lice to have to contend with tomorrow.' "

One smoggy afternoon while he was holding court at the pool he suddenly stopped short and beckoned me to follow him to the parking lot. Horror was in his face.

"H-how old was the chap, avick?" he asked hysterically.

"Which chap, Brendan?"

"The c-chap, t-the c-chap that the c-captain buggered!"

"The captain, Brendan. Which captain?"

"*The* captain on the Norwegian ship."

"Hmmm! Twenty-five."

"Twenty-five . . . ahaaa . . . B-b-but yew said he was f-fifteen, s-son."

"No, Brendan, you're mistaken."

"M-m-mistaken!!??"

"Yes, Brendan, I said he was twenty-five but *looked* fifteen."

"L-l-looked f-fifteen!"

In the cavernous recess of his eyes Brendan's horror and confusion were burgeoning. He twitched anxiously. "F-f-fifteen," he reiterated.

"Fifteen, Brendan. Now you've got it."

With great reluctance, he charged back to the area where he had been holding court and threw himself down on the concrete. He seemed to be undergoing extreme difficulty in reconciling his thoughts as he looked skywards and mumbled to himself. Then he bolted up off the ground and headed for the upper lot. When he turned and found me following him he quickened his pace.

Brendan was now undergoing a great deal of difficulty in deciphering what was real and what was fantasy. His face had assumed a hue of lime-white. His eyes had become gelid and deep set in their cavernous sockets. A look of sheer dread came over him. Once again I suggested to him to ease up on the "malts." He ignored my harsh words and continued to guzzle the liquid madness as though it were the very meaning of his life, the savior of his soul. "Alcoholics have a habit of dying of alcoholism," he reiterated each time that he bent his elbow. He had now turned to gulping down triple shots of straight Jack Daniel's. Each drink was as usual downed in a single draught. Staggering along the boulevards, Brendan developed a habit of stopping short and making grotesque faces at the passers-by. "You really hate me, don't you," was his favorite retort to those who stopped to look.

In spite of the extreme difficulties that he presented when I was left to take him in tow, I still regarded him as the most lovable and entertaining fellow that I had ever known. However, owing to my own dire need of rest and the need to discontinue losing body weight, I was sometimes forced to leave him wandering aimlessly on his own. But most often within the hour of our severance from one another, a familiar knock would come to my hotel room door.

One early morning I opened my door and discovered Brendan standing naked in the hall. He was grimacing and clutching his crotch. His shoulder was tilted almost to the floor.

"What's wrong, Brendan?" I asked, "is your balls getting too big for you to carry?"

"Cud yew get a thrill out of watching a six-year-old boy undressing avick?"

"Only if the six-year-old was you, my sweet."

Brendan's face lit up with delight. He picked up his clothes and hastily departed. An hour later I opened up to a clatter of kicks and thumps and found him with arms outstretched, his head tilting to one side, then in a flash he was doing an imitation of a kamikaze pilot falling to his death aboard some U.S. naval vessel. The ship suddenly exploded, sending bodies and debris flying. The improvised battleship was the floor of my room. The bodies and debris were my room furnishings. Brendan lay dead for a time, then returned to life, a smile as wide as a cow's arse on his face. "Did you like that avick-ho?" he asked getting up from the floor.

"That was fuckin' jayzus marvelous Brendan. A real tour de force."

On another occasion I opened the door of my room and found Brendan spewing great words of endearment while undressing himself. Minutes later we were heading north on Wilcox Avenue, our two heads bent in silence. I had once again refused to sodomize him. "We'll stop in here and pick up a present for the other aul cow," he said as I followed him into a camera mart. "Give us a camera and a few rolls of film," he barked at the bespectacled salesman.

The salesman went into explicit detail to describe the names and the prices of dozens of different models of German and Japanese cameras that he had in stock.

"Listen, mister," Brendan roared into the man's face, "If I wanted a sermon on the mount I would have went to Jerusalem. Save the fuckin' sermons for the savages and give us a fuckin' camera before I take my business elsewhere." The man took down an uncomplicated-to-operate camera and began to explain to Brendan how to insert the film.

"Do yew think yur talkin' to a fuckin' bogman who cums from the wilds of Donegal?" Brendan snapped. "Just wrap up the fuckin' thing and let me worry about insertin' the bollixin' film." Brendan threw a roll of money on the counter, picked up the camera and headed for the Montecito.

"Here, I brought yew a present," he said to Beatrice, handing her the camera as we walked into the apartment. She beamed with delight.

"Oh just what I wanted, now we can have our picture taken."

"Naturally isn't that what cameras are usually meant for. I'd expect even *yew* to understand that."

"It's lovely, Brendan," she said excitedly. "Are there any instructions?"

"Instructions!!" Brendan barked, "d-didn't I get yew the simplest fuckin' camera in the cuntin' store, yew press a button! What more is there to know. How stupid can yew get? Do yew want me to take it back?"

"That's O.K., Peter will show me how to operate it," she said.

"I'm sorry, Bea," I interjected, "the man gave the instructions to Bren."

Brendan was now the star of oodles of curbstone playlets.

It is universally well known that Irish persons of the older generation have a habit of twisting and distorting their syntax, nouns and vowels, often rendering the names of people, places and objects difficult to understand. The city of Los Angeles is by no means the most likely of places to meet one such personage. However, one early morning as I was in the process of dragging Brendan north on Hollywood Boulevard, we came upon an old lady who was fleet-footing her way west. Instantly she recognized Brendan. She stopped short, froze, genuflected and blessed herself.

"Oh Mr. Beehang," she sputtered, "what a lovely surprise, and shur wasn't it just the other day that I got all through readin' yur luvly Catholic book. Now sir," she went on in her benevolent voice while clutching her breast, "I don't like to be asking you sir, because I know that writers are like doctors, lawyers, ships' captains and the likes, they don't like aul ones to be askin' them niggling questions and so early in the mornin', but since we're all here together, I don't mind askin' you, would you ever be writin' a sequin to *Boston Boy* Mr. Beehang?!"

The tips of Brendan's hair were oscillating to and fro on the boulevard, his fingertips were down to his toes, his right jacket pocket was adjacent to his trouser cuff. With great effort, he straightened up to answer the lady's question, while mimicking her every word and nuance.

"W-well ma'am, since I haven't read the luvly Catholic book of yur prayers, I am not in a position to answer yew, b-but yew c-can jot down yur name and phone n-number and give it to P-Peter there, and if I do get around to reading the book and writin' the sequin I'll be sure to let yew be the first to know. Now I thank yew m-ma'am for yur kind concern and w-with that I'll bid yew good day."

Charging in and out of supermarkets eating up everything in sight became another of his favorite sports. One night after the two of us had spent over an hour in a famous supermarket gorging everything in sight, the manager of the store hurried over and told us to leave "quickly and quietly."

Brendan puckered his lips, opened his shirt to the waist, crossed his legs daintily, and in a feminine sexy voice said, "If my name was Kim Mansfield or Marlyn Mowhawk yew wouldn't be so fuckin' quick to tell me to cunt off, would yew?"

Driving around and lunching at seafront restaurants became another delight. Southern California's shores are known to be infested with practically every known predator of the sea. The prospects of being mutilated or devoured stimulated him. "Would yew be a nice girl," he said to a waitress in a seafront restaurant, "and get me yur luvly manager." When the gentleman arrived, Brendan asked, "Listen avick, but

I was just wonderin' if yew permitted diving from yur balcony? I'd like to go for a dip."

"Sir, not only do we not permit diving," the host shrugged, "we don't recommend swimming. Around here the sharks have a habit of hiding in the weeds!"

Brendan thanked the man, then waited until he departed, then *he* disappeared. A few minutes later, I found a pile of familiar clothing rolled up in a ball and sitting in a corner of an outside balcony. Some fifteen minutes later, Brendan reappeared, walking up the beach, his penis erect.

Late one night Beatrice phoned and begged me to go down to the boulevard and take Brendan home. "*You* know where to find him," she said. I found him in the Comet. From all appearances, I deduced that an anonymous ominous call had been made to Beatrice.

Brendan held tight to the end of the bar with both hands. He refused to budge. To afford himself an extra margin, he undid his belt buckle and let go his pants. To add to my upheaval, the management was threatening to phone the cops. Brendan was insisting that I answer a very important question. He wanted to know if I had ever fornicated with a five-year-old boy.

"Yes, yes, of course I fucked five-year-old boys in boxing clubs, lots of them, didn't I tell you before that that is what boxing clubs are for."

"Good man," he stuttered, pulling up his pants and following me to the car without further ado. Beatrice stood waiting outside. "We'll go for a ride," Brendan insisted.

"A short one," I said crisply.

Beatrice placated him with sympathetic talk. "Don't worry now, pet, everything is going to be all right as soon as we get home. You'll have your supper and a good sleep."

"I don't want any supper, I don't want any sleep," he barked as he attempted to leap from the car. I jammed the brakes. My engine sputtered and conked out, right in the middle of Hollywood and Vine. To preserve my battery I doused my lights. An argument ensued.

"Listen mister, I don't know what class of cuntin' rags that yew've been reading but I d'don't only make h-headlines in H-Hollywood, b-but all over the c-cuntin' world, ask any postman," he shouted into my face.

"He's right Peter, Brendan's right," Beatrice shouted. "Brendan gets letters from Australia, Africa, France, Germany . . ."

My car refused to budge. I began to roar at the top of my lungs into the mouths of the Behans. "*Oist lomsa, anois* [Listen to *me* now]! Now I have something to tell to the two of you, you pair of fuckin' overgrown children who have obviously no respect for maturity and feelings of others." Then to Brendan, "Listen mister, insofar as *your* big fuckin' fame and publicity is concerned, I don't give a diddly fuckin' squash about it. My car is stuck. I have to get it goin' again. That, and only that, is my immediate concern. If you don't like it, you can go and fuck yourself and get out, O.K."

The day was suddenly saved. A light panel truck carrying a gaggle of bottle-waving boisterous Mexicans chanced along going north on Vine and smashed into the rear of my car. The blast was literally the boost that I needed. Quickly I turned over the engine and got the car started. We drove to the Montecito and dropped Beatrice off. The always nocturnal Brendan insisted on going for an early A.M. stroll.

Hollywood Boulevard is commonly known as the "Walk of Fame."

Brendan was a master tactician at developing instant little escape valves when he felt pensive and very ill at ease.

Dashes up and down the Walk of Fame spitting, then mashing his spit onto the face of the pink and charcoal terrazzo stars that bore the names of the illustrious was one such outlet. "Go 'way yew dirty little swine, yew, the only reason why yew got yur name inscribed in the gutter in the first place is because yur mother taught yew how to spread yur legs when yew were bending down to pick up the soap," he roared at a star.

"Here avick, cunt over here and feast yur eyes on this load of shite, wha," he hollered when scrutinizing another star. "Yew can bet yur sweet ballox that this big-titted, buck-tooted whore has a cunt-shaped pool in her backyard."

Posters bearing blown-up photos or portraits of John Wayne and Walter Winchell also drew his most savage invectives and blasts from tin cans, stones and whatever other debris that he could find.

"Gwan, gwan, yew fascist, war-mongerin' cunt yew."

I joined him in the reverie and vented my wrath by gathering empty cans, stones and other debris and hurling them at the posters. At that point in my life I had not yet heard of Winchell and was never a great fan of Wayne's.

I said good night to Brendan and went home to catch up on some much needed sleep.

An hour later I received a desperate call.

"Can you get here at once, Peter, it's very urgent. Brendan is doing some writing. I'm delighted, b-but now I don't know! There's a big fella here who says he's John Dillinger. He's bothering Brendan, he won't let him work; he keeps looking over his shoulder and telling him to change this and change that, for God's sake come right away."

I arrived and instantly recognized the tall heavy-set former movie star. He was Lawrence Tierney, the actor who portrayed John Dillinger, the famous American gangster of the nineteen thirties. Around Hollywood, scuttlebutt had it that Tierney was still playing the role in public. Tierney subsequently became infamous as a drinker and a brawler, the type of individual that Brendan loathed.

"Excuse me sir," I said to the actor, "I'm Peter Arthurs. I'm Brendan's bodyguard. [Brendan threw me a wicked little glance.] I'd appreciate it if you would leave *quietly*. There's important work going on here and we don't want intruders."

"No kiddin'," the big man said in a mock Irish brogue as he circled the room like a nocturnal cat preparing to leap.

"Close the lid on the typewriter," I said to Brendan who was standing motionless and petrified. Brendan locked the machine. The actor continued to circle in a clockwise motion. Just as I was about to let go a right-handed punch his look softened.

"Hey, what is it with you two. I just came up to see how things are going and to wish you good luck on your new play. I'm an actor, I'm Lawrence Tierney." He extended his hand. I shook it. Brendan ignored the hand.

"Now that you've wished us well and yew see how it is goin', I'll ask yew to kindly fuck off," Brendan said crisply. Tierney departed.

Brendan opened up the machine and went back to his writing.

A few hours later, Tierney phoned in to offer his apologies and to invite us to a party in his fiancée's home. Brendan accepted.

"This is Brendan Behan and this is Peter Arthurs, they're two homosexuals," Tierney said to his lady friend as she opened the door of the house.

"What did he mean by that?" Brendan asked me, a look of horror creeping into his red face.

"It's O.K., Brendan," I said placatingly. "It's like he said, he's an actor—it's his only talent." Tierney shot me a menacing look.

The five of us sat down to dinner. Later I played with their dog. The dog became excited and horny. "Go way you fuckin' mangy little faggot you," I shouted into the dog's mouth while pushing it away from my leg. Another look of horror crept into Brendan's face.

"What in the name of God are you calling the poor animal a name like that for?" Brendan demanded.

"Look!" I said pointing to the dog's hard penis.

We departed and drove home in silence.

I wanted to ask him why he was so grossly upset, but to ask Brendan Behan a civil question and expect a civil answer under such circumstances was tantamount to throwing a handful of rocks into a duck pond and expecting not a single quack.

Since Brendan insisted on spending many of his nights in my room, and since I had proven myself a genuine friend who adhered to his every whim, one late night I insisted upon talking about myself, my life and my long-range plans. Brendan grunted, groaned, twitched and snored. His pattern of snores was uneven. Unquestionably he was awake. A ploy to get him to sit up and listen was needed. I thought of my youth when I was a boy growing up in the Christian Brothers schools. I thought of the lean, mean days when I gladly permitted some of those same degenerates to molest me and all for the purpose of not having to absorb pain-wreaking, hand-swelling slaps from their canes for committing the crime of coming late to school after attending to one or more of my family-supporting chores.

For the next half hour I sat talking to the snoring figure, my eyes riveted to his every twitch and tremor, my ears recording his every grunt and groan. Obviously he had no intentions of engaging me in conversation.

I continued to talk in a low monotone, elevating my tone only when going into sketches of how the Christian Brother's hot bated breath made my penis stand erect and how his lips slurped and swallowed my juice of life. In a flash Brendan's eyes were open and as big as saucers. "D-do yew tell me that avick? Is that a fact now? wha!" I continued my story.

Then I checked my watch, made a face and said, "Oh fuck it, Brendan, I almost bollixed it up. I have to go, I have to meet a lady named Pennie Rua for lunch. See you later." I charged out the door and down the hall. Brendan, never a man to give up on a good story, was in hot pursuit.

"W-what happened then avick, what . . . happened, w-w-what?"

"What happened when, B.? To who?" My voice trailed off just as the elevator door was closing in his blue-tinted face. The naked, stricken little man cursed and twitched, his ample stomach heaved.

VII

A guru, a pariah, a genius, a singular man of the theater, a man of raves, a man of wisdom whose writings took precedence, a spiritual and temporal powerhouse, alas; the ideal paradigm of the new avant-garde and the antibourgeoisie school of writers that was burgeoning in America; this was how the majority of the younger cadres of interviewers who flocked to the Montecito looked upon Brendan. Many of these curious youngsters were not even remotely aware of the name of one of his works.

With open arms he welcomed them. He felt ill at ease with the superintellectual left-wingers who bombarded him with questions on the topics of the need for abortion, on recession, hunger, nuclear warfare and police brutality. The younger stalwarts looked upon him as a burgeoning symbol of socialistic simplicity and unpretentiousness, a modern-day messiah and the final word on the subjects of hypocrisy, injustice to the poor and the disenfranchised, immoral attitudes and other aspects of the surrounding bleakness and the entire catalogue of human woe.

When the emotional need to do another reenactment of the Glasnevin shooting incident struck him, he summoned his youthful cadres to his apartment—his theater in the oblong—where he quickly disrobed and cleared the living room of furnishings. Here he had the refuge of his strategic command post: the bathroom, a place to run to when the questions became too intense and difficult to deal with. The cryptic, tough-talking, suspender-snapping, piratically swaggering Brendan took to the floor with great pomp and pugnacity. They listened to his speeches. They laughed deferentially at his jokes and puns. In the presence of the young and the naive, he displayed a unique way of two-blocking and making his eyeballs recede as an extra exercise to convey the illusion that at heart he was an exceptionally sensitive soul. His expressions ran the gamut, ranging from the most amiable to the most savage and alienating. His preferred pose and posture was that of the quiet man who was holding in tight rein his true emotions, but somewhere deep within the dark folds of his schizophrenia lay an explosive, potentially dangerous homicidal animal in some ambuscade, ready and capable of being dangerously triggered, once the key figure in some far-off real-life drama was tinkered with.

"Great, man. Thanks, Mr. Behan. Brilliant. Great interview."

These were the most common of accolades given him.

His reciprocations were to mimic their remarks: "Great man, Mr. Behawn." [Here he yawned.] "Come again Mr. Beekman, coming is good for you Mr. Beeswax, it's good for your nerves, Mr. Beebang. It's the only toddy for the body Mr. Beebunk. Coming endears the soul and fortifies the mind Mr. Beehive. Shur the only reason why any of yiz is here in the first place is because I happen to be somebody with a name. If I was selling fish and chips in the lobby, would yew be here wha!" Brendan exuded an arrogance born of a very private and unique rightness, yet the youngsters generally saw through him and laughed hysterically.

The evolution of life, the passions and the full capabilities of the human mind, modern civilization, Irish guerrilla warfare and his own holistic vision of the physical world held no real, deep interest for him. Neither did he care about the signal tragedies or disasters of the times. Brendan was obsessed with his own intrigue, treachery and trickery, childhood fantasies as opposed to literal creations. He was a circum-navigating consummate artist, constantly yammering and refusing to answer the questions put to him.

But Brendan's improvisations and truth-stretching theatrics were genuinely entertaining and gladdening of the heart.

Each time that he retold the stories of his shooting and bombing missions, like the one to blow up the *King George V,* he emerged an even greater public hero. The streets of Dublin were littered with bodies.

(In 1941, the *King George V* went on to further fame by sinking the mighty *Bismarck,* the pride of Hitler's navy. Brendan never made mention of this historical fact.)

He claimed to have shot at two police officers from a distance of fourteen yards. When asked, how he, a masterful tactician in the arts of guerrilla warfare missed at such a short distance and why he was not sentenced to *life* or to *death* for these near *murders,* Brendan went into a paroxysm of coughs, excused himself, dashed into the bathroom and left the door ajar while he gurgitated, listened and peered. Minutes later he reemerged and continued his gabfest.

"Did I ever tell yew the yarn about the little old American lady who went into a Dublin library and asked to see a book on Irish guerrillas. 'Well,' says yur woman behind the stick, 'gorillas in Ireland . . . divil a one I ever saw, shur the climate here is not at all suitable for those sort of beasts.' "

In Dublin in the middle fifties the Catacombs was a place of late-night meeting for the younger intellectuals, the avant-garde artists and hangers-on. A segment of Dublin's homosexuals and lesbians also hung out at the decaying, mortar-swelling club, which came to life during the wee hours of the mornings. Brendan became a vital part of its adrenalin and history. "A marvelous aul kip," he said, while toasting his glass. "Yew could go there at any hour of the night and find men havin' women, men havin' men, and women havin' women. Shur amn't I writin' a book about it at the present," he told his cadre. "I'm in the process of immortalizing the place. Used to go there a lot to drink with me buddy J. P. Donleavy the aul *ginger man* himself. Did you know that one day I decided to invite mesself along to his house in Bray, to have a feed of rashers and eggs and a cup o' tea. A bit later J. P. went out for a walk. When he returned he was surprised to find that I had altered several pages of his draft on *The Ginger Man*. He was livid, I might tell yew. B-but I'll also tell yew this much, he soon changed his tune once the book was published, and might he well, it's one of the biggest best sellers on the market! *Up from the Catacombs* is what I'm calling me book!" he explained jubilantly.

When he had had enough or felt that the interviewers were becoming too clever, his poetic ways of ridding himself of them were opulently put to the test. "Now if yew'll excuse me, b-but I do have work to do, for although they say that work is death without the dignity of dying, I must return to it. If I don't, I'll never be able to get together the price of me grog and me grub. Providence protect us from geniuses and God be with the working class amongst us."

The execution of Caryl Chesman, an execution that was still fresh in the memory of most Californians was another topic on which he held forth. He vociferously attacked the American jurisprudence system. During the long hard battle by lawyers and organizations to save Chesman, Brendan's anticapital punishment sentiments came to world attention. So did his anticapital punishment play *The Quare Fellow*. His remarks coincided heavily with the views offered by those who worked hard to save Chesman. Brendan savagely denigrated the policies of the state of California, particularly Governor Pat Brown and the judge who presided over the case. "Shur when I was in San Francisco didn't I meet the priest who attended him just before the whores dropped the murderin' pellets."

Brendan was a walking encyclopedia of Judaica. With ease he could explain and clearly distinguish between the Talmud, the Midrash, Mishanal, and the Cemara, an accomplishment that many of his Jewish friends and associates could not fully lay claim to. He was also well versed on Jewish heritage, festivals, feasts, customs, traditions, culture, folklore, rituals and beliefs, Jewish Nobel prize winners and other great world-renowned personalities all the way from Genesis to Harry Houdini. Brendan was always jolly and jubilant when in the company of his Semitic friends. He felt that he was being understood, appreciated and totally accepted. He regarded the Jewish people as the intellectuals of the universe.

Around the Hollywood Jewish community, Brendan displayed a habit of stopping short in the middle of his gushes. "Me wife here was born in Ireland but her mother's an Austrian Jewess who was forced to flee her country when the little corporal started to run amok. She finally wound up in the land of the sow and the cow where she married and had Beatrice."

One day I said to Beatrice, "Beatrice I don't understand. You go to mass all the time but you're a Jewess."

She burst out laughing and explained to me that her mother was born in Silesia of a German father and a Polish mother. Her own father was born in northwest India and met her mother in Germany when he was there on a scholarship. Her mother was a domestic economy student and a Lutheran who converted to Catholicism.

Another of Brendan's cherished little acts was to carefully select a hot acquaintance, call him on the phone, make an appointment to meet at such and such a corner and at such and such a time. (To keep in Brendan's good graces one had to be always on time.) Brendan himself showed up minutes ahead of schedule. For the next several minutes the vaudevillian man carried on an uninhibited flow on a variety of topics. Carrying on such conversations with the width of the famous boulevard between him and his interlocutors was a stand-out. Bits and pieces of dark secrets and information that he had recently garnished from a media man were quickly elaborated upon. The names of moguls and movie stars were loudly mentioned.

In spite of his extreme imbibing, he remained a periodic theatergoer, reader and pursuer who was always on the lookout for fresh material to be inserted into his writings and his monologues.

One night the author of *A Whisper in God's Ear,* took us to a performance of his hit play. "The play will definitely never make it to Broadway," Brendan reassured his contemporary in a raucous roar.

"Why do *you* only write about yourself?" the other author inquired with a hint of anger.

"Write about mesself!" Brendan snapped, "I write about any cunt that I find interesting enough to write about. One of these days I might even write about yew, but I doubt it!"

During intermission, Brendan repaired to the middle of the street.

An elderly lady recognized him and charged over to him with pencil and playbill in hand.

Brendan took hold of her book and pencil and burst into one of his frothy denigrations of his colleagues with particular emphasis on the Irish. "What! Paul Vincent Carroll, indeed, the man is nothing more than a pseudointellectual, an imitator of O'Casey. James Joyce! A phenomenon. A thirteen-pound turkey who tried to lay an eighteen-pound egg. Hemingway, a typical Madison Avenue mucker, a conjurer of trivia and small talk. He should've stuck to ambulance drivin'. Truman Capote? Never heard of him, what does he do?" he snapped charging back into the theater.

At the conclusion of the play, the author asked Brendan why he made the negative analysis of this work.

"Listen, mister," Brendan roared as he stormed through the lobby, "do yew think that I have nothing better to be doing with me valuable time but to be goin' about editing other people's tripe for them. It's in the madhouse I'd be, if I listened to *my* critics." Then turning to me, "Cum on avick, let's cunt off home before this place gives me a case of the galloping gout."

Restaurateurs, bell captains, waitresses and waiters elbowed one another to take Brendan's orders. He always ordered the largest steaks on the menu. As all know, Hollywood is a fantasy dream world to which tens of thousands of beautiful young men and women flock to be immortalized on film. To keep body and soul together until that all-important phone call comes through, those in waiting work part-time as car hops, waitresses and typists. Some of them sell their bodies or make pornographic films. They also have a reputation for making brazen passes at the famous who sup at their places of employment.

Where their passes at Brendan were concerned, their beauty and their boldness were all for naught. Brendan Behan had no prurient interest in the fair sex. "Shur the only reason why the whores even look at me is because I happen to be Brendan Behan. Bloody lot of little bitches," he said, pushing a waitress away who had rubbed her thigh against his elbow in a well-known Beverly Hills eatery.

Drunk, Brendan displayed an enormous hostility toward those who looked sexually adjusted. "Fuckin' lot of sluts, they'd peddle their cunts to an ape for a bit of actin'," he snorted.

He never entered a crowded bar, restaurant or theater lobby with another person, least of all I, who topped him by six inches. In his two neat feet he stood a shade under five foot three. He carefully selected his time to make his entrances. All entrances were presented as debuts. His places of preference to eat were Ollie Hammond's, Musso and Frank's, the Brown Derby, the Cock and Bull, Slade's and many other bourgeois hangouts in Beverly Hills and on the "restaurant row" called La Cienega.

At the entrance to these swank eateries the sight of Brendan backed up by Beatrice and me as he stood on the tips of his toes, his thumbs twiddling behind his back, his eyes scrutinizing the emblazoned menus on display in the windows, was commonplace. But Brendan's gaze was misleading. Deviltry was in his soul. Brouhahas in posh eateries were another specialty. His pencil-thin eyes were in actuality peering around the rim of the menu for purposes of getting a more in-depth view of who was inside prior to making his entrance.

Brendan could gobble up to twelve to fourteen steaks per day. Beatrice and I once calculated that Brendan had already eaten up a whole herd of steer. No sooner would Brendan have eaten up his dinner, he would attack the contents of Beatrice's plate, then mine. Another three orders of steaks and chops would be ordered. I learned to eat fast.

In these eateries he foraged deep into his celebrity and put himself across as an implacable enemy of cant and hypocrisy. He derived special pleasure out of hopping from table to table and signing food-stained napkins for old ladies.

"Take that now and may yew be the grandmother of a bishop," he would say, then turning to me, "Shur I suppose they'll sell it or put it in a frame wha!"

"They'll hang it in their bathroom Brendan," I said, "where else?"

Those who made a major fuss of him were doubly rewarded by having their dinner checks picked up and paid for.

One morning I received a very frantic call from Beatrice. "For G-God's sake Peter, whatever you're doin', stop it and rush over as fast as you can. How quick can you get here?! Is your car still runnin'?! Can you be here right away?! Hurry like a good boy!! For God's sake hurry."

I looked at the clock. The time was one forty-five A.M. I had not had more than a full hour's sleep since I left the apartment.

"Oh thank G-God you're here," Beatrice said opening the door.

"Where's the quare fella, Beatrice?"

"Oh no, no, no, P-Peter for God's sake be careful, don't let him hear you, you know how he hates that word," she lamented.

I made my way down the hall. The apartment was in chaos. Brendan was nowhere to be seen. Beatrice remained behind me. "Where is he, Beatrice?" I asked. I received no answer. On the floor of the kitchen, the living room and along the hall, several pieces of meat were in evidence. Suddenly, from the tiny dressing room adjacent to the bathroom, Brendan appeared. He was naked. His cock was erect. His face was aflutter with madness. He dripped with sweat. His black shiny hair hung down over his forehead.

At first I thought he had just returned from a dip. But the wages of his heavy drinking and his plunge into decrepitude were evident. Brendan's severe diabetic condition played havoc with his serious drinking. His sugar was unbalanced. His paranoia exacerbated. The atmosphere was manic, threatening and absurd. Suddenly he began one of his clockwise charges around the room.

"The window, the window, Peter," Beatrice cried, as Brendan approached the rear wall.

I ran to the window and spread my arms. Each time that Brendan got set to pass Beatrice, she ran behind me for safety. Brendan, I deduced, was off on another of his alcohol-induced short-circuiting, pleasure-pain-extracting tantrums, his prized indoor recreational activity. He finally threw himself down into his favorite chair, selected a rag from his pile and read and snickered. A sequence of familiar little noises was audible. When I felt safely reassured that he was set for a time I went to the bathroom and doused my neck with cold water, then unzipped my pants and sat on the commode. A flurry of screams and shrieks went out.

"P-Peter, P-Peter, quick, quick!!"

I darted into the living room and found Brendan pummeling Beatrice. I pulled him off of her.

Brendan's hands were the hands of a well-nourished eight-year-old boy. In a fight they were totally ineffectual. They were incapable of battering the stuffings out of a jelly donut.

An amused little look appeared on his porcine face.

"How many more times will I have to tell you to leave her alone?" I said, glaring down into his glistening eyes.

I returned to the bathroom to finish the second half of my call to nature. Another medley of shrieks went out.

This time I pulled him off of her and sent him pirouetting into his chair. "This is the last time I'll warn you," I said returning to the bathroom. Another medley of bleeps, blurps, and giggles went out just as I was about to sit down.

I ran into the kitchen, pushed Brendan down and took inventory of Beatrice's arms and found that there were no contusions in evidence. Then bending down to pick up the pieces of meat and liver, a profusion of questions entered my brain. Was I being had? If so, by whom? By how many?

I rinsed the meats under the spigot and placed them on a plate.

Drunk, Brendan's eating habits had undergone a major diversification. No sooner would Beatrice have placed the fried steak in front of him than Brendan picked it up, pushed it into his mouth and all the way down his throat. His eyes bulged and shone. His face and neck took on a vast discoloration and blew up to gigantic proportions.

On a number of frightening occasions I rushed to his side to extricate the steak, but Beatrice with a flurry of hand gesticulations waved me away. With all of the meat now hidden from view and asphyxiation imminent, Brendan reached up and extricated it, placed it on the plate and nodded to Beatrice who in turn cut it into eight pieces.

Brendan's eyes went back into their sockets, his natural coloring returned. He ate in silence without looking at either of us.

Having carefully observed the various pieces of steak as I placed them together on a plate, it dawned on me that the steak was originally one of unusual enormity. No salivation or teeth marks were in evidence. Beatrice out of fear of him choking to death committed a cardinal sin. She had cut the steak in two. Brendan, seeing the fresh cut in the steak flew into a rage. Beatrice, frightened to death, then phoned me.

Beatrice discarded the cut steak and put another one on the stove. We sat down to eat. I felt like a pivotal character in a convoluted plot.

"I must go home and get some sleep!" I said to the Behans as I finished my meal.

"Oh, have another cup of tea, there's plenty," Beatrice said beseechingly, while ladling out the steaming liquid.

To get a few minutes' sleep I sat down on the commode and dozed off. But in a flash, like a thirsty dog on a hot afternoon, Brendan was in the bathroom pursuing his old line of question. "D-d-did yew ever fuck a four-year-old b-boy in a b-boxing club?"

I pushed him out of the bathroom and closed the door in his face. He pounded on the door. "H-how old was the youngest b-boy that yew ever fucked in a b-boxing club avick . . . tell me, tell me, tell me!!" he moaned.

I opened the door and pushed him away, but again he returned.

Each time that he returned, he appeared more intoxicated than the time before.

"What the hell do you want?" I yelled at him.

He whispered and moved closer as though there was something special that he wished to convey to me. I turned my head, bent down, and let out a roar. Brendan sank his teeth into my neck, just below the right ear. Blood seeped from the bite mark.

"Y-yur a strange b-boy P-Peter Arthurs, a peculiar l-lad, a q-quare fella," he shouted as he stood poised with feet spead as though challenging me to chase him into the bedroom.

"Fuck off," I said calmly and went back to my commode, and shut the door.

From the slit in the door I watched him as he went into another of his tantrums.

Brendan was like a rare cootie, lying down, jumping up, going into a tizzy, careening and falling. His short stubby arms and bloated legs flailed and twitched like the tentacles of a beached baby octopus. His head spun and whinnied. His bizarre hornet of moods and proclivities was fascinating to watch.

"Will you come and sit by the window," Beatrice said to me, forlornly.

As Brendan lay writhing, mumbling and twitching, Beatrice talked about *Cork* and Joan Littlewood. She lived in fear that the very talented English director would go off on some big excursion before Brendan would finish the play. The play would then have to be handed over to some other director who was less knowledgeable of Brendan's fantasies and dreams.

In public, Brendan had spoken violently of Joan. "People are always cummin' up to me and saying, 'Brendan, isn't it true that without Joan Littlewood you would not be who and what you are?' To a certain extent this is a fair statement, but then again if it wasn't for me, Joan Littlewood and the West End wouldn't be what they are. Eaten bread, like drunken wine is soon forgotten. Fuck Joan Littlewood," he barked with great hostility.

However, sitting there by the window listening to Beatrice while away the night, it became quite obvious to me that he very much depended on the great lady for the success of *Cork*.

Privately he very much believed in the "auteur theory," particularly where he and Littlewood were concerned. In better moods he had said, "The difference between me and Dylan Thomas is that he wrote *Under Milkwood*, I wrote under Littlewood."

Littlewood, according to Beatrice, had a unique talent for getting the most out of her actors and for setting the entire cast into the precise consistency of mood and acting style essential to Brendan's writings. *She* and *she* alone could do the job. Brendan raised his head from the floor.

"If it's all one and the same with yiz, I have even heard rumors to the effect that she writes me plays. I don't give a shite who writes the fuckin' things, just as long as I get the lolly. In New York, when I had the last cuntin' thing on the stage that she purportedly wrote, I received three thousand dollars per week. Not bad for an editor, huh, Peter? She can write all me fuckin' plays for that kind of lolly if she wants."

Brendan's play material was autobiographical, drawn from his dreams and manifestations, then judiciously placed in the hands of a lady who was acute enough to draw from his zesty exuberance, shape it, package it, and put it on the boards. In so doing she skillfully deleted his wickedness, his dryness and his often humorless didacticism and enervation. I deduced that Joan had all the capabilities of making literature out of trivia and madness if necessary.

"Shur I suppose the lobby is full of mongoloids waiting for me autograph, and me picture," Brendan suddenly moaned raising his head again.

"You'll manage, Brendan, you'll manage," I said pushing his head down and patting him on the shoulder.

At this point in time Beatrice had made it a habit of begging me to be more selective with my words. Being acutely aware of his supersensitive acoustic powers, Beatrice beckoned me to join her in a chorus of compliments. "No doubt Brendan has a little extra fat on his stomach there Peter, but if you look at his arms and shoulders you will see that he is still in good physical condition. Don't you agree that he could still give the best of them a good thumpin' if he had to," she said nodding her head.

"Oh yes, to be sure, B., I'd hate to be the one who had to wind up on the wrong end of one of his punches! Brendan can still put them away when he needs to. *Borstal Boy* is such a great book, I sure wish that *I* could write a lovely book like that," I concluded.

Brendan moved, smiled, chuckled and prattled. "Yew will dear boy, yew will."

I lay down on the floor beside the window and slept the sleep of the dead. Beatrice slept on her chair.

Brendan was now primarily reduced to a state of almost immobile wretchedness, lying supine on the floor of either hotel, grunting, groaning and making profane sighs and anguished moans about "my sufferings in life." Seldom did he make any attempt to be cooperative or deferential. His antithetical sexual roles were causing him severe mental stress.

Beatrice and I were also down to our bare essentials, emotionally as well as physically. I was breaking out in hot then cold pneumonialike sweats. The fear of a relapse or an infection to my eyes or nose frightened the titters out of me. I became an insomniac, but made the irrevocable decision to let Brendan founder if he would not get his act together. For me, the countdown was on.

On Wednesday June 7, I received a desperate call from Brendan.

"Can yew get here at once avick?' " he asked gruffly.

"Be right over, Brendan," I said and sped to his hotel.

Brendan was dressing to kill but obviously out of his gourd, zipping from one room to the other, pushing his wife against walls and instructing her to "fetch me me socks, root me out a suit, me blue silk one and a clean shirt and tie." His sudden bright-eyed cognitive, sapient transition greatly surprised me. He was a man of enormous resilience.

"Where are we off to today?" I asked.

"I have to go and see some fuck-faced cunt," he barked.

"Which fuck-faced cunt are we meeting?" I asked Beatrice.

"Ask Brendan," she said in her usual cautious manner.

"I already did, Beatrice, see you later," I said and moved towards the door.

"W-where d-do y-yew think yew-re goin'?" Brendan snapped, putting on his cufflinks and tiepin.

"To see a cunt-faced fuck," I said and hastily departed.

Later that evening I found a message in my hotel pigeonhole. John the hotel clerk informed me that Brendan had been trying desperately to reach me. "He's been calling all evening, sounds like something big is in the wind," he concluded. I phoned immediately.

"Peter, me aul scholeara, is it yurself?" Brendan said bubbling with excitement. "Wasn't Beatrice and mesself just talking about yew and saying why isn't the boy here havin' his supper with us? Listen me aul son, b-but I have a great idea," he went on with great jollity, "why don't the three of us jump in yur jalopy and cunt off down to Mexico for a few days, the bit of outing will do us a world of good wha!"

I asked him which day he had designated for us to make the trip. "Tomorrow," he barked with great aplomb.

I explained with great detail that that was "quite impossible and out of the question," since Pennie Rua had arranged a big house dinner party in my honor.

"Fuck the party," Brendan sharply responded, "there'll be plenty of parties for all of us when we get back here," he bellowed. I hung up. Then I phoned Pennie and explained my dilemma.

"Listen, Peter Arthurs," Pennie said in her commanding voice, "don't you realize that you are a very lucky boy, you are traveling in the company of a very famous and much sought-after man. If Behan wants you to drive him to Mexico, you drive him to Mexico, don't worry about my party. There'll be plenty of parties in the future, be careful with the Mexican water; don't get diarrhea, luv and kisses, call when you get back, bye."

I phoned Brendan and informed him I could leave in the morning. I was then invited for dinner.

When I arrived at the apartment I discovered a plethora of newspapers carrying the news of Brendan's court appearance earlier in the day. Brendan's face was aglow with the delight of an undertaker's who had suddenly found himself with a deluge of bodies after a drought.

Great words of contrition and endearment abounded.

I picked up the papers from beside his feet and began to read.

"Put on the pan and a jug of java, a ponger of your precious poison for the boy," Brendan ordered the excited Beatrice. "Eat up, eat up me aul son, in the days of old when pigs were bold and turkeys chewed tobacco . . ."

Brendan smashed ahead with his poetry while I immersed myself in my reading. Photos of him ostensibly drinking coffee and shaking hands with media people flourished.

At the Los Angeles Courthouse his impeccable attire and manners shocked many. He was the epitome of the Irish continental, gallant and suave gentleman, polite with dignity and grace as he apologized and thanked everyone for being so understanding and putting up with his drunken boisterousness in the renowned pizza parlor the week before. Brendan made front-page and centerfold news: "BEHAN'S SPIRITS STILL UP AS HE PAYS FINE"; "BEHAN FINED: APOLOGIZES FOR BEING A NUISANCE."

Judge Delbert E. Wong fined him two hundred dollars on the battery count. Brendan asked the judge to offer his apologies to "The good people of Los Angeleeze."

Later, outside of the municipal courthouse, he posed for photographers and swore that he harbored no ill feelings towards the law. By the same token he made it crystal clear that he did not make it a practice of praising cops. "No, byjayzus no, I wouldn't exactly refer to them as my class of people. American cops, Russian cops, Chinese cops, or any other kind of cops. They're all the bloody same. A right thieving lot."

Another tabloid showed him accepting a fifty-dollar bill from a reporter called Wally Burke. Brendan explained that in his haste he forget to pocket a sufficient amount of money to cover the charge expenses. The bill was meant to pay for the fifty-dollar charge for being plain drunk. Burke, who worked for the Los Angeles *Herald* and *Examiner*, described Brendan as being one of the most colorful personalities to come to the shores of California in eons. He also described him as being massive of physical stature.

VIII

Bright and early the following morning the three of us piled into my heap of dilapidation and headed for the border.

The merciless sun pounded the hillsides and the hood of my car. Its blinding, battering heat assaulted the windscreen. Village after village shone white and glistened like a mirage in the mica-hot day. The normally two-hour ride took in excess of five hours to negotiate. At Brendan's insistence we stopped at every coffee shop, bar, restaurant and mission along the way. Brendan told and retold of his bombing and shooting escapades. Coming up close to the Mexican border, disaster almost overtook us.

I drove along at a comfortable fifty miles per hour, millions of tiny dust pebbles churning up under my wheels and clashing against my windscreen. Far away in the dust-blanketed sun-dappled distance I spotted a convertible loaded down with a mottlement of bottle- and banner-waving youngsters. The car was coming at an alarming speed and traveling with bulls-eye alignment into my path. My heart pounded. The traffic on the north lane was very heavy. I had nowhere to run. My window wipers refused to function. Dust and dirt caked my windscreen. The other car suddenly disappeared. My palpitation rate eased. Then in a flash the car reappeared. The rapid approach was becoming a reality. A living nightmare. It now dawned upon me what was taking place. The driver of the souped-up jalopy was challenging me to a game of chicken, an old California highway sport. The driver of the car that pulls out of harm's way first is the loser and the chicken.

I decided to jam on the brakes and try to abandon the car but remembering Brendan's cantankerousness when given orders and Beatrice who sat dozing in the rear of the two-door sedan, quickly I shifted my foot from the brake to the gas pedal and pulled to the left. The right front fender of the hotrod nicked my right rear fender. We wound up in a pile of mud on the right bank of the highway. *"Chick-een, covardo, maricon"* the hopped-up youths screamed as the two cars passed one another.

Brendan sat and picked his nose. Beatrice was a portrait of a ghost in blue and white wax, *"Blazes, blazes, blazes,"* she moaned.

Brendan shook like a whore in a confessional. "The s-shower of d-dirty little l-low-life scuts, w-what in jayzus name was that all about?" he grumbled.

"That, dear Brendan," I said, "is what happens when some attention-grabbing silly son of a bitch steps out of line and attempts to gobble up a little extra by forgetting the principles of life and lets a little drunken bravura go to his brain."

"Y-yew don't s-say avick, y-yew don't say," he groaned.

My larynx was still somewhere down in my lungs. "While our lives are still intact, let's heave this mass of junk out of the muck," I suggested encouragingly.

Brendan sat picking as Beatrice and I pulled and pushed and finally got the heap back onto the highway. A few minutes later we were rolling across the border into the dusty town of Tijuana, where we were greeted with a splatter of billboards announcing the inexpensive quickie divorces and life's other sundries that could be had for new low bargain rates.

We checked into the Cesar Hotel on Revolucion Street. Outside on the curbstone a swarm of mustachioed pimps clung like bats to the wrought-iron railings. "Ah señor, queek, queek, I have fur jyou berry berry nice jyung gerl or jyung boy wheech eber jyou like, it's no cost jyou too mouch señor," one of the pimps announced.

Brendan's eyes sparkled. His ears piqued. "We'll get our rags parked, then see what yur man has in his stable," he said beckoning me to pick up our bags and follow him into the lobby. Then quickly he turned to the flesh peddler and assured him that we would be in touch with him shortly. Brendan then turned to me and asked me to join him in the lobby, "in a matter of minutes."

Seconds later I trekked back to the lobby, but Brendan was nowhere in sight. In the wanton heat I caught a faint glimpse of him fleet-footing it down Revolucion Street. Beatrice was going like a gazelle in hot pursuit. I picked up the tempo and caught up to her. She was panting, puffing and on the verge of collapse. "Oh t-thank G-God you're here, Peter, bless you," she said. "Quick, r-remember what the chaps from the UPI said about the jails and the cops down here. Quick, catch him before it's too late, before he gets taken in."

I vividly recalled the warnings of Joe Finnegan, who had pulled me aside and advised me to look out for number one in the likely event that Brendan would find the virgin territory too irresistible. "The cops down there have a strange way of losing keys," he had said with a nudge and a wink. I recalled my own days in jails, in Venezuela, Guatemala, Brazil and Honduras. I quickened my pace and finally caught up to the fast-pacing Brendan. His face reflected a composition of fear, hysteria and determination.

Beatrice closed the gap. "Oh t-thank God you got him in time," she muttered as she stumbled, exhausted against the wall of an adobe building.

The three of us stood for awhile, catching our breath, then we continued on down the main thoroughfare, passed a variety of stores and photo-taking shops, then came upon a pair of eager-eyed boys who held a camera in their grip. Alongside of them stood a weary looking ass supporting a cart. "Berry nice pectures for you señor, four for teen dollar," one of the boys said. Brendan jumped up on the cart and donned a Mexican straw hat bearing the legend, "Zorro." Beatrice followed him onto the cart. I followed Beatrice. Brendan became upset and switched his position to the back of the emaciated ass. The ass flinched and buckled. The boy uprighted the animal. Beatrice and I donned our hats. Our picture was snapped.

A few minutes later Brendan was up to his unction in a brouha ha with the confused boys who were struggling to understand his Irish idiom.

"Listen youse two little scuts," he bellowed into their confused sweaty faces, "do yiz think that yiz are dealin' with some fuckin' culshie savage from the wilds of Wicklow?"

A police officer who was stationed in a wooden police hut some twenty yards away approached and in a surprising unaccented voice, said, "Yes, is there anything that I can do to straighten out your problem, sir?"

The officer's perfect English took Brendan by surprise.

"Well, sir," Brendan started, "I mean to say it's really all one and the same to me how much I pay to have me picture taken, but sir, if there is anything that I can't stand, it's a pair of fuggin' delinquents who are obviously trying to rob me, you see, sir, I originally . . ."

"Oh, I'm sure we can get it all properly resolved without further embarrassment to you," the officer said calmly, a smile on his middle-aged face.

Again Brendan was numbed. He composed himself and went on.

"Yew see, sir, when I was in New York with me play, I always took taxis; now New York cabbies as they are affectionately referred to, have a reputation for—"

"Yes, yes of course Mr. Behan, I am very much aware of the reputation of New York's cabdrivers. Such thievery does not exist in Mexico I can assure you, Brendan. I'm sure it doesn't exist in your wonderful little country either."

Brendan was again taken aback but beamed with delight. He reached into his pocket, extricated a roll of notes, peeled off a fifty and handed it to the officer. "I would be greatly honored if yew would take your charming wife or your mistress," he chuckled, "to dinner and have a bottle of wine on me, sir," he said to the cop, then handed two twenty-dollar bills to the boys plus another ten for the photos. We hastily departed.

In Woolworth's, Beatrice purchased a heavy sweater, which was the equivalent of an Aran Island sweater, in the pattern of the Aztec. Brendan purchased a bright paisley tie and a pair of bright-colored hand-made moccasins. He donned the tie and shoes, stuffed his brogue shoes into Beatrice's handbag and handed me his Donegal tweed tie, "Here avick, yew can wear that two thousand years after my death." He also handed me a fifty-dollar bill. "Don't go puttin' that in the Saint Vincent de Paul box now," he ordered.

"Don't worry, Brendan, I'll keep the tie safe," I said stuffing it into my pocket. "Two hundred years from now I'll wear it in remembrance of you. I'll also keep some of this to light a candle for you," I said, pointing to the bill.

Word that Brendan Behan had landed in Mexico spread like tar on fire. Within a few hours newsmen and photographers from San Diego and other surrounding areas flooded into town and caught up to us in the bar of the Cesar. Tape recorders were activated, flashbulbs blinked. Brendan danced the blackbird, sang a medley of bawdy Dublin ballads, told tall tales, played his harmonica, joked and regaled his beholders with a host of very entertaining impressions that included Mussolini, Churchill, Toulouse-Lautrec, the babushka-clad old woman of Connemara, Hitler and others.

When Brendan had finished his Hitler impression, he stepped to the center, snapped his suspenders against his chest, winked and quipped, "Aye, but there's a thing or two to be said about us aul house painters."

Once again he proved himself a man of rare mimetic recall, a sparkling wit and a brilliant entertainer. His viewers, consisting of an ever larger group of foreign tourists as well as Americans, clapped, "Bravo, Bravo, Brendan Behan." The entrance to the restaurant and the sidewalk was jammed with pushing, shoving Mexicans. With a jubilant wave and a gush of perfect Spanish, he ordered champagne by the magnum.

In another lightning-quick stint he was on his knees and on his back doing another series of impressions of corpses in caskets, every politician in Irish history, mouthing platitudes and oaths by the dozen, then he finished up his one-man circus with taking the piss out of the Abbey Players and denouncing their historically pious attitude towards sex. The viewers rolled on the floor.

His overall performance was worthy of the high accolades and the standing ovations that it received. "Bravo, bravo!"

In a matter of minutes Brendan had become a conjuring, clowning tour de force. A diabolic wit. An apocalyptical madcap. An extravaganza. A bonanza. A hurricane of approvals exulted his every move.

When the fury settled, he inquired from the media people, "Who is Ernie Kovacs?"

He was informed that Kovacs was a cigar-chomping showman whose showmanship had no boundaries. "Nothing in moderation," was his motto. He was a TV personality, zany, witty, bizarre, an oddball. He had rid the media of old preconceived notions of what humor was and wasn't. He combined his own genius with contemporary TV technology. He jumped barriers of convention, time and place. He had a major following that consisted of Hollywood's top connoisseurs of comedy and inventive and creative artists. Most of his sketches were wicked and malicious abuses of the very arena that he worked in. Brendan shuddered and chirped, "I'm looking forward to meeting him next week."

"So am I," I chimed in, in an audible voice.

Then the media bombarded him with a series of personal questions. "Mr. Behan, why do you only write about yourself? Is your new play the same? Is it autobiographical? Is there sex in it? Are you doing a sequel to *Borstal Boy?*

He reciprocated by launching into a series of satirical denunciatory skits on the senility of current American and European politicians and church ecclesiastics. But the boys from the press were dogmatic and pressing. They wanted to know a little more about what it was that engendered his specific type of writing. Beatrice became violently upset. Brendan twitched and fidgeted.

"For God's sake, Peter," she begged, "do try to get them to go away. Brendan has given them enough for one night!"

"The trouble with yew lot is that yew take this fuckin' writin' lark too seriously," Brendan quipped in his characteristic, offbeat manner. "Shur I only write the cuntin' aul things when I'm skint. If it wasn't for that I wouldn't be bothered. Shur didn't I write the other cuntin' aul thing [*The Hostage*] in twelve days. There's Peter there, he'll tell yew, wha!"

"And that's a fact," I said gingerly.

"Next week I have to return to Hollycock, to finish up me new play. Now I'm making a valid point, and that is to say that any cunt who can write, even a postcard in a kip like that, what with phones ringin' and parasites runnin' all over hell, asking yew to do this for them and to do that for them—" We charged out of the eatery and home to the Cesar, leaving the newsmen stunned and disappointed.

Less than half an hour later, the haunted voice of Brendan was on the phone begging me to accompany him on a lonely stroll into the dark night of Tijuana's sexual underworld. Now the truth and the agony beneath the carapace of jollity was again rearing its anguished head.

"P-P-Per, P-Peter, is it yurself avick. Will yew cum to the lobby and we'll go to a nice place that I've been tipped off about." Brendan went on to explain that he had made a deal with one of the pimps to produce a young boy. The rendezvous was to take place in a side-street seedy hotel.

I hesitated awhile, then in a lightning-quick gush I said, "Listen Brendan, this fuckin' quagmire is crawling with low-life louts of gendarmes who have nothing better to do but to patrol the streets, looking for fast-buck suckers the likes of us. Fellas with a few bob in their jeans. Know what I'm saying, Brendan? Whether you're drunk or not, it makes no difference, it's into the cuntin' slam you go. Next morning, before you see the light of day, you're told to appear before another lout of a judge who tells you to fork up a hundred or else!!"

I waited a second or two, then heard his distraught voice, "Listen yew, *will yew for fuck sake cum down cum down cum down cum down cum down. Will yew will yew will yew fuck fuck fuck fuck.*"

I felt sorry for him. His thirst for the companionship of the very young was insatiable. I turned in for the night, but within a few hours the horny little man with the gargantuan appetite was back on the phone.

"*Eist liomsa a cara peadair* [Listen to me my friend, Peter]," he whined, "the other c-cow is out to m-mass, um u-up here in me r-room, cum-up-cum-up-cum-up. I have something g-great to t-tell y-yew, s-something marvelous. It's a-all arranged, me s-son, y-yew'll be d-delighted avick, cum-up-cum-up-cum-up."

"Be right up, B." I went back to sleep.

Ten minutes later the phone rang again. "H-how much longer am I supposed to w-wait for y-yur f-fuckin' jayzus eminence, d-didn't I t-tell y-yew to cumupcumupcumupcumup."

"I'm saying my prayers, Brendan, join you later," I said and listened.

"WILLYEWFORTHELOVEANDHONOROFSWEETMOTH ERO'DILAPIDATEDFUCKINCHRISTCUMUPCUMUPCU MUPBEFOREIGOFUCKINJAYZUSMADINMEHEADAISU RROUNDEDBEAPACKOFSAVAGESALTOGETHERCUMU PCUMUPCUMUPWILLWILLWILLYEWYEW..."

I hung up.

Along about eleven o'clock Beatrice called. "Brendan says that we're to meet in the coffee shop for a light lunch. Come down." We waited for Brendan while we sipped in silence. "Brendan is never on time for his meals," Beatrice moaned.

"Anything the matter, Beatsie?" I said in a gentle voice.

"Oh no, nothing."

She continued to smoke and sip. Then in a surprised moment, she turned and said, "P-Peter do you know if there is much homosexuality in bullfighters?" Her question took me slightly aback. I hesitated awhile, then answered in a matter-of-fact tone.

"I don't know any of them fellows personally, Beatsie, but in my humble but profound opinion, it only stands to reason that since the stuff is rampant in boxers, wrestlers, footballers, union goons, gangsters and dock wallopers . . . well, what I'm saying Beatrice is this—these chaps are as graceful, poetic, elegant and sleek as Macy's models and sometimes twice as dandy. There simply has to be a bit of the stuff in their genes."

My opinion brightened her face.

"Bless you, good boy, you will explain all of that to B.B., won't you."

"I will, I will dear Beatsie, but surely he is well aware of these universally well-known facts, isn't he!?"

"Oh yes, yes, yes o' course but I'm sure he'd like to hear it from you," she said, shifting uneasily.

At one P.M., we were visited by a battery of reporters. At Brendan's instructions we piled into my car and headed for an unknown destination. The conversation that took place between Brendan and two media people, one of whom was a female, was about bulls and bullfighters.

"Have you seen a bullfight before, Mr. Behan?" asked the lady.

"I'm a working class writer, yew can call me Brendan," he chuckled. "In answer to your question, yes, yes, indeed I have, in Ireland."

"In Ireland?" asked the befuddled lady. "But I was not aware that they held bullfights in Ireland . . . ?"

"They don't. Yew see this was a fight between two bulls. They were fighting over the affections of a cow."

A burst of laughter went up. I took driving instructions from the man who was the most geographically informed.

"Which one of the bulls won, Brendan?" the lady enquired with delight.

"Both of them."

Another round of applause went up as the media folk scribbled into their pads.

I turned down a dusty street thronged with barking canines, squawking fowl and wandering pigs and people with melodious voices who were flooding in from every artery of the tepid city. Packs of hawkers and vendors charged the excited crowds, attempting to sell them plastic eyeshades, straw hats, souvenirs, sombreros, faintly chilled Coca-Colas, and stuffed dolls that scarcely resembled sacred matadors and infamous bulls. The massive round bullring lay ahead of my windscreen.

"Are we going to a bullfight, Brendan?" I asked with joy.

"No we're going to purgatory or maybe yew thought we were goin' to make our first holy communion?" he barked.

We took our seats in the barrera directly behind the *burladero,* the section of the ring where the matadors, at the conclusion of each fight, lure the well-beaten bulls, then at the sound of the *aviso* and with well-placed pinions, deliver the final thrusts of the sword. This is the "moment of truth."

Brendan sat on my right. Beatrice sat to my left smoking, fidgeting and trembling.

All around us, in the Plaza de Toros the tension of the day was rising to a crescendo. Tacos and Coca-Colas were gobbled and guzzled in the heat of the noonday sun.

Somewhere above the far reaches of the solidly packed arena a trumpeter rose and sent out the clear, shrill, high call, known as the *pasodoble,* the distinctive piece of music which denotes that the ceremony of the drawing of the bulls is over, the *corrida* [bullfight] is about to begin. The *fiesta brava* was on. With eyes glued to the gates of the arena we watched in anticipation.

A stream of matadors, flanked by their phalanxes of toreadors, picadors, and banderilleros, marched proudly to the center of the ring, their bedazzling suits of lights glistening in the solemn splendor of the perfect day. A raucous burst of applause from the aficionados went up and swept down from the steep banks of the great arena and reverberated through its concrete-and-steel under-structures.

"*Los toros, los toros, los toros, Viva la Mexico,*" they roared as the brave youngsters took their ceremonial bows. The bulk of the matadors moved away with a brisk pace. One fighter remained. The svelte-figured boy took his muleta in hand. To the surprise and the glee of the roaring fans, the daring youngster took up a kneeling position, his back and the outstretch of the cape to the bull pen.

In a ferocious burst of fury, a frisky young black bull was on the sand, then in an explosion of savage rage, its horns bent downward, it plunged headlong into the full spread of the quivering muleta, missing it by mere inches.

"Bravo bravo, los toros, los toros!" The crowd roared in ecstasy.

The streamlined beast, baffled by the inexplicable disappearance of the object of its angst, kicked and snorted into the hot white sand, then regrouped its small senses and made another charge, this time its wide-rimmed horns missing the *fenomeno* by fractions of an inch.

Here now was raw, undeniable courage. Here was the miracle of the muleta and the taut muscle of the brave and the brutal at work.

Multicolored umbrellas were opened and sashayed in the breeze. Hats, scented handkerchiefs and ascots were flung in the air. Shrieking voices filled the arena. However, approximately one hour later Brendan, Beatrice, the men from the media and I looked at each other in despair. Something had gone awry. Beatrice smoked incessantly and shook from head to toe. "You will be a good boy and keep a very close watch on your man for me, won't you," she reiterated, time after time.

"I will, I will, I will!!"

The contests of the day were not up to par. Murmurs of despair were heard. Death hung heavy in the humid air. The courageous but less than impeccable bullfighters were experiencing a tough afternoon in the boiling arena. The stubbornness and the brute power of the animals were taking their toll. Matadors were gored and tossed like wet mops into the shimmering air. Despair was etched in the frustrated faces of the fighters. Sprays of sand went flying into the bleachers when the more determined of the fighters took up a position between the shimmering capes and the walls of the arena. Brendan was suddenly ashen-faced and quiet as a church mouse. A look of fear, the same look of fear that I had witnessed on the day of his arrest, was creeping into his eyes.

"D-did yew ever fuck a bullfighter avick!?" he whispered nervously.

"No, I never fucked a bullfighter, Brendan, but when I was a boy growing up on my grandmother's farm in County Cavan, I used to fuck the bulls."

"F-fucked the b-bulls up the arse, but w-wasn't that a dangerous c-class of a thing for a young chap to be doing," he stuttered, a look of utter perplexity in his face.

"Not when you know what you're up to Brendan. You see I only fucked the bulls in their noses. This way I enjoyed the advantages of having my arsehole licked by their tongues while I was letting them have it in the snot box. In so doing I reaped the ultimate benefits, all without running the risk of getting a horn between me ballox and me juggler."

Brendan's face froze as though he were working his brain to put the incident into its perspective. The men crouched and attempted to pick up our talk.

Suddenly, the reason for Beatrice's extreme nervousness was clear to me.

There and then I made an irrevocable decision: should the bold Brendan muster all of his resources and jump into the arena at an opportune moment, the moment of truth, to stop the matador from delivering his golden thrust, or perhaps to commit the act himself, when the last bleeding bull was toppling to the sand, he would do it without my assistance. That much was settled and decided in my mind.

As time wore on, the look of fear in Brendan's face became more graven. The sanguineous puddles that mottled the original white glistening sands were bountiful. The tempo of the day took an upturn when one of the matadors knelt and kissed the tip of a horn. "Bravo, bravo, bravo," a matador stood rigid between horns and the wall below us. Had the wind risen and furled the muleta or had the now distraught animal miscalculated the edge of the boy's cape, his bowels would have wound up in Brendan's lap. By the change of expression on Brendan's frightened face, it was obvious that Brendan's bullfighting plans for the day went the way of the Irish jaunting cart. Beatrice looked relieved.

The newsmen talked of Hemingway's affinity and macho attitude towards the sport and hoped that Brendan would come up with some unusual, titillating comments for the tabloids. But Brendan merely groaned and referred to the whole affair as a "big fuckin' outdoor, hamburger-making scheme. The matadors are a pack of wild eegits," he spat. "I've seen enough to turn me stomach for one day, cum on," he ordered us, "before I develop a case of the head staggers." We quickly departed. Our day had been a memorable one: a day when only brave bulls had died. *Deo gratias!*

Back at the Cesar Bar, Brendan ripped a red cloth from a table and did a series of not-too-elegant impressions of a bullfighter at work. In a sudden change of venue he became a gored and dying bull. His antics were met with few bursts of approval. He vociferously condemned the art as "an ignorant man's passion."

The manager graciously requested that we leave. "Shur didn't I drink in better caliber whorehouses," Brendan cracked and walked to the door. Just as he was about to ascend the stairs, he was confronted by a tall hulking man with a Bronx Irish accent.

"I saw your play in New York, Behan," the man intoned in a gruff voice as he peered down unmercifully into Brendan's sheepish face, "I didn't think very much of it, I might add."

Brendan slapped the man on the shoulder and invited him to the bar. The manager hurried over and reiterated his expulsion order. Brendan advised him that he was imminently expecting "a stampede of very thirsty colleagues from Hollywood. Needless to say they'll be looking for a well to drink from. They don't know the layout," he went on in a surreptitious manner, his eyes darting mischievously. The manager beamed, shook Brendan's hand and informed his bartender that his previous eviction notice was forthwith rescinded.

Drinks were ordered. Glasses were drained. Conviviality abounded. Brendan gulped glass after glass of soda water. The talk between the two new friends concerned Irish plays, players and playwrights. The man made Brendan privy to the fact that he was a police officer and in Mexico on business. His job was to apprehend an escaped, convicted murderer and bring him back to New York. Brendan finished up his soda water and in a low, low whisper, informed the man of the law that if he ran into the chap he would not only "tip him off but I'll give him the fare to fuck off to Brazil or wherever else that they don't have extradition treaties with your capitalistic sex-conscious country."

The verbal battle continued, Brendan shifted the weight from the ball of one foot to the other while he picked his nose and mimicked the frenzied man's accent. The argument boiled over into the topics of politics, religion and early American settlements. The berserk policeman rattled off a host of (names of) Irish-born who had made their impression indelible in the sands of the new world.

"People who are compelled to abandon their homelands in search of a better way of life are troglodytes and low-class scum," Brendan cut in, slowly raising his eyes to the level of the man's nose, *"I'm* here at the invitation of Hollywood moguls and Broadway producers."

"And *my* ancestors came over on the Mayflower," the officer snapped.

"And so did syphilis," Brendan quickly replied. Then he chuckled a snide little chuckle, politely excused himself, spirited through the doors and laughed his way to the top of the stairs.

The day was not a total loss.

We spent the next couple of evenings attending the local dog and horse meets. Brendan was in fine fettle, sporting his new colorful attire and a sideburn that was shaved one inch higher than the other. At the dog meet he barreled ahead with his tall tales.

"Did yew know that I once made me livin' be dopin' greyhounds in Dublin. The chap that I was in partnership with was an albino chap, that's a chap whose eyes and hair is the same color as his skin." He talked and turned his head from one side to the other, periodically lowering his voice as though the conversation was being monitored by J. Edgar Hoover himself. "However one night our game came to an abrupt end. Yew see the albino chap and mesself were in the process of drivin' the mutt to the track when lo and behold, weren't we suddenly stopped be a holy communion procession in progress. Well, to make a short story long, we had given the whelp a springer, a shot of lightning liquid, if yew follow me meanin' (he winks), but be the time that the procession had passed the effects of the stuff had worn off, then the four-legged cunt went into a deep sleep. Slept like a whore in a confession box. He was the last dog in the race. The little ballox never even left the box for reasons that the effects had been counterproductive. Just lay there sleepin' his cunt off. Even the hare was taken by surprise," he concluded with a grin and a chuckle. "Luckily we didn't end up doing twelve months in the Joy (Dublin prison), if it wasn't for the fuckin' aul rosary rally, the souped-up whelp would have met himself twice before he got halfway round the first turn of the turf. Wha! But shur what odds, shur the Irish only go to greyhound meets because the booze is better and the conversation is of a higher intellectual quality.

"Did yew know that I am the only playwright on record that was ever barred from his own play. Why, says yew. Well, one night outside of the Wyndham Theatre in London I decided to tell a few yarns and sing a few songs for the buskers. At the time of me singin' wasn't me play ready to be performed. The people who filled me cup with silver, were the same people who saw the play a half-hour later. Why did I do it, yew ask! Well, shur wasn't I once a busker mesself. Under the circumstances, I felt that it was the natural thing to do.

"Now I'll admit that I'm a fellow with a great deal of fame, my fame has enabled me to sleep in better beds, but I'll tell yew this much, I don't sleep any better . . ." Here Brendan stopped and stared into the faces of his listeners for an interminable period. Then in a totally different mood he went on.

"Shur didn't fuckin' aul Princess Margaret laugh herself to death and almost fall from the balcony during a command performance of me play."

Brendan was particularly proud of this documented incident. In late 1941, after he had been released from Borstal servitude and deported to Ireland as persona non grata, he was instructed that if he returned to England he would be incarcerated. In the ensuing years when he traveled to France and to other European countries he was forced to land in England, and he was temporarily locked up. In October 1958, with the major successes of *The Hostage* and *Borstal Boy,* the British begged him to appear on their television networks. Brendan became much more famous in England than he was in Ireland.

Kenneth Tynan, a leading English theater critic, hailed him as a possibly even greater dramatist than O'Casey. In his Hollywood monologues, Brendan described England as a "fucking dreary aul hole, filled with chancers that would rub butter on a fat pig's arse." The forthcoming London premiere of *Richard's Cork Leg* was a ceremony that "I'm not looking forward to. Be the same token now, even though I'm known to be a man who does not lie, I'll admit I have the occasional propensity to stretch the truth," he concluded with a mischievous wink and a nudge.

During the London West End run of *The Hostage,* Dominic, Brendan's brother, also had a hit play running in that noble district. A precedent in theatrical history was set. Brendan never made mention of this.

"A fella says to me the other day in Hollycrud, a fuckin' aul kip of a place up the road a bit where I've been holed up writin' a play, wrote two full acts in a matter of five days wha! Not bad for a former busker, huh! Ask Peter there. Well anyways, says he, 'What is yur play about Brendan?' Silence. 'What is it about?' says I, 'It's about sex, religion and politics, is there anything else worth writin' about,' says I. But to be honest with yew, that's only the half of it. What really happened was this. On me way to America I told a joke to a steward on the boat. He laughed his ballox off. There and then, says I to mesself, anything that can get a laugh on a Cunard ship, should be on Broadway. I decided to make a play out of the cuntin' thing. I'm callin it *Richard's Cork Leg.* It's an old line of James Joyce's. Not that I'm a fan of that inferior-minded, degenerate cunt. He should've been hung, in my estimation . . . for desecrating valuable paper."

At these meets Brendan exuded a rare charm, an ebullience and an enormous human sensibility that I had not before observed. He lavished on me handfuls of ten- and twenty-dollar bills. "Here avick put a few of these on the nose of a winner and whatever yew do, don't give them to the nuns or the clergy. If yew do, I won't make a movie star out of yew."

His handouts were lost on a bunch of losers. He offered me more.

"I can't accept any more of your money, Brendan. I feel ashamed."

"O.K. me aul son," he said dolefully and put the money back into his pocket. But sensing his hurt and humiliation I accepted another handful of twenties and placed them on another horde of slow joggers.

Brendan displayed an uncanny ability for ferreting out old, run-down but interesting bars and restaurants where equally interesting citizens gathered to reminisce and play their musical instruments. Most of these dilapidated eateries were off the beaten track and far from the eyes of niggling tourists. He discovered one such place located several blocks from the main thoroughfare. It became our favorite late-night hangout. Each night along about eight o'clock a gaggle of Mexican hombres attired in sombreros and national costumes gathered and strummed until the wee hours of the morning. At Brendan's request they played and replayed his favorite song, "Guadalajara." Each time that he reheard the piece he handed each member of the quintet a ten-dollar bill. Tears welled up in his eyes and rolled down his puffy cheeks. Taken aback I asked Beatrice why he was crying so profusely. But she instructed me to "ask Brendan."

Brendan sat glumly and refused to answer my question. In an attempt to perk him up and change his mood I switched the conversation to another topic.

"Brendan," I said with caution, "I'm curious to know about the mechanics of good writing, the initial approach to take when getting a book into its first workable drafts."

"What in the name of fuckin' jayzus would the likes of yew be wantin' to know that for?" he snapped.

"Well, I too, like you sir, aspire to write. I have traveled far and wide. I may have a thing or two to tell to the Bellcuddy and the Connemara bogmen who read your works." My reciprocation was delivered in a lightning-quick burst.

"Look, will yew, for the love and honor of poor aul sufferin' fuckin' jayzus, not be goin' on with such shite, yew have as much chance of becummin' famous as I have of gettin' to heaven. Leave the writin' to the writers and stick to yur own way of carvin' yur livin'," he yelled into my face.

"I didn't say that I wanted to become famous, Brendan, neither did I say that I wanted you to get to heaven, I merely said that I aspire to write and since I've developed a great deal more enthusiasm as a natural consequence of being in your gracious company and in the shadow of your genius, and importune I felt it appropriate to ask. However, I assure you I will not bother you again with such trivia. *Slainte,*" I said, as I toasted with my glass of soda water.

Brendan was now into his fifth day of sobriety. His nerves were in rags. "That crucial day, the 'crisis day,' " Beatrice again reminded me with caution. Brendan hadn't had a drink since the day of his court appearance.

"I didn't cum here to be bothered with bullshite," Brendan snapped as he put his feet up under him and sat for a time dozing.

"Then may I suggest that we listen to music, the only real international language, the natural cauterizer of men's phobias, the soother of their souls, the lifter of sagging spirits and the bringer of compassion and understanding. *Skol. Salud,"* I said, tipping and clinking my glass with his. "You are a weaver and a shatterer of myths, are you not, B.," I continued, "I am a lover of the Latin beat; became inculcated with it when I dredged the Bay of Maracaibo. I am curious, B., obviously you are deeply enthralled with the piece "Guadalajara." Any particular reason?"

Brendan fidgeted, and went deeper into despair. *"Jayzus mother of fuckin' Christ on high,* b-b-but did I c-cum here to eat me supper and to listen to a bit of music or did I cum here to hear a fuckin' sermon on a mount and to be drivin' into some fuckin' madhouse, be a great poet the likes of yew," he roared, his food splattering all over his lapels.

Brendan suddenly stood up, slammed down his napkin, called for his check, paid it and stormed out of the restaurant. Beatrice and I followed him into another restaurant.

"Would you like to order now, sir," a crisp waiter asked.

"No, we came here to view the bottles on the shelves," Brendan roared into his face. The waiter disappeared. Brendan squirmed, twitched, then looked in the mirror and spotted four well-muscled youths in a booth behind us. Their gazes were concentrated on him. "What the fuck are yiz looking at?" he hollered at their reflections.

"Nothing much," one of them shot back.

The crispness of the boy's answer sent Brendan into a paroxysm.

"What are yew, some sort of smart cunt?" Brendan roared.

"No, I'm a playwright, a faggot playwright," the boy snapped threateningly.

"I never heard of yew," Brendan shot back. "Yew mustn't be much of a playwright."

"That's because you haven't stopped talking about yourself for long enough."

Brendan snapped his fingers and called the waiter back. "We decided to cancel our orders; we don't like the kind of people who eats here."

The waiter looked perplexed. "But sir, you haven't ordered anything yet."

The four American youths snickered and giggled. Brendan shuddered and shook.

"Now I know where I've seen you before," I said to the boy who had engaged Brendan in the adder-tongued dialogue. "I've seen you in Gimbels . . . at the knicker counter. Let's step outside, I'd like to get a look at your knickers. I'll bet they're maroon."

"Never mind, fuck them," Brendan snapped. The three of us arose and headed for another bar.

One morning Brendan cut short our breakfast and ordered, "We'll go for a spin in the country."

We came upon a small mucky village of low-roofed houses that were made of straw, discarded sheets of galvanized tin, twigs, ancient bedposts, dry fern, bedsprings, slats of wood, bricks and sun-dried clay. The village lay low and deep, set in off the main road.

"Will yew pull off for a bit and get a gander at what the gentry below is up to," he sputtered as he spotted a gaggle of dirt-encrusted little children at play. A few older denizens sat dozing against an adobe wall. Another coterie of older folks, dressed in sandals, straw hats, and multicolored cloaks and tattered sombreros were piling some home-made hand-painted pottery onto a cart. A horde of mangy dogs and hungry fowl wandered about pecking, barking and clucking in the sunbleached mud.

The air was moist, tacky and laden with a heavy tang of despair, deprivation, starvation and slow death. Further down the slope, another cadre of old ones were crouched around a cauldron stirring its contents and talking softly. An indefinable odor permeated.

A diarrhea of snot-nosed, naked, hunger-bloated urchins paraded themselves before us and attempted to sell us a variety of sapless, weatherbeaten bananas and other fruits. When they realized that their sales potentialities were minimal, they proceeded to scratch their scabby limbs and rub their potbellies to indicate their earthly wants. We handed them a fistful of coins. Their eyes came to life and glistened. *"Muchas gracias, muchas gracias, señor,"* they shouted. Brendan patted them on their touseled heads as they darted away amongst the ruins of their precious, rusticating abandoned cars, plywood shacks, and clotheslines. Lines laden with tattered clothing furled and billowed in a refreshing breeze.

A few of the smaller children, those who were less apt to become frightened, remained to stare up into the face of the little impeccably dressed man who stood transfixed and glaring at them. The sight of the handsomer naked hungry boys sent Brendan into a fit of utter despair, self-hate and fear. He seemed traumatized beyond repair.

Across the street was an open-air bodega. Beatrice and I purchased soft drinks and sat on a wooden bench drinking them. I watched Brendan as he stood there frozen and flush of face. A few of the more daring of the urchins reached out and touched him. In a flash he charged over to the car, jumped in and yelled to me, "Cum on P-Peter, let's get away from this godforsaken place." He held his arms tight around himself. His head was in his chest. He shivered from head to toe. His fear and hysteria were omnipotent.

We drove back to the Cesar and sat glumly in the coffee shop.

"Just exactly how does a playwright go about setting up a play?" I asked, hoping to strike up a note of conviviality.

"Will yew for cuntssake not be goin' on about such bullshite."

"Look, B.B.," I said solidly, "there's no need to get testy with me. I'm just trying to help you, O.K."

A heavy mood came over him. "Let's cunt off to Ensenada," he suddenly chirped. We piled into the car.

"But I don't know where Ensenada is, Bren!" I said as I started the engine.

"Yew don't!?" he said victoriously, "but I thought that all yew big fuckin' professional seamen knew where everywhere is. I'll show yew. Drive down that street," he ordered with complete self-assuredness.

A half hour later we arrived at a barren strip of land along the beach. From all appearances a great deal of construction had once been in progress, then abruptly abandoned.

"We'll pull over and go for a dip," he sputtered.

"But we have no togs, B."

"*Togs* are for old ladies and seamen. Who gives a fat ballox about togs!" he snapped as he barreled out of the car.

The day was idyllic. The sun's golden rays glistened and danced on the azure blue water. I spirited down the beach and began to do a series of push-ups and sit-ups, then sat for a time gazing out at the endless rim of the sea. A medley of screams and shrieks shattered my reverie.

"Quick, Peter, quick, over there, over there."

I straightened myself up and focused in the direction where she was pointing. I caught a glimpse of Brendan as he was struggling hard and being battered by the inexorable pull of the sea. I rushed over and jumped into the seething foam and wrapped myself around him. We struggled against the undertow while I dug my heels hard into the sand. Finally the surge and pull was broken. I got him back up onto shallower ground. "That was a close one, B.," I said jubilantly, "but not to worry now, fuck it, it whetted the appetite, what say we call it a day and cunt off home to the Cesar?"

"Why don't yew mind yur own small business," he hissed.

"Next time I will!"

"Yew didn't even get yur hair wet," he quickly rejoined.

I ran back to the water's edge, scooped up several handfuls of water and doused my hair. "Is this wet enough for you now, B.?" I asked with affected irritation.

Brendan belched, farted and dressed.

"Good boy Peter, bless you," Beatrice said, as she sighed and leaned on the car's fenders.

We drove off, then came upon a vendor. Brendan gobbled up a belly full of tacos, colas, chili beans, tortillas, pork ends and something that tasted like roasted cactus.

"You shouldn't eat so much of that junk, B.," I said, "it'll spoil your appetite, not to mention the fact that you are at the moment digesting a gutful of weeds."

"Well shur if everyone in this cuntin' world was as clever as yew are, they would have to abolish the whole medical profession, wouldn't they," he snorted as he sat down in the car.

For the remainder of the evening Brendan was forced to stay close to the hotel lobby. On one or two occasions, he ventured out onto Revolucion Street to see what was happening, only to be forced to run back to the bar bathroom as swiftly as possible.

The following morning Brendan was well again. We took a preprandial stroll on the main drag. Much to his delight he discovered that he was more famous than he had envisioned as he waved at those who called out his name.

"Hello, Señor Beekman; Hello Señor Beekman; Sank you, Mr. Beehong."

Sauntering over to a coterie of tourists he launched into another of his one-man gabfests: "An aul ballox of a reporter who makes his livin' lying to the New York theater crowd says to me one day, 'Listen Behan, we made you and we can break you.' 'You did and you can says yew! Well,' says I, 'if it wasn't for people like me, fellas like yew would be sellin' snowballs to little old senile ladies in the wintertime.'"

Brendan posed, romped and commented and opined on everything from Lux soap to bunion pads, African rhubarb to Norwegian sardines, nuclear warheads, monogamy, and the ludicrousness of heterosexuality as the sole sexual excursion in life. He proselytized for homosexuality and talked about Oscar Wilde as though he were his former mentor.

A short, swarthy man carrying a tray of highly polished junk jewelry suddenly stepped into his path. The man gaped at him in awe. Brendan attempted to push on past the peddler, but the man was dogmatic.

"Usted es un artista Americano," the man shouted excitedly.

"Look will yew fuck off before I take that lot and heave it up your arse," Brendan roared into his leathery face, while pointing to the tray that was fastened to the man's chest by a length of sash.

The man quickly apologized and moved off. We spirited ahead. Brendan suddenly stopped, turned, ran back to the man and said crisply, "How much do yew want for the lot?" The man looked frightened, then attempted to run. Brendan took hold of his elbows and began to shake him until some of the jewelry fell out of his tray, then in his finest Spanish, he shouted into the sun-sapped face, *"Oiga Usted Señor le pregunto a Usted . . . Cuanto valle ellote completo?!"*

A look of delight came into the hawker's face.

"It's just a load of polished shite," I said warningly.

"Mind yur own business," he said pushing me away.

Words were bandied. A bargain was reached. Brendan handed the man a roll of green bills. The glittering jewelry was stuffed into Beatrice's handbag.

"Mia gracias, mia gracias," the ecstatic hawker shouted as he charged down Revolucion Street. *"Mia gracias, hombre."* The hawker quickly disappeared.

Back at the Cesar bar we placed the cargo on top of our lunch table. Brendan wound up and set the watches in motion. "This watch we'll give to Dessy, God luv him, the brooch we'll hand to Celia, Joan will luv the necklace, God bless her aul heart, the two rings will go to—"

"I still say it's a concoction of pure unadulterated shite."

"Listen, did I wake up this mornin' to spend another day in *yur* fuckin' crucifixion factory?" Brendan snapped.

Suddenly I found myself rocking back and forth with hysterical laughter. At first, I thought that he had purchased the trayful of glitter as a token of gratitude to the man for his recognition of his celebrity. I suddenly realized that Brendan was genuinely of the belief that the stuff had a redeemable value.

"Look B.," I said picking up one of the watches and peeling the frayed tinsel from its girth. Crumbs of artificial gold glittered and trickled to the floor beside his feet. "See what I mean, B., that little poxy-faced Mexican cunt gave you a royal fuckin' and him only a mere commoner." His eyes bulged at the sight of what was under the exterior of the watch. With a furious swat of his hand the contents of the table were swept into Beatrice's handbag. Then he charged up the staircase bumping into everyone cursing and spuming and forgetting his lunch.

Brendan's nerves were like old piano strings ready to pop. If he was destined to break out on the booze, today would surely be the day. Again I recalled the words of warning from Finnegan. At the breakfast table we eyed one another with surreptitious intensity.

"Today is the day for me," I said.

"Today is the day for yew for what!?"

"I'm out . . . o-u-t, out."

The Behans eyed one another in characteristic fashion.

"He means he wants to leave today," Beatrice said cautiously.

"We'll hire a car." Brendan spumed.

"Oh no, we'll go with Peter," she said, patting him gently on the leg.

"He's right," Brendan suddenly said. Then with a flash of jollity, "Shur if we stayed here any longer wee'd roast our ballox off, let's fuck off back to Hollyfrock."

"Today will be luvly Pete, we've had enough," Beatrice said with a smile on her face. The three of us sat, sipping and beaming.

"Three o'clock is pullout time," I said sharply cutting through the silence. "I can't risk a dark highway with that load of rust, not to mention the hotrod degenerates who stalk the highways at night."

Now that the date and the hour were firmly agreed upon, I proceeded to verbally lay out a few more of my previously thought-out decisions. "We won't make too many stops along the way, and no drinking booze." Another flurry of eye-to-eye confrontations ensued. We sat for a time.

"Beatrice and I were just saying avick, that another day's outings would do us all the good in the world," Brendan interjected, clipping the tip from off his cigar and changing his venue.

"I'm sorry B., my early morning decision was irrevocable. I'm out at three sharp. The car is shot, the tires are barely in existence. We'll be lucky if we make it home in one piece." Brendan sighed and lit his cigar. "I have neither the desire to tangle with the fascist highway patrol or the chicken-fuckers who await us, B."

"Fair field and no favor avick," he finally said with a smile that was half smirk. "Certainly, me aul s-son," he went on, "shur wasn't it only half an hour ago I was saying to Beatsie, an' me wedgin' me way into the jax, let's cunt off out of it says I, before we die of dehydration." I detected a twinge of malice in his voice. "If we stay here any longer, says I, we'll cook in our own juices."

At three P.M. sharp we began loading my car.

"Peter Arthurs, Peter Arthurs." My name was being called out. I turned around and spotted Carol Poland, a voluptuous young lady who once worked as a secretary in the Seafarers International Union hall in Brooklyn. She was subsequently fired because she broke down while following her former boss's funeral cortege. The man was married to another woman.

"This is Carol Poland and this is Brendan and Beatrice Behan," I began as I attempted to do the honors.

"This is Peter Arthurs," Brendan said to Carol, interrupting my spiel, "and I am Brendan Behan. I am a direct descendant of a sixth-century king called Conal Cearnacht; Peter here is formerly a MacArthur. The MacArthurs were of Scotch heritage, but their blood lineage is vague in the history books."

We shook hands and departed after agreeing to meet in Hollywood. Carol informed me that she was pursuing an acting career.

Standing in line to pass customs I suggested to Brendan to let me do the talking. Brendan was traveling on an Irish passport. A limited visa. I was traveling as a U.S. citizen. Brendan sat in the rear of the car.

Suddenly he went into a tirade that almost seared the paint from my dashboard. "I-I-I m-mean to s-say it must have been a grand fuckin-jayzus experience in life to have traveled the length and breadth of the great big cuntin' world the likes of which only a firm-minded and stalwart lad the likes of yew could have done. Indeed . . . such a m-m-marvelous gift in life for any man to have been endowed with. Isn't that so," he said vehemently to his fright-filled wife who sat frozen in the sun-baked seat beside him. "But I'll tell yew this much avicko" his voice rising, "and this will probably cum as a s-surprise to yew, b-but yew are not the only one who ever stood in line at Woolworth's passport counter and made an application for a permit to travel. No byjayzus yur not."

The blazing Mexican heat seared the interior of the car. At that crucifixion point in time, the long line of cars in waiting behind me were honking their horns demanding I move up and fill a vacuum. I couldn't. My engine had stalled. I jumped out from behind the wheel, ran back to the car behind me, and pleaded with the driver to give me a boost. "I have a very sick lady in the car," I lamented, mopping my brow, "she is immediately due to have her baby, she wants to have it at home, in L.A.!" The driver nodded with sympathy. I got back into my car. "I too have had a few experiences with the customs and cops and others who purportedly represent our mad fuckin' society," he continued as I released the handbrake.

"Listen, Brendan, I'll thank you to put your pacifier back in your mouth until we pass these customs, O.K.! Also I'll thank you not to have so many wasps for breakfast in the future."

The driver behind me gave my fender a bump, I turned the key, pulled the choke and hit the gas pedal. The khaki-clad customs officer gave us a sweeping scrutiny and waved us north.

Along the route, at Brendan's insistence, we stopped at dozens of eateries and newsstands. As usual he held forth. "I mean to say shur any intelligent cunt can tell yew that the fastest and the easiest way to kill a culshie is to tell him a few funnies, then put the whore between a pair of starched white bedsheets, if the bit of humor doesn't kill him, the cleanliness of the bedclothes will. They can't stand the sound of a bit of laughter." Brendan's tune hadn't drastically changed. "Now I know for a fact that the average poor cunt who has to go out to sea to earn his kip, may indeed wind up well traveled, but so what, he hasn't learned anything has he, and why not, you might ask! Well it's because he spends the bulk of his liberty time in some whorehouse or some gin mill at the head of a rat-infested wharf wha!! Do they ever go inland to study the people or their cultures? No! Before they know it, it's upgangway time and back out to idiots paradise, the middle of the ocean. It's the type of an existence that wouldn't suit me atall atall! But so be it. Each cunt to his own."

In the coffee shop an ominous silence prevailed.

"Brendan's a pure one hundred percent right," I announced, clapping the nails of my thumbs lightly. "What Brendan just said is what I have been saying to so many for so long. However, I sincerely doubted if my meaning was ever taken in. That, of course, was because I was never blessed with the elocution that my great friend and landsman here was. Merchant seamen are basically and essentially nothing but low-life flotsam, a bunch of drifters, hooligans and perverts frightened of life and for that reason are forced to go down to the sea in filthy rust buckets, called ships. A tangle of bowsies whose blood is only in their knuckles. My sincere thanks to you, my landsman," I said tapping his teacup with mine. "To your ambrosia."

"What sort of work do *you* do, sir?" the coffee shop owner asked. "Are you a writer?"

"No, thank God, I'm a seaman."

We drove off and came upon a newsstand, where Brendan discovered a newspaper showing him riding the ass on Revolucion Street. He beamed with delight and handed the seller a large bill.

The paper was the San Diego *Union.* The portion of the picture of Beatrice and me was blocked out. The headline read "Irish Playwright Brendan Behan in Mexico."

"B-but the bastards cut me out," I complained with bitterment.

"Ah now son but don't get it up," Brendan chuckled, "shur we should all be famous at least for a month, then pensioned off. What say we go home avick, this place is putting years on me."

Brendan's one-hundred-dollar investment had paid off handsomely. The Mexican police officer had performed his duty well.

We passed a smattering of arbors, bosky retreats, then came upon an ancient stucco building with a small steeple on top of it that may have once housed a mission bell.

Brendan begged me to stop.

We spirited into the solemn quietude of the mission, an ancient tiny ruin of worship. Its walls were asplatter with Spanish and Mexican paintings and a large crucifix. Its narrow pews were rough-hewn benches with uncovered knee-boards. Scattered here and there were dozens of brochures and other pamphlets that graciously bespoke the house's history and once-significance. Sprinklings of little old black-shawled ladies who had dropped in to spend a coin and to utter a prayer for their dead or dying occupied the pews as they knelt and bent their hoary heads in solemn prayer. Brendan scooped up handfuls of the printed literature. Later he visited the rectory and asked to speak to the abbot. The two men strolled about the grounds for a time, exchanged views and spoke of the trying times that the world was harrowingly undergoing. The abbot was allowed to talk freely. Brendan listened attentively to the holy man's every utterance. Finally the abbot mentioned the exhilarating word, "Brendan." Brendan's eyes danced and sparkled as he quickly ripped a piece of a brochure from his pocket, autographed it, handed it to the monk and saluted him: "May yew be the father of a handsome altar boy," as the car sped from the scene.

Back on the main highway I clamped my foot down hard on the gas pedal. The hands of the speedometer rose sharply and reached eighty-five miles per hour. The torque pulled the wheels from one side of the tarred road to the other. The wheels struggled hard to hold the dangerous curves and bends of Western Avenue. The dilapidated Buick swayed to and fro, bounced, careened but held to the course. The stench of burning oil and overheated rubber permeated the car's interior.

Brendan's beady little eyes glistened with a combination of reverie, fear and malice. In the rearview mirror Beatrice prayed and trembled. Sporadically her lily-white hand crept up over the back of my seat, tapped me on the shoulder and silently indicated to the speedometer. I paid the gesticulations no heed and rattled ahead.

Blankets of dust churned up and encrusted my windscreen. To achieve a little visibility I was forced to stand in a crouching position and wipe the outside of the window with a rag. Then I passed the rag to Brendan. "Here B., you probably want to brighten your view." The rag remained in his lap, untouched where it had landed. Brendan was suddenly sullen, silent and scared.

The arid glitter of the day had dissipated. Dusk was now quickly establishing its ominous presence. The jalopy sashayed and performed better than I had anticipated, but the punishing potholes were taking their toll. I pushed down harder on the accelerator. A stretch of road repairs in Western Avenue caused the car to bounce, zigzag and shudder. The engine sputtered and coughed as though it suffered from chronic emphysema. A headlight blinked and went out.

At Beatrice's painful insistence, I finally eased my foot from the pedal, "I'm just trying to make it to Hollywood before the vultures on their motorbikes come out to prey, Beatrice," I excused. "The hulk is on her last legs and I'm just hoping to make it in before dark," I said with further apology. She sighed with relief.

Finally we made it to the Montecito. In the apartment we ate in silence. Brendan then hastened to his favorite chair and scanned the pages of a rag. A chorus of little bleeps and snorts went out. They were the specific type of snickers and snorts that he emitted when the heady wine of some small emotional victory was won, or at hand. But when? where? I wondered, as I bade the Behans good night.

In the recess of my soul I could not bring myself to deny Brendan his small, unimportant (to me) victories, victories that I felt I could well afford to lose, without too much stress or strain. Besides, something much more important than a cargo of childish pranks was now uppermost in my mind.

It was the big star-studded, upcoming blowout to be held in the palatial home of Ernie Kovacs.

I spirited home in sheer ecstasy.

IX

On Wednesday, June 14, I did not hear from the Behans. This did not bother me since I was amply aware that Brendan was an egoist supreme and could not forgive me easily for not joining him in the proposed tryst with the boy in the seedy hotel the Sunday previous. Spats, even of an insignificant nature, were things to be thoroughly dealt with in his maharajah mind.

I looked forward to the party at Ernie Kovacs' and meeting the host of stars whom I fantasized about since I was a boy. My heart thumped with joy. Thursday June 15, at approximately three P.M., the phone rang. With boyish ebullience I picked up the receiver and said "Arthurs residence."

"Oh hello, Peter." Beatrice said with unusual frivolity.

"Great Bea, great. How's the form, dear girl, how's Bren?"

"He's great Peter, marvelous."

"Put him on Bea, like the lovely girl that you are."

"He's busy right now. Oh I almost forgot to tell you, we had a great time last night at your man's, and oh! didn't we meet your girlfriend, she looked so smashing. She was dressed in very casual clothes, must be her style."

I almost said the only girlfriend that *I* have in this town is your husband, when the name Kim Novak crackled across the wire.

Was I suffering auditory hallucinations?

"I said to Brendan, Oh Brendan, Peter Arthurs should be here now to see 'his girl friend.' She's so beautiful. She was with her boyfriend, a director, a Mr. Quine."

My confusion mounted. I was speechless. "A Mr. Quine?"

"And oh! Guess who else was at the party, Elizabeth Taylor. She's so small, Peter, a little bit of a thing. She and B.B. talked for hours about their illnesses; I couldn't get a word in edgewise. Later on, says I to B.B., there is the one woman in all of Hollywood who can command a million per pic. Don't *you* think she's a good actress Peter?" Beatrice continued to talk incessantly.

My heart began to race. "Beatrice, my dear, you will have to excuse my ignorance but I don't understand. What 'your man's house' are you referring to, where did you meet Kim and Elizabeth?"

"Ernie Kovacs' house . . . we were at Ernie Kovacs' house last night . . . that's where we met them," she said in a low-keyed voice.

"B-but B-Beatrice, y-you must be mistaken, the party at Kovacs' is not until tonight, t-that's why you're calling me, to d-drive you and B. there!" Silence.

"Oh no, the party was last night. Ernie sent a limousine to get us. That's why you didn't hear from us yesterday."

My heart pounded. Suddenly I felt old and haggard. Brendan had deliberately lied to me about the date. Now the tyranny of reality was taking hold. I had been had. Beatrice's voice reappeared on the wire.

"The reason I called is to tell you that Brendan wants you to come at once and drive him to Hollywood Memorial Cemetery, he wants to see some more graves before he gets back to *Cork.*"

My tongue dried, shriveled and clung to the roof of my mouth. My heartbeat was pushing my lungs out of my chest. A swell of pain rose in my chest and skittered down my left arm. My hand trembled and went numb.

In Mexico, Brendan had made mention of the fact that he wanted to see the graves of Tyrone Power and Rudolph Valentino. Their remains are in Memorial Park Cemetery. Another cemetery that he dearly wanted to visit was the Los Angeles Cemetery for Pets: dogs, cats, rabbits, hamsters, iguanas, goldfish, birds, parrots, snakes and lizards. We were informed that some of the wittiest inscriptions in existence were carved on the headstones in this place of eternal rest.

"H-Hollywood M-Memorial C-Cemetery . . . the b-bastard wants me to drive him there, does he?" I shouted into the receiver. "Yes, yes, t-tell him t-that I'll drive him there to be sure. I'll even go to the b-bother of leaving him there. Tell him I'll make a statue out of him."

My hand went totally numb. The phone slipped from my grip and fell to the floor. I darted out of the room and fell down the fire exit then charged up Wilcox Avenue. I made the nine-block dash in a matter of minutes, slipping and stumbling several times along the hazy route. The palms of my hands were raw and bleeding. I went up the rear elevator in the event that Brendan might try to make a fast getaway.

Murder was in my mind. Mayhem was in my fists. For a considerable period of time I had been aware that Brendan was an evil, sadistic, and sadomasochistic game-player. But in my boyish brain I never perceived that *I* would be selected to absorb such a hurt. Numbness flooded my every nerve. My heart pounded like an eggbeater out of control. Never had my faith, trust and confidence been so brutally violated.

I pounded on the door to the apartment. No one answered. My knees buckled. Finally the door was opened. Beatrice tried to block my entry. "Here Peter, be a good boy and get these groceries in Hughes for me, then the three of us can sit down to eat," she said attempting to push a wad of paper money into my hand. I pushed on past her, careened into the living room and found Brendan sitting naked on the settee with the phone in his hand. The name Jim Downey was being mentioned plentitudinously. He scratched his scrotum and talked without looking at me.

"Tell the overstuffed leprechaun to get off the phone," I said to Beatrice.

"Oh he'll be finished in a minute," she said timidly, "he's talking to Jim Downey in New York."

I darted over to him, stood directly above him and attempted to force him to look up at me, but all to no avail. He merely continued to talk, pick the cretinous matter from his nostrils, roll it between his thumb and index finger and flick it past me.

"S-smashing Jim, smashing, they were all there, the whole fuckin' lot of them, every cunt and fuck face in smogsville. Jack Lemmon, Elizabeth Taylor, Laurence Harvey, Eddie Fisher, Shirley MacLaine, Edward G. Robinson, Kirk Douglas, Groucho Marx, and oh yes, there was another one, a big-titted one, oh, what in cunt's name is she called! She's the one with the head of cauliflower on top of her head. (Brendan scratched his scrotum and played with his erected penis) . . . oh, never mind Jim, I'll think of her name later."

I turned half a turn, picked up my left hand with my right hand and stuffed it into my left pocket. I would keep Brendan's victories for the day down to a minimum!!

"The lady's name is Kim Novak, Brendan."

Brendan ignored my assistance and continued to pick and scratch.

"I mean the whole shebang was a marvelous affair, a great success, but shur I still say that the lot of them is nothing but a shower of ill-mannered nobodies, but so what says yew, they treated me royally, that's what counts, right Jim, and why shouldn't they. I might decide to do something for them, one of these days, the talentless bunch."

Citric little smiles seeped in and out of his porcine puss. Never before, in the macramé of his complex and complicated mien had I seen Brendan operate with such cool and savage efficiency. His timing was as accurate as an Accutron; his portentous little pauses followed by his picks, rolls and flicks, incisive moments of silence, then loud raucous saurian-tongued remarks were convincing. "Mohawk, yes Jim that's it, that's her name, Mohawk, Kim Mohawk!"

I was the joker playing the losing hand. The Devil was the dealer. His satanic majesty was holding the trump cards. He was unbeatable, the master dealer of the house. I had made the horrendous mistake of taking the master on at his most wicked game and in his own house. With all of his buffoonery and lampoonery Brendan was intent, serious, skilled, steady and consistent. The man was deadly. During the many weeks of our friendship, his quintessential public line was "If there is a thing in a human being that I go for it's their weakness; once I find it, I'm a devil." His second best line also came to mind, the line that captioned his name on the Broadway playbill for *The Hostage,* and on the cover of his autobiography, *Borstal Boy.* It was the line that lent so much to the furthering of his legend, the solidification of his immortality, and the concreteness of his image in the minds of millions. "I respect kindness to human beings, first of all, and kindness to animals."

I made a few feeble attempts to interject a word or two, but on each occasion he raised his voice an octave or two in range and drowned me out. His eyes glistened with triumph. His blubbery face was inebriated with an electrifying vengeance. Never before had I witnessed such a magnitude of evil machinations in him. A sense of paralysis swept over me. I was about to sit down in infinite weariness and defeat, but on second thought, realizing that he would then be in a greater position to eye my misery I decided to adhere to Beatrice's wishes and run to Hughes for the daily dairies.

In Hughes a number of conclusions came to mind. Brendan was a festering mass of evilry and spite. With a fair amount of talent and an ego that was unstoppable, he had carved for himself a niche in the scrolls of famous men. But the basic thrust of his celebrity was rife with alcoholism, lies, deceit, fear and malice. Brendan had succeeded. He was the unstoppable lie. He had the right amount of savagery to succeed. His well-publicized courage was of a nihilistic nature, a derivation of self-destruction and a need to destroy those whom he needed most of all. Those who would not cotton to his whims would suffer his brand of opprobrium.

Back in the hotel lobby a thought suddenly emanated in the base of my mind. "Did Brendan receive any long-distance calls today?" I asked the switchboard operator. "He told me to inquire, to keep him posted while he is in and out."

I was quickly informed that no long-distance calls came or went on that afternoon. My curiosity was satiated. I was fast becoming a Behanologist.

I rapped hard on the apartment door. I handed Beatrice the two bagfuls of groceries, the change and the checkout slip from Hughes, then pushed on into the living room, where none to my surprise I found Brendan stretched out naked on the settee with phone still in hand, "Yes, Jim, sure, sure, they're after me night and day to write this and write that for them . . . hmm . . . I'll take your advice . . . hmmm . . ."

"Who is he talking to now, B?"

"Oh he's still on the phone to Downey," she said, avoiding my eyes. Jim Downey was the New York restaurateur who operated the famous steak and chop house on Forty-fourth Street and Eighth Avenue. It was there that the parties for the opening and the closing of *The Hostage* took place.

Brendan slammed down the phone and ran around the room emitting a familiar cacophony of sounds; farts, burps, snorts and snickers. His tumescent member was standing straight out as though it were another limb. We made no eye-to-eye contact. Beatrice packed the foodstuffs into the refrigerator and deep-freeze.

Brendan continued to flounce around in his miasma of ecstasy, his unruly hair grazed by, directly under my flaring nostrils. Then he stood in the center of the floor with legs apart. He picked his nose with both hands. I decided to sit down and get a different perspective on the carnival in motion. However I did not sustain that position for long.

Brendan suffered from a condition called aerophagia. Ordinarily, in order to release his intestinal gases with ease and in relative silence he was forced to squeeze his buttocks together with one hand while he picked his nose with the other. Now as a natural consequence of his spread-legged position, his farts, instead of popping out one or two at a time, fizzed out in long steady streams. A look of sheer delight suffused his harlequin face as he let go stream after stream of flatulence. I paid him a wink of confidence and approval which he portentously reciprocated. The scatological show went on. Seconds later he was back and doing another of his familiar three-hundred-and-sixty-degree runs of the apartment. Then he rerouted his course and ran backwards, knocking over furnishings and spouting scatological interpolations of his devising that pertained to the talents of the celebrities with whom he had dined the night before. "A fuckin' bird-brained lot, a talentless pack of fuck faces. Who do they think that they are inviting *me* to their pigsty."

Seconds later his nose was dipping into the freezing depths of the refrigerator. A contemplative silence prevailed. Beatrice was ashen-faced, a frozen figure of fright. Brendan made a series of deprecating remarks while he checked the foods and their stamped prices against the prices on the oblong checkout list from Hughes. In his reverie, he had clearly forgotten that he was sober and that the groceries were paid for by him, by virtue of the fact that Beatrice had given me a twenty-dollar bill he had previously given to her to give to me to make the purchases.

Suddenly his mind was clear. A look of horror swept over him. He dashed into the bathroom, sat on the commode and observed me through the jamb of the door while he sporadically lifted his legs one at a time to unleash his gasses. He rubbed his hands together in frenzied glee while making fiendish little remarks to his wife about the virtues of my dream girl. "Wouldn't yew say that that big white-haired cow that we met at yur man's last night probably saw more ceilings than anybody else in Hollyfuck wha!?"

"W-which actress do you mean, Brendan?"

In a flash he was up and out of the bathroom, a wad of toilet paper sticking to his buttocks and trailing on the floor. "What are yew, fuckin' deaf or what? Did I say anything to yew about an actress, I d-distinctly recall asking yew about a cow!"

I jumped to my feet and affected a look of disbelief.

"That's right, Beatrice! Brendan is right, he didn't say anything about an actress, he was talking about a cow, a white-haired cow, didn't you hear him?"

Another series of eye-to-eye confrontations among the three of us ensued.

"God I'm awfully sorry Bren," I said with utter concern, "but it is quite obvious that you didn't enjoy the blowout last evening, but that's the way the mop flops, don't worry B, another party will crop up soon. You're a famous man!" I picked up my prized scrapbook from the coffee table and prepared to go.

I had left the scrapbook containing my most cherished photos and newspaper clippings there days before. Stories concerning my seafaring career from the *SIU Log,* pictures of me boxing at the New York CYO and comments regarding my punching ability by the famed Olympic coach Pete Mello, were carefully placed alongside the photos. My hopes were that Brendan would, in his leisure time, read the write-ups and become impressed.

The picture-story of me as the first and the youngest member of the first U.S. maritime upgrading school in history, was on page one of the book. The U.S. Coast Guard had failed me on the very first question. "Give date of birth." I was *then* seventeen years of age. The minimum age allowed, to be granted an able seaman's ticket, was nineteen but, by virtue of the fact that I had accumulated more than the required seatime to sit, the Coast Guard granted me permission to sail as an acting A.B. until such time as I reached the age of nineteen. I had made history, a precedent.

"Ah yes, avick, yes, I got a glimpse of yur photos," Brendan mumbled as I readied to go. "Luvly aren't they Bea," he said to her without looking at me. "Too bad, I didn't have the time to read yur clippings, I'll bet there's a few good ones amongst the lot and why not, shur yew're a great boy who traveled far and wide and at a tender age, yew learned a lot about life I'll say that about yew avick," he continued in mock determination.

"There's nothing very compelling or of any real world-shattering interest in this book, Brendan, no sex stories, no politics, no shootings, no bombings, nothing like that, in comparison to others, my life reads like a nursery rhyme."

A snide look crept into his face. He dashed into the bathroom and opened the door of the medicine cabinet. I spoke to Beatrice and opened the door. But in my mind's eye, something was askance. My intuition told me to stay. Brendan was contemplating his face as though it were a rare treasury of bone and gristle, standing on the tips of his two neat feet, peering long and hard into the tilted mirror, carefully and meticulously scrutinizing every crack and crevice of his well-battered nose, his small pouting mouth, his fat immobile face—a face that appeared as though it had been stuffed with a barrelful of overripe melons. Sporadically the small laser eyes roved far enough to take in my middle-of-the-living-room reflection. Clowning and taking the piss out of his friends and imaginary enemies was Brendan's only real link to the world of normality. It was his stage where he could be himself. A place where he could be home and far from the fears and the phobias that haunted him. Here he was conducting a never-ending game of coming to grips with his sexual madness. In his most vainglorious moments he genuinely believed that he was truly in possession of an androgynous beauty that could attract both males and females.

He picked up his electric razor and began to shave carefully, meticulously, running the razor up and down, back and forth, along the edges of his thick sideburns.

The razor was a gift that he had been given a week before for delivering a brilliant dissertation on the subjects of social ostracism, the inequities of American society and man's inhumanity to his fellow man.

The air was stagnant, soundless and eerie. I approached the bathroom and stood in the vestibule observing the shaver at play. I shook my head, "Tch," reached over, picked up the plug attached to the razor's cord and inserted it into a socket on the wall, "There now, Brendan," I said reassuringly. "Now you will get a better shave, a closer one, albeit one of a slightly noisier nature."

His face froze. His eyes blinked and winced. His jowls sagged. He reacted as though he had been doused with a saucerful of white hot vinegar. His face contracted with fury. His hands gripped the razor harder. He was on the verge of an apoplexy. Our two heads were side by side in the tilted mirror. Brendan quivered. He closed the mirrored door tight. My reflection disappeared.

In a violent fit he slammed the razor down hard onto the porcelain sink, sending its mechanical entrails all over the bathroom. Then he stormed out of the room and into the bedroom where he went into a paroxysm of shouting and swearing. *"Slan leat a gcailin"* [Good-bye, woman] I said to Beatrice and hastily departed.

On my way home I opened my book and discovered that the clippings and the photographs had been very much tampered with. The photos were very much out of sync with the stories. They had obviously been taken out, and later reinserted.

I hurried home to the Wilcox to sit and ponder and do some major personal inventory-taking. I arrived at a number of sobering-up conclusions about myself, Brendan Behan and our bizarre relationship.

Under the influence of intoxicants, Brendan had proven himself a master at revealing himself in obfuscated snippets. Nothing would have given him greater pleasure than to publicly come out of his closet and make a full declaration of his sexual proclivities. It would have been the triumphant moment of his life.

His small good nature and comedy were redolent of sickness and malice. I finally realized the true, stone cold, glittering opaqueness of Brendan Behan. He labored so desperately to carve for himself a Jack London image, simultaneously worrying himself into tatters that somehow, someday, his world-renowned reputation and stalwart fits of profane dialogue might be exposed.

I felt genuinely sorry for the tragic little buffoon with the gruff sardonic exterior, who labored so furtively to fool the world and to belie the lonely, frightened little wretch beneath the myth.

I soaked my aching body in a hot downpour of water and lay down to sleep the sleep of a fool. I masturbated my warm yellow seeds of wrath onto the blue and white legend inserted on the bed clothes: Hollywood Wilcox Hotel, Hollywood, California. Then sighed and fell off to sleep.

A short while later the predawn somnolence was shattered by the phone. I looked at my Baby Ben clock and discovered that it was just after five A.M.

I picked up the receiver no more than half an inch and dropped it back into its cradle. It rang again.

"Yes, who is it and what the fuck do you want?"

"Listen to this avick," a familiar gruff voice said, then in a profusion he prattled ahead. For a while it sounded as though he were reading from an old Boris Karloff film script. Brendan was reading newly inserted pieces from *Cork,* which included sketches pertaining to Forest Lawn Memorial Cemetery, credit cards, the Harlem Globetrotters, Bonnie Prince Charles, shots below the belt at Evelyn Waugh, fornications on tombstones, happy reunions on gallows, a hangman staggering "under the influence," a shooting episode, ashes blowing in a hero's face, and a few familiar blasts at the inevitable Irish priests and nuns. However, Brendan's stand on homosexuality and homosexuals had obviously softened. "Well me aul son, what do yew think of that?" he chirped, culminating his reading. I didn't answer.

Silence, then a cacophony of despairing mutterings came over the wire. "Jayzus holigan fuckin' Christ, am I surrounded by savages and—" I hung up. The deadly seriousness and the consistency of the man never ceased to amaze me. I went back to sleep. Again I was awakened.

"Sounds like a ton of fun, Bren," I said as I put the phone to my mouth. Then I hung up.

Half an hour later the phone rang again. This time Beatrice was on the wire. "Listen, Peter," she whispered in a confidential voice, "your man is in a very good mood this morning. When you come over for your breakfast be sure to bring your two books. I think he's up to autographing them for you this morning. The breakfast is on the table, your togs are here. See you in a few minutes. *Slan leat.*"

"I won't be able to come today, Bea."

"W-why P-Peter?"

"I'm shipping out."

"But shur there's nò ships in Hollywood."

"No, but there are in Wilmington."

"Wilmington?!"

"Wilmington, Bea . . . Wilmington, ask B., he knows where it is."

Half an hour later a knock came to my door. I opened up and found Brendan in the hall. He was nervously clutching a handful of manuscript. "P-Peter Arthurs, P-Peter, Peter, g-great b-boy, h-here, I have something luvly to show yew," he mumbled, pushing his way into my room.

Brendan sat down on the floor adjacent to my bed and read all of his latest insertions. Then he lapsed into a long litany about the inadequacies of his wife and how much he desperately wanted her to return to Ireland, alone. "She's fuckin' useless. Why won't she leave me be!"

"It's your life, B.," I said.

For the next few minutes he sat patting his manuscript as a blind man might pat a precious dog. Then in a burst of ebullience he told me of a great plan that he had conceived and was ready to put into operation.

First, he would, with great warmth, convey to Beatrice that he genuinely desired to adhere to her wishes and return to Dublin, via the train route from Los Angeles to New York. The second half of the journey would be made by Cunard ship to Cork, then on to Dublin by train.

Brendan's eyes were aglitter with mischief. "At the last minute, just before they're about to pick up the gangway, I'll conjure up some fuckin' excuse about having to meet some chaps from the press, then it's down the plank and up the dock. While yur woman is headin' the other way be water to the patch of witherin' shamrocks, I'll be headin' back this way be air, then its yew and me, me aul son, we'll get it up while the gettin' is still good and plentiful. Be the looks of things these savages out here are willin' to buy up any cuntin' thing that I trow on paper, wha! They're like sows grovelin' at a swill barrel." He rubbed his hands and stared me in the eye as though he was awaiting a crescendo of applause.

I looked at him with a long, hard look. "She's your wife, B., it's your life, your choice." His face dropped. His chin sank to his chest. Hysteria swept over him. He quickly departed.

Along about noon I received another call from Beatrice. "Brendan says you're to come at once, it's very urgent, two men are coming!"

"I can't, Bea, I'm packing to drive to Wilmington."

"But you can wait for a day or two, surely."

"Give Bren my regards."

"One of the men coming is yur man, Mason, James Mason."

"What has James Mason got to do with me? Or Brendan for that matter?"

"I don't know Peter, but Brendan will be terribly upset if you don't come, be a good boy and be here soon, won't you."

I went looking for my car then realized that I had left it in the Montecito lot.

"The men are here Peter," Beatrice said opening the door, "the tea will be ready soon."

The apartment was in a state of quietude, save for the intermittent hustle and bustle of rattling pots and pans.

Two men, one tall, dapper, dressed in a neatly creased gray pin-striped suit stood solemnly looking out the front window; the other, resplendent in typical California casual wear, sat on the settee.

Brendan sat in his favorite chair picking, wincing, snickering, and reading a rag.

The man in the pin-striped suit turned and eyed me in a slightly accusatory manner. A sneer was building on Brendan's face.

A glut of questions and answers flooded into my brain.

The two quiet men were from the Los Angeles Police Department. Detectives! Brendan had called the cops! On who? For what? Someone had stolen his three-quarter finished manuscripts! Who? Why? The dirty rotten son of a bitch, either hid or destroyed his only copy, then phoned the fuzz and blamed me!

Tension mounted. The opaque and puzzling silence bore on. Silence pervaded. Finally Brendan jumped to his feet, slammed down his rag, and said to the dapper gentleman, "My name's Behan. Brendan Behan. This is me wife Beatrice and this is Peter Arthurs. Now sir, what can I do for yew?"

"Ah yes," the sophisticated-looking man said in a distinct British accent, "I'm Hugh French and this is Tim O'Leary, a friend, a screenwriter. I'm here to represent James Mason and Albert Finney, two fine actors who are great admirers of yours Brendan, dear James is presently on the island of Catalina filming *Lolita* with Peter Sellers—"

"State yur business, sir," Brendan interjected crisply.

The suave Englishman flinched, and informed Brendan that Mason was chomping at the bit to play the part of Pat, the caretaker of the brothel where the action of *The Hostage* takes place. "Finney wants to portray the title role in the same film." Tim O'Leary, he was informed, would, with his O.K. and writing assistance, write the screenplay. The film, according to French, could be shot in Dublin, London, Hollywood or anywhere else that Brendan desired, and preferably in a place where it was most conducive to *his* tax-avoiding needs. "We'll save you all we can, Brendan," French assured him.

"Great," Brendan barked. "If there is anything that I can't stand, it's ladling out good hard-earned money to degenerates called tax collectors. Always a pleasure to beat the cunts at their own dirty game."

"Great man," French said, with enthusiasm.

"However there's a problem or two, I'm afraid," said Brendan as he made his way to the refrigerator. He extricated two bottles of Tuborg beer and a bottle of whiskey from its shelves, then set about pouring a percentage of the beer from each bottle onto the floor then spiking the beer with substantial amounts of whiskey and pushing it into the lapels of French's suit.

"Thank you Brendan," French said. "However I don't drink and neither does Tim." An apologetic chuckle followed the announcement.

Brendan forced the spiked bottles into the man's hand. "Go on, go on for jayzus sake, it will do youse a world of good. Shur didn't I enjoy two cases of the same concoction this morning before I sat down to do me work wha!" Brendan roared.

The contents from the beer bottle splattered all over the outstretched hands of the protesting man. "Go on, go on for fucksake," he reiterated, "divil a harm it will do yiz. It's merely a small one, a gentle toddy for the body." Brendan insisted. French again declined in his suave gentle manner and extricated a handkerchief from his pocket and wiped away the frothy substance from his clothing while Brendan barreled into a spiel on the bombing, pimping, terrorist and shooting incidents of his early youth in Ireland, England and France.

"Great man, Brendan," the flushed Englishman said, regaining his composure.

Brendan then gave a lecture on the immediate need for laws to imprison the pedophiles. "From what I've been told and I might add, I only get my information from the best of sources, but I hear the condition and the cowardly swine who indulge in these criminal acts are both rampant in England, whereas over here, these sheepish fuckin' Yanks, shur the bit of the other [homosexuality] seems to go down well with *them!* I always trow a bit of it into me plays when I'm writin' one of the cuntin' things. I only write the fuckin' things when I'm out of lolly."

The two men nodded in affirmation.

"Now about the wonderful *Hostage,*" French insisted, a hint of frustration evident in his voice.

"Oh no no no," Brendan sputtered while coughing up a wad of saliva and spitting it into his handkerchief, then carefully examining the fruit of his labor. "M-Mason is much too fuckin' bourgeoisee for the role of Pat. Pat is a very special sort of Irish gentleman. As for Finney . . . too teethy, much too teethy. If there is anything in this fuckin' jayzus world of the theater that I can't stand it's an actor who depends upon his teeth to portray a character," he said while clacking his teeth together and opening the door to let the men out.

(The three of us had, days previously, seen the film, *Saturday Night and Sunday Morning,* starring Albert Finney. Brendan had commented on Finney's "fine set of molars.")

French suddenly shifted the conversation to another topic: Winston Churchill. "Yes, yes, indeed Brendan," he sparkled, "he's like yourself, a great man, a great wit, a genius, a very charming fellow, a treasury of words. He has a bit of the Irish in him. Hs great-grandmother was Irish. I'm sure he'd be most flattered and delighted to meet you, he has a very charming collection of geegaws and trinkets that you'd adore . . ."

"He's a fuckin' aul greasy ballox and a warmonger," Brendan sharply interrupted. "If youse want to talk to me, call me in Europe. My address will be on the front page of every newspaper, just ask any postman or policeman." Brendan bellowed, pushing the men out. "They're a right lot of fuckin' chancers and chiselers," he said to me, turning his head and indicating the departing men, "they'd rub butter on a fat pig's ballox."

"Great man, pleasure," French said as he depressed the elevator button.

"Will yew cunt in out of that for fuck sake," Brendan roared at Beatrice who was in the hall bidding the men good-bye.

Beatrice returned to the living room. Brendan rushed after her. "Listen yew," he barked into her face, "what in cunt's name were yew standin' out there makin a fool out of yourself over those two fuckin' eegits." Then he moved to hit her as she flinched and ducked behind me. I put my hand up, stopped the brunt of his blow, held an uncompromising look and departed.

Approximately one hour later Beatrice called. "It's very urgent Peter, he wants you to do something for him right away."

"But I have a lot of things to do and a long drive tomorrow, also I have to find a way to get rid of the car. I need the money."

"Your tea is on the table," she said fretfully and hung up.

I drove to the Montecito. "Oh thank God you're here. Bless you." We sat at the table in morbid silence, save for the sporadic gulps of tea that were taken in by the three of us.

Three minutes went by. No one spoke. Five. Seven. Eight. Nine. Ten. Brendan was full of angst and growing angstier by the gulp.

Finally he looked at me. It was a lightning quick, reptilian blink of the eye.

Beatrice with cup to mouth caught sight of the blink. Quickly she lowered her cup, "Brendan wants you to do something for him," she said.

"He does . . . hmm . . . I understand you want me to do something for you, Bren, something very urgent. What is it?"

"Yes, yes, indeed I fuckinwell do," he said, his anger rising, his chest heaving, "I would like yew to convey to the one sitting beside yew that if it's all one and the fuckin' same to her arse, I'd like to go for me swim and to a picture show, but I'll be fucked if I'm gonna go to either of them without me bit of grub, first. Furthermore, yew can tell yur one that if she keeps skitterin' and footerin,' and trickin' and rootin' for the rest of the cuntin' day, it will be too fuckin' late. I'd like to get to the cinema to find out why the Japs lost the last world war before the slant-eyed cunts get the chance to start the next one. I don't consider mesself a war strategist by any fuckin' means or measures but even an aul eegit like me knows that it's more than a good possibility that the sneaky-looking fuckers will. Who knows, maby this fuckin' kip will be next? If that shower of poxy little punces don't do it, the fuckin' earthquakes will." Then he went back to drinking his tea.

The three of us sat in trancelike, benumbed, laborious silence, then cutting through the hiatus: "Beatrice, Brendan ardently desires to go for a swim and to see a picture show. The name of the show, I do not know, neither do I care. Now to get on with it Bea, Brendan would be fucked rather than go on an empty stomach, no fun in that wha! Furthermore, he wishes me to convey to you that further fuckology and trickology will slow up our chances of finding out why and how the Japs lost the last war. Furthermore Brendan feels that there is a strong possibility that the poxy-looking sons o' bitches might attack again. He feels that Hollywood might be the attack zone. The attack could come imminently. But if we are lucky, that is to say, if we get a move on and get our ballox in gear, if we are in a well-structured cinema when the attack comes . . . well, who gives a rat's diddy, wha! Bea, you get the picture, Roger, over and out.

"Tell Brendan that I'll put the tea on right away, Peter."

"Beatrice is about to put on the tea, B."

"Marvelous, marvelous, marvelous. Thanks be to the merciful and the accomodating jayzus on high, amen," Brendan said sighing and blessing himself.

"Amen, amen, Brendan," I joined in, blessing us both and sighing in unison.

Beatrice chuckled, beamed and readied for supper, "Will you tell Brendan it won't be long, Peter."

"It won't be long, Brendan."

We ate voraciously. "Will yew cum here avick," he said, beckoning me to follow him to the bedroom. Once more I refused to sodomize him. We donned our togs, "Let's get the fuck out of here," he bellowed. "This fuckin' kip is puttin' barnacles on me." We went to the pool.

Brendan went into another of his non sequiturs: A wicked attack on the perils of pedophilia and a vicious vilification of Harry Truman and his dropping of the A-bomb on Japan ensued.

Back upstairs we ate, then drove to a downtown cinema. I took my driving instructions from Brendan, who sat with road map in lap, pointing with hs finger. "Park the heap over there, son."

I parked the car behind the cinema, then marched up to the box-office and purchased three tickets. On the marquee, the words *Hiroshima Mon Amour* were emblazoned. The majority of the grim-faced patrons standing on queue were Japanese and Japanese-Americans.

Brendan quickly ferreted out those who were speaking in Japanese and went into another fiery condemnation of the "Savage and unnecessary bombing and slaughter of innocent people, the fuckin' piano player should have stuck to his piano playing and left the bombing to those who knows how and where to bomb."

Brendan told of his own bombing campaign in Liverpool and re-enacted the shooting incident at Glasnevin.

An usher led us to our seats. The movie started. Brendan continued his frothy attack on the, "piano players and pedophiles of America."

A well-spoken Japanese gentleman who was sitting in the front row turned to Brendan and informed him that he came to the cinema to see the film and not to be harassed by anyone, ". . . particularly by a person who was nowhere near the cities of Hiroshima or Nagasaki at the time of the bombing."

The man's sharp admonition upset the easily intimidated Brendan. Nevertheless, he beamed with delight in the profound knowledge that his celebrity had not gone unheralded. The usher came over and advised me that I would be asked to leave if I was not quiet.

I assured the intense youth that I would remain mute for the remainder of the show, then turned to Brendan and said, "Bren, I really want to see this historical documentation."

"Certainly avick, certainly, shur won't it be an education for yew. Something to talk about besides sex when yew go back on yur boat."

X

I sorely wanted to return to the sea but my decision to try my hand at acting was too overpowering.

The tenor of our friendship had changed. No longer was I Brendan's votary. Gone was the awe of yestermonth. Brendan was still the principle of Hollywood's greatest one-man treasure hunt. The news of his return from Mexico was well publicized. Word had spread that *I* was his business and publicity arranger. My phone rang incessantly. Propositions were made. Questions were asked. "Is it true that you are the real writer? Is Brendan dying? How sick is the great man?" Business luncheons were proposed.

Brendan foraged deeper into his celebrity. Articles heralding him as the most rowdy, rambunctious, roistering Irishman to come to Hollywood leaped from the shelves of the newsstands. Brendan rejoiced, but his main interests lay in the rehearing of shipboard arsehole banditry stories.

Again and again I asked Brendan to utilize his importance and introduce me to studio casting personnel. My requests were reciprocated with quick owllike blinks of his eyes and curls of the lip. "Certainly, avick, certainly, isn't that what friends are for, for helping one another, shur without yew, I'd be a nomad . . ." And such was the iconography of our lives.

In 1958, I had been locked up of my own volition in the psychiatric unit of the Staten Island Marine Hospital. Life had suddenly become too difficult to cope with. At the clinic, it was suggested to me that I

155

enroll in a dramatic arts class. The purpose was to bring me out of my shell and into the mainstream of American society, where I could meet, talk, and deal with women on a one-to-one basis. In 1959 I enrolled at Stella Adler's workshop in New York. I had informed Brendan of my previous schooling but never of the impetus behind it. Brendan's ego was too brittle. His dependence upon me was too great.

Brendan succeeded extravagantly in putting himself across as a true heterophiliac. His appeal to women was phenomenal. They saw him as a passionately unfeigned, supersensitive realist, ultra-vulnerable. His iconoclastic smirk encouraged the enthralled to believe that life is merely a temporary rendezvous.

Brendan was aware that his sexual myth was profoundly established in America. It was a source of legend as enormous as his characteristic sense of humor. He continued his unabashed dalliances with elegant and eloquent ladies whenever the opportunities presented themselves. He sulked and fumed when his pinchings were rebuffed and graciously accepted platitudes and ministrations when they weren't.

His presence was like magic. Actors revered him and his theatrical ingenuity with an incredulous awe. His hubbub of Montecito visitors grew. He was outgoing, charming, whimsical, amusing and iconoclastic. Each and every expectation was fulfilled. He delighted in talking about his revisions of *Cork*. His listeners were dazzled by his verbal facility.

The tumescence of his enormous sexual prowess and personal lechery stories and his purported insatiable need to seduce the wives of his own best friends was always at the center of his embellishments. Amongst the more emancipated, Brendan was snickered at. His yarns were regarded as heinous and small-boyish. But Brendan was so filled with his own satyriasis, he smashed ahead like a steamroller building steam.

Brendan was an inveterate nudist. One morning Brendan and I engaged one another in an unusually intensive question-and-answer conversation. Brendan typed and talked. His questions were coming like the staccato bursts of machine-gun fire. I labored hard to keep up with his volleys. Curious, I arose, stood up behind him, peered over his shoulder and read the contents of the page in progress. No correlation between what we were talking about and what he was working on was evident.

Suddenly, the lid of the machine went down hard. He charged out of the room and depressed the button for the elevator. Seconds later he was back in the room donning his socks. Then he went down for his dip. Minutes later he returned and sat on the settee naked, save for his dripping wet socks, spitting through his teeth at every object in the room.

I headed for the door. My departure was quickly curtailed by a cacophony of roars. "I don't recall giving *yew* permission to leave," he bellowed. I sat down in the kitchen, mute. Brendan returned to his typewriter and picked up the conversation on the exact thread where we had left off, half an hour before.

The interview continued with revved-up intensity.

One morning after he had made a desperate grab for my genitalia, I rejoined, "I'm sorry B., but at present I am studying the book of Christian Science, the knowledge and science of the mind as opposed to the handbook of shipboard buggery and masturbation better known as hitting the flying fish between the eyes or flipping one over the wrist. Jerk off, B., masturbation is therapeutic and good for the introspection; as for myself, *I'm* trading in the pussy market this week."

Brendan grinned with wounded eyes, then ran to jot down my idiom "What did yew say they called that stuff avick?"

"What stuff, B.? Who? When?"

His eyes blazed. He put down his pen and paper. "We'll go for a drive and maybe a dip," he announced.

We drove to a seafront restaurant. Brendan took photos of Beatrice and me. Beatrice took pictures of Brendan and me, I took photos of the Behans.

In the restaurant, the imperial-voiced Napoleonic figure of Brendan moved and came on strong of personality and deliverance, like a man who believed that the world moved silently in his shadow.

"Lobster and caviar should be taken with white wine, shellfish and crab should be eaten with burgundy wines. I mean to say, I very much consider mesself a city dweller, no, no, I don't care to write in the country, I prefer to stay in the steel-and-mortar jungles, that's where me raw meat is, my material, what's more, I can tell yew that all this chat about the birds and the bees and the quietude of the country is pure bullshite. I for one never got any intellectual stimulation out of talking to those pesky little cunts. Me mother once worked as a maid in a house where Yeats used to come to eat. He'd eat anything that wouldn't eat him first, says she. That is anything with the exception of the parsnips. No, he couldn't do with the parsnips; he was forced to turn his nose up at them. 'Madam,' says he to her, 'what class of a peculiar pudding have you concocted today?' Do you know what was in the puddin. Well I'll tell yew . . . parsnips . . . then he proceeded to put sugar in his soup and salt in his coffee.

"No, the art of good conversation is a thing that I have always truly cherished. However, I am sad to say that only in America is it a murdered cause. Murdered by American lunatics." Then he sat down beside Beatrice and me and went into a sullen mood.

"I'm goin' for a dip," he suddenly announced.

"Oh no, no, no," Beatrice shrieked. "P-Peter don't let him go, will you not, didn't the manager say that the water is infested with sharks? Tell him Peter, tell him."

"Sharks or no sharks, um takin' me dip," Brendan snapped.

"Oh no no no Peter, don't let him."

"Now, now Bea, if he wants to go for a dip it's his prerogative. Bren has enough smarts to stay clear of the weeds, the weeds is where yur man said that the whores hang out. Here, Bren," I said handing him my steak knife, "put that between yur teeth when you go in, that will chase the fuck-pigs away. Besides I'm gonna keep nix for you, if I see one of the big cunts coming, I'll give you a shout, in the meantime I'm gonna finish me dinner, cheers."

The saga of the swim and the sharks ended on that note. He sat and sulked.

Next to a good boy-buggery story the type of yarn that boosted Brendan's sagging spirits was a rollicking good funereal story with all of its sanctimonious thrills and dirgeatorical frills.

Home once more, "I'd sure appreciate it if you would invite Carol Poland to your house for dinner, Bea," I said. My ulterior motive was to hopefully get better acquainted with the voluptuous lady. For years, on ships of the SIU banner I had fantasized over the beautiful girl. Now with Brendan's cooperation I could make a profound impression on her.

Brendan was on the threshold of nixing my request when I informed him of the reasons for her dismissal from the SIU. His eyes glistened. "B-bring the poor g-girl over r-right away," he demanded. "Maybe she can spin a yarn or two that will put some blood into the other c-cuntin' thing [*Cork*]."

I phoned Carol and invited her to Brendan's house. We spent the next three hours talking and sipping tea. However, much to Brendan's chagrin, the lady would not divulge her past.

"F-Frank S-Sinatra is a great friend of ours," Brendan attempted. "He called today and asked me to do a bit of writing and some casting for his next film."

"Oh I hope you will let me read," Carol said, bubbling with enthusiasm.

"C-certainly, c-certainly, and why not." I tried to talk to her of our old days in the Brooklyn-based headquarters of the SIU, but again the lady showed no interest in the subject.

Finally Brendan arose and extended his hand to the lady. I drove her home, then returned to the Montecito where I found the Behans both in a dour, sullen mood.

Brendan was in his living room chair. Beatrice sat in the kitchen. "What's all the ecstasy about?" I asked. Silence. "Maybe I should go home."

"Y-you didn't tell B-Brendan why you pissed in the blackberries," she moaned putting down her cup.

Brendan was a lover of my childhood stories. On a variety of occasions I started and deliberately halted one such story, one that very much interested and excited him. It was a true story about one of the more titillating things I did in the slum ethic of my youth to raise money to keep my drunken father in his liquid spirits.

Collecting wild blackberries from the branches of public bushes in the wilds of Bellurgan and Crossmaglen, two of Dundalk's rural districts, then selling them to a man named Hutchinson, became a seasonal chore. However, to boost the amount of recompense which I received for my pickings, I devised a method of adding an additional undetectable weight to the bucket. Split seconds prior to it being weighed, then dumped and reweighed, I would draw my overcoat over the top of the bucket and piss into it. The money was doled out commensurate to the final weight. The purpose of not urinating into the bucket at any other time prior to seconds before I reached the head of the queues was because the liquid would descend to the bottom and become detectable. The bucket's total contents would then be invariably returned to me.

The blackberries were ultimately stored in huge wooden barrels and kept in a warehouse for shipment to England.

One day "Hutchie" arrived at his warehouse and discovered that the bottom of one of his barrels was leaking. He opened the lid and inhaled a God-awful odor that quickly cleared his sinuses. My jig was up. I had been drinking an overly excessive amount of water prior to getting on queue to sell my wild blackberries. Unwisely, I had passed the patent on to all of the kids in the neighborhood. The upshot was disastrous.

I told and retold the story to Brendan, always cutting it short just as I had urinated into the bucket. The specific reason for the act and the conclusion of the story remained a mystery to him. Brendan tried just about every scheme and ploy in his copious book of schemology to get me to unveil the crux and the culmination of the yarn. Now at that time it might have caused the end of our friendship, they begged me to unleash the conclusion to the blackberry bucket saga. Under no circumstances would I ever.

Later that evening Andrew Pollette, a movie producer, arrived and asked Brendan to write a comedy film script on the Irish Rebellion.

"C-certainly avick, b-but how much would be in it for me?" Brendan asked petulantly.

Pollette assured Brendan that he would receive, "a good pay-check" for his services rendered, then departed. Brendan went back to doing what he liked to do when the strain of sobriety was too overwhelming to cope with: perusing and discarding newly purchased hardcover books.

He seldom read past the thirtieth or fortieth page of a book, then flung it into a waste disposal. "Another fuckin' aul Yank hacker with a childish propensity for violence." In the course of a single evening,

1949 at age 15   1950

1951

Somewhere in the Indian Ocean
enroute to Djakarta, Java, 1953

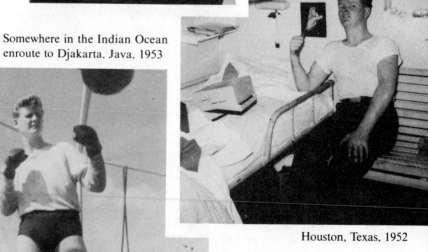

Houston, Texas, 1952

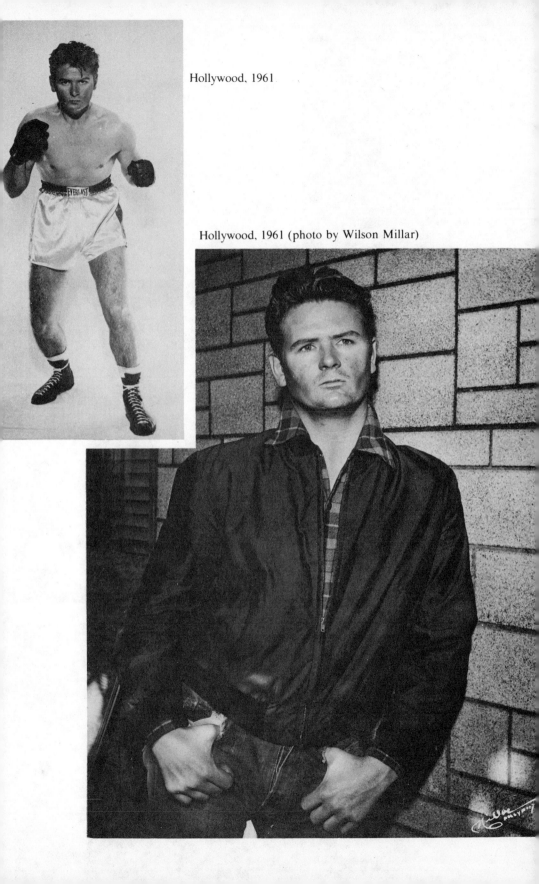

Hollywood, 1961

Hollywood, 1961 (photo by Wilson Millar)

Arthur Miller and I chatting in the hall between the Chelsea Hotel and the El Quijote.

The celebration for the Broadway opening of *The Hostage* at Tim Costello's Steak House, 1960. (*Left to right*) Celia, Brendan's sister-in-law and real-life model for Theresa of *The Hostage*; a beaming Brendan; famed publican, Tim Costello; an unusually happy Beatrice; and Art Buchwald. (Courtesy of the New York *Daily News*)

Arthur C. Clarke and I in a Chelsea bookstore.

Brendan interrupting a performance of *The Hostage*: "Yiz are makin' a muck of me play."
(Courtesy of the New York *Daily News*)

Beatrice and Brendan having "a
quiet pint" during more
propitious times.

Just before we departed, a somewhat guilt-ridden looking Brendan turned to the officer, thanked him and said, "I'll have you to know that I was treated a damn sight better than I was in most other places that I temporarily lodged at." (Courtesy of UPI)

A well Band-Aided Brendan and I being interviewed by the media seconds after he was sprung from his Hollywood cell. (Courtesy of UPI)

The rumpled and crumpled Brendan, myself and Beatrice outside the police station. (Courtesy of UPI)

Brendan, Beatrice and I outside a
southern California seaside
restaurant in 1961.

The Montecito Hotel swimming pool.

The Hollywood Wilcox Hotel.

Hughes 24-hour supermarket where Beatrice went for her early morning supplies.

Brendan, Beatrice and I in Mexico, 1961.

Brendan's last supper in Los Angeles at the Pacific Union Railroad Station, 1961. *(Left to right)* Beatrice, TV director, Michael O'Heirleighy, Brendan, Laurie Shields, Arthur Shields, myself and "The Man," police officer Kenny Vils.

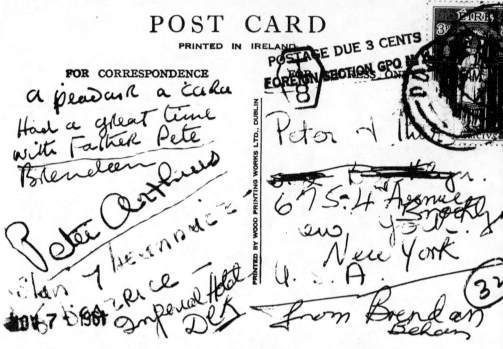

POST CARD

PRINTED IN IRELAND

The postcard I received from Brendan in the fall of 1961, signed by my father and Beatrice.

What I believe to be his final portrait in America.

The last picture of Brendan in America, July 3, 1964. Beatrice and Rae Jeffs are to his right and left, respectively. (Courtesy of Wide World Photos)

Brendan doing what he did so well, holding court for the media at a London airport after his arrival from Paris in 1962. (Courtesy of Wide World Photos)

Brendan's funeral, Dublin, March 22, 1964. (Courtesy of Wide World Photos)

Brendan discarded up to ten or fifteen newly purchased hardcover books. In his mind's eye, the books' authors were mere graduate students, clerks and dilettantes of the "writing game" and writing nothing more compelling than their own dreams, hopes and fantasies.

Brendan never wrote letters. He was an inveterate postcard writer—up to a dozen cards per evening. Usually he signed each card twice. Once in English. Once in Gaelic. The cards that he selected were usually the bawdiest and gaudiest on display.

At the end of each day I was handed my usual handful of cards. "Here avick, will yew stuff these little fuckers in the tin can on the corner. This way the culshies will know where we are, in the event that the catafalque country starts to sink into the Atlantic Ocean and they need someone to trow them a life ring."

One night I said to him, "Brendan, I never see you writing letters to anyone; any particular reason?"

"Well, son, it's like this, when I'm gone there'll be one or two opportunists about, looking to break into print by writin' about me. Not that I mind. But I'd like to think that the whores are out there pickin' and shovelin' for their material just like I had to do."

Brendan's remark was still jarring about in my brain as I counted ten postcards. I decided to keep the cards for posterity, then stuffed them into my pocket. I hastened home to the Wilcox. On the corner of Wilcox and Selma I underwent a change of mind and dropped the now historic messages into a mailbox. My Christian Brothers-inculcated code of ethics thus afforded posterity a smidgen of good luck.

My interest in staying close to the Behans was waning. Brendan's phone calls were coming in over the Wilcox switchboard like hailstones on a galvanized roof.

"Is that yurself avick, I was just wonderin' if yew'd like to cum over for a splash in me backyard puddle." Or . . . "Ah, there yew are me aul skilleara. I was just saying to me missus maybe the boy would like to go for an aul punch-up at the Y. Shur wasn't it there that I had the great fortune to meet yew." Or . . . "Listen me aul son, but I just called to find out if yew'd like to go for a bit of a ramble on the boulevard and get a gander at the fruitcakes on parade, wha?" Or even . . . "Ah me sound man." Then in a clandestine voice, "Listen avick, but I think I know where we can get for ourselves a couple of Judies (whores) and a rub of the relic."

I had had enough of Brendan Behan and his Mickey Mouse malice.

"Listen B., I really appreciate your concern but you see, I'm a very simple and basic sort of a fellow, I'll say good-bye and good luck to you and above all, good luck to *Cork. Slan leat.*"

Very late one night I received a call from Beatrice, "Oh, listen Peter, Brendan said to tell you that a friend of his from Dublin, a chap called Eddie, is coming tomorrow to take us on a big outing to Knott's Berry Farm. He says it's lovely there . . ."

Then Brendan's voice came over the wire, "Ah, there yew are me aul china, listen, this chap who is the son of a Dublin publican friend of ours is comin' tomorrow. We'll have a smashin' time of it, cum in the mornin' for yur bit of grub, shur there's loads and lashings and full and plenty, isn't there B., wha? Well avick, I was thinking, while the other one is out havin' her communion or whatever she does have so early of a Sunday mornin', yew and I can be havin' our swim and the aul chat . . ."

I hung up the phone.

Minutes later I looked out my window and saw the Behans fidgeting with my car's windows. I watched for a while then went down to the corner to get a closer look.

Brendan's Mexican straw hat was perched incongruously on his head. Outfitted with sunglasses and a stick in hand, he was poking through the rear window of my locked car and desperately attempting to fish some articles from the backseat. I peered around the corner, then made my presence known. Upon seeing me he charged up Wilcox Avenue as though the car were about to explode. Beatrice remained.

"Yes, is there anything that I can do for you Bea?" I asked amiably.

"Oh yes Peter, Brendan wanted to get his things out of your car."

"Yes, of course Bea, I'll open the door for you," I said extricating my keys from my pocket, opening the door and pushing the seat forward. Brendan watched from afar while he picked his nose and stood with legs crossed.

A month-old compilation of togs, towels, camera, combs, socks, shoes and other personal items were scooped into her handbag. "*Slan leat a peadair* [Good-bye, Peter]," she said as she joined her frightened husband.

"*Slan leat anois a gailin* [Good-bye girl] and give Brendan my fondest."

The two figures made their way north on Wilcox. I went home.

Approximately one hour later I received a call from Beatrice, "Brendan says you're to come at once, it's very urgent, you will come, won't you Peter? Your supper is getting cold."

I drove to the Montecito, where I found Brendan sitting in his sartorial chair like the proverbial prince of despair, picking his nostrils and stuffing the matter into the measureless maw of his cavernous navel.

On the floor beside him was an opened national magazine with a full-spread colorful caricature of Brendan. It depicted him as a glassy-eyed, overstuffed leprechaun with a bulbous nose, a wreath of shamrocks around his neck, a huge bottle of whiskey held tight to his breast, a gold belt studded with diamonds around his waist, and a crown of jewels on his head.

An adjacent story spoke of him as a schemy buffoon, a flash in the pan as a dramatist and a sad little man who was riding for a big fall. I laughed aloud as I read and reread the wicked attack. We drove off.

At Knott's Berry Farm, in a photo gallery, I pointed out to him a blown-up photo of an American folk hero named Johnny Behan. In a fit of rage he tried to rip the photo from the wall. Then, to bolster his spirits we sat down on a bench on either side of a huge, wooden Indian maiden with a pair of enormous breasts. A passing photographer snapped our picture. Brendan fondled, sucked and peered around the huge bust for the benefit of the photographer. Then he became upset when he saw what I was doing. I was doing the same thing to the lady's left bust that he was doing to her right.

Throughout the afternoon I took several photos of the Behans. Finally, "No no no, no more pictures," Brendan shouted. Beatrice in a fit of hysteria ran up to me, jammed her fingers into the lens of my camera and said "Please Peter, no more photos, Brendan doesn't want you to take any more photos, for God's sake put the camera away."

Later that evening we were invited to the Gay Nineties Bar for dinner and drinks. Brendan was a sensation as usual, surrounded by a bevy of beautiful scantily clad waitresses. He sang, danced and talked tall and tough. Oscar Wilde and his sexual preference was his theme. "I mean to say, who cares what people do with their sex lives? Children under the age of fourteen excluded naturally. Shur isn't it a natural class of a thing for matured people to do, isn't it a known fact that sailors on ships, Norwegian ships in particular, have the occasional bit of a go at one another . . . there's Peter, there, he's a chap who went to sea on Norwegian ships and at an early age, he'll tell yew, go ahead son . . ."

"Gee, Brendan, I'm sorry," I said in pure confusion, "but you must be mistaking me for someone else, I never told you anything of the kind, although I vividly recall in detail my telling you of my years on Norwegian ships and all of the stories of fights, explosions, fires and whorehouse anecdotes!"

He went into a paroxysm of stutters and stammers. Then he charged into an adjacent club, called the Roaring Twenties, where he sat down and gave the impression of a man in the hibernaculum of his dotage.

Later we drove to the famous twenty-four-hour Hollywood Supermarket, a wee-hour-of-the-morning hangout for starlets, body builders and others who live in the hopes of getting picked up by love-starved "in" people. Invaluable casting tidbits pertaining to upcoming movies and TV series are exchanged for services rendered. It is also a congregating depot for the nouveau-riche who flaunt their external symbols of success. Brendan excelled in taunting this particular stratum.

Brendan had a very sharp eye for eccentric faces and backgrounds and for new ears. His one-liners abounded.

"I fear God, not to mention the scorn of womanhood.

"They say that to have a play of your own produced on Broadway is an honor worthy of the highest of accolades. May I say that I, for one, am happy to have savored such a bestowal. Me play *The Hostage* was recently produced in that Big Apple. I made three thousand dollars per week. Not bad for a workin'-class writer!"

Hordes of voluptuous young ladies flocked to him and in return were warmly caressed by his arm around their waists. "Ah, me darlin' daughter. Me sweet child of love." He pinched their breasts and goosed them, back and front.

Suddenly he spotted an old, haggard-looking black lady who was slumped against a fast-food counter; he then charged over and immediately went to work, digging deep into her background. The old woman looked wizened and tired of life. Brendan carefully scrutinized her broad black features and frizzly hair. She appeared traditionally negroid of feature and voice. She sported a grin equally as gap-toothed as Brendan's. Brendan let loose a bombardment of questions, until such time as each and every speck of knowledge pertaining to her ancestral background was sucked from her brain.

Finally he struck gold. Much to my surprise, the old woman had one-sixteenth American Indian in her blood. He beamed with triumphant delight, then quickly departed and rejoined the younger coterie. I charged over to him and tugged on his sleeve, "Listen Bren, but I wouldn't be surprised if that old lady is starving half to death; she's definitely up against the elements."

Brendan eyed me with disdain, excused himself, ran back to the counter, ordered a plateful of french fries and threw them down in front of the sparrow-looking figure. "Here 'yar granny, get them into your aul guts and may yew be the mother of the first black and red bishop."

The woman eyed the plate's greasy contents, then pushed it across the counter with a sigh and a mutter.

His eyes blazed. "Will we c-cunt off out of it."

We returned to the car. I turned over the engine. "Excuse me, Bren," I said, "but there is something that I very much have to do." I got out and walked over to the woman. I looked at her several times, moved my jaws, bent over, smiled into her face, received a wan smile in return, extricated a few napkins from a container, moved my mouth again, waved my hand, returned to the car, shot Brendan a very enigmatic look and drove away at a fast speed.

The strain of sobriety was once again playing holy havoc with his nerves. A look of extreme perplexity crept into his face.

"W-what d-did s-she say avick, w-what d-did the aul cunt want?"

"What did he say, B. . . . hmmm . . . what did the aul transvestite want?" Slowly I looked into the rearview mirror at Beatrice, then back to Brendan. "Hmm . . . what was his game . . . hmm . . ." My voice was barely audible.

In a fiery little huff Brendan climbed out of the car when we got to the hotel, muttered a few oaths, then charged up the hill from the parking lot and disappeared. Just before he stepped into the lobby he stopped, looked back at the car, muttered and spat through his teeth. I genuinely did not expect to ever see him again. Neither did I care.

June 20. Late in the evening Beatrice phoned. "It's very urgent Peter; Brendan wants you to come at once."

I found the Behan apartment in a complete state of flux. Suitcases, shopping bags and brown paper bags that were chock-full of clothes, books, Mexican pottery and other paraphernalia were lying all over the floor. "Your supper will be ready in a minute," she said dolefully. Brendan was in a complete tizzy, tearing around in his nakedness and muttering, "Who do these big cabbage-headed fuck faces think that they are." On a few occasions I asked either of the Behans to fill me in on what was going on, all to no avail.

A glut of questions and answers ricocheted through my mind. First and foremost—what *was* going on!? Had the Behans finally decided to call it a day? Brendan's clothing was still in the closet. Beatrice's was packed. She was leaving! He was staying! He wanted me to drive her to the airport! The train station? Wherever.

I went to the bathroom and pissed. At once Brendan came bursting in and grabbed hold of my cock. My hot piss splattered all over his hand, the walls and the floor. "Listen avick," he said clandestinely, "just keep in mind what I told yew the other day. I'm only goin' as far as the Big Apple with this one, then it's right back here, so yew hold on now, yew hear."

I flushed the toilet and watched him in the mirror as he charged around the rooms. As usual, his arms and hands were buzzing and gesticulating like a broken windmill. His limbs looked tinier and frailer than ever before. They seemed to protrude at an unmerciful angle without vestige of grace or rhythm. His leonine head looked so enormous and totally out of proportion with the rest of his body, I wondered why he did not topple over onto the rug. His outstanding pot belly was so protruding it made him appear even more gnomish than he really was. Puttering about in his birthday suit, while inserting the index finger of one hand into his huge gaping belly button and the other index finger into his rectum, Brendan looked like a pile of uneven, well worn tires searching for old alignment and a retreading device.

Even when he tried to be impeccably dressed, Brendan still looked like a mobile rummage sale.

A small, bemused smile flickered in and out of his face. It was that old familiar "Here look at me now, shur no matter what I've said or done, I'm not really a bad aul whore after all, am I" type of smile. The familiar little hint of self-doubt again in strict evidence.

In good physical trim Brendan could never have weighed more than one hundred and fifteen pounds. He was usually photographed when in a state of creeping intoxication and in the commission of disturbing the peace. In so doing he gave the universal impression of being massive of stature. His bloated face embellished his bigger-than-life image. His overall appearance was a poorly composed mismatching of uneven bits and pieces. The lower half of his body looked more disproportionate and truncated than before.

My intuition forewarned me that he was up to some evilry. His slitty eyes were aflutter with mischief. The corners of his mouth twitched. He appeared dizzy and on the verge of toppling over, but he spirited ahead. Suddenly he stopped, crossed one leg over the other, dug a finger deep into a nostril, grimaced, came up with a wad of snot, held it up to the amber glow of the light, turned it, carefully scrutinized it, "D-d-don't yew agree, *BEAAATRICE,*" he shouted to his wife, who was in the bathroom, "d-don't yew agree that the fuckin' aul white-headed c-cow, the one that we met at K-Kovacs', the one with the head of cauliflower on top of her head, is a—"

I bolted up out of the settee, charged across the room and forced him into the dressing room beside the bathroom, without ever touching him.

"B-be the same token now, but she must be a very lovely girl all the same," he said, lowering his voice an octave.

Suddenly he was on the phone to Ernie Kovacs.

"Me wife felt that it would be a good idea to throw a goin' away party in me honor tomorrow at the Pacific Railroad Station, she'd like you to cum avick."

Minutes later he was compiling a list of Hollywood names to be invited to the party.

"Why don't you invite Lawrence Tierney," I said.

"Listen avick, just in case our paths never again cross, I'd like yew to know that if there is anything in this world next to a drunk that I can't stand, it's a loud-mouthed drunk!"

"How about inviting Maureen O'Hara?"

"Maureen O' who?"

"Maureen O'Hara."

"Never heard of her."

Brendan was back on the phone chatting with Groucho Marx and a host of others he had met in Kovacs' house.

"I'll bid you adieu," I said rising to leave.

"Oh you mustn't go yet, Peter, I want you to help with the packing, also B. wants to talk to you," Beatrice shouted. "There is a few things that he wants you to have. Sit yourself down!!"

Brendan autographed a sketch that had been made of him at the Gay Nineties and gave it to me along with two crisp one-hundred dollar bills, "Here avick, take this, yew'll be needing some getaway money after I'm gone."

"What about the jewelry," Beatrice said.

"Oh yes," Brendan said, pointing to the array of frayed jewelry that adorned the coffee table. It was the jewelry that he had purchased in Tijuana, "Go on avick, pick over it and take what yew want, take the whole cuntin' lot. We bought it for someone else, but we decided to give it to yew, didn't we Beatrice!"

I picked up a handful of watches and looked at their faces.

"But if I use these watches, Bren, I will become even more confused than I already am, here take a look, each face has a different time on it," I said showing him the confusion of frayed tinsel.

"What about the rest of it," he said with a wan smile.

"But I can't wear brooches or necklaces, Bren, I'm not the type."

With one fast sweep of my hand I pushed the lot into the garbage can. "There Bren, now we have that piece of insignificance resolved." I walked to the door.

"Oh you will be here to drive us to the station tomorrow at twelve won't you like a good boy," Beatrice exclaimed.

I departed without answering, then drove to the Wilcox.

"There's an urgent message here for you, Peter," John the receptionist, said. "It's from your pal Brendan." I phoned immediately.

"Listen avick, but where did yew say in the cauliflower country that yur man's people cum from!?"

"Whose people? What man?"

"The other greasy ballox."

"Which greasy ballox?"

"The fuckin' aul ballox that yew good-naturedly but foolishly gave up your chair to on the plane."

Suddenly it dawned on me who he was talking about.

Sometime during the month of September in 1960, I had flown from Mexico City to Los Angeles to join the supership S.T. *Erna Elizabeth.* Just as the plane was about to take off, the captain approached me and asked me to give up my seat in the rear of the plane to accommodate "a gentleman." After the plane was airborne the gentleman approached me and thanked me for forfeiting my seat. Upon hearing my Irish brogue the gentleman sat down beside me and asked me to translate some words into Gaelic. He told me of his heritage.

He was Pat Brown, the governor of the state of California.

"Limerick, Brendan, I think they're from Limerick. See you."

"Hold on, avick, there's a luvly woman who wants to tell yew something."

"Brendan wants you to drive us to the station," Beatrice pleaded, "Please be here at twelve."

A couple of days later a very wickedly worded article savagely condemning the conditions of the Los Angeles youth reformatories appeared in one of the local rags. The article was an open, indignant letter to Pat Brown.

Its author was Brendan Behan.

Wednesday, June 21, eleven A.M. The phone rang. "Peter, Brendan wants you to come at once."

The pandemonium of the night before was still in full bloom. Brendan careened around the apartment biting the paint and the wallpaper from the door frames, paintings and the walls. "The big fuck-faced cunts, the dirty cunt-faced fucks," he shouted as he chewed, spat, snorted and farted.

Clearly he did not want to leave Hollywood.

Beatrice was shaking like a leaf. Brendan was now into his fifteenth day on the dry. The train journey to New York would take up to four days. "But I know that as soon as the train pulls out of Los Angeles, he'll go back on the malts," she lamented.

"Cancel the train," I said. "Take a plane."

"Oh I can't fly, Peter, the claustrophobia is so nerve-wracking; it's O.K. for Brendan, he just gets drunk and falls asleep!"

"Stand up to him, Bea, fight back, here let me show you how to put across a few jabs and hooks," I said picking up her hands and feigning a few punches. We shadow-boxed for a few seconds. Hysteria seeped into her face. I turned and found Brendan standing in the hall with his legs crossed, picking, chewing and snickering. "What does Lawrence Tierney do for a living?" he suddenly snapped.

"He's an ex-movie star."

"Get him on the phone, I'll get him a job before I leave."

I phoned Kim Novak, whose number I had just gotten from Joe Finnegan. I received no answer.

"Get *me* a job before you leave, B."

"Listen yew, let's get one thing understood before I leave this kip, under no circumstances do I want yew to go around these studios mentioning my name when I'm gone, do yew hear?"

"If you want me to drive you to the station I suggest that you put your shirt on your back, your pants on your ballox, your shoes on your feet and get the show on the road!" I sharply reciprocated.

"Root me out a suit and me Mexican paisley tie," he ordered his wife. In the lobby we were met by Pennie Rua, who gave us both a pair of topaz cufflinks.

I packed Beatrice's bountiful purchases into the backseat, then started for the station. For approximately fifteen minutes, Brendan sat speechless. Beatrice dozed beside her bags. Brendan reached over and turned on the volume control button of the radio. No sound. Suddenly it dawned upon him that the radio was not functioning. A scowl seeped into his wattled countenance.

Brendan rattled off a number of his old anti-Cavan folk jokes, let go a few below-the-belt shots at the "inefficiencies of the Dundalk branch of the IRA," then launched an attack against the virtues and the talents of my favorite movie star. My right foot hit the brakes, the car skidded, careened, bounced and made a few scorched impressions on the freeway before coming to a sudden halt.

Pottery, books, chinaware, maps and other colorful brochures and paraphernalia went flying all over the back seat. Beatrice was flung halfway over the back of the seat. Brendan was plastered to the dashboard.

Suddenly I heard a police siren. I looked in the rearview mirror and discovered that I was being followed. I hit the gas pedal hard and tried to outrun the law. Brendan crossed his legs and beamed with brattish delight.

"Don't overly concern yourself, Bren, I have just the antidote to cool the heels of this shiny hillbilly," I said reaching into my breast pocket and extricating a small white card that was given to me by Kenny Vils. One side of the card bore the legend, "Los Angeles Police Department." In pen and ink on the other side was "Thanks for the favor, see you in the shop. Sig: Kenny Vils."

The motorcycle barracuda pulled me over, gave my car a look of sheer disgust then read and reread both sides of the card. "I'm in a hurry to meet your colleague," I said.

"Yes, sir," the officer said crisply, "come on I'll give you an escort." The policeman gave us a special courtesy escort all the way into Union Station. "Park your cycle and drop in for a bite and a drink," I said to the man of the law. "My colleague here has an affinity for cops."

In the main dining room of the station we were met by Vils, Arthur and Laurie Shields, TV director Michael O'Herlihy and a cadre of newsmen. The media bombarded Brendan with questions that ranged from the upheavals of African politics, to the age-old questions: "Brendan, do you think that the Arabs and the Jews will ever settle their differences, and what is your opinion about the possibility of the Irish Catholics and the Protestants getting together?" Next he was asked to comment about his liver.

Brendan banged his fist on the table and said, "What liver, I have no liver, it's as hard as that. My intestines feel as if they've been washed with sulphuric acid." To another newsman he said, "I'm only going away to avoid the earthquake season. I'll be back in September that is providin' this kip is still here of course."

Then he went on to denounce the Los Angeles Police as being like all other cops, "a wee bit screwy." We proceeded to the platform.

The train that he was scheduled to leave on bore the legend, "Placid Waters." On the platform Brendan was given a cup and saucer and asked to pose for the photographers, but when one of the more serious-minded newsmen felt that his answers lacked news-making substance, a plot was quickly hatched. The scenario was verbally written. Action!!

A reporter from KTTV is the director. The train moves out. Brendan discovers that his manuscript of *Cork* is missing. The Behans go into a speechless frenzy. Brendan blames Beatrice. It is suddenly discovered that I am in possession of the manuscript, the only copy in existence. The Placid Waters picks up tempo with speed. I run after the train. The cameraman is on my heels. My hand is reaching out to Brendan's hand. Beatrice holds on to her husband's back. The action is intense. The manuscript is mere inches from the grip of its worried author. I quicken my pace and the script is saved. An expression of gratitude sweeps over the faces of the Behans. The train moves on and dissipates into a cloud of smog. I give my address to the newsman and inform him that I would like a copy of the film to give to my theatrical agent. Later that evening the Los Angeles *Herald* and *Express* tells the story of the going-away blowout.

"BEHAN (HIC) OFF TO EIRE." Wally Burke announces, "Ireland must be heaven 'cuz Brendan Behan comes from there."

Brendan reciprocated by saying "I love Los Angeles and its people, including the Hollywood stars. The film community was very kind and hospitable to me."

In my room in the Wilcox I lie down on my bed. Waves of depression, uncertainty and insecurity sweep over me. I feel like an umbilical cord without a baby. I phone Kenny Vils and tell him that I want to become an actor. "Can you get me an agent, Kenny?" Kenny makes an appointment, calls me back and instructs me to go to the offices of a friend, an agent, a man who once made movies in Ireland and Scotland with Alfred Hitchcock.

"Do you have any experience? Any footage? Showcase?"

"Yes, I most certainly do, Sir." I inform the prospective agent of the KTTV film footage, taken at Union Station. "It was aired last night on television."

"Ah, wonderful. Go home and wait. We will call you."

"Thanks a mil, this is the opportunity that I've waited for all of my life!" I sit and wait.

A few days later I moved into a small studio apartment on the corner of Olive and Sunset Boulevard. Mrs. Arney, my landlady, extended the courtesy of putting her private phone at my disposal. I wired the number to the Algonquin Hotel on Forty-fourth Street in New York, where the Behans would be staying.

On June 24, by way of an introduction from David Greggory, I gained access to Columbia Studios and met a horde of stars.

As I stood there on the *The Notorious Landlady* lot, looking into the cat's eyes of the beautiful girl of my fantasies, panic, hopeless insecurity, and fear assailed me like a school of piranhas. My throat dried up. I practically swallowed my tongue. My knees buckled.

"My name's P-Peter A-A-Arthurs . . . I'm Brendan Behan's . . ."

The great lady, sensing my misery, extended her hand, shot it out and prevented me from toppling to the floor. "H-hope we meet again sometime Miss N-Novak-k . . ." I staggered to a door at the other end of the lot. The movie star stood waving as I quickened my retreat.

Sunday, July 2. Mrs. Arney awakened me. "You better come to the phone right away," she said with great concern. "The caller refuses to give his name, but he seems to be in terrible distress!" I dressed quickly and crossed the courtyard to her apartment. "Hello."

"P-P-Peter A-A-Arthurs. Is it yurself avick!?"

"Yes."

"P-P-Peter its H-H-Hem . . . H-H-Hem . . . s-shot h-himself, P-Peter h-he's d-dead, P-Peter."

"Get hold of yourself, Bren. Now what seems to be the problem?"

"H-H-Hem, H-H-Hemingway is d-dead P-Peter, he shot himself a few minutes ago in K-Ketchum—"

"Well don't worry Bren, that was inevitable, concern yourself with *Cork,* and your return here."

"Y-Yes P-Peter Arthurs . . . I-I w-will, g-good b-boy."

"Listen, B.B. this will warm the cockles of your heart and tickle the tone and temper of your testicles. The other day I went over to Columbia Studios and was introduced to Richard Chamberlain, Laurence Harvey, Jane Fonda, Richard Quine, Burt Lancaster, Ernie Kovacs, Jack Lemmon, and guess who else, B.B.?"

"W-who avick?"

"Kim Novak. Beatrice was right, Bren, she sure is a beauty. Can you blame me for being mad about her, and oh yeah, I was a big hit, they crowded around me and wanted to know just how I was associated with you."

A period of not unusual silence ensued.

"W-what did y-yew s-say avick?"

"Oh I just told them that we were . . . we were . . . hmmm. I didn't say much, B., no point in . . . I just said that we were two . . ."

Brendan's anxiety was palpable over the wire. "I also had soft drinks and sandwiches with the carpenters, the propmen, and the grips, you know B., our type of people, the real salts of the studios, the one and only type of—"

"L-listen yew, I fuckinjayzuswell hope that yew're not out there in that cesspool using my name to get in with that small-time shower of charlatans. Don't yew recall when I left there I gave yew strict instructions that yew were not to—"

"Hold on, B., hold on, you're getting your pussy all lathered up for naught. First of all it was my other writer friend, David Greggory, who by virtue of his friendship with a chap who works in the story department, made the introduction. It wasn't necessary for me to use your good name."

"Then how did the whores know that we knew each other?"

"Oh, they probably saw your name or your photo in the paper beside mine," I said matter-of-factly. A period of silence followed by a gush of indecipherable invectives, then Beatrice's voice cut in.

"Oh hello, Peter, it's awfully hot and humid here in New York. Is Hollywood still smoggy? Brendan is bashing away! I'm hoping to get him home to Dublin in a few days. He hasn't touched *Cork* since he left Hollywood! So far no word from Joan. *Slan leat.*"

Brendan's voice reappeared. "Are yew still there avick?"

"When are you going to make the big U-turn, B.? Did you book her passage yet?"

"Shur I can't, shur amn't I fucked, like a fuckin' sow with a ring in its nose, I'm bollixed, I have to go home to the weed country with your woman!" Then a scuffle at the other end of the wire broke out and the phone went dead.

A few hours later I read of Hemingway's suicide, which apparently had taken place just a very short time before Brendan called me. Mary Hemingway, Ernest's widow, upon hearing the fatal shot ran downstairs and found the body. Most of the skull was blown away. All that remained was a few teeth and the lower part of the jaw. A shotgun and two spent cartridges lay next to the body. Mary then phoned the police and Leonard Lyons, the New York columnist. Lyons called Brendan.

A few days later when it became apparent to me that I was going nowhere in the acting business, I packed some of my belongings into a cardboard carton and left them in the care of Kathryn O'Mara, the secretary to Richard Quine, director of *The Notorious Landlady.* Then I drove to Wilmington and checked into the Don Hotel.

The local junk dealer informed me that I would have to give him twenty dollars to have him take the Buick off my hands. No deal. I thanked him profusely and moseyed on down to the SIU hall and checked the rotary board. Shipping was still tight but I was now in possession of a "killer card." I posted a notice on the bulletin board announcing that a Buick in excellent condition was for sale. Jim Foti, a former shipmate of mine from the *Erna Elizabeth,* permitted me to flop for a few days in his home on L Street.

Out of curiosity I phoned Jim Downey in New York and was informed that Brendan had been picked up by the police and for his own protection had been placed in the psychiatric branch of the New Jersey State Hospital. The police had found him barefooted and wandering aimlessly.

For the next few days I alternated between sleeping in the backseat of the Buick and in the front room of Foti's house.

On the morning of July 31 on the ten A.M. call I "threw in" on an A.B.'s berth aboard the S.S. *Lasalle* and got the job. The Waterman C.2. was inbound from the Far East and heading for the Gulf Coast. I decided to abandon the Buick on a side street. Just as I was in the process of removing the license plates, a fellow SIU man ran up to me and informed me that a drunken Mexican was in the Tradewinds bar waiting to buy my car from me. I sped to the scene and quickly informed him that the car was a "Beaut of a transportation piece," and well worth the eighty-five dollars that I was asking. He eyed me suspiciously and did a bleary-eyed study of the car's wheels and body, then he sat behind the wheel. My heart pounded.

"Señor, I weel geeve jyou ten dollars for the pile of jonk."

"Tell you what I'll do, champ," I said mustering all of my salesmanship, "lay a double sawbuck in the old palm and the baby's yours. She's a pip man, a real pip, no shit."

"Feefteen."

"Twenty, señor."

"Feefteen, hombre.

"Fifteen, sir."

The drunken longshoreman smiled, wiped his brow and laid three five-dollar bills in my quivering palm. I sighed and handed over the ownership papers to him, then went down Avalon Boulevard to an old familiar cathouse, rented a portion of much needed pussy, purchased a case of beer and headed up the gangway of the *Lasalle*.

Some two blocks from where the Waterman C.2. was berthed, I caught a last glance of my once proud Buick. The car was parked at the end of a narrow street next to a waterfront warehouse. Hundreds of deep, sledge hammer indentations were in ample evidence all over the car's hood, fenders and body. I deduced that the car's present owner had suddenly become enraged at something or other in regards to the auto's performing ability. I hurried up the gangway. An hour later we "let go" and headed for the Panama Canal. The smell of the sea air was refreshing and invigorating.

XI

August 23. Port of New Orleans. The officers and crew of the S.S. *Lasalle* were informed that the ship was going into lay-up status. In accordance with the union-company cargo ship agreement, I was paid the equivalent of a first-class air travel ticket back to Wilmington, L.A., the port of engagement. En route to the airport I had a change of heart and flew to New York.

During my travels in California with Brendan, I had caused severe damage to a number of expensive cars. Some of these damages were deliberate. On a number of occasions the owners of these cars jotted down my license plate number as I was speeding from the scene. I felt that the police would be, by now, looking for me.

I checked into the Belvedere Hotel on Forty-eighth Street, then subwayed to Brooklyn and registered for a ship.

On September 7, I secured a job as A.B. aboard the S.S. *Topa Topa,* a Waterman C.2. bound for the Orient. I had another change of heart and paid off and signed on aboard the Liberty lumber-carrier S.S. *Marymar.* The *Marymar* was bound for the West Coast. Again, I cut short my plans by paying off in the port of Philadelphia, and headed back to New York. For the next several days I worked around the clock as boatswain, consultant and rigger in Todd's shipyard in Hoboken, New Jersey, aboard the supership, *Transeastern.*

In Downey's I was informed that the film version of *The Quare Fellow* was about to get under way in Dublin. My interest in acting was again renewed. I forwarded a telegram to Brendan and Beatrice inquiring if a part in the film would be relegated to me. A few weeks later I received a letter and a postcard from the Behans.

The card was from Dundalk. It was signed twice by Brendan, once by Beatrice and once by my father. Beatrice assured me that my part in the film was being spoken for. Then I phoned my Brooklyn friend, "Duke," and was informed that the charges in Brooklyn against me were probably dropped.

I subwayed to Park Slope and checked into a familiar rooming house on Union Street where I rented a familiar room. I lay down on a familiar sweat-and-bile-stained mattress to contemplate. The atmosphere in the room was muggy. A big blue-bottle fly flew in the window, buzzed about, just above my head, careened off the walls and flew away. Streaks of oil that were once the residue in the cargo tanks of the S.S. *Transeastern* surfaced on my arms and legs. The whir of a police siren shattered the outside quietude.

On or about November 7, I called Irish International Airlines, booked a flight and flew to Dublin. I checked into the Wynn's Hotel on Pearce Street and dashed off a message to Brendan. Bright and early the following morning a familiar set of thumps, kicks and ear-defiling shrieks awakened me. I opened the door. Brendan was partially drunk, rumpled and crumpled, but looked remarkably hale and chipper. He greeted me as though I was the second coming of Christ.

"Listen yew," Brendan said in a characteristic pseudocaustic manner, "don't yew know where yew are, don't yew know what this is, this is a hideout for fuckin' aul priests and nuns! Here take these and stuff yur ballox into them," he said picking up my jeans from the back of a chair and pushing them into my bare chest. "Yur cummin' home with me. Begod avick, I'll be afraid to go to sleep tonight, for fear that I'll wake up and find that I was dreaming."

Downstairs in the lobby our paths were crossed by two priests. "What are youse atall atall?" Brendan asked. "Are youse brothers or fathers or what is it, shur I can't tell be the cut of yur jibs," his face screwing up in a histrionic smirk.

"Well, Brendan," one of the elderly men said, "surely you will agree that you are a man of rare intellect, will you not?"

"I doubt very seriously if anyone with a sizable degree of intelligence will give yew an argument on that, sir," he retorted perfunctorily.

"Well now," the priest went on in a kindly fashion, "true, Brendan, you cannot tell what we are by the cut of our jibs, but surely you can tell what we are by the cut of our collars."

The priest's alliteration took Brendan by surprise. A smile crept into his face.

"May yiz be the fathers of bishops," he said extending his hand. We made a left swing on O'Connell Street and sped over O'Connell's Bridge, Brendan in the lead carrying my suitcase. We proceeded in silence, then suddenly, "Listen avick, b-but I meant to be asking yew, b-but h-how old did yew say that that chap was, the c-chap on the Norwegian t-tanker, or w-where was the ship heading for atall atall. . . ?"

"Brendan you're fuckinwell drunk again."

We spirited ahead in somber silence. Then he stopped short, turned sharply, looked me in the eye and in an exuberant voice said, "Well, so what of it? Drunk! Certainly I'm drunk, at least I hope I am, for if I'm not, it's one hell of a fuckin' physical impairment that I'm stuck with and will be stuck with till me dying day."

When Brendan made the sharp turn to chastise me, the corner of my battered suitcase hit one of the decorative columns of the bridge and caused my personal belongings to spill out all over the windswept bridge. Hastily we gathered up my oil-stained clothing and continued south.

"Cum on avick," Brendan roared as he hailed a taxi, pushed me into its backseat, then instructed the driver to make a series of turns.

Before I realized what was taking place, I was being given a grand tour of the city of Dublin; a city that I was not familiar with.

"Over there avick," Brendan pointed out, "that is the post office where the proclamation of Irish independence was read on Easter Sunday, 1916. It was from there that the Great Rebellion was launched . . . There is the house where the great O'Casey grew up . . . There is where Wilde lived . . . over there is where Michael Collins hid his secret documents and guns . . . How old did yew say yew were when yew left the Dealgan boxing club? There's Holles Street, the hole where I was born . . . How old did yew say the chap was, the chap on the other ship? . . . It was in that ugly-looking monument where I first met my father, behind a row of steel bars . . . There is Nelson's Pillar . . . Here is where Sheridan hung out. . . ."

Later we returned to Lower Grafton Street, where Brendan got into a fierce brouhaha with a big hulk of a Cavan policeman. Brendan had gotten into another argument with the taxi driver over the fare, then in a moment of disgust he threw a ten-pound note into the man's face "Keep the change yew cur yew," then he pulled my suitcase from the cab and crossed the street against a red light. The police officer, who was on traffic control duty, ordered Brendan to wait until the light turned green. Brendan made a derogatory remark about the man's manhood, fatherhood and the intellectual capacities of his mother and the county in which the officer was born. Next the officer stormed over to us and upon learning of his antagonist's identity remarked, "Oh, what would you expect . . . It must be nice to be able to get drunk so early in the day." Then he went back to his post in the middle of the street. No arrest was forthcoming.

"Cum on, son," Brendan said as we moseyed up Grafton Street. We stopped off at McDaid's, Davy Byrne's, and the Bailey, three well-known pubs where pseudos, actors, actresses, radicals, would-be poets, patriots, and malcontents sip and wait for phone calls from their agents, or the dispensation board.

Brendan polished off fifteen to twenty double Irish whiskeys, chased by glasses of soda water. Each huge drink was downed in a single draught. "This will cure me worms," he chuckled as he downed each setup of malts. We dined on oysters and crabmeat.

In a very short period of time I became fully aware of the fact that Brendan was by no means a big Dublin favorite. During the drinking spree he savagely slagged his contemporaries and made known his desire to return to Hollywood. "It's nothing but a quagmire crawlin' with Judas Iscariots, eagerly waiting to crucify me on high. The same chancers would drink porter out of a policeman's boot."

In one of the pubs, the Bailey on Duke Street, I repaired to the gents', and when I returned Brendan was nowhere in sight. My suitcase with many of its contents still bulging from its side lay in the corner of the pub. I went outside and found Brendan in a melee with a pair of Trinity College students.

"Hold on for a bit, and we'll make it a foursome," I shouted as I took off my jacket and rolled up my sleeves.

"You stay out of it, it's none of your fuckin' Yank business," one of the juiced-up youths exclaimed.

"But I intend to make it my fuckin' Yank business," I interjected as I pushed the tousle-haired bully off the curbstone.

"This man is neither entitled to his money or his fame, he has his plays written for him," the other fellow butted in. "Ask him who Joan Littlewood is."

"Joan Littlewood is my aunt," I said, "if she had balls she'd be my uncle."

"Yew, watch your mouth," Brendan barked at me. Seconds later I picked up my suitcase and we hailed a taxi to Ballsbridge, a bourgeois suburb of Dublin where Brendan owned a Georgian house.

We popped into a pub called Cole's, where Brendan ordered another ten or twelve double Irish whiskeys and a jug of soda water. He talked for hours about America and Hollywood. "I had to get away from the fuckin' aul kip!" he moaned to the patrons. "Couldn't get me play wrote, they were callin' night and day, 'Mr. Behan will yew write this and will yew write that.' 'Away with the fuckin' lot of yiz,' says I, 'I have me own work to do. Even if I hadn't, it wouldn't make matters any the different, for youse are nothing but a horde of fuckin' chancers and snake charmers who would rob the coat off a mange dog,' says I." With characteristic ease, Brendan then went on to drop a load of the most illustrious names in the film colony.

Just as we were about to depart he introduced me to his neighbors, "This is a great friend of mine, his name is Peter Arthurs," then clench- ing his fist and shaking it in the face of an ancient drunk, "He's a handy boy to have on your side when the natives get restless, if yew follow me meanin'." Brendan then went on to tell of his "infamous battle with the Hollywood cops." The spectators watched in awe as Brendan relived the historical battle.

We departed. Brendan was now heavily intoxicated but still insisted on carrying my bag. We crossed over Ballsbridge. Beneath the bridge flowed the river Dodder. The Royal Irish Horseshow grounds lay on the left side of Anglesea Road. A low-lying grey stone wall lay on the right. Further on up the road was a tier of two-storied red brick buildings. The distance from the bridge and the first house was approximately two hundred and fifty yards. Brendan grew more helpless with each step. "Which house is yours, B.?" I asked. He didn't reply, he merely sighed from fatigue and the weight of the liquid madness coursing through his veins. Then he dropped my bag and threw himself onto the top of the wall. Degrees of intoxication crept up on him.

"Look over there avick," he suddenly exclaimed with jollity, "I'll bet there's a ship sinking further down the river."

Perplexed and looking in the direction where he was pointing, "Brendan that river doesn't look deep enough to float a mattress, what in jayzus name are you on about?"

"Look avick, look, did yew ever hear tell of a pack of rats swimming towards a foundering ship?"

I looked again and discovered a swarm of fat rats swimming towards the bridge. On the other side of the river was a flour mill that bore the legend "Johnson, Mooney, and O'Brien."

"Well, Brendan," I chuckled, "that's life, that's how it is, all one and the same, a lifelong pursuit of a good bellyful and a place to flop. The rats got theirs and we have ours, what say we head for your flop?" I was dying from jet lag and the week-long around-the-clock stint of tank cleaning in the bowels of the big supertanker in Hoboken. "Come on," I said, taking hold of my bag in one hand while putting my other hand around his shoulders in an attempt to drag him the remainder of the journey.

But Brendan was stubborn. He clung to the wall and pushed me away with his leg. "Yew never explained to me why yew pissed in the blackberries," he exclaimed in a sullen manner.

"I will dear B., I will, but not this minute. I'm dead for the want of rest."

We came to a house with a small square garden with an iron fence around it. Attached to the gate was a small plywood board with the word "Cuig" [Five] stamped on it. I opened the gate, listened to its groan and stood the semi-paralyzed Brendan up against the door, then rattled the letter box to muster Beatrice's attention, all to no avail. "Beatrice must be out," I said to the snoring figure. "Have you got the key to the door?" He continued to snore. Then I did a fast rummage of his pockets and came up with a big black key.

Brendan went into a spasm of coughs that seemed as though he was about to come asunder. On one desperate occasion he tried hard to say something but phlegm and other impedimenta prevented him.

No sooner had I opened the door, than a big tortoise-shell cat was purring and rubbing against my shoes. I crouched and allowed Brendan to flop across my shoulder, then went in search of a bed or a sofa. In the parlor I found a comfortable-looking high-backed mahogany chair and placed Brendan in it. Then I went in search of Beatrice. "Beatrice . . . Beatrice . . . Beatrice . . . it's us." The hallway was littered with unopened letters, postcards, telegrams and empty bottles. A huge poster of a svelte matador administering the final thrust into the neck of a bleeding bull adorned a wall. Plaques honoring Brendan for his generosity and literary achievements adorned the walls of the living room. A stuffed duck with Shelley Winters' name on it sat on the mantlepiece. The invitation to Kennedy's inauguration ball stood open and proud beside it. On a landing, halfway to the top of the house, I found a small room. The guest room, I deduced. A bathroom lay adjacent to the room. Up another short flight of stairs were two more rooms. The master bedroom and a room that was obviously Brendan's den. This room was a veritable rat's nest, aflutter with books, an omnipresent sheaf of poems, a jumble of unfinished manuscripts, publishers' periodicals and brochures, smatterings of notes, a copious amount of souvenirs, books of slang, posters, and other appliances and paraphernalia of the traveled writer.

The presence of Brendan was everywhere. It was as though the domain was packed full of foreboding memoirs and old hurts, some perhaps a little too painful to have to live with. The walls of the oblong room were a museum of theater memorabilia. A huge bronze bust of Brendan stood tall and daring in the right-hand corner. Two single beds were placed in the center of the room.

Outside on Anglesea Road a scurrilous wind rattled the windows. The blustery winds of winter were in the air. The powerful wind caused the house to shudder and tremble as though a giant hand was attempting to lift it by its roots.

I hastened down the stairs with the intention of carrying Brendan up to the master bedroom, undressing him and putting him to bed, but upon observing his deep snores and his curled up, fetuslike position in the chair, I decided to let well enough alone and go to bed.

A few hours later I was awakened by a figure approaching my bed, like some strange malediction in a horror movie. I bolted upright and let out a roar. "Ahhhh . . ."

"It's O.K. me aul son," a voice blurted, "it's only mesself."

A splatter of something hot was suddenly spilled all over my face. I jumped out of bed, put on the light and found Brendan clad in a collarless, long-tailed shirt. He was holding a large saucepan in his hands. "Here avick," he said, "I brought yew some hot food to put in yur guts. Yew didn't eat all day, yew must be lost with the hunger."

I slurped up the hot liquid and discovered that I was eating a potful of strange-tasting tomato soup. "What else is in the soup?" I asked the ghostlike perpendicular figure.

"I just thought yew would like a little extra nourishment avick, so I trew in a few eggs," he said with a face full of seriousness and pride.

We spent the next few hours sitting talking on the side of the bed. Brendan made clear his deep-seated disdain for the land of his birth. He ardently desired to return to Hollywood. He hadn't written a single word of *Cork* since he'd departed. Under no circumstances would Beatrice accompany him on his return. On several occasions during our discussion, I asked him where Beatrice was, but he merely nodded his head and kept her whereabouts secret.

Exhausted, I fell off to sleep, only to be once again awakened by Brendan who was kneeling on the floor sucking and biting my penis. As usual his mind was far away, meandering into exotic vistas of his masturbatory fantasies. I reached down and grabbed a handful of his hair with one hand and his Adam's apple with the other, then squeezed until he let go of my cock. I sighed with relief and begged him to go to his room. Huffily, he went off.

With one hand cupped around my swollen genitalia, the other hand lying across my heart, I lay awake and wondered what sort of man I really was. My pores exuded sweat and smatterings of black oil from days before, the residue from the tanks of the *Transeastern*.

Early daylight seeped in through the back window. Gusts of powerful winds and heavy rains lashed the walls and windows. Upstairs the sounds of Brendan's shrieks accompanied by the crashing of furniture were heard. I went back to sleep.

Early in the P.M. I awoke, got out of bed, checked Brendan's room and found it in a state of complete disarray. Books, snippets of reworked notes, empty bottles and other objects were strewn around on the floor. Brendan opened his eyes and attempted to talk, but phlegm and other mucus prevented him. Then I crept downstairs and gathered up an armful of letters and telegrams. The telegrams were mostly from European and British theater and film producers who wished Brendan to become involved with productions outlined. Others demanded that he sober up and take care of business. Some of the letters were from French, English, German and Swiss psychiatrists. One of them guaranteed Brendan a period of treatment which could reduce him from being a chronic alcoholic to a moderate drunk and a much more productive writer. One letter in particular caught my fancy. It was from Sydney, Australia. It read:

Dear Mr. Bebum:
Don't you think it's about time that you wrote a serious play and called it the *Fuckin' Idiot*.
If and when you do this, needless to say, *who I* feel will be just right for the title role.

The letter was signed,

A fellow Irishman, living in Aussie and genuinely earning his living.

I threw the letter into the fireplace.

A short while later Dr. Terence Chapman, Brendan's doctor, arrived, gave Brendan a vitamin injection and departed. Brendan reacted as though he had eaten a bellyful of live wasps. I heated up a potful of tomato soup, (the only soup that was available) then fried up a concoction of bread, potatoes, and a few bits and pieces of meats and liver that I found in a small tin box nailed to a wall on the outside of the house. A small garden some thirty to forty feet in length separated the rear of the house from the river. With the sounds of my feet, a fauna of little mice scurried down to the edge of the garden and took up refuge along the banks of the Dodder. Storms of little birds cried, careened and settled on the edge of the roof.

We ate voraciously. "Great boy," Brendan muttered as he attacked the food.

After we had finished he turned to me and blurted, "Cum on out of that son, let's fuck off out of here."

I phoned for a cab and minutes later we arrived at the "Forty-foot," an archipelago of rocks that is used as a male bathing spot in the district of Sandy Cove, a Dublin suburb. I had never before been to the lonely deserted cove but was familiar with it from reading James Joyce's *Ulysses*. No other bathers were in sight.

Brendan quickly disrobed and beckoned me to do likewise. A gaggle of cawing seagulls careened over our heads as I disrobed in the icy chill of the Irish winter with nary a bare arse in sight. "Let's go in and get our ballox wet," he stammered as he mounted a high rock and plunged into the frigid waters. Wave after wave of cruel wintry swells continued to muster all of their savage fury and pound the well-worn, salt-encrusted rocks. Brendan did a number of dives then disappeared below the cold grey surface. One minute passed, two, three, four. A heavy mist blanketed the cove. Finally far away in the misty distance a black glistening head appeared clinging to a rock. I sighed with relief for I was just about to make a searching leap into the icy depths. My skin had now taken on a hue of dark blue.

Brendan reemerged, climbed up from the lower line of rocks, walked over to me and began to fondle my genitalia, which had shrunken up to a piece of skin and crawled up into my abdomen. Brendan's penis was fully erect.

"But B., how can you even think of sex, much less get an erection, in this kind of eskimo weather," I said perplexedly, while shaking like a madman on a witness stand.

"Yew don't mean to tell me that it's cold," he snickered. "Here take this," he said as he handed me his heavy handmade Swedish sweater.

"But I have to insist on having it back, it's not mine, avick. I only got a loan of it from Joan Littlewood."

A ship's foghorn was audible in the distance as we donned the remainder of our clothes. Brendan phoned for a taxi and I was taken on a tour of Killiney, Bray, Greystones, the Sugar Loaf Mountain and the patch of Wicklow where there are fourteen different shades of green growing in the grass. "This is where I first learned the use of explosives, here is where the IRA used to dump their victims after they shot them and wished to dispose of their bodies." Here was Irish primitive beauty at its best. The curve of the Dublin Bay and the layout of Dublin City were amply in evidence. Oodles of tiny white thatched-roof cottages, their chimneys sending up spirals of clear white smoke, dotted the lush landscape. Later we moved on to Glendalaugh and its vale. We took in the bountiful sights while the wind whistled through the branches of stately chestnut trees. Then we repaired to a quaint restaurant, where I quickly guzzled down a half dozen shots of Irish whiskey and three bottles of Guinness. Brendan sat, goggle-eyed and amazed. This was the first time in our friendship that I had imbibed so heavily in his presence.

Far out across the phosphorescent sea, flotillas of great ships, riding north of the Banba and west of the moon carried exiles and textiles to and from foreign lands.

We began our trek back to Ballsbridge. "Where is Beatrice these days?" I asked in a low-keyed voice. We spirited onwards in silence. "We had a marvelous aul time of it above in Dundalk with yur great aul chivalrous father," Brendan blurted, "did yew get the postcard that we signed in the Imperial Hotel?"

"Yes, indeed B., I picked it up before I left." An hour later we were back in Coles. Brendan ordered a dozen doubles and scoffed them up in single draughts.

"It'll cure what ails me," he muttered as he swallowed glassful after glassful.

Finally, reeling under a heavy load, I dragged and carried him across the bridge and began the final two-hundred-fifty-yard struggle homewards. Later, we christened this stretch of land "The last leg."

I put him in his chair, then said, "I'm goin' up to take a nap, B.," but he insisted that I sit in the living room and retell him a few more stories of my early life, sexual discoveries and shenanigans on board ships and in boxing clubs. Finally he willed himself to sleep.

A few boggling subjects rattled my brain. First, my funds were low. The airfare from New York had eaten heavily into my after-taxes six-hundred-dollar payoff from the tank-cleaning gig. Was there genuinely a part for me in *The Quare Fellow?*

Our friendship was once again bedrock solid, but patience was a virtue that had to be slowly cultivated and nurtured around Brendan Behan.

Living in Brendan's home, I had to quickly accustom myself to his variety of thumps and kicks on the front door. Brendan seldom squandered precious drinking time by giving unnecessary explanations. For example, a series of rapid quick kicks indicated that he was with a cadre of hangers-on whom he did not wish to entertain in his home. This type of knock was meant to be ignored by me. Brendan subsequently groaned, apologized for not being in possession of his housekey, then led the gaggle back to Cole's or wherever he picked them up and quickly found an excuse to rid himself of their company prior to shuffling back to Cuig.

A slower, heavier banging on the door foretold me that he was outside, in a drunken stupor and about to collapse. Under no circumstances would he put his hand in his pocket, extricate his key and open the door. The heavy black key reminded him of darker days.

Through trial and error I learned to open the door inches at a time while slowly putting my right shoulder forward, then in one lightning-quick movement I opened it all the way and allowed the drunken Brendan to flop across my right shoulder. My next move was to turn, kick the door shut with my left foot while I precariously balanced myself on my right foot. Next, the journey up the narrow staircase began.

One afternoon, approximately fifteen minutes after Cole's had closed for the evening closing hour, "the holy hour," as Brendan called it, I opened the door, caught the snoring, falling figure, and began to negotiate the stairs. Then, while I was in the process of making my familiar left turn to mount the three final steps that led to his bedroom, Brendan began to flail his arms and kick his feet. "Bejayzus avick, yur working wonders like a nag under a bale of hay, but I must get mesself a glass of buttermilk."

My knees buckled. I reached out to grab hold of the banister, but missed it. I began to fall, then with both hands I grabbed hold of the door frame. However, in my panicky haste I lost grip of Brendan's thighs. He slid from my grasp and clattered down the stairs, the crown of his head hitting each and every step all the way to the floor.

For the next fifteen minutes he lay in an unconscious state at the foot of the stairs, a flabby amoebalike pile of blood, bone and gristle. Panic surged through my every artery. I phoned Terence Chapman. "He's out cold, doctor, he's undoubtedly suffered a concussion, maybe worse. Can you come over?"

"Keep a close eye on him for a while," the doctor instructed me.

In a matter of minutes Brendan was sitting upright and picking his nose. "W-where did yew say the buttermilk was avick?"

"Listen, B.," I said with ultra-concern. "Fuck the buttermilk, do me a favor and let's cunt off down to the nearest hospital and get yourself a head X-ray."

"Do me a favor avick," he sharply reciprocated, "and don't overly concern yourself, I'll eat the cabbages that'll grow on your grave."

"When you're down there munching, B., do yourself a mite and don't look up, at least not with your eyes open, for more than likely I will be pissing on the dandelions that's growing on *your* grave."

Brendan jumped to his feet and jotted down my words, "Good man avick, that's smashing, that will go grand in me play."

For the next few days, Brendan and I took daily trips to the Forty-foot. He did most of the swimming and drinking. I watched and waited. At home, I did the cooking. Brendan gobbled up everything that I put before him. On a few occasions he gobbled up the potatoes before I had a chance to wash and peel them.

One day while I was in the process of readying a huge omelette to share between us, Brendan stormed into the kitchen, reached over and swallowed up all of the raw eggs, shells and all.

Later that evening, in a very sullen mood, he said to me, "Cum on son, I'll introduce yew to a great aul ballox who will love yew. Talk to him about yur travels in the East, he'll go mad over yew, he will be-jayzus, he will."

We spirited down Morehampton Street at an unusually fast pace. Brendan remained mute and sullen. Finally we came upon a four-storied somber grey Victorian building. The numbers "43" were riveted to the door. A long narrow path, cutting through a well-manicured lawn, led to the door.

"Up there, avick, go up there to that door, rap hard on it and the Dalai Lama will let yew in, go on, son, go on," he said as he hurried away with a cacophony of snickers.

I rapped long and hard on the door. No one answered. I rapped some more. Suddenly I heard some footsteps on the stairs. In a flash I vividly recalled the early A.M. hours of June the first, when Brendan had been drunk and making peculiar references about the Dalai Lama. Not knowing who was about to open up, I decided to abandon Brendan's charade. I ran down the path and headed home.

Later that evening Brendan asked, "Well avick did yew see the high priest? What did he have to say for himself? Did he give yew his blessing?"

"No B., I didn't see him, no one answered the door."

"Oh, it's O.K. son, yew'll see him some other time," he said mysteriously.

Brendan continued to imbibe heavily. In Ireland, according to courtesy and tradition, he who does the buying of the spirits is entitled to hold the floor indefinitely. Cole's was his favorite hangout, but during the hangover early hours of the mornings, we took long walks along the waterfront. The bars in the Gresham and the Shelbourne hotels were his favorite morning hangouts—sanctuaries for the elite and the super-rich.

Brendan showed no genuine love for and desired no intimacy with Irish peasantry. The aspect of his nature to accept himself as the guest of honor was amply displayed in these elite hangouts. He acted the part of the verbose thesaurus, guffawing in Dublin slum idioms and lending his own fragrance to his every expression and shade.

In these particular pubs he was virtually guaranteed a continuum of heavy arguments, brouhahas and melees. Brendan seldom associated himself with Dublin's working class. The company of Ballsbridge's upper middle class with their exclusivity and gentility he found more suitable. Ballsbridge streets shone with an eloquent cleanliness and grace, unparalleled elsewhere in the city.

The early Irish mornings gradually became crisp, chilly and foggy. Sprinklings of rain and frost filled the air. I wondered if my bones and my blood would be able to stand up to the oncoming wrath of an Irish winter, my first winter in Ireland in almost fourteen years. My trips to India, Africa and South America had long ago thinned my blood and melted my marrow. We took long walks along the quays. The somber sounds of tramp colliers, puffing tugs and other Liffey River traffic reverberated.

Taking care of the hard-drinking Brendan was mind and body draining.

One day I announced that if I couldn't get a "solid yes" in regard to my part in the film, I would have to make the U-turn home to New York. Brendan became disturbed and bellicose, "Shur surely yew can hold on for awhile longer until the other one gets back!"

"Which other one, B.?"

"The other one avick, . . . yur woman."

One day Brendan advised me that Joan Littlewood would "more than likely be calling in to check on me play, be sure to watch what yew say," he barked.

One early Sunday morning Brendan awakened me, slipped a handwritten note and a five-pound note into the palm of my hand and told me to fetch him "a bottle of much needed medicine. Yur woman will get me meaning," he chuckled pointing to the address on the front of the folded paper. The short letter was addressed to Dolly Fawcett, a famous Dublin publican who sold very watered-down portions of whiskey to Sunday morning stragglers and croakers. I taxied to the North Wall shop where I made the sleazy purchase, then hurried back to the dehydrating man.

"Here, B.," I said proudly as I handed him the unlabeled bottle.

"Great boy, avick, yur handier than a crucifixion on the hill of Calvary. Now, son, will yew get yur father a glass for him to drink out of?"

"To be sure, B." I turned my back, stepped out of the bedroom and began my descent of the three steps to the bathroom. My trek was quickly curtailed.

I heard a clatter of flying glass. I dashed back into the room and found a hail of broken glass lying all over the room. Other fragments were gradually coming to a halt. Brendan lay motionless, his fingers were intertwined as though he were dead. A smirk was etched in his blue, leaden countenance.

I picked up several pieces of green broken glass and clearly deduced that they were pieces of the bottle that I had moments before handed to him. No smell of the very potent Irish grog was evident. No damp stains were visible on the pillow or the bedclothes!

Finally I realized what had happened. Brendan had swallowed the entire quart of spirits in one quick draught. I looked down at the corpulent figure, bent my head, held my ear over his mouth and listened hard. His face was suddenly blotched and blue. The rhythm of his breathing was agitated. His eyelids spasmodically fluttered. I wondered if he was going into a diabetic coma.

In a lightning-quick flash he reached up with both hands, took hold of my ears and practically pulled them from my head. *"Kill me, kill me, kill me* and be done with it, Peter Arthurs. Peter Arthurs, I luv yew, I luv yew, I luv yew." Then he raised his head and attempted to suck my eyes from their sockets. But I managed to get my thumbs around his Adam's apple and choke him into semiconsciousness. He lay still. Just as I was about to lie down again, in another burst of fury, he got his mouth inside of mine and was in the process of biting my tongue out when I managed to stop him by depressing his jugular vein. Minutes later he fell off to sleep. When he awoke, I informed him of my decision to return to New York immediately.

Brendan careened out of bed, dressed hurriedly and said, "No, no, no, wait avick, wait, we'll go for a ramble, there's a luvly woman down the road who wants to see yew. Hold on, son."

I went to the bathroom and smeared my eyelids, ears and lips with a heavy layer of after-shave talcum powder. We headed down a maze of windswept streets. Neither of us spoke. Dogs barked in the distance.

"W-where is the Burlington Hospital for Female Disorders?" Brendan asked a bespectacled man who suddenly crossed our path.

The man gaped in awe as though he was observing an ogre and wiped the rain from his glasses, then leaned his elbow on a letter box, stared Brendan in the eye and said in a low serious voice, "In the name of sweet mother of jayzus, sir, do you mean to tell me on this rainy Sunday evening with the bells of the church pealing out into the city, that a man of your integrity and world renown is not aware of the whereabouts of the Burlington Hospital for Female Disorders?"

Brendan shifted his weight from the ball of one foot to the other, stared up into the craggy face of the ancient Dubliner and said, "Well sir, at least it would appear that yew read the tabloids and the periodicals and keep abreast of world events, not that they do yew any good, however in regards to your latter remark, I must say this, b-but do *yew* think for a solitary moment that if a man such as I had even the slightest of inklings as to where the Burlington Hospital for Female Disorders is located, I would ask a fuckin' four-eyed eegit the likes of yew, particularly on a wet Sunday night and the bells of the novena chiming out as yew so stoutly stated."

The two Dubliners eyed one another then moved off.

Further on down the street Brendan waved to an ancient, ashen-faced man sitting on a stoop. The man beamed and returned the wave.

"Shur I suppose that's the only real pleasure the poor aul ballox has in life," Brendan muttered as he nodded a second time to the old man. "I mean to say he must be delighted every time that he gets a wink or a wave from a man like mesself. Wha! I wonder what he does for himself when I'm away in America or in some other fuckin' aul kip writing one of me plays."

We continued ahead in silence. Anger suffused his face.

"I'm sure he's delighted you're home from America again, Brendan."

His face softened. We quickened our pace. Later, we came upon a small red brick building.

"Cum on son, let's fuck off in here," he said.

"But we can't go in there, B., that's a convent."

"Cum in son, cum in." A horde of nuns approaching in stolid phalanx swept through the passageways. I followed him down a narrow hallway and into a room. Two figures were sitting up in chairs. One of them was Beatrice.

"Oh there's Peter," she exclaimed exuberantly. "When did you arrive? Oh thank God you've come. Bless you. *Cead mile failte romhat abhaile* [A hundred thousand welcomes to you]."

We kissed and hugged. "But why are you in hospital, Bea? What's wrong? How long are you here?" I asked.

"I found the word, Beatrice," Brendan exclaimed joyously, cutting through my profusion. "I found it in the *Britannica.* Now I can get back to *Cork.*"

"Oh thank God," she exclaimed. "This is Desmond MacKey and this is Peter Arthurs," Beatrice said, introducing me to the man sitting in the chair.

Brendan had once told me that on the day that he was expelled from the island of Ibiza for his public denigrations of Franco, in his haste he had mislaid the only copy of *The Hostage.* Desmond was in the immediate vicinity and chanced upon the script. Thus, *The Hostage* went on to greater heights.

I shook hands with the gentleman while I pulled the collar of my raincoat up around my chin, to hide my swollen earlobes and scratched neck. Then MacKey and Brendan went out into the hall to chat. Beatrice in a subdued voice gave me a verbal list of things to do and not to do at Cuig.

A. I was to get all of the high protein that I could find into Brendan's guts.
B. I was to feed Beamish. Beamish was the big furry cat that had greeted me when I first opened the door.
C. I was granted permission to use the downstairs bathtub, but only

on condition that I remembered to shut off the expensive over-head electric heater which I could use while bathing.

D. Under no circumstances was I to allow any of Brendan's friends into the house without him being there personally. According to Beatrice, "local chancers" were in the habit of coming to the house and claiming to be old IRA friends in the hopes of getting a handout and a flop.

E. I was not to be too overly generous with the local gypsies.

F. I was to be sure to phone the rat exterminator.

She informed me of the physical layout of the house and hiding places where dozens of watered-down vials of whiskey were stashed, ready to be administered to Brendan on an hourly basis. The purpose of the watered-in-degrees whiskey was to eventually wean him from the bottle and get him back to *Cork*. Beatrice also instructed me to keep a "sharp eye out for the garden." Brendan had a habit of falling down and sleeping his drunks off there when there was no one to open the door.

I assured the lady that I would have him off the "gargle" and back at the typewriter by the time that she returned home. We departed and went home.

On at least two occasions per day for the next three days, Beatrice phoned in to find out how much food Brendan had eaten the day before, how many vials of the watered whiskey I had administered and how much of *Cork* he had done.

"Everything is fine, B.," I assured her. "B. is sober as a bishop saying a high holy mass, and is presently working diligently on *Cork.*"

"Bless you, be a good boy and stay, won't you!"

"I will dear B., I will. *Slan leat.*"

Whenever Brendan answered the phone, he immediately handed it to me and said, "Here avick, it's for yew." Beatrice only wished to talk to me.

Brendan's attitude was perceptibly more subdued than it was in Hollywood. No longer was he making frothy and vociferous calls for the passing of laws to imprison pedophiles. The tone and tenor of his demeanor was quieter. His accent slightly changed. He referred to Los Angeles as Los Angeles, Beatrice as Beatrice.

Brendan was a fellow who obviously pulled no stops and employed every tactic to fit the farce. Around Dublin and from IRA friends I learned a lot about him.

He was born into a middle-class family. His grandmother owned a row of tenements. His uncle was deputy mayor of Dublin. The Behans did not hurt for want. But in public he kept secret this aspect of his background for reasons that the Irish proletariat wit and humor is of a much more recognizable and appreciable substance than the wit of the middle or upper classes. The lower-class wit is faster, unexpected, outlandish, highly improbable and delivered in a staccato manner. The shock and insult thus takes on a more stunning, sulphuric, quicksilvery charge.

His linguistic features and foibles were the hallmark of Brendan's fame and style. But he was not as unique as he purported to be. "I must say, I didn't exactly lick me words from the bricks of Dublin," he had boasted in Hollywood. Nevertheless, the repetitive Brendan was a Dubliner who to a large extent inherited and utilized the traditional Dublinesque expressions and inflective rhythms of that specific Irish idiom. He had not invented the total language that he utilized, as he claimed to have done.

Brendan's real gift was in combining being a "chancer," a plagiarizer, and an adept arranger and rearranger. In so doing, he had successfully put himself across as a possessor of a uniquely raw, brutal, profane, lyrical idiom.

To a great extent it can be truthfully stated that his success and his literary life started with his Liverpool arrest and conviction. At the exact time of the arrest, Brendan was in possession of a suitcase full of explosives with which he was purportedly about to "blow up the King George V." Brendan was later convicted and sentenced to three years in Borstal detention. He served a little over two years of his sentence.

The suitcase contained a glass fountain-pen filler, a handful of toy balloons, a few ounces of potassium chlorate and sugar, and a bottle of sulphuric acid. In those days, these small IRA incendiary devices were made by injecting a quantity of the acid into a balloon covered with potassium chlorate and sugar. When the acid had eaten its way past the frail rubber, it came into contact with the potassium chlorate and the sugar. Everything in the immediate vicinity was ignited. These tiny but effective bombs were deposited in letter boxes and sent through the post.

In court Brendan boasted that he had been dispatched to Liverpool to carry on the struggle for the rights of the Irish workers' and small farmers' Republic. The adjutant general of the Dublin-based headquarters of the IRA subsequently denied Brendan's claim to have been dispatched. Rumors abounded that Brendan had even concocted the whole scheme knowing that he would be followed by sea from Dublin, arrested and imprisoned. Another story permeated that it was himself who had informed the cops of his whereabouts.

His "murder" of the two Special Branch officers was the second most important episode in his life.

However, in deep contrast to what he reported, I also discovered that the actual shooting did not take place at the cemetery gates, but at De Courcey Square, a spot that is considerably far from the cemetery's entrance.

The shooting itself was also vastly different in reality from Brendan's entertaining fiction.

Each Easter Sunday the IRA holds an annual march in memory of their fallen blood brothers. On Sunday, April the fifth, 1942, Brendan was in phalanx with his comrades. They were, as usual, being closely watched by the Special Branch, a segment of the Irish police that keeps a watch on the movements of that guerrilla organization. The parade finally dispersed. Two detectives grabbed hold of one of Brendan's colleagues. Another IRA officer grabbed his gun and got set to fire at the cops, but for some unexplainable reason, didn't. "Use it, use it, fire, fire!" Brendan roared, "*I'll* shoot the bastards, give it to me." Then he peeled off his jacket and coat, pulled the gun from the IRA man's grip and fired two shots, each shot missing by a very wide margin.

When he was asked by his Hollywood interviewers to explain how he, a highly skilled guerrilla, proficient in the arts of guerrilla warfare, missed at such a distance, Brendan chuckled. "Well since yur a luvly girl I'll tell yew. Any man, guerrilla or otherwise, who misses a pair of fuckin' cops at a distance of fourteen yards deserves a year in the pokey for each yard . . . and that is what I got—a fourteen-year sentence! Did I tell yew that the luvly daughter of the judge who sentenced me sent me a teapot for me weddin' present. Isn't that right, B.B.?" he had shouted to Beatrice. On another occasion he claimed that he was presented with an electric coffeepot.

In those sensitive days of the war when the British and the Germans were locked in a fierce struggle for victory, Irish politicians cried out for the incarceration of all IRA members and "movement sympathizers." Internment camps were opened up all across the land. The least excuse to put these ardents under lock and key sufficed.

The IRA officer who pointed the revolver at the policeman was a known crack shot. In pulling the gun from his hand, Brendan may have saved the policemen's lives.

In retelling the story, Brendan further explained that for the next few days, while he was "on the run" when the order was put out to shoot him on sight, he earned his living by holding up penny tosspits, sleeping in cemeteries and "puncin'" off local prostitutes and pawning "everything I got hold of." Later the cops closed in and captured him after a blazing gun battle. "Youse wouldn't have got me so fuckin' easy if there wasn't an army of yiz," he declared, as those moments of history were reenacted by Brendan, a ketchup bottle in his right hand, his clothes lying in a willy-nilly fashion on the floor. I also learned that his gun-battle yarn was a farce. By order of the IRA high command, his gun had been taken away from him prior to his arrest, an arrest that was made without any ado on his behalf. Also, during this period, all pawnshops in Dublin were closed, due to a strike.

One day he turned to me and asked, "Where is the rest of that fuckin' dishwater that yew've been feedin' me with?"

"As they say in Texas, B., it's all drinked up. You should get into the practice of spilling a few down your boots at night. This way you can wring your socks out over your mouth in the morning, B."

"Well shur fuck it, avick, we'll get more," he barked.

"No more, B.," I said, "if you don't get back to *Cork,* I'm on to New York."

For the next three days he worked hard on the play, rising at five-thirty each morning, cooking breakfast for us, then sitting in front of the typewriter. Once again my boyhood stories became the cathartic force for his writing. To allay his always palpable sense of panic I embellished heavily. My well of yarns was running dry. Once again Brendan sobered up under my influence and mentorship.

One morning I informed a hungover Brendan that I had seen an army of rats cowering at the foot of the garden. "Better call the local exterminator," I advised.

"Oh never mind son," he chuckled. "They're only hangin' in till the current subsides, then they'll cross the river for their dinners. In the meantime, why don't yew look in the box and give them what's goin'. Can't expect to the poor little fuck-pigs to swim the river on an empty stomach, wha."

I went outside, cleaned out the makeshift refrigerator and threw the scraps to the rats.

"Did they thank yew at least?" he quipped as I walked up the garden.

"No, but they send their regards to yew. The commander-in-chief said something about fuck the begrudgers and long live the Republican playwrights."

Brendan giggled self-indulgently. "Good boy, good boy."

We sat down and ate our fourth breakfast of the day.

One afternoon Beatrice called and announced that she was being discharged from the hospital. "I'll be home in an hour," she said gleefully.

Hurriedly I washed up the mountain of dirty dishes and scrubbed the mounds of dried up excrement and stale urine from the two bathroom floors. Brendan's aim was usually off when he was drunk.

Beatrice moved into the room on the lower landing. I moved into Brendan's den. The early morning clatter of the typewriter keys awakened me. Beatrice sometimes served me breakfast in bed.

One evening in Cole's, Celia, who was Beatrice's sister and the lady who created the role of Teresa in *The Hostage,* turned to me and said "You're a quare fella."

"A quare fella? Why do you think I'm a quare fella?"

"Oh it's not me who thinks you're so queer, it's Brendan. He doesn't understand you, he says he can't make head nor tail out of you."

"I'm sorry to hear that Celia, I'll do what I can to mend my queer ways."

"Oh no, no," she exclaimed excitedly, "why bother, it's just that your antics and some of the things that you say baffle him," a strange little smile creeping into her beautiful face.

On the day of her arrival home, Beatrice phoned Arthur Dreifus at the Shelbourne Hotel. Dreifus was the director and coauthor of the *The Quare Fellow* film. Bryanston films, Pathé in America and the Irish Film Finance Corporation were its producers. James McKenna, the author of *The Scattering,* assisted with the scenario. Patrick McGoohan and Sylvia Syms were the stars. "Peter Arthurs is a very close friend of Brendan's, a great inspiration to him," Beatrice said to Dreifus. "He came all the way from America." An interview was arranged. I taxied to the Shelbourne Hotel, the place where the casting was going on.

"How much film experience do you have?" Dreifus asked.

"Quite a lot," I lied. "I also studied under Stella Adler in New York. Also, in Los Angeles there is a lot of important footage of Brendan and me."

I was cast as a prisoner and told to report on the fifteenth of November to Kilmainham Prison, the historical lockup where the insurgents of Easter Sunday, 1916 were imprisoned and shot by the British.

One afternoon, as Beatrice and I were sitting down to tea and biscuits, the phone rang. Beatrice picked it up, handed it to me and said, "Here Peter, it's for you."

"Listen, Peter Arthurs," a chill voice said, "irrespective of what your financial circumstances are, you have to move out of that house. *Move out at once.*"

"Who the fuck are you?" I asked.

"Move out at once," the voice repeated.

"Why? What for? What have I done wrong here? Who are you!?"

A period of silence followed, then the voice was back.

"You made the mistake of turning up Brendan's collar! You're a fool!"

"What's so fucking horrendous about turning up Brendan's collar? Where and when am I supposed to have committed this terrible atrocity?"

"The other day, when the two of you were getting into a taxi, on Ballsbridge." The phone went dead.

I reflected for a moment then recalled the incident.

"Who was that calling?" I asked Beatrice.

"An old IRA friend of B.B.'s."

"What have I done so terrible that I have to pack up and go?"

"Oh, it's not your fault, Peter," she exclaimed apologetically. "It's B.B. You know how he is, you know how he feels about you. He doesn't want you, above all people in the world, to watch him while he destroys himself."

"But he's not even drinking now, he's working on *Cork.*"

"But don't worry Peter, I have made arrangement for you to move into number 27. It's just down the road, the woman who owns the house is Petronella O'Flanagan. She's a columnist for the Irish Press. Also she wants you to go over to Borough Quay to her office to be photographed and interviewed for her Sunday column. Hurry like a good boy."

"Oh fuck it all, B., I'm going upstairs to pack my rags and fly home to New York," I said in disgust.

A few minutes later I came downstairs with my suitcase.

"Here, Peter," Beatrice said, handing me a pair of grass cutters.

"What are these for?"

"Brendan wants you to trim the lawn."

"Trim the lawn! Fuck the lawn. I'm on to New York," I said, moving towards the door.

"But won't you have some tea before you leave, you can trim the lawn first, then wash up and have your tea. B.B. will be along very shortly."

I adhered to her wish and spent the next hour clipping the hedge and trimming the grass. Then I ate and moved into 27. As I was walking out the door, Beatrice turned and said, "Brendan wants you to come every evening at six for your tea. You will come, won't you."

One evening Beatrice arrived home in a state of slight intoxication. She looked drained, wan and helpless. I greeted her with enthusiasm, but she merely charged past me and threw herself down onto the dining room table. Then she sobbed hysterically. Minutes later she lifted her head, dried her tears and poured out her upset to me.

Brendan had invited her to a pub and proceeded to become stotious. She begged him to come home but he ignored her entreaties. "The gypsies are living a better life than I am," she moaned. Then she calmed down and went on in a winsome voice. A rush of compassion swept over me for indeed I totally understood her sense of aloneness, and the incompatibility of her marriage. Obviously, she felt like a surrogate wife and camp follower. I listened attentively to her railings against her husband, patted her gently on the back and promised that I would talk to Brendan. She sat upright, and stared stonily into space. "Oh, it's no good Peter," she lamented, "it will always be the same, he won't change. He's bent on destroying himself and me too if I let him." Never before had I seen her in such a state of unhappiness. Life with the ineluctable, inept man was fast becoming a living torment. Suddenly a strange illumination came over her and she went to the kitchen and prepared for supper.

The local Anglesea neighbors affectionately referred to Petronella as "Petro." Living in her impeccable spit-and-polish home was a charm, save for the unspoken agreement which I had with her concerning her cat Gigi. Gigi was a big, furry, prize-winning, spoiled animal who was obviously aware of her beauty and importance in her home. Whenever she decided to meander into the kitchen and park herself next to the hearth, I was obligated to depart. Gigi was repelled by my strangeness and made known this chilling fact. The remainder of my evenings was spent sitting in Cole's with Celia or at the Behans' fireplace sipping tea.

For the next several weeks I arose early in the morning and bussed to Kilmainham, where I donned my prison garb and earned my two pound five shillings per day by walking in and out of scenes, always far from the sensitive lens of the motion picture camera. I grew weary and longed for New York.

One morning, out of misery and mischief, I walked across Kilmainham Square, swiped a bottle of milk from the windowsill of the Kilmainham Pub and drank it. The lady who owned the pub saw me and called the police. I anted up the price of the milk and the charges were dismissed. Later, in the prison infirmary, I got into another heated entanglement with fellow extras over their derogatory remarks concerning the "disgusting and shameful" international escapades of Brendan. Sometime later a few of the officials from Irish Actors Equity arrived and were calling for my dismissal from the lot. "What nationality is your passport?" Eamon Brennan, an actor in the film and an Equity officer, asked me.

"Don't worry about my passport," I snapped, "I'm an Irishman by birth, worry about your own fuckin' passport." A few of Brennan's fellow actors overheard me and called for my ouster.

That night at the supper table I informed the Behans of my problems on the set.

"Serves yew right," Brendan rejoined. "An intelligent lad like yew, the next time that yew steal anything in a bottle, at least make sure it's good grog, this way if yew get arrested at least yur getting arrested will be for something worthwhile."

Bright and early the following morning, as the stark greyness of dawn was replacing the dark of night, I was awakened by a strange silhouette hovering above my bed. I turned my head and found Brendan kneeling on the floor.

Brendan's body reeked with body odors. He never bathed except when he went for a swim. He began to bite my testicles, then my thighs. I jumped out of bed. "How the hell did you get in here? Does Petro know that you're here?" I shouted. "If she finds out about this, I'll wind up on the goddam street. Get out quick."

"I'll wait downstairs for yew," he moaned and tiptoed down to the street. Crossing Ballsbridge, "Cum with me," he demanded as he pushed me into a taxi, then he instructed the driver to take us to Kilmainham Prison.

"Why are *you* going there, B.?" I received no answer.

In the prison compound, the area where the bulk of the shooting was being done, Brendan confronted Arthur Dreifus. "Listen yew," he roared into the birdlike face of the bespectacled director, "when I promise someone that I will do something for them, I usually do it. Apparently *your* word is as good as your ability to direct."

"What seems to be the problem, Brendan?" Dreifus asked.

"Well, in case yew have forgotten, mister, this is Peter Arthurs, the same boy whom yew promised to give a part to in the film! Why isn't he getting his part?"

"But he's working, he's earning money every day."

"I'm earning ice cream money," I said. "I didn't fly all the way from New York to earn snotrag money. I came here to get myself established in film."

"But you're working as a prisoner," Dreifus cried.

"Yes, but I'm miles from the camera."

"What sort of a part is that?" Brendan heatedly interjected.

"But he's too healthy looking to put him close to the camera," the distraught director rejoined.

"Listen, mister," Brendan said, "b-but it would appear to me that yew sir are slightly misinformed about prison life. Yur taking a load of fuckin' gobshite for granted. Yew see, sir, I myself happen to know a thing or two about prisons and prisoners. Since fuckinwell when do all prisoners have to look like scarecrows or something that the cat dragged in off the street?"

There and then the role of Murphy, the sub-chief warder, was written into the scenario.

"Let me show you something great, Brendan," Dreifus interjected, attempting to change the subject. He led Brendan out into the exercise yard where a gaggle of propmen were digging a hole in the ground. It was the "quare fella's" grave. A bleak, shabby-looking coffin lay adjacent to the grave. Dreifus patted Brendan on the back.

"Am I surrounded by a pack of fuckin' eegits and American savages," Brendan snapped into the man's face while putting his two hands up to his eyes as though he were Dracula, shielding his sight from the daylight. Then he charged out of the yard.

Later I was instructed to report to wardrobe to be outfitted with a uniform of a different nature. The following day, at my request, Brendan returned to have a series of photos taken with me in my two-striped navy blue uniform.

For the remainder of my footage I was cordially referred to as Mr. Arthurs, artist. When I was to be used in a scene, my name was called out over a megaphone, "Mr. Peter Arthurs, will you please report to the compound." And such was the saga of my days in Kilmainham Prison, a grey fortress of a building, which was then being restored as a national monument to the brave fallen men of 1916 whose remains lay planted in the soil of the exercise yard.

Violent scenes were written into the script for me. My most violent moment arrived when I was instructed to kill the prisoner, Mickser, with a pisspot. The killing occurred during the hanging sequence, as the "quare fella," the off-camera protagonist of the serio-moral-anti capital-punishment plot, was being led to the gallows.

My killing performance was so brutally and believably played, I got a standing ovation from the stars and the extras who stood in the wings.

One year later, in the Carnegie Cinema in New York's Carnegie Hall, the scene was dropped from the film. "Why?" I asked the tuxedo-clad producers in attendance. "Too violent, much too violent," I was informed.

It is my emphatic opinion that the murmurings of literary genius are in this play. Here was Brendan Behan at his best. Only occasionally, as in the dialogue of Dunlavin who referred to sexual offenders as "sex mechanics," did Brendan manipulate the penumbra of his phobias and his sexual tastes. The range and depth of the work's true climate and meanings were abundantly in evidence. It reflected the true passions of an author who was sensitive, real and well in tune with what he was writing about. I felt proud to have been a part of this great work.

Sunday, November 26, a full center-page article about me, my present employment and vignettes pertaining to my background appeared in the *Irish Times.* The author was Petronella O'Flanagan. With great zeal and boyish delight I charged up to Cuig and pounded on the door. Brendan answered.

"Brendan! Brendan! Did you read today's paper? Did you see my picture?"

"Yes, yes, yes," he snapped and shut the door tight in my face.

For the next two or three weeks a spate of colorful stories and other photos concerning my past, present and probable future appeared in the Dublin and Dundalk papers. My name was becoming a household word. My time and my autograph were being sought after.

One night as Brendan and I were tearing down Burlington Road, a little girl came up to me with paper and pencil in hand and asked for my autograph. I gladly complied. Without deigning to look at Brendan she thanked me profusely and ran away. Brendan and I continued on in glum silence. On that particular evening I was not invited into Cuig for my usual dinner, "Shur I'll see yew tomorrow avick," he said as he slammed the iron gate that led to the house.

One night along about the middle of December, as the three of us sat eating our supper, I announced that on the following day I would travel to Dundalk "to see my father."

The Behans eyed one another surreptitiously.

"Yew won't find him in Happy Valley," Brendan said.

Happy Valley is the nickname for the neighborhood in Dundalk where I grew up. The neighborhood consists of two narrow streets lined with red brick houses. The streets are called St. Patrick's Terrace and St. Bridgid's Terrace. One street crosses the other. My family lived at number 1, St. Patrick's Terrace, in a private house built by my grandfather, Nicholas Arthurs, at the turn of the century. For three generations the Arthurs families lived there and brought up their saplings.

"But I don't understand B., my family has lived there for almost sixty years. According to my grandfather's will, the house is mine."

"Yur aul fella is presently residing at 25 Mary Street South," Brendan said without looking across the table.

An hour later I caught the Dublin-Belfast express and disembarked at Dundalk. Minutes later I was pounding on the door of number 25 Mary Street South.

My father, a man whom I had not seen in many years, came to the door. In a drunken haze, he looked long and hard at me as though he were ogling a UFO. Obviously he was suffering from a severe hangover. "Which of yiz is you?" he enquired. "Are you the Peter fellow who bes at the boxing in America? Or are you the Gerry fella who lives in London . . . no, no, no, begod you're the Michael chap, the chap who is on the Norwegian ships. Cum in avick."

"Well, sir," I said, "my name is Peter Joseph Arthurs. I bear the same name as you do. I am your second son, I live primarily in America. What are you doing in this rat trap of a house? Did you sell the family house in the Valley? And if so, why? According to my grandfather's will, that house is mine! I demand to see his last will and testament! Where is it?"

"You'll get nothing here, neither will yew see anything. You're a no-good blackguard," my sodden parent roared. "You think you're a big fuckin' Yank movie star do you now, with your big fucking face in the papers. Well, you were always a no-good blackguard. The only thing that you will get here is the prongs of a pitchfork in your face," my father said as he tried to slam the door shut in my rain-splattered face. I kicked the door in, but my entrance was suddenly stopped by the prongs of a pitchfork at my neck. I pounded on the window until my father's alcohol-stained face appeared.

"Go away, go away you dirty low-life scut, get, you," he shouted, "go away before I call the Qardai Siciona [police] and have you arrested, you whelp." I deduced that my father had sold my house and drunk the money. Forgery was one of his lifelong ways of affording himself his wherewithal.

Disgusted, I eventually returned to Dublin.

"Well, me aul son," Brendan chuckled ebulliently as I landed in, "shur I suppose your poor aul fella was delighted that a man like mesself came to pay him a visit, wha!"

"Certainly B., certainly. Sure aren't you the only international celebrity that either of us ever knew."

"Great man, avick, great man!"

"However B., don't be alarmed, I did not mention to him that we were living in sin."

"Sin avick?"

"Sin, B."

"What sin me aul son?"

"Well B., surely you would consider our relationship to be somewhat unorthodox to say the least, if in fact not downright bizarre."

One evening Beatrice brought me to 43 Morehampton Road. There she introduced me to her father and mother. Her father was a very self-contained man in more ways than one. He virtually lived in a self-made bed; boarded up with two-by-fours and plywood sheets.

He ate, drank, slept, shaved and entertained his guests there. I learned that he was a renowned playwright, painter and muralist whose work was on display on the walls of Davy Byrnes and other renowned literati hangouts in Dublin.

We talked at length of India, Africa, the Near and Far East and his travels in Tibet. Suddenly it all came back to me, Brendan's spree in Hollywood. His mention of the Dalai Lama.

"Then you must be the gentleman whom Brendan refers to as the Dalai Lama," I said as I sat looking up at the face of the huge man who was languishing in bed.

"Poor aul dear Brendan," the man said as he burst out laughing. "Will he ever stop drinking and fighting with his friends?"

"Only when he's dead I'm afraid."

We shook hands and parted.

One night Mrs. Cole, the lady whom I met at the swimming pool in Hollywood, phoned from the airport and announced that she was on her way to Rome "to see some clients." Would Brendan meet her at the airport, as she had some important things to discuss?

"Tell her to cum to Cole's," Brendan instructed me, "tell her we'll roast a goose for her. Also, Mr. Cole will give her her hole."

"Can't someone pick me up in a car?" Mrs. Cole lamented.

"Tell her that all the cars around here have flat tires," Brendan chuckled. "Tell her to take a taxi or to jog it."

A short while later in the snug of the pub, Mrs. Cole was giving out to Brendan a verbal list of the books and plays that she wanted him to have ready for her when she stopped off on her way back from Rome. Brendan closed his eyes and dropped away in willful slumber. He snored and prattled.

"Who is this cow and how is she connected to B.?" I asked Beatrice, in a whisper.

"Oh she's his agent in America," she said, "she must be doin' O.K. for herself, she lives in the Waldorf-Astoria."

I said, "Have no fear, Mrs. Cole, I'll be sure to get your works for you and in the chronological order of your desires. Have a ball in Rome and be sure to visit the Leaning Tower of Pisa. Get as close to it as you can."

The lady departed in a huff after admonishing the lot of us for not paying her the courtesy of picking her up in a car when she arrived. Then turning to the barman, she verbally blasted him for not having a napkin at her disposal, "to wipe the chicken grease from my fingers."

"Lady," the country barkeeper said in a stern voice, "this is Ireland. In this country napkins are things that mothers use to put on babies' arses." She departed. Brendan instantly came to life.

"Is she gone?" he muttered looking around the bar.

"She's off to Rome, B."

"Good, I hope they canonize her."

A few minutes later, Liam, an old IRA colleague of Brendan's, entered the bar and put "the touch" on Brendan for three hundred pounds. Brendan lapsed into another fit of snores and prattles.

"Listen B.," I said half shouting into his snoring alcohol-stained face, "I've been here now for over a month, I need a rub of the relic. Where can I get a Judy?"

"Cum with us," he said beckoning to Liam, "let's get the poor boy fixed up before his balls get rusticated and fall off."

The three of us drove to the corner of Burlington Road, Dublin's red light district. Liam parked the car. Brendan pointed to a pair of ancient-looking doxies who stood smoking, silhouetted in the amber glow of a street lamp. The December night was drizzly and misty. As I approached the two women I suddenly realized how old and shopworn they were. One of them, the older one, put up her hand and spread five fingers in my face. I rushed back to the car.

"Well, avick," said Brendan, "did she take the sting out of your knickers? Did yew get yur hole?"

"Get me hole my arse," I said. "I wouldn't touch either one of them with a cattle prod. The only way that I would attack either one of those World War One relics with *my* cock would be if I was wearing a deep sea diver's suit and had a fistful of tetanus shots in my pocket for probable rust infection."

"Great luvly gab, son," Brendan said as he jotted down my remark.

The IRA man drove off. Brendan and I walked home in the rain. "Walking in the rain is good for the soul as well as for the mind," Brendan chuckled. The saga of the pursuit of the pee-hole ended on that note.

Along the fifteen-block route, Brendan told me of his love and admiration for Liam, who was a former IRA colleague who till this day carried a policeman's bullet around in his chest. "The dirty cowardly bastards shot him at point-blank range one night as we were driving home from a raid."

He slagged the city of his birth and referred to it as a "useless airmail postage stamp, a malicious village full of begrudgers and sneering fuck faces who would begrudge a dying dog a bone. A citadel of gossip, incestuous interplays, small discussions and smaller charades."

The two pound six per day that I was earning did not cover my living expenses. On a number of occasions I attempted to borrow money from Brendan. He turned me down. All of my prized belongings: my camera, watch, ring, tiepin, cufflinks, and other extras were now in hock. I left the tickets in the care of Petro. On December the eighteenth, Beatrice, Petro and Celia threw a farewell party in my honor. Brendan was then in hospital for alcoholic gastritis.

On or about December the nineteenth, 1961, I flew to New York, deplaned at Idylwild Airport, taxied directly to the SIU hall and shipped as able seaman aboard the sulphur-carrying Cities Service-owned and -operated T.2. tanker S.S. *Bents Fort*. The *Bents Fort* was trading between Cartaret, New Jersey, and Brownsville, Texas.

XII

On February 4, 1962, the S.S. *Bents Fort* docked at Petty's Island, Philadelphia, to discharge her cargo of black sulphur. George Mc-Cartney, an SIU representative, boarded the vessel and informed me that Brendan Behan—now in New York—had been frantically phoning the SIU hall to learn of my whereabouts. "He sounded real uptight, Pete," McCartney said.

I charged down the gangway, found a public phone box on the dock and called the Algonquin Hotel. I was quickly informed that Brendan Behan was no longer welcome to stay there but was staying at the Bristol. I asked the clerk why he had been ousted but was informed that it would be unethical for him to tell me.

I thanked the desk clerk for his assistance, assured him that the hotel had taken justifiable action whatever the reason, then phoned the Bristol.

"Is t-that y-yurself avick!? Good man. Where are yew? Never mind, get here at once, how long will it take yew?"

"Well, it's like this, B., I'm over here on Petty's Island outside of Philadelphia. I'm on a tanker. We just got in from Brownsville. I doubt if I can see you this trip. It only takes sixteen hours to unload a T.2 and—"

"Fuck the tanker, fuck Philadelphia, I have something more important here for yew. Cum over cum over cum over . . ."

"I can't, B., you see according to union rules and Coast Guard regulations, I am obligated to give the skipper a twenty-four-hour notice."

"Fuck the Coast Guard, fuck the skipper, just tell the fuckin' aul ballox that yur poor father just dropped dead beyant in the carbolic country and yew being an only son have to fuck off home to bury the poor cunt."

"I'm not sure that is a viable enough reason to be able to—"

"Listen avick, will yew for jayzus sake get off the fuckin' shite pot and cunt over here before I go out of me fuckjayzus head . . . amn't I just after saying to yew that I have something of great urgency to talk to yew about?"

"Is it in connection with the film, B.? My close-ups?"

"Yes, yes yes yes yes yes. C-cum on o-o-over r-right away s-son, will yew will yew will yew. *Forfuckinjayzussake quick quick quick quick . . .*"

"Be there soon, B., don't get your foreskin caught in the wringer."

I scrambled up the gangway, darted up the ladders of the midship house, entered the master's office and said, "Excuse me Captain Riddle, but I just received some very disturbing news. My poor father just died in Ireland, God rest his soul. I have to pack up and plane it to Dublin. I have to hurry home to bury him, sir. It's imperative that I get off the ship." Captain Riddle threw his head into the palm of his hands, shook his head, muttered a few words regarding the upheavals of being a ship's master, then made out my discharge and handed me my wages.

When I arrived at the Bristol, I found Brendan naked, sitting in a corner of his room on the seventh floor. Two pages of the *New York Times* were spread out on the floor beside him. On top of the paper were three piles of steaming food; a heap of Chinese spare ribs, a mound of egg rolls and a load of chicken chow mein. A very distraught-looking man dressed in a bellhop's uniform stood against the wall with his hands in his pockets. "Excuse me, sir," he said. "My name is Davies, I'm the head bellhop here. Do you know Mr. Behan personally?"

"Not really, but maybe I can help. What is it?"

The bellman pushed a piece of paper into my hand and said, "Here will you get this money from him. He refuses to pay me. If I don't collect, I'm out six dollars and eighty-five cents." The bill was from the Huey Yuen restaurant.

"Why won't you pay the man, B., he's only a poor bellhop?"

Brendan picked the ribs, sucked the egg rolls and gorged himself with handfuls of chow mein.

I went to his clothes closet, took his passport from the inside of his jacket pockets, extricated an Irish five-pound note from between the pages and handed it to Davies. "Here," I said, "that will more than cover it, keep the change."

The bellhop smiled and departed. Brendan threw me a wicked glance, made a few extraneous noises and continued to eat. I sat down on the floor beside him and helped myself to the plentiful food. "Well now, B.," I said exuberantly, "what's all this great news that you have for me about *The Quare Fellow* and my close-ups."

Brendan snorted, burped, farted like a storm trooper and ate as though every Chinese foodshop in America was immediately due to burn down. Grease, rice and egg-roll stuffings rolled down his cheeks. A half-empty bottle of Jack Daniel's sat adjacent to him. He reached up, jerked his food-and-sweat-drenched shirt from the back of a chair and wiped his face and fingers with it, then threw it into a corner.

Suddenly he was shuffling around the room backwards, knocking over furniture, then he threw himself down on the floor and lay on his back and counted the months of the year on the tips of his fingers, "February, January, December, November, October, September, August, July, June." He suddenly stopped, gazed out the window and did a recount of the months. "June, July, August, September, October, November, December, January, February," gazing up at the ceiling. A look of doubt came over his face as he groped on the floor for another well-picked rib then began to suck on it.

In the meantime I did a fast inventory of the room. No clothing, save for one suit, one shirt and one overcoat existed. No toilet articles were in sight. The well-chewed manuscript of *Richard's Cork Leg* lay on top of the chest of drawers. "You traveled light, B.!" I said.

Brendan counted, pondered, recounted, and picked, then he got up and sat on the commode. "She might be right, she might be right," he blurted.

"Right, B., who is she and why might she be right!?"

"Listen avick," he said with great intensity, "there's a one in this town who's about to shite a baby into the world and says it's mine! What do *yew* think avick?"

"How would I know, B.! I very much doubt it, but go on, who is she? What else does she do when she isn't on her back?"

"I'll call yew in the mornin'," he said as he beckoned me to the door. I reflected for a moment. A flurry of thoughts rattled my brain.

"Listen to me, Brendan," I said excitedly, "am I to understand that yew have some broad who is yelling pregnancy and that *that* is the reason why you conned me into giving Captain Riddle Diddle that big fuckin' cockamamiedoodle story about my dad being dead and on his way to the big bucket? Have you no soul, Brendan? No respect? What! ... are you aware that I got a measly forty-eight days work out of that scow, don't you know that just about everything that I own of any worthwhile value is in half of the hockshops in Dublin; Petronella O'Flanagan is holding my stubs in the event that I do not get back in time. I don't even have the fuckinjayzus money to eat or to pay my rent!"

Brendan was running and flailing his arms, then he stopped.

"Here avick, over here, look down there," he said pointing to a red-facaded restaurant on Forty-eighth Street, "anytime that you want to fill yur gut or empty yur bladder for that matter, just go down there, eat and drink yur ballox off and sign the chit, I'll pick it up later. Jack Leipsig, the owner of the grease-pot, is a personal friend of mesself's."

"And what about the rent for this firetrap?"

"Don't worry son, yew won't wind up on the bowery, see yew in the morning, don't go getting drunk now."

I departed and rented a room for the week in the hotel.

The following morning I was awakened by a banging on the door. I opened the door. Brendan made a lunge for my genitalia. I let him play with it for a while, then pushed him away.

"No, no, no," he shouted as he grabbed for my cock.

"No need to get nutty with me, B., my cock is mine. If you want to fondle a cock, fuck with your own, that's what it's there for, O.K.?"

We ate breakfast in the coffee shop in the rear lobby, then took a brisk walk up Park Avenue. "Here avick, let's go in here," he said, entering the lobby of a sparkling highrise apartment building, then we boarded an elevator and went halfway to heaven. We disembarked. Brendan depressed a doorbell. A young, very pregnant girl opened the door and greeted us with a Dublin accent. Brendan muttered and threw himself into a wickerwork chair and began to read a newspaper which he had picked up off a table.

"I'll make some coffee," the girl said on her way to the kitchen.

The half-acre apartment had a panoramic view of Central Park. On the walls of the elegantly furnished place taxidermy abounded. Scattered around were small tables containing typewriters, books, Indian carpets, wooden idols, flags, jungle geegaws, spears, and unfinished manuscripts. I traipsed about. The formidable array of stuffed heads of the big-game animals seemed to be glaring at my every move from the high walls. "This has to be the home of some big-game hunter or writer," I blurted in astonishment.

"Doesn't he know," the girl said to Brendan with confusion.

"Doesn't I know what," I asked.

A medley of little snickers and snorts went out from behind the paper as Brendan pulled it closer to his face.

"My name is Valery Danby Smith," the girl said extending her hand, "and this is Ernest Hemingway's apartment. Now that Mr. Hemingway is dead, the apartment belongs to his wife, Mary. I was Ernest's secretary. I am now working with Mary. We're presently working on a photo and caption book. Brendan is writing the captions."

"That's very interesting," I said. "I have always been a great admirer of Mr. H. I'm a seaman. I also—"

"I came here to talk about babies, not about books or ships," Brendan cut in. The girl beamed and nodded approvingly. I deduced that this was the girl whom Brendan had spoken of the night before. Whispers were exchanged. We departed and made our way east, where Brendan depressed another doorbell.

"Who resides here," I enquired. Again no answer. An elderly lady with a heavy north European accent opened the door and let us in. "Oh Mr. Beehank," she exclaimed, "pleeze to me you, come en, come en." We walked up a flight of stairs to a large elegantly furnished room. A little boy was crawling around on the floor playing with books and toys. A silver-haired man warmly greeted us. Then a slender-built, red-haired lady came in. I instantly recognized her. She was the heroine of the film *East of Eden*. Her name was Julie Harris.

Coffee and biscuits were served. The conversation revolved around the filming of *The Hostage*. Brendan brought up the subject of homosexuality. Harris and her family changed the topic to plays and players. Brendan was adamant. Harris opined that the renowned aggressiveness of the American woman largely contributed to the rampancy of homosexuality. Julie was very anxious to play the part of Teresa. The man sitting beside her, I learned, was her husband and the coproducer of an American production of the play. Finally we departed.

For the next several days, Valery came and went at the Bristol. Her growing dislike for me was in evidence, but Brendan flatly refused to take her to Broadway's famous watering holes if she would not agree to my presence.

Brendan's feelings about becoming a father were mixed and intense. For example, he would start out a day by thumping his chest, extolling himself for the viability of his much tested spermatozoa, while slagging his wife for her inability to bear him a child. "Shur no home is a home until it's lived in by a wee chiseler or two, wha!" By midafternoon he would be savagely denying that the baby "about to enter the world" was his. Towards nightfall, as Brendan was heavily into his cups and the ubiquitous dark was closing in, his attitude once again took on a new lease. "What! . . . shur, who cares? . . . So what if it's not mine! . . . It's his! . . . It's hers! . . . It's somebody's! . . . The fact of the matter is, that it's a baby! . . . We were all babies at one time or another . . . We are all products of a woman's womb and a man's loins . . . Certainly I'll give the wee chiseler me name and proudly so. . . ."

In a very short period of time, the pub crawlers of midtown were hinting that the baby was actually Hemingway's, and that it was for that reason that he committed suicide. Brendan was a drunk who couldn't differentiate between night and day. He was impotent, gullible and the "perfect setup" for such a wool-pulling deal. Along the Great White Way, laughter and jokes abounded.

One night, to impress her, Brendan took Valery to Harlem, to Sugar Ray Robinson's nightclub. Brendan introduced Valery to Robinson. "What line of work are you in," Robinson purportedly asked Brendan. Brendan took Valery by the arm, heaved her into a taxi and took her back to the Bristol and proceeded to knock over furniture and savagely desecrate the morals and the principles of every black man in America. " 'What line of work are you in' says he! The dirty-looking buck-toothed black-faced fuck, if it wasn't for the presence of yur woman and her up the spout [pregnant] I would have there and then thumped the shite out of the spindly-looking cunt," he snapped.

The name Johnny Lombardo suddenly came to his mind. "Where is that other fellow . . . Lombardo or Lombago or whatever his cuntin' name is. Get him here quick," he said, "get him, I'll give him a check for ten thousand dollars if he will go up to that fuckin' coalbin and thump the teeth out of that big fuckin' spook."

"Will you make the check out for a pair of fives, B., and I'll chip in and do a bit myself," I said. "Come on B., I know where to find Lombardo."

In the cafeteria of the SIU hall, I introduced Brendan to Johnny Lombardo. The two men talked briefly, then Brendan turned to me and said, "Let's go home avick." The subject was dropped.

Johnny Lombardo was a Pennsylvania-born formidable pugilist of the fifties. He fought bruising battles with many of the leading welter- and middleweight contenders and world champions. One of the champions was Sugar Ray Robinson. The fight took place in Cincinnati in April of 1955. I was then Lombardo's sparring partner, roommate and personal friend. Lombardo lost a very hotly disputed split decision. The judges who voted in Robinson's favor were loudly booed and criticized. Lombardo and I then went to Venezuela to box local fighters. But our partnership soon dissolved. Lombardo returned to the rings of Miami, New Jersey and New York. I remained in South America.

Developing on-the-spot friendships, jotting down the addresses of his newly acquired friends, then dropping in unannounced, became a favorite caper of Brendan's.

One afternoon as we were on our way home from the Upper East Side, Brendan suddenly began pulling me up a flight of steps. "We'll go in here for a minute," he said, depressing a door bell. A very clergy-looking bespectacled gentleman allowed us in.

For two full hours Brendan talked like a self-testing pneumatic drill. The man sipped mint tea and listened attentively. Suddenly Brendan jumped up, ran across the room and threw himself into a chair in front of an ancient typewriter. Then in a frenzied fit he was extricating wads of precious notes from his pockets and placing them on either side of the machine. He beamed with delight as he typed rapidly. Suddenly a dark scowl swept over his face and he began to curse and punch the keys with his fists. I moved closer to find out what had angered him.

Blood, phlegm and snot saturated the paper napkins that his former thoughts had been scribbled on. Brendan had developed profuse nose-bleeds and violent fits of hacking and coughing. I made a habit of stealing fistfuls of napkins from every coffee shop and bar that we visited. These were meant to be stand-by notepads, but in his haste and confusion, he would dig into his pockets and soak up the sudden gushes with a wad of napkins that he had previously used to make notes on.

Brendan was now in a swivet. The defenseless typewriter continued to absorb the brunt of his rage. I pulled him from the chair, apologized to the gentleman who was brushing tears from his eyes while looking dolefully at his heirloomic typewriter, then dragged him down the steps. "I honestly don't think we should invite ourselves back here again for a while, Brendan," I said, as I pushed him into a taxi.

The following morning Brendan and I were heading west on Forty-sixth street. Brendan was moving at a faster pace than I. I finally caught up to him on an upper platform of the Port Authority building as he was about to board a bus to Hoboken, New Jersey. "Cum on son, cum on," he barked impatiently as he dug his quivering hand into his pocket to pay our fares.

"Absolutely not, Brendan, I refuse to board the bus until you tell me who we're visiting," I said, as I stood on the platform.

The driver of the vehicle ordered Brendan to either pay up and sit down or get off. Brendan got off and paced up and down the platform, his hands wringing behind his back, his mouth flapping and denigrating the current crop of Irish youths for their insensitivity in regards to the feelings and the needs of their elders. The bus departed.

Suddenly it came to me. New York's bars did not open until eight A.M. The time was seven-thirty. The ride to Hoboken would have taken seventeen minutes. The bus stopped directly outside an all-night cafe that catered to the twelve-to-eight shift, shipyard workers. With a little enthusiasm and fortitude he could have guzzled up a bellyful of malts before the first bolt on the door of one of his New York haunts was released. The option to hightail it back to the Big Apple and get an additional load on, or to finish up the job in New Jersey, would be up to him, depending upon his mood. Now, all was lost. The next bus would not pull out until a quarter to eight. To take it would be counterproductive. Some thirty minutes of dehydration lay in the balance. Brendan ranted and raved and acted as though he were a man who had missed his own funeral. I hastily departed.

The exigencies of becoming a papa were too overpowering for Brendan. He imbibed more heavily than ever before. His health went into a fast decline. Seldom did he sleep. Fits of delirium tremens were coming rapidly. His need to dash to the steam bath at the Hotel St. George was intensified.

Brendan was a steam bath freak. Prior to entering the hot steamy emporium he would careen around the locker room, drink up to two gallons of water, then enter the tiled cubicle and throw himself down onto the sweat-covered floor, where he sat for hours at a time, talking.

One day as I was standing outside of the steam bath, a big black man dashed out of the steam bath and said to another sweat-oozing man, "Isn't that Brendan Behan in there? I recognize his voice from the Jack Paar show."

The swimming pool of the St. George was located on the lower level of the hotel. The hotel is located in Brooklyn Heights. The pool was the largest indoor saltwater pool in the world. In the fifties and sixties, the steam bath, hot rooms, gymnasiums, basketball courts, locker rooms, shower rooms and the vast labyrinth of dark, narrow hallways were a virtual playground for the homosexuals who flocked there daily. The pool was closed in the seventies and has since reopened as a private facility. The hotel itself is being renovated, but parts of it still serve as a refuge for welfare recipients, drug addicts, gamblers, hobos, hookers, and hundreds of patients put out to pasture from New York's mental institutions.

Brendan and I became daily communicants of the pool. Another gaggle of daily patrons who flocked to the pool were the taut-muscled, coffee-colored, clean-limbed Hispanic youths of New York. Many of these broad-minded ethnics allowed the older homosexuals to fondle them for a fee. For these teenage boys, this was an easy way to earn a few extra dollars.

Brendan took advantage of this situation. These were the specific type of clear-complected youths who sent his eyes aflutter. On a number of occasions, when Brendan had suddenly disappeared for a considerable period of time, I would eventually come upon him sitting on one of the long wooden benches in the locker room, or in a kneeling position behind one of the supporting columns in the basketball court, sucking the cock and caressing the buttocks of a well-constructed teenager.

Another aspect of the layout that very much appealed to Brendan was the three diving boards at the deep end of the pool. The high board was his favorite. From that lofty perch he recited poetry and reenacted the famous speech that he made from the dock on the day that he was sentenced to three years of Borstal servitude. "Here goes fuck all," he shouted as his feet left the forty-foot board. Minutes later, Brendan resurfaced in the middle of a coterie of small boys at the other end of the pool. His togs were always missing, floating off in some other region of the pool. Brendan's problems, fears and phobias were temporarily forgotten. But on the days that his deep dark fears surfaced, in a fit of morbidity and despair he threw himself down onto one of the wooden racks and sat sullen for hours at a time while his eyes roamed and glared painfully at the young carefree boys who were prancing, shouting, laughing, horseplaying and diving. Poor Brendan, his bitter bile of a life was a terminal, torturing soul-searing condition. On a number of occasions when his superego gave way to his libido, when he was in the throes of following a very small boy into a dressing area, I grabbed hold of him and prevented him from carrying his emotions further.

One evening, after he had spent a particularly lengthy time in the steam bath, sweating profusely and touching as many limbs, cocks and brown torsos as humanly possible, Brendan emerged from the room, his two eyes bloodshot and out of focus. He staggered and wobbled from the sudden loss of body weight. "Where in jayzus name am I, avick, atall, atall?" he sputtered.

"Come on, Brendan," I said, "let's get out of here and get some grub and liquid sustenance into our guts." We dressed hastily and crossed Clark Street to a restaurant, where Brendan gorged two huge sirloin steaks, a fifth of Jack Daniel's and a case of Tuborg. Then, reeling under the heavy load, he staggered down Clark Street to Columbia Heights, where he mounted a set of steps leading up to a four-story red brick house. A pair of black carriage lamps adorned either side of the door. The house was on the Brooklyn Promenade, overlooking New York harbor. Brendan kicked the glass door of the house and did a spate of derogatory name-calling. "Come out, come out, come out, yew aul whore yew, come out before I smash the door and come in." No one answered.

A few minutes later in a fit of dulcet doom, he walked down onto the promenade, where we sat in ominous silence. Brendan grew drunker by the minute. He talked of death. His own death. "I'd like to get a heart attack in me sleep," he said. "It seems like the least painful way to go. A small price to have to pay for it all."

"Let's go home," I suggested. He didn't answer. "Who owns the house that we came from?" I asked.

"A writer."

"Which writer?"

"A Yank writer."

"Which Yank writer?" I received no answer. (Ten years later I discovered that the house belonged to Norman Mailer.) "Let's go home," I suggested.

"No, no, no," he cried.

"Shur the other one will be there hanging about like a vulture. Everytime that I stop short and turn around, shur isn't she there like Lazarus at his own wake, hanging feet first out of my arsehole."

Finally we boarded a subway and I took him to the home of Eddie Iversey, a friend who resided on Fifty-seventh street in the Bay Ridge section of Brooklyn. At Brendan's insistence we stopped off at another pub where he gulped ten straight shots of J.D. and six bottles of T.B.

Brendan sat sullenly in Iversey's living room and grew drunker by the minute, while Susan, Eddy's eight-months-pregnant wife, cooked steaks and watched Brendan in awe.

Susan placed a huge plateful of steaks in the center of the table. Brendan's eyes glistened, he reached over, picked out the largest steak and stuffed it into his mouth. His eyes, throat, and neck bulged. Susan became hysterical and rushed into the bedroom. "He's O.K.," I whispered to Eddie, who sat dumbfounded, in a state of shock.

A short while later Brendan reached up and extricated the meat from his mouth and placed it on the plate.

"Cut the meat into six pieces," I whispered to Susan who had come back. Brendan ate voraciously and in silence. We departed and took the subway home.

Somewhere in the vicinity of Greenwich Village a swarm of trainee police cadets boarded the train.

Brendan ambled up to a big beefy-looking cop, looked him seriously in the eye and asked, "Excuse me sir, but is it true what they say about yew chaps who make up New York's finest?"

The man instantly recognized Brendan.

Brendan beamed cherubically. The youthful Irish officer-to-be smiled in anticipation of Brendan springing the age-old line about St. Patrick banishing the fabled snakes and ordering them to New York to become policemen. "Yes, Brendan, and what is it that they are saying about us?"

Silence prevailed.

"That yiz are all a pack of fuckin' queens in drag."

The officer's face crumbled in disbelief.

Brendan blinked, twitched and acted as though he were eagerly awaiting the answer to the most important question he ever posed.

"What are you, some sort of a wisearse little creep?" the man bellowed.

Brendan reacted as though he were appalled by the youth's reciprocation. "You don't have to get so fuckin' impertinent," Brendan shot back, "after all I only asked you a civil question. It *is* part of your job is it not? Tch! tch! tch!" The rattle and roar of the train sent the two straphangers banging into one another. "Come on Peter," he chuckled in mock disbelief. "Let's get off of this electric sewer before these juvenile delinquents prevail upon me to call up city hall and register a citizen's complaint."

We got off at the next stop. After the subway doors had closed, Brendan thumbed his nose at the very vexed man. We took the next train home.

In the lobby of the Bristol, Valery sat waiting. At the sight of her, Brendan sighed and moaned. Her baby's deliverance was no more than a few days away. She looked gloomy and beside herself.

To add to his grief and sexual hysteria, a coterie of beautiful, effeminate-looking, olive-complected Spanish dancers had moved into the hotel. The boys were in New York to perform at a number of Latin clubs in the metropolitan area. Brendan was beside himself with misery and glee, running around the floors in the raw, banging on doors, spuming in Spanish and working frantically to get me to entice the boys into one of our rooms.

Brendan's boy-homoeroticism was becoming unbearable to him; he began to talk incessantly about Oscar Wilde and his similar sexual conflicts. Wilde had traveled to America in the 1880s and stirred the imagination of that era with his dazzling language and intellectual brilliance, without his sexual conflict being known to the public.

Not only did Brendan sorely resent Wilde for his mastery of repartee, his vital genius, coruscating conversation and infectious wit, he also resented the fact that he succeeded opulently as a playwright, as well as a celebrated public figure—without the aid of any collaborators or the mass media. Brendan also bitterly resented Wilde's heroic self-defense against the powerful "Black" Marquis of Queensberry and the entire hypocritical English Victorian establishment. Wilde's contumacious court actions ultimately exposed the frailties of his flesh and rendered him an expiatory sacrifice and whipping boy. This was a martyrdom that Brendan painfully envied, as he contemplated his own less sensational court appearances.

Brendan, a man who never truly abandoned himself for the love of another, genuinely loved the legendary Wilde. Once he confided to me that he had gone to the trouble of climbing the high wrought-iron entrance to the Père-Lachaise cemetery in Paris to visit Wilde's grave, only to be chased by the gendarmes because it was after hours. Through his vociferous public denunciations, elliptical twists and injudicious statements, Brendan desperately sought to conquer the intellectual God of his understanding.

As the wintry days passed and no orgies were manifested, Brendan's sexual angst deepened. He reveled and suffered as he observed the ethereal youths at work in the hallways; stretching, flexing, and doing a series of limbering up exercises.

One afternoon Brendan chanced along and found me talking in my limited Spanish to one of the dancers. Instantly, I lowered my voice and bent my head closer to the boy's ear. Then I waved the lad away. Brendan looked at me in horror, much as Jesus must have looked at Judas in the Garden of Gethsemane.

Valery's distrust of me rapidly burgeoned. "Why don't you get away from us, why don't you go back on your ship," she yelled at me while B. was at the gents' one night as we sat opposite one another in the Blarney Rose on Sixth Avenue.

"But we're all good friends, Val, I wish you no harm, indeed, quite the contrary. Brendan is a good friend and admirer of my dad, they're the same exact type of people, honest."

"But who did he know first, you or your father?"

"O.K. Val, as soon as B. comes back I'll split, then the party is yours." Brendan returned.

"Excuse me, B.," I said apologetically, "but it appears that a problem is developing. Valery has just made known her disgruntlement with me. I'll leave and bid you adieu," I said as I arose.

"No, no, no, yew can't leave," he roared after me while throwing his arms around me and pushing me back into my chair. "Leave this boy alone," he shouted into Valery's face, "he's my friend, he's everything to me. In the future yew're not to say anything to vex him."

Valery threw her face into the palms of her hands. Her elbows rested on top of her ample girth. The three of us sat glumly nibbling on our pickles and hamburgers.

On February the ninth we celebrated Brendan's thirty-ninth birthday in the Monte Rosa. Brendan was sullen, dour, gruff, and cross-grained. Viola, Jack Lipsig's wife, in an attempt to perk up his descending spirits, ran into the office and emerged with a Delft teapot. The girth of the pot bore the legend, "Brendan Behan, his teapot." "Here, Brendan," she said placatingly, placing an October 1961 copy of the *New York News* in front of him. "I'll bet you remember this."

On the cover of the frayed yellowing newspaper was a full-page photo of a drunken Brendan who was in the process of disrupting a performance of *The Hostage.* "You're making a muck of me play," he had roared from the rear of the theater. The Cort Theatre was located next door to the Monte Rosa. Brendan sighed with boredom, then with a quick, violent smash of his hand, he sent the teapot and newspaper flying. At the time of the incident in the theater, the box office sales had been sagging. The following day they picked up considerably.

"Oh Brendan Behan, how could you do such a terrible thing," Viola lamented, gathering up the teapot. Brendan reached down, picked up the paper, tore it into shreds and sent it flying about in a hail of confetti.

Along about the middle of the month, Brendan informed me and just about everyone else who resided in Midtown that Valery was in the New York Infirmary Hospital having their baby.

During this time, in the early hours of the A.M., in states of extreme drunkenness and total exhaustion, Brendan burst into my room and shouted, "Peter, Peter, c-cum on s-son, let's go to the George for our dip."

"But Brendan, it's only four A.M., the pool doesn't open until eleven."

The pool and its surrounding facilities had become his second home, his sanctuary from his responsibilities, those dimly-lit, sweat- and disinfectant-smelling rooms and hallways where nameless, faceless, sweet-limbed youths abounded. Here the darker side of his psyche would remain a secret. This haven, where the sounds of glug and slurp were heard in huddling hallways. No one asked for an autograph, no one cared who owned the appendages that were being groped for. Cock was king and the trappings of youthful bloom were all that mattered. Verbal eroticism was unheard-of. Physical foreplay was the prize. Stallions stalked while passive ponies lay motionless and face down on sweat-slithery hard wooden benches eagerly waiting to be pounced on. Leaking valves and rusticating pipes hissed and spewed brownish water as the old, the young, the fat and the frightened groped, gaped, gawked, took their chances, and reached for fistfuls of flesh. Periodically a feeble, ill-at-ease fellow will slip and fall on the soap- and semen-slippery floor and end up with a cracked rib, a torn cartilage or a brain concussion.

Here in this fleshy, grapple-and-grope emporium, romance is nowhere in existence. Nudity is the stark equalizer, and come is the name of the sport. Silence prevails while tricking in the maze is rampant. Once in a while, a tension-ridden sound explodes, a head pops up and a groan of surprise or look of sheer shock is overheard or witnessed.

My presence and the sight of the hordes of the no longer physically attractive men who lined the white-tiled walls of the pool, eyeballing prospective youths, assuaged Brendan's misery and confusion. Brendan's sexual orientation was roused to rut as the boys poured into the pool, their tanned, bulging bodies parading before his slitty eyes, like a phosphorescent glow in the gloom. The sight of the beautiful apparitions of God-given well-developed human masterpieces hewn by the hands of nature was the one and only antidote for his low-lying spirits. On the occasions that his outstretched, groping hands were sharply rebuffed, Brendan became afire with pain and mortification. The terrible enemy within was abundantly evident in his suddenly crestfallen face.

In the washroom the sight of his own bulging stomach and toothless grin sent him reeling into deeper travail and mental vexation. Like a dying dog, he wandered into the labyrinth, in a somnambulistic haze, to live for a time in a wicked, sodden, bleary-eyed world that he was amply familiar with. His involuntary reactions to the small catastrophe would be his own deep dark secret to cope with.

One early morning Brendan came bursting into my room and shouted, "Cum on, me aul scholeara, cumupcumupcumup, there's a luvly woman that I want yew to talk to. Wait there avick," he said pointing to the outside hallway, "I'll be back in a sec." Then, a flurry of heated orders were given to Mae, the elderly Dublin lady who operated the switchboard during the hours between midnight and eight A.M. Brendan was calling for the long distance operator. "Cum in, cum in," he shouted, "go on son, talk to her," he said handing me the phone.

"Hello, hello, is that you Peter?"

I recognized the voice. "Where are you, Beatrice?" I asked.

"Where am I? Where do you think I am? I'm in Dublin, where else? I'm certainly not in America and don't intend to be!"

"Why will you not come over, B.?"

"Why will I not come over!? I wasn't invited, that's why! How is yur man? What is he doing? Is he writing? Good thing I didn't wait for him, good thing I decided to eat my dinner. . . ."

"What do you mean, B.?"

Beatrice then went on to explain how one day, directly after lunch, Brendan excused himself and said that he had to go down to Cole's "to meet a friend. I'll be back for supper," he assured her. Later Beatrice ate her supper alone, while Brendan dined on an airplane far out over the North Atlantic.

"Do your best to get her to cum over," Brendan whispered.

"B., B. wants you to come over, so do I. Will you come?"

"If he invites me, I might," she said. "But let him do the asking. He's a man, isn't he! However I probably won't come, Peter, it would be very crowded with the three of us, Peter."

"How do you mean, B."

"Oh come on now, Peter," she said in a harsh tone, "don't you above all people go getting the same as the others!!"

"I still don't follow you, B," I lied.

"I'm talking about Valery. She's in the hospital, isn't she? Does he still believe that the baby is his? Tell him what a goat he is, won't you for God's sake, before it's too late. Can't you get him on the next plane before he becomes the laughingstock of New York. Watch the windows like a good boy, won't you! And keep the manuscript safe."

"Slan leat."

During the weeks to come, Beatrice made fifty to sixty transatlantic calls, sometimes calling up to four times in a twenty-four-hour period. Under no circumstances would she talk to Brendan.

"What did she say avick? Is she on her way? Will she cum wha?"

"What did who say, B.? Who? What in the world are you on about?"

Word was now circulating around town that Brendan's future was in the hands of a young, shrewd, baby-faced thinker. A manipulator. *I* was being referred to as a "shark."

One afternoon I received a call from a lady who begged me to talk Brendan into giving her and her husband a story and some photos. The pair were husband and wife. He was a photographer, she was a writer. "Call me later," I said. "I'll see what I can do," I said to the woman.

While I was in the process of putting down the receiver, I overheard a man's voice: "The little drunken son of a bitch is surrounded by sharks and this guy is obviously the biggest shark of them all. O.K. honey, be up in a minute, soon as I dry this batch."

The phone went down. I called the number that they had given me.

"Oh, hello," the female voice said, "you called so soon, I know it's good news."

"Great news," I said, "my name is Arthurs, *Peter Arthurs,* not shark, sharko, or sharkey."

"Oh no, no, you don't understand, you see I was talking to my husband. He was in the basement. That's where he does his developing. I'm so sorry. I didn't mean any harm. Oh, we need the story so desperately. I'm just getting over a heart attack, my husband has—"

"Bye-bye lady," I said. "I'm not running a benevolent association for slanderers or broken-down photographers. Get a plastic heart."

I hung up. Minutes later the phone rang. "Oh Mr. Arthurs, I sincerely hope you will reconsider and—"

"Fuck off, lady."

One morning Brendan introduced me to a man named Perry Bruskin. Perry had been the stage manager for the Broadway production of *The Hostage.* Later that afternoon Perry phoned and said, "Peter, how would you like to see *The Hostage?*"

"*The Hostage?!*"

"Yes."

"How? Where? When?"

"Tonight, any night."

"Perry, *The Hostage* went off over a year ago! What are you talking about?!"

I was informed that *The Hostage* was currently running at the Circle In The Square Theatre in Greenwich Village.

"The Circle In The Square Theatre in the Village! Since when?"

"Since February the fourth."

"February the fourth?"

Perry introduced me to the cast and to Shelley Winters.

Much as I expected, the play was totally chaotic; a very bubbly bouncy type of musical, chock-full of political chicanery, social hypocrisy, jibes, jokes, limericks, bubbling performances, music, hustle and bustle, and filled with the same type of Svengali razzle-dazzle that made Brendan famous.

However, many of its cheap, below-the-belt shots at the Irish were irksome. The overall directorial craftsmanship was brilliant. The prancing, sashaying, guffawing character called Rio Ria that was played by a big burly black man in boxer's attire was the perfect symbol of what Brendan wanted to believe about pugilists. I personally felt that the character lacked real believable muscle and power. He wallowed in thematic trivia and lampoonery. The overall power of the play desperately depended upon the total talents of its smaller players.

"How did yew like the play?" Brendan asked.

"Ask Perry," I said caustically. "I already gave him my review."

One night in the famed Cedar Tavern on University Place in Greenwich Village, Brendan held court until early morning. He was preaching to a mixed bag of New York's avant-garde writers and artists. His staccato outbursts came in their usual, frothy, loudmouthed manner as he projected his chemistry and banged the drums of war.

Approximately once each half hour, he interrupted himself to call for a law to imprison pedophiles. Finally he excused himself and went to the bathroom. Sam Dilberto, the co-owner of the bar, eased over to the entrance of the toilet and awaited Brendan's reemergence. "Brendan," said Sam, putting a friendly arm around him, "Come on, what say we call it a night. You've had more than enough for one night, tomorrow's another day, go home, get some shut-eye. Be a good guy."

A look of perplexity suffused Brendan's face. "But jayzus avick," he said to the burly bar owner, "I haven't had a drink all day."

The two men stood eyeing one another in stark confusion. Brendan was telling the gospel truth. On that particular day, he hadn't had a drink. A lightning-quick transformation came over him. He went back to his seat, sat down and remained glum for the remainder of the night.

An irksome female had by now gotten into the fray. Her name was Beverly Bently. She was an aspiring actress and Valery's closest friend. One day Beverly turned to me and in a very bold, cold manner said, "You worry too much about Brendan. Why don't you go away and forget about him. We can take care of him."

Later that same day the phone rang. The caller was Valery. In my Behan best I said, "Yes, this is Brendan Behan, what in fuck's name can I do for yew?"

"Oh, I just called to say that Beverly wants you to write in a part for her in your new play."

"Tell her she's too concerned with the nonsense called acting," I said abruptly, "but I'll see what I can do for her."

Brendan was coming apart at the seams. Beatrice, by way of the transatlantic wire, made me his guardian, his "keeper."

"He's on his last legs, better come over," I warned her.

"Call Jim Downey, he'll help you get him into hospital," she said. "You sign the papers. I'll keep in touch. *Slan leat.*"

I phoned Archie Downey, Jim's son. "I need your old man's assistance Archie. It's Behan, he's dying." Archie gave me his father's phone number in Miami. I called immediately and reversed the charges.

"Mr. Downey says he never heard of you," the operator said.

"Please tell Mr. Downey that the call is an emergency one, it concerns the life and possible death of Brendan Behan."

Downey's voice came over the long distance wire. "Look here, kiddo, I'm down here on vacation, why are you bothering me? Throw the animal into the Liffey River."

"But the Liffey is in Dublin, Jim, this is New York." I hung up.

One evening along about five o'clock, Letty Cottin, Bernard Geis's promotion and subsidiary rights director, called me to say that she was coming over right away to buy some new clothes for Brendan and to get him spruced up for a few radio and TV appearances. Geis was Brendan's publisher. Brendan was in debt to him for approximately twenty thousand dollars. I gave Brendan a quick scrub, polished his shoes, and combed his hair with a damp towel. I also clipped his nails. Letty arrived promptly, "Let's go to Cy Martin's," I suggested.

Martin's was one of the most elegant haberdashery stores on Broadway. Its window was aglow with autographed photos of famous baseball players and movie stars. Brendan eyed the pictures disdainfully.

Inside the store Brendan quickly disrobed and charged around in the raw, cursing and knocking over racks of expensive clothing, then he reenacted the Glasnevin shoot-out, improvising the gun with a shoe tree.

The bespectacled salesman pulled the curtains, doused the lights, asked a few female customers to leave, then locked the doors. "Please tell Mr. Behan to at least put on his shorts," the man pleaded, while he wheedled, and coaxed Brendan to dress.

"But look," I said pointing to Brendan's urine- and excrement-caked clothes that lay in a pile on the floor, "he has no shorts, you have drawersful of them, sell him a few pairs, Letty has an American Express credit card, she will pay for them."

Brendan's measurements were taken and a couple of complete outfits were purchased. A dozen shorts were included in the purchase.

The off-Broadway production of *The Hostage* was breaking all previous off-Broadway records. Brendan's royalties were being spent mostly on doctor's bills. Another road company considered me for the role of the Russian sailor. Brendan wouldn't hear tell of it. "He's too Irish-looking, much too Irish," he said to Bruskin. Brendan refused to talk to lawyers, producers, directors, doctors and agents without my presence. He had by now a full contingent of doctors attending him. Dr. Alter Weiss was the honcho. The very attentive doctor talked seriously to Brendan about his health and suggested a rehabilitation program. Brendan wouldn't hear tell of it. "Such a program wouldn't fit in with me present plans." He gave me a strict regimen of pills and other medications to administer to Brendan, but Brendan took his A.M. pills in the P.M. and his P.M. pills in the A.M. In so doing he conveniently did not have to own up to his fatherly and literary responsibilities.

Beatrice kept up her barrage of calls. "Keep trying to get him on the next plane out, won't you Peter," she begged. "If you are lucky enough to succeed, don't forget to pack *Richard's Cork Leg* and make him take his medicine." I assured the very distraught lady that I would try.

One night a very young bovine girl arrived from San Francisco to talk to Brendan. Brendan was out. I greeted her. "I want to do the part of Colette in the next road tour of *The Hostage*," she cried. We ate supper in the Monte Rosa and later went to bed, where I made love to her.

"Go easy with my breasts," she said.

"Why?"

"They're sore."

"Why are they sore?"

"I just had a baby!"

"Whose baby?"

"Brendan Behan's."

"Where did you get pregnant?"

"In Los Angeles."

"In Los Angeles. Where in Los Angeles? What date?"

The girl looked at me in disbelief, dropped her eyes and sat silently.

The following day I introduced her to Perry, but the then director of the play confided "she's too young to portray the tough-talking Dublin doxie."

The following day the disturbed girl flew home to San Francisco without ever meeting Brendan Behan.

One Saturday night along about the end of February, Mrs. Cole, the agent, phoned in to advise me that she had arranged for Brendan to spend Sunday on Huntington Hartford's Paradise Island in the Bahamas, "The sea, sun and sand will do him a world of good." I wholeheartedly agreed. Brendan was ecstatic. The celebrity plane was leaving at seven-fifteen in the morning. Another plane, the one carrying the noncelebrities was leaving at eight o'clock. "I'll be traveling with Brendan on the celebrity plane," Mrs. Cole informed me. "If you are coming you will have to travel on the eight o'clock flight. You are not a celebrated person." Brendan agreed.

"So why are *you* traveling on the early plane?" I enquired.

"*I'm* his agent, I'm a celebrity," she stated flatly. "I'm depending on you to have him prim and proper and at the airport on time. Call you early in the morning, bye."

"Will do, Mrs. Cole, be sure to call!"

Very early in the A.M. Mrs. Cole called and said "Put Brendan on, there are a few last-minute details to be worked out." I excused myself and returned to the wire.

"Brendan says to proceed to the airport, he will meet you there." I hung up quickly.

Minutes later, she called again. "What's all this intrigue about?"

"Well Mrs. Cole, you said you were depending upon me to get him up and out, so he is in the bathroom, shitting, showering and shaving or whatever else big celebrities do when they are in the process of making a grand entrance. Do you wish for me to disturb him!?"

"No, just tell him to be there!"

"I will, dear woman, I will. Call back if you have a problem!"

The lady called back. "Listen Pete, something irritating has just come up. The staff out here at the airport insists that I am not a celebrity and refuses to allow me to board the celebrity plane. I want to talk to Brendan."

"Hold on, Mrs. Cole, hold on." I lay the phone down for a time.

Then I returned to the wire. "Brendan says that since you are his American representative, you are very definitely a celebrity. A celebrity of major magnitude. You're to be granted space on the celebrity flight at once. He says to tell you that if the whores' melts don't let you board that fuckinjayzus contraption, *he* will not travel! Pass the message to Hartford."

"Why doesn't he tell me that himself? Why will he not come to the phone? What is all this about!? Put him on right away."

"Mrs. Cole," I said resignedly, "Brendan Behan is presently in the painful process of getting into his tuxedo and I'm sure that I do not have to relate to you, particularly at this ungodly hour of the A.M. how B.B. feels about tuxedos. Tuxedos are not exactly the attire or the bib of house painters, or working-class writers. Now you know how much of an aversion he has for zippers, hooks, and such mechanical contraptions. Do you wish for me to disturb him? Call back in fifteen minutes, *please! please! please!*"

I hung up, then picked up the phone and instructed Mae that Mr.

Behan did not wish to receive any more calls this morning. "He's wiped out, Mae. O-U-T. Out."

"How right he is," said the kindly Dublin lady, "shur the half of them must be drivin' the poor fella out of his wonderful, God-given, gifted mind, bad cess to them, by God I can tell you this much, they won't bother him anymore this live-long night."

"Thank you, Mae, and a bed in heaven to you."

We slept until two P.M. Brendan's sleep was considerably sounder than mine.

Sometime during the hours of the very early morning, with the aid of a safety pin, I scraped the contents out of three of Brendan's vitamin capsules and reloaded them with a powerful sleep-inducing potion that I had taken from another set of capsules, then handed him a glass containing several fingers of Jack Daniel's. "Here B., take this, this will do you a world of good and help you to get some good sleep to boot." The role of Nurse Nightingale was becoming a coveted role.

When he finally awoke, he reeled around the room and asked, "What time is it?"

"Two P.M., B. Did you have a good kip?"

He staggered about, went into the bathroom, tilted the mirror, eyed me coldly and sputtered, "Yes t-too g-good I'm afraid, if my memory is still serving me right, I kind of remember that I was supposed to be doing something this morning." He began to do another of his three-hundred-sixty-degree runs of my room, spuming, fuming, and screaming a conglomeration of indecipherables, then he went back to the bathroom. Standing on the tips of his toes and leaning into the mirrored door, Brendan kept one eye on the blackheads that he was supposedly squeezing from his chin. The other eye remained riveted to my reflection in the mirror. Hysteria was in his eye. His lips quivered. His hands trembled. The intuitive man was aware that he was supposed to be somewhere. Somewhere very important! Where!!?

He was also aware that he was supposed to be doing something! Something very important! What!!?

Suddenly it dawned upon him! The tyranny of his sudden remembrance was now in his bulging eyes, his drooping jowls. I moved closer to him until our two heads were adjacent to one another. Brendan was suddenly consumed in a fit of near collapse. I put a reassuring hand on his shivering shoulder. "Oh that reminds me, Brendan," I said gingerly, "today is Sunday, the day that you are supposed to be on Paradise Island in the Bahamas serving as the guest of honor in the home of Huntington Hartford. However, needless to announce, things turned out slightly different, as you can see," I said loosening my grip, "Shit man, you were sleeping so fucking soundly I just didn't have the balls to awaken you. But then again, B., me aul Cavan ma always said, 'Nothing like a good night's kip, when the body is in need of repair.' Besides I'll bet that that fuckin' sun-cooked island is at the moment being stampeded with singers, dancers, movie stars and hordes of others from that bird-brained walk of life. Wha! I mean to say, who needs them, right B.?" I went on while patting him gingerly on his hunched-over back. "Also, the whores melts might have succeeded in getting you drunk as a skunk. You might have wound up with a broken leg from a fall in the white-hot sand. I'd never have forgiven myself had I awakened you. A mishap like that would have gotten you onto the front page of every paper in America. And why, may I ask, should *you* be the one to go out and get a ton of valuable publicity for that lot, that shower of ingrates, a swarm of fuck-faced chancers who would step on their own mother's left tit, all for the sake of getting their plastic jibs onto some rag. Let them do their own pick and shoveling, right, B.?" The mirror door was suddenly blurred with Brendan's bated breath. His chest heaved as he struggled under its weight. He had so dearly looked forward to the sycophancy.

"Be happy you're here, B.," I said while moving briskly towards the door. "Soon as you freshen up a bit with a good wank and a shower, you'll be back on the old terrain, on Forty-eighth Street where you belong, amongst the church-going Irish-American working class. Our class, the real salts of the city. See you later," I concluded and quickly departed, leaving Brendan to his faith.

A few days later Mrs. Cole called in to say that she had had a wonderful time on Paradise Island. I assured the lady that I would be "more than happy to relay the message to the great man. Brendan was simply too tuckered out to attend," I apologized.

XIII

Michael M. Murphy was a personal friend of mine. He was also an FBI agent, the specific type of law enforcement officer that Brendan Behan feared and loathed. Murphy wanted to meet Brendan. Mary, Michael's fiancée, was an actress who very much wanted to do the role of Colette.

The Intermission Bar was located next door to the Cort Theatre. One night in the Intermission, I introduced Brendan and Murphy. The intuitive Brendan was instantly aware of the man's occupation.

"I saw your play next door," Murphy said to Brendan.

Brendan, with glass in hand, stared up into the riveting face of the big burly agent, frozen like a frog looking into the jaws of a boa constrictor. In a flash he darted from the pub, charged across the street and into the lobby of the Bristol. "What the hell's the matter with *him?*" Murphy asked, as we watched from the window.

For the next few minutes we stood looking out through the dust-encrusted, neon-lit window. Brendan was performing the same type of exercise from the vantage point of the Bristol lobby. The staring episode went on interminably. Then I went across the street and into the lobby. Brendan ran to the rear of the lobby like a little boy cowering from a wicked schoolteacher about to spank him.

"It's O.K., B., he's a personal friend of mine, his fiancée's an actress. She's presently trying for the role of Colette."

Brendan stared at me. Paranoia was in his eyes. His empty glass was still in his hand. Then he threw the glass to the floor and charged into an opening elevator.

An hour later he was back in the predominantly black bar shouting down and denigrating sheriffs, clansmen, rednecks and John Birchers.

A short while later, two elderly ladies were walking up Forty-eighth Street with theater playbills in hand. Brendan, upon eyeing the bills, dashed out of the bar, grabbed the bills and autographed them. "Did I ever tell you that *my* play *The Hostage* was the only success around here in years?" he asked.

"Brendan, did I ever tell you that I regard autographing books and pamphlets as the world's number one idiotic ritual?" I said.

The fear of being institutionalized in a fit of madness was now uppermost in his mind. He continued to rant and rave and talk as though he was a prophet born for one purpose only: to bear witness to the truth. "Rubber-room" were his most dreaded words. He quickly jammed his fingertips into his ears whenever I made mention of them. He was vividly aware that Beatrice was urging me to hospitalize him. What he was not aware of was the nature of institution I would commit him to in an emergency. Would it be a community of the mad? In public, he spoke frothily of madness as though it were the proof of elegance and the stormbird of the eccentric's, the genius's, the revolutionary's and the Irish dramatist's consciousness.

Brendan's madness, miseries and intense paranoia continued to propel him to ever greater heights of fame. Sal and Mike Mineo continued their pursuit of *Borstal Boy* as a film project. Andy Pollette flew in from Los Angeles in the frail hopes of getting even a few pages of rough draft. Requests for him to write feature stories about New York poured in from national magazines.

Pollette hung around for a few trying days but finally gave up in despair. Prior to his departure he assured me that my immediate future would be financially secured if I could get Brendan's name on a few sheets of typing paper. The Hollywood screenwriters would fill in the rest. I thoroughly assured him, "I will do my damndest." Unfortunately for both of us he returned to Hollywood without the cherished papers.

Alter Weiss called and ordered me to keep Brendan walking and swimming. I was to take charge of Brendan's pharmacopia. But Brendan was sinking to the level of a human semaphore who lived in a misty fog. Playing the role of the dying king in his coffin became another pastime. Seldom did he close the door to his room. "Cum in cum in, cum in," he shouted whenever he heard a pair of footsteps in the hall.

One night Letty Cottin came to the hotel with a female friend. "I want to talk to Brendan, it's very important," she said. "Will you bring him to the lobby?"

"He's up in his room," I said, "goupgoupgoup."

"Oh no," she said while stepping backwards. "I was up there already and he closed the door and asked us to get into bed with him. I had to get out of there in a hurry."

"Tch tch, Letty, how naive of you. Just go on back up there and let the pair of you put your arms around the poor man, he won't touch you, he's harmless, he's just very lonely."

Minutes later the two ladies returned to the lobby, beaming and twittering. "You were so right, Peter," Letty chuckled, "poor Brendan, he only wanted us to lie down beside him for a few minutes and put our arms around him."

Brendan continued to display sporadic and remarkable recuperative powers. One morning at approximately five A.M. I was awakened by the phone. "Get up here right away, me aul son, I have a great yarn to tell yew, cumupcumupcumup . . ." I hurried up the fire escape and found Brendan beaming with rare ecstasy. He was sweating profusely while dressing.

"What's the big news, B.?"

"Cum on son," he said joyfully, "we'll go for a ramble."

We hurried eastwards in the chill of the bone-cold early A.M. Then we sat down on the steps of St. Patrick's Cathedral. He remained mute. Sitting there beneath the spiraling gothic arches of that lofty house of Christian worship, I wondered what was on his mind.

"What's this early A.M. constitutional all about, B.?"

He remained mute, a benumbed look on his angelic face. Suddenly he decided to talk. "Bejayzus avick, b-but do yew know what it is, b-but d-didn't yur one give me a right fucking bollixing, the best bit of plating that I ever heard of, wha! She sucked every drop out of me. I couldn't get away from her, she grabbed hold of me balls with one hand, jammed the fingers of the other hand up me arse and held tight until she got it all, every last fuckin' drop."

His mind was far away in another orbit as he prattled on and retold of the blow-job that he had had minutes before. The young lady who had given him what sounded like his first blow-job was an actress from the off-Broadway production of *The Hostage*. On several occasions, unbeknownst to Brendan, she slipped into the hotel and gave me the same savory treatment.

Brendan's unique ability to put himself across as a potent puncher and worldly figure never ceased to fascinate me. In Hollywood, in Dublin and in New York on countless occasions he told and retold of his "lean, mean days," the elixir of his youth when he worked as a pimp in Paris, in Harry's Bar, "a sleazy place where Fitzgerald, Hemingway, Mailer and Faulkner hung out, shur what's a fella to do when his readies are low wha? . . . I had to write pornography for the local rags, to keep body and soul together. Shur doesn't hunger make pornographers out of us all."

On the cold grey steps of the revered Catholic shrine, named in honor of our patron saint, the tale of the blow-job went on. "Begod avick, it was luvly . . . we'll have to get her again wha . . ."

Then his jowls suddenly sagged. Horror was in his eyes and the twitch of his lip. The thorough ingestion of the semen suddenly disturbed him.

Brendan was suddenly morose and depressed.

For some time I had been aware that the disease of alcoholism was threefold: spiritual, mental and physical. The theory is that the spiritual aspect is the first to go and the last to come back. Alcoholism I learned was a great exacerbator of feelings of low self-esteem. Depression, paranoia and hysteria are other symptoms. As he talked, his feelings of low self-worth sounded as though they were at their lowest ever. His despair, misery and depression became more palpable. A quick energizer was necessary. I reminded him that, had it not been for his incarcerations, fears, phobias, sufferings, courage and talents, hordes of actors, producers, directors, stagehands, grips, cameramen, and even writers would be jobless and probably be behind the eight ball with their mortgage upkeep.

Brendan's face suddenly lit up into a cherubic glow. His eyes glistened and shone. "Good man avick, good man," he chirped and banged me on the side of my leg with his fist. I pursued my source and enlightened him to the fact that a great many individuals who had never before seen the light of day or even expected to, were now in the process of relishing the physical and mental comforts that only a modicum of success in the theater could bring: "All as a normal consequence of your determination and will to succeed," I assured him.

"And what about those who were finally able to settle down and marry and subsequently bring new life into this world," I quickly interjected in a subtle tone.

Brendan's head was now leaning over onto my left shoulder. His ears were cleaving to my words. I deliberately spoke in low-keyed, fast monotones. I wanted to be sure that he was listening attentively. Brendan was not one who ordinarily took kindly to words of comfort.

"Let's get the fuck out of here, my ballox are frozen and crawling up my arsehole," I said. "I feel like Dracula on the day that he missed the last bus to fogsville," I said as I moved off at a rapid pace, leaving Brendan sitting numbed on the steps.

"Wait for me, hold on," he shouted as he ran to catch up to me. Brendan then said that he would settle down and work prodigiously on his play. Freshly typed pages of *Cork* littered the floor and furnishings of his room, but his period of productivity was of a short-lived duration. On that afternoon he guzzled up two bottles of Jack Daniel's, chased with white wine and pink champagne.

Early the following morning, I was awakened by an ear-defiling clatter of kicks and thumps. "Get up avick, getupgetup."

We spirited south on Sixth Avenue. "Where are we bound for, B.?" I stopped short. "Brendan," I said crisply, "if you don't tell me where we're going, I'm making a U-turn."

A period of silence ensued, then suddenly he growled, "Well, if yew must fuckin' well know, we're on to Burton's to buy mesself an overcoat, some fuckin' Mafia ballox stole me other one." Brendan had left his overcoat behind in an Italian barbershop the day before.

We spirited ahead at a faster pace. On the corner of Twenty-third Street and Sixth Avenue I stopped short. "Brendan, Burton's is on Grafton Street, and I can assure you that there are no corners of Grafton Street within three thousand miles of this asphalt jungle. What you need is a swimsuit and an oxygen tank. You're as fucked up as a Chinese fire-and-boat drill." He stopped short several paces in front of me, looked skywards, sighed and fell against a building.

"O.K. me aul son," he groaned, "we'll fuck off b-back to the Bristol, where's the car?"

"The car Brendan? . . . I sold it Sunday to a Mexican playwright."

Brendan's alcoholic slip was showing. His incredible intakes were causing irreversible insult to his brain. We taxied back to the Bristol. Later that night Mae made an urgent call to my room, "Come down avick, right away, there's a quare-looking fella pulling your man out the door!"

I charged down the stairs and found Brendan being pulled throug the lobby by "a friend."

"Where are you taking him, Bernie?" I demanded reprovingly.

"Oh, just up the street, to a friend's place," he said casually.

I reached over, released his grip on Brendan and said, "A friend's place? What place? Where?"

"Look, Peter," the man said coldly, "this friend of mine opened this joint a few months ago, see, and it's going down the tube, it's a swell bar, but he can't get it moving. I promised him a little publicity, know what I mean?"

"I know just what you mean, Bernie, but we have a problem. You see I promised Beatrice that I would look after Brendan and that is what I intend to do. Good night."

I took Brendan to my room and put him to bed, then phoned Phillip Auditore, and had him sit up with him while I got some sleep.

In spite of his rapid decline, Brendan continued to weave his glittering little webs of wickedness. He managed to get Valery and Mae into a brouhaha with each other. Valery accused Mae of listening in on her phone conversations. "I never would have suspected her," Brendan said with utter disbelief.

His macabre humor was surfacing. One day as we were heading south from Beverly Bently's apartment, I turned around and discovered that I had been talking to myself. Brendan was nowhere in sight. Down the street several wooden barricades were cordoning off a series of holes in the street that were being dug by one of the city's utility corporations. I walked over to one of them that was shaped like a coffin and found Brendan lying on his back with his hands joined as though in death.

"Will you for fuck sake get to hell up out of it?"

He arose, shook the mud from his trousers and continued on foot. "Your carbolic wit sometimes bothers me, B.!"

"So what of it," he snarled, "I'm for the big jump soon anyway."

Valery and I were getting along in our own icy way. Whenever she spoke to me, her words came in short, crisp, staccato volleys. Brendan sneered, giggled and grunted. Our at-odds type of relationship sent him into pirouettes of ecstasy.

One day I took it upon myself to go to the hospital on my own and for her own sake pleaded with her to put her baby up for adoption. "One of these days he's only going to fly away and forget about you," I said warningly.

"Get out of here," she yelled. "What would you know about Brendan Behan." I departed a wiser man.

Brendan's spirits continued to sag. Fatherhood panic, sexual hysteria and delirium tremens took over.

One day the manager of the Bristol phoned me and said, "Listen Mr. Arthurs, we have a great deal of respect for your friend Mr. Behan, but if he is to remain as our guest, he will have to keep his clothes on and stay out of the lobby."

"Be right down, sir, please don't call the cops."

I found Brendan running around in the lobby with his pants down by his ankles. A pool of vomit lay on the floor. I was informed that Brendan had pinched the breasts and goosed the derrieres and the vaginas of some very elderly guests. "I don't want to have to ask him to leave," the manager moaned, "he's such a sweet, talented man."

As I was about to drag him to the elevator, Brendan went into a tantrum, pointed out the window to the marquee of the Cort Theatre and shouted, "I'm Brendan Behan, I'm a genius. I had two plays running at that theatre over there."

Brendan was partially right. *The Quare Fellow* had been produced off-Broadway.

"Please take him upstairs," the desperate hotel manager cried.

"Come on B., let's go," I said crisply. But Brendan was adamant. He refused to budge until I answered an important question.

"But do y-yew get a t-thrill out of w-watching a s-six year old b-boy u-undressing?"

"Yes, yes, yes yes come on come on come on . . ."

He pulled up his pants and followed me to my room. While Brendan slept I read the almost-finished drafts of *Richard's Cork Leg*.

The play was typical Brendan vintage: bold, bawdy, crudely energetic; cartoonery and political angst abounded. I was more than pleased to find that my long-ago early-morning Hollywood chats had had a profound impact on its confused author. My spur-of-the-moment theories and impromptu gushes had added spirit and exuberance to the discursive plot. Brendan's well-concealed lavender was now surfacing more dramatically in his work. The mention of the word queer was rampant, but in a compassionate manner.

Brendan's health was barreling downhill at an alarming rate. Bernie Geis, Letty Cottin, Jack and Viola Lipsig, Perry Bruskin, Mae and many more were begging him to join the fellowship of AA. "Listen, but if there's anything that grossly displeases me, it's listening to boring drunk-a-logues," he barked. "Furthermore. I do not need to be twelve-stepped, goose-stepped or stepped upon in any other form or fashion," he concluded. The subject was dropped.

One day I turned to him and said "B., I just now heard of the horrible death of Ernie Kovacs." Kovacs had died in a car crash.

"He didn't cum to me fuckin' party at the Pacific Railroad Station," he growled.

"How can you be so fuckin' wicked," I asked.

"Well shur, if that's how I am, says yew, then I feel obliged to state that that must be a part and parcel of me metier and mien, and to those who don't like it, I say to them, fuck off."

"It doesn't bother me, B., if and when I get to that junction in life I won't be around, but then again *I* feel morally obligated to state that I can't be *all* right, either. How could I be? Taking into consideration the very nature of some of those that I take into my friendship. . . ."

In Dublin Brendan had once told me that he had thrown Virginia Mayo and Michael O'Shea out of his house merely because they were slightly intoxicated: "If there is one thing that grossly disgusts me it's a drunk and disorderly person. Women in particular."

One morning Brendan burst into my room, "P-Peter, P-Peter, Peter, guess what, s-son . . ."

"P-Peter, Peter, Peter, what, what, what?"

"P-Perry Bruskin wants me to play a part in the new road company production of me play. What do you think avicko?"

"Forget it Brendan, you're no actor, besides you wouldn't last three performances. You'd get drunk and fuck up. Then you'd wind up with a lawsuit up your arse." A sudden wave of overwhelming desolation swept over him. Brendan was the most frustrated actor that I had ever known. He made a few piteous moans, then lapsed into a spell of coughing and retching that wracked the whole of his body. Tears ran down his cheeks. His face became sepulchral.

Brendan was now spoiling for fights. He was aware that Art Carney, the Irish-American comedian and TV actor, was a nightly communicant at Eddie's, a bar located next to the Huey Yuen. Brendan sorely desired to engage Carney in a verbal shoot-out, but Eddie the bartender, sensing Brendan's intentions, barred him permanently from the pub. "Fuck yew, I've been trown out of better places," Brendan snorted.

Another night when on the way home from a party at Geis's house, Brendan spotted Jack Dempsey standing on the corner of Forty-eighth Street and Broadway. "Oh there's me aul friend Dempsey," Brendan said, "I'll go over and take the piss out of him."

"Go ahead, B.," I said, "I'll wait for you in the lobby."

An hour later Brendan arrived home, his head, eyes, ears, nose and teeth still intact. I took it that his meeting with the former heavyweight mauler was one of conviviality.

Brendan's knack for becoming the star attraction of curbstone playlets was a thing that was still very much intact. One morning as we were making an exit through the hotel lobby, an elderly Irish lady who was living in the hotel suddenly slipped on the step leading onto the curbstone. Brendan dashed to the rescue and prevented the lady from falling. Upon becoming aware of the chivalrous man's identity, the lady looked him in his bloodshot eyes and said, "Well now, even in this day and age, it would appear that there is still a bit of chivalry left in this rat-infested jungle, even if it does come from a dirty rotten bowsie, the likes of yourself." Further on down Broadway another fan informed him that he looked "well and prosperous." "A mere temporary condition," he assured the lady.

A short while later another idolator stopped Brendan and said, "Good morning Mr. Behan."

"What's so fuckin' good about it," Brendan barked.

At Bookmasters we perused the books in the bountifully displayed window. Books with photos, sketches and the name Oscar Wilde abounded. "Hey, Brendan," I said excitedly, "I never realized that Oscar Wilde was an Anglo-Irishman. I always thought that he was pure Irish."

Brendan turned savagely, looked me up and down as though I were galvanized with a leprotic substance. "Are yew fuckin' mad is it, or what? *Oscar Wilde an Irishman!* Is that all that the fuckin' Christian Brothers taught yew beyant? Oscar Wilde was no Irishman, Anglo or otherwise. Oscar Wilde was a Dublin writer like mesself," he roared at the top of his congested lungs while hacking and pounding his chest with his fist.

One afternoon in an attempt to bring him together physically I took him to the McBurney YMCA on Twenty-third Street. We punched the heavy bag, did a few calisthenics, swam and steamed ourselves out in the sauna. Then we repaired to the showers. Feeling uptight for the need to piss, I pissed in the waste trough and watched the iodine-colored substance slowly run to a scupper that was located directly in front of the huge glassed window where a heavily muscled lifeguard dressed in a bikini was sitting, reading a body-building magazine.

Brendan and I were the only ones in the shower.

The voyage of the urine to the digestive under-currents of the great metropolis was slowed considerably by a congealment of mucus, shredded pubic hairs, discarded soap and other wastes. The thick-muscled, eager-looking sleuth suddenly spotted the foreign flow, then darted out of his coop and traced the stream to the immediate area where Brendan was showering. (I had moved to the farthest spigot.) Brendan was not aware of the proceedings. His eyes were focused on a well-built boy who was diving from the deep end of the pool. The eager beaver looked at Brendan, sighed and waved his hand in disgust then went back to his coop without uttering a single word.

"What is that muscle-bound cunt on about," Brendan barked.

"Oh, who gives a shite. His boyfriend probably cut off his supply of cock," I chuckled.

Brendan nodded his head in agreement.

In another effort to curtail his decline I took him on an excursion of all of my old haunts. "This is the famous doghouse," I said as we sat down in the cafeteria of the Seaman's Church Institute at 25 South Street. A heavily tattooed former shipmate of mine ambled over and asked me to introduce him to my famous landsman.

"Why so many pictures?" Brendan asked, indicating his graffiti.

"Well," said the amiable man, "it's reassuring to know that I have at least a few things that the customs, the shipping commissioners, the unions, and the faggot priests who run these fuckin' green- and red-eyed whores can't steal from me." (The green- and red-eyed whore remark pertained to the Institute, a building regarded by seamen as a stationary ship. Red and green are the colors of a ship's navigational lights.)

Brendan beamed with delight. "That's a fuckinjayzus great bit of stuff. Will I squeeze it into *Cork,* avick, wha?"

"Squeeze it into *Cork,* Bren. Why not? You squeeze everything else into *Cork.*"

We traipsed in the door of the Norwegian Seaman's House at 52 Hansen Place in Brooklyn. "This is the house where Thor Heyerdahl planned the expedition of the Kon-Tiki," I said. "It is also the place where the Norwegian Council sent me to live when I arrived here on March the twentieth, 1950, aboard a burning Norwegian tanker called the S.S. *Belinda.*"

From there we went to the SIU hall in Brooklyn, where I introduced him to a number of my former shipmates and union representatives.

At Stavenhagen's pawnshop on Fifth Avenue, I redeemed an Omega watch that I bought in Barcelona in 1959 and hocked on December the nineteenth, 1961, for purposes of getting up the carfare to make it to Carteret and to the *Bents Fort.* "Here, B.," I said, "take ye this, for this is my flesh and this is my blood . . . No, no, B., forgive my indecencies, I'm just cuntin' you about. Take this watch, I want you to have it as a token of my friendship and my esteemed regards for all of the good fortune that you have brought me. Wear it well and go with God."

Brendan smiled and strapped the watch to his wrist. We taxied down to Red Hook, a known Mafia neighborhood. Brendan had a very keen sense of geographical awareness. He became petrified. "Let's get to jayzus out of here," he cried, while shaking like a wet puppy dog, his eyes darting. Brendan lived in mortal fear of the Mafia. He honestly believed that the brotherhood would get wise to his sexual bent and blackmail him. We subwayed home.

One very early morning just as dawn was driving away dark, I was awakened by a whole lot of tugging below my belt. I was lying on the floor. Brendan's lower half was still in my bed. His top half was hanging over the bed. His two hands were astride my hips. He was sucking my cock and snoring simultaneously. My genitalia was saturated with blood.

My heart pounded with fear. Quickly I got up, slowly made my way to the shower and turned on the spigot. Finally I looked down and sighed with relief. Everything that I hoped for was intact. I toweled myself off and went back into the room and found Brendan sitting on the side of my bed wilting, tilting and snoring. Saliva oozed from the corner of his quivering mouth. Blood dripped from his nose. I took hold of my cock, played with it, and masturbated into his sweaty, bloody, crucifixion face, then I sat down in a chair directly in front of him and waited and watched. He continued to wilt, tilt, snore and bleed. A congealment of blood, snot, sweat and semen dripped onto his chest. He uprighted himself.

Suddenly his eyes were open. He stopped snoring. We eyed one another with intensity. "No, no, no, why, why, how, how," he screamed as he ran naked into the hall.

I did not see hide nor hair of him the remainder of the day.

Very early in the A.M. the following morning I awoke, got up out of bed and collapsed on the floor. I took the receiver from its cradle and tried to call the switchboard. I couldn't. I lost my voice. Then I did a series of quick depressions on the cradle's button. Minutes later Davies burst into my room and found me sitting on the floor flailing my arms and legs.

He wrapped me up in a blanket, led me to the lobby, ordered a taxi and instructed the driver to drive me to the Polyclinic Hospital on Fiftieth Street. I alighted from the cab, then staggered down a corridor that seemed to be six million miles long. When I reached the emergency ward I did another series of arm and leg flailings.

The effeminate nurse who was in attendance mistook me for a junkie, injected my arm with a hypodermic needle and sent me to the land of the leal. When I awoke I was informed that my loss of speech and stability was due to a very excessive amount of coagulated dirt, lodged in my ears. I deduced that a major amount of dirt had gotten into my ears as a consequence of my spending so many long nights sleeping on my floor next to the door while Brendan slept in my bed. The nurse washed my ear drums, gave me a box of penicillin tablets and informed me that I was free to go. I wrapped my blanket around myself and walked the five blocks to the Bristol. I felt happy and carefree. Never before did the neon hieroglyphs of Broadway glisten and say so much.

"There's a very quare-looking fella above in Mr. Behan's room," Mae said to me in a clandestine manner as I entered the lobby. "He says he's a priest, but mind yurself avick, he's as drunk as Pontius Pilate."

"I'll be careful, Mae, thanks."

"Who the fuck are you?" I asked the naked, slender-built man who was lying in Brendan's bed.

"And who are you?" he responded in a benevolent tone.

"Never mind who I am, how did you get in here?"

"Oh, you have an Irish lilt. You must be that great man they call Peter Arthurs, the man who causes Brendan's eyes to light up and sparkle every time that your luvly name is mentioned."

"Who are you, mister?" I asked in a sterner tone.

"I'm Father Jacobs," the man said wrapping himself around me.

"Father Jacobs . . . hmm . . . but how do I know that you are a genuine man of the cloth?"

"There," the man said pointing to a bundle of clothes that lay on a chair. The black vestments of a priest were lying beneath a green-colored shirt. I picked up the shirt and looked at it. On the left side of it, the legend read "Sal's Auto Repairs." A smattering of dried-up oil stains mottled the front of the shirt.

"Apparently you do a little moonlighting on the side, father. Then you are the man who Brendan refers to as his Jewish priest." We embraced.

The phone rang. "Hello," I said.

"It's the quare one, uptown," Mae said warningly.

"Don't worry sweetheart, I can handle her, put her on."

The voice of Valery came over the wire. "Don't go away," she said, "Brendan wishes to speak to you, it's very important."

Then Beverly Bently's voice cracked across the receiver. "Are you still holding? Don't go away, Brendan is coming."

"Listen yew, what's this load of ballox all about, and who gave you permission to go running to hospitals telling people to put their babies up for adoption," Brendan roared, "and who told yew that it was O.K. for yew to call up a pair of fascist cunts the likes of Walter Winchell and Frank Farrell and tell them about my personal business?"

For several minutes, Brendan lambasted me and accused me of letting the world know that he was the father of a three-week-old boy. But something was amiss. More than anything, Brendan wanted the world to know of his parenthood. Also, to be pilloried in print was a thing that did not disturb the stones in his kidneys.

"Be right over, B.," I said putting down the phone.

"Oh, that must be Brendan asking you to do something very wonderful," the man of God exclaimed joyously.

"Excuse me, father," I said, "I have to make an emergency call. Something very urgent just came up, I'll keep you posted."

I made my way east on Fifty-second Street.

By the time that I began my ascent of the steps to Beverly's apartment my thoughts were clear. Brendan's tit was in the wringer. He needed an out! A brouhaha of sorts would be the ideal antidote to fit the fandango. I banged on the front door. Beverly opened up, then attempted to slam the door in my face. My right foot prevented her from doing so. "Where's the whore's melt, where's the son of a Dublin bitch," I roared as I smashed on past her and into the bedroom where I found Brendan lying in bed wrapped in a Japanese kimono. His hair was closely cropped. A smirk as large as life lit up his face at the sight of me. "Behold Samson and his two Delilahs," I said.

The newborn baby lay in a crib in the corner of the room. Brendan jumped out of bed and began to pummel my chest with his fists while Beverly and Valery worked on the back of my head with a pair of high-heeled shoes.

"Listen you, you dirty rotten little son of a bitch, if you don't pack your fucking rags and shite off back to Dublin, I'll break your fuckin' head," I roared into his face as I bent his head across the mantelpiece. Unable to restrain himself, he burst out laughing into my face. I put my face against his, to hide his revelry.

I returned to the Bristol. Two hours later I was awakened.

"He's here in the lobby with two quare-looking ones," Mae warned me. "The sweat is pouring out of him . . . wait . . . wait . . . Be God he's asking for his bill. What in God's name is the poor man up to? The quare ones must be drivin' him bloody mad!"

"It's O.K., Mae, he knows what he's doin', talk to you later." I put down the phone then took the manuscript of *Cork* from between my mattress and boxspring, then darted up the stairs, opened the door and placed it conspicuously in the center of the floor of Brendan's room. Brendan had a strange penchant for leaving his unfinished manuscripts behind. He once left the only copy of *Borstal Boy* behind in the London office of the BBC.

I ducked onto the fire escape and watched and waited. The elevator clanged open. Out stepped a very disheveled, smiling Brendan. Seconds later he reboarded the elevator with a brown paper bag that contained all of his possessions.

I went to my room and slept like a bear.

Hours later I was again awakened. "This is Mike Wardell from Irish International. I've called about our beloved—"

"Yes, yes, Mr. Wardell I know, I know, you've called about our beloved Brendan. He is presently halfway out across the Atlantic Ocean in one of your safest planes and in the hands of your most competent stewardesses. Thanks a mil, see you." I hung up and laughed myself to sleep.

The phone rang. "This is Jack Lipsig."

"Be right over, J."

Jack informed me that a bill for almost two hundred dollars for my food and beverages had not been paid. I felt like screaming. "I'll take care of it J., just as soon as I finish another tank-cleaning stint." Later, the manager of the Bristol advised me that I owed two weeks' back rent.

On March the twentieth, I flew to Norfolk and shipped as butterworth rigger and chemical sprayer aboard the supership S.T. *Erna Elizabeth.*

XIV

In the months to come I engaged myself in the cleaning of an armada of tankers, S.T. *Thetis, Ocean Ulla, Cantigny, National Defender* and many more. I did not hear from the Behans.

I read that *The Hostage* had been elected by the French theater critics' association, *Le Syndicat de la Critique Dramatique,* as the best play of the season. The film version of *The Quare Fellow* was due to premier in the Carnegie Hall Cinema. I was about to become a celebrity! I purchased a Countess Mara tie and a suit and shoes to match.

Brendan Behan's Island, Brendan's latest book, had been published, well reviewed, and chosen by the Book Society as their October choice.

November 25, 1962, Eddie Mooney, an SIU vice president, phoned and informed me that Albatross Tanker Corporation needed a relief bosun on their supership S.T. *Erna Elizabeth.* I was their choice. I accepted the position.

November 26, very early in the A.M., the unloaded supertanker *Amoco Delaware* barreled out of a soupy fog and smashed headlong into the fully loaded *"Ernie Liz."* The midship house on the starboard side was caved in. The starboard lifeboat was draped across the cargo manifold, located some fifty-five feet aft of the midship house. Thousands of barrels of oil coated the Narrows. We spent the next three weeks in Todds Brooklyn shipyard undergoing extensive repairs. The crash made international news.

On Christmas Day, I received a plethora of letters from Beatrice, Celia and Petro. They all inquired about my well-being. Brendan, according to Beatrice, was imbibing even more heavily. His health was a thing to be gravely concerned with. The completion of *Cork* was no-where near.

The exigencies of supertanker work were wearing me thin.

On January 28, I decided to bring a degree of simplification into my life by resigning as ship's bosun.

On January 31, I took a job as a watch-standing able seaman aboard the Liberty ship S.S. *Marymar.* On February 5, while standing gangway watch at a Greenpoint Pier in Brooklyn, I lost my footing in a spill of bunker sea oil. I received a well-bruised shoulder, a strained back and a mild concussion. The medics at the USPHS (United States Public Health Service) clinic issued me several vials of medication, a home physiotherapy program and a word of caution: "Get plenty of rest, your body needs it." I assured the professionals that I would adhere to their warning. I checked into the Bristol Hotel.

One morning along about the latter part of the month, I was awakened very early. "Yes Mae, what's the big news."

"He's here! He's here! Your luvly fella is here! He's here for you! He's cum back to you! Yiz are together again! Indeed yiz are, yiz are a great aul pair! He's got himself a luvly room on the fourth floor above and he's on the phone, talk to him, go on, talk, talk, talk . . ."

"Is that yew? Where are yew? Are yew here? What floor are yew on? How long will it be before yew can cum? Cum up cum up."

"What's up, B., welcome to cockroach junction. What's doin' in Dub?"

"It's the other one, yur woman, she went and put a fuckin' shyster onto me. I wuz good enough to give her child me name, now she wants me money. Um surrounded be fuckin' savages, fascists, begrudgers and Judas Iscariots, *Cumupcumupcumup!*"

"Be right down, B."

I charged down the stairs and found the door to his room wide open. A tall, dark ultraresplendent, suave-looking gentleman stood inside the door. He seemed to be talking to himself. "I'm only concerned with little Brendan," he kept saying in a strained voice.

"Who are you and where's Brendan?" I asked.

"Who are you and what do you want?"

Suddenly I heard a scuffling sound on the floor. I stepped into the room, walked around to the other side of the bed and found Brendan down on all fours, crawling about on the carpet, picking up well-picked chicken bones, sucking on them, throwing them under the bed and muttering oaths.

"What's with the picnic, B.? A little early in the season for *that,* isn't it?" He looked like a beached baby whale in rags.

He beckoned me to join him on the floor and out of sight of the man.

"That's the c-cunt avick, that's the big fuck face that yur woman has shoved onto me," he indicated with his thumb while picking up a very dry looking bone and draining its last dregs with a single slurp.

"Great man, B., great man, you've done wonders! Maybe next time you'll go for the adoption bit, wha!"

"Holyvinegarfuckinjayzus, is it a sermon I'm getting at this crucifixion hour of the mornin' when all good Christians are in their beds?"

"Listen B.," I whispered, "I have a plan. I think I know how we can get rid of Bella Lugosi. Tell him you lost *my* watch and *your* passport and we have to find them right away, tell him you have to fly to Paris and Rome to give a lecture."

Brendan beamed at the suggestion. "I c-cant seem to f-find the fuckin' things," he blurted in despair. "How can I tell what time it is without me watch! Did you find me passport, son!"

"We'll find it later," I said in a tone of affected resignation. "Let's go down to the coffee shop on Sixth Avenue, we'll get a bit of sustenance into our guts then we'll return and pick up the forensic search."

"Great man, avick. Will yew join us?" Brendan suggested, getting up off the floor and turning to his antagonist.

"But I'd rather we sit down and talk about little Brendan."

"Cum on, me aul skin," Brendan insisted. "The bit of fresh air will do no harm."

The triumvirate moseyed east on Forty-eighth Street, then south on Sixth Avenue. We entered a workingman's pub, thronged to capacity with early-morning comers and goers.

Once inside in the warm balm and the noisy din of the smoke-glutted, bellicose arena, Brendan moved swiftly. "Did I ever tell yew what I said to my aul pal Gene when I met him in the New York Athletic Club," Brendan asked a bearded man as he put his arm around him. " 'Yew lost the title be the long count when yew refused to go back to the neutral corner, Gene,' says I, 'If it wasn't for that, yew would still be heavyweight champion of the world!'

" 'Yur a proper Eisenhower with balls,' says I to fuckin' aul Truman, when I put me arm around him in the Red Lion."

Brendan's performance was blithe and buoyant.

"But I thought you agreed to talk about little Brendan," the bored attorney lamented, his anxiety graven in his face.

"Must be a great occupation, being an attorney," I said reassuringly to the man. "By God, one thing about you chaps, you have to have a lot of patience and perseverance. See you later," I said and departed.

I went back to the Bristol and did a series of back- and shoulder-strengthening exercises on the floor, then went on to lower Broadway, where I employed an attorney and brought suit for one hundred thousand dollars against Calmar Steamship Corporation for injuries sustained.

In the days ahead Brendan's state of physical and mental health plummeted to new depths. His delirium tremens were coming more rapidly, his nosebleeds more profuse, his hysteria, angst and paranoia more intense. He believed that the FBI, the CIA, the Attorney General's Office and every law enforcement agency in the land was monitoring his every vowel.

On the occasions that life with him was totally untenable, or when I felt that it was time to throw a jolt into him, I announced that I was due to "ship out." The majority of these threats were nothing more than playlets. Brendan's madness was incipient. Its incipience was my adrenalin, my blood of life.

One afternoon a few hours after Brendan had once again succeeded in talking me into getting off the train and heading back to the city, I came across him in the hotel lobby. He was chatting up a couple of his idolators. "Shur what can I do with him, shur he follows me everywhere and when I stop short, shur don't I turn and find the poor boy hanging feet first out of me arsehole, wha! But shur then again, the boy has to have someone in life to look after him. Shur jayzus wouldn't he be nowhere without me."

I pivoted and crossed directly in front of him, "Hello Brendan," I said casually, "If you're talking about the Irish, I sincerely hope you will be a good guy and put in a truthful word for *me*. See you," I said and left him in benumbed silence.

On another occasion as we were subwaying to the SIU hall, Brendan as usual was begging me to get off and make a U-turn back to Forty-eighth Street. In final resignation he turned and said, "Besides, Beatsie told me to tell you to take care of me for her!!"

A period of lugubrious silence ensued. "I know, *she* also told *me* to tell *you* to explain to *me* what *she* said, but up until now, *you* didn't, and so, dear Brendan, I say to *you, you* take care of *yourself* and above all trust no one, *no one,* least of all *yourself!*"

I got off and left him sitting, picking and sullen in silence. The train roared away. I returned to the Bristol alone.

Valery was becoming more dogmatic in the pursuit of her child's future wherewithal.

"B-but as soon as I finish me play and get me divorce from the other aul c-cow everything will be as right as rain," he implored.

His dashes to Geis's for additional advances were becoming more frequent. His need to subway out to the St. George was being hampered by a sudden fit of claustrophobia and mortal fear of subways. Becoming trapped in an inferno below the city suddenly had become another phobia.

I flatly refused to discuss any further my boyhood buggery and boxing club stories. As the days passed, Brendan's ability to cope was sorely diminished. He merely sat in the lobby of the Bristol, waving, raving and chatting amiably with the hordes of ghosts that crossed his alcohol-and-drug-veiled line of vision.

The manager of the hotel called me up on the average of three times per day to tell me to take Brendan upstairs and out of his lobby. Brendan was barred for life from Tim Costello's, Jimmy Glennon's, and practically every bar in New York. Even Jack Lipsig also made known his desire to disenfranchise him from his eatery. Valery's hatred of me grew wicked. Brendan was quickly becoming the leper of Forty-eighth Street. His life was dwindling into meaninglessness, yet he somehow maintained a smidgen of spirit while his explorations into death became a misery to behold.

Dark thoughts came and went, unbidden, in the night. This was surely the walpurgisnacht of the once smug man who had so proudly proclaimed, "In my judgment there is no bad publicity, with the exception of the mention of your name in the obituary column."

Brendan did not fear death. He feared the life hereafter. He lived in the twilight of his early-life inculcations.

As his gait slowed and his lists to starboard increased, his death rattles and his shuffling down the long grey corridor to his demise were in ample evidence. Late each night, early in the A.M., glimpses of Brendan being carried or dragged up Forty-eighth Street by a pair of friendly priests were commonplace. On most of the occasions the priests in question were different from the ones who dragged him home the night before. Brendan's dash, pomp, style and bravura had all but vanished. So had the majority of his friends.

One night in Downey's, just as Brendan was in the pitiful progress of approaching a table where Jim Downey, Jr., was sitting, Jim stretched out his hand and said, "That's far enough, bum. Get out of here, you drunk, and don't come back." His words cut deeply into Brendan. Like a dog he traipsed out the door and returned to the Intermission, his last bastion, his only water hole on Broadway. Sitting at the bar, looking at his reflection in the mirror he talked lugubriously about his famous parties in Downey's. His listeners were few.

Beatrice's transatlantic calls became forlorn. During one of these calls she broke down and cried pathetically. "Oh Peter, can't you get him into hospital or home on a plane? Is there no one who you can call on for help? Jim Downey? Jack Lipsig? Bernie? The police? Have you not contacted his friend the police officer Paul Burke in New Jersey?"

"You better come over and take him home, B., he's going to die here in this cold, grey, merciless jungle," I warned her.

Brendan had now switched to drinking Guinness stout and champagne, a combination that increased his hallucinatory outputs.

One night in the Huey Yuen after we had gobbled up a ton of ribs, rice and chow mein, Brendan got into a melee with the Chinese owner. In the language of the Gael he claimed to have given a waiter a ten-pound Irish note to cover the bill. Now he demanded his change. The host became hopelessly confused. Brendan, eying a bevy of French airline hosts who were sitting in a corner, began to scream insult and threat at the proprietor, in French. The airline employees, realizing who the hysterical man was, burst over and patted him affectionately on the head and shoulders. Brendan adored being petted by people in uniform. Any kind of uniform. He derived a sexual satisfaction from fondling buttons and braid. In France, Brendan Behan was looked upon as a great writer, a man of destiny.

Brendan now lived in fear of entering the Bristol lobby and what the possible consequence of his arrival there might entail. "Will yew be a good chap and take a look and see if the woman with the bundle is in there," he asked me as we got set to make our entrances.

The sight of Valery and her one-year-old son horrified him.

One day I emphatically announced, "This is it for me, B., I'm out as of today."

"Yew seem to be suffering from some sort of a chronic out condition," he bellowed. "O-out, out where avick?"

"I'm out on a ship today, B."

"What ship, where are yew going?"

"I didn't get the boat yet, B., I haven't gone to the hall, yet."

Brendan pleaded with me to hold on until Beatrice arrived.

"But there is no guarantee that she'll come, B., then what?"

He followed me to the SIU hall and pleaded with me to get off at every stop and do a quick U-turn. As usual I adhered to his wish.

One night, Captain Harold Sharpe of the *Erna Elizabeth* phoned in and informed me that a big tank-cleaning job on the vessel was upcoming. Would I take Brendan along as a tank cleaner just for the fun of it. "He can sign on as a librarian," Sharpe suggested. Sharpe was an avid fan of Brendan's. He had read his works, seen pictures of him and me in recent issues of the *SIU Log* and through the seafaring grapevine got hold of our address.

"But I'm only here on a limited passport, I can't earn money outside of literary royalties," Brendan informed Sharpe. Brendan sorely wanted to make the trip.

"Don't fret, B., it's all arranged between Captain Sharpe, Port Captain Bennet and Eddie Mooney. You can sign on as a librarian!"

Brendan suddenly eyed me as though I reeked of panther's piss.

He went into a catatonic trance. In a sudden blur of four-letter epithets, I was out the door of the Monte Rosa. I looked back and found him standing outside the restaurant shouting, "L-librarian . . . l-librarian . . . l-l-librarian, laminated jayzus, now I'm a fuckin' librarian."

Brendan's days of cogitation were nearing their end. The insidious effects of his boozing were taking their toll. His cataleptic trances increased. His storytelling continued but with very palpable valedictory rings to it. He had become a perambulatory skeleton, a man who was in the cataclysmic spring of his dotage. He was a living breathing cesspool of misery and grief. Gone was the lordship of old. His pep and piety had evaporated. The neighborhood laundries and dry cleaning stores refused his business. His liver was almost gone. His paunch more protruding, his kidneys were infected, the detritus of tears, blood, vomit and alcohol on his lapels were always in attendance. At the age of forty, he was a weather-beaten curio, an ancient drayhorse. His eyes became increasingly gargoylish, his battered countenance twisted into a rictus; Brendan was a desiccated wreck. Betimes he looked at me as though I were the cause of his downfall. He honestly believed that he was blameless for everything in life. Staggering around Forty-eighth Street he looked like a decayed sorcerer on his way to a black mass. Gone was his poetry. Beleaguered by fatherhood worries and creative aridity he turned to anyone who would lend him a thin ear.

Total exhaustion replaced exhibitionism. His remarks and comments were nothing more than insult to art, logic and reason. To most, he had become a dour, burdensome, overbearing buffoon, a derelict and an insufferable liability. Yet I made no attempt to alter his life-style or to curtail his imbibences. I merely assisted in the altering of his attitude to own up to the tyranny of the fate that awaited him. One day in my room I said with enormous ebullience, "Listen B., you have to learn to take this death lark for what it really is. It's only a fuckin' practice after all."

"A practice! A practice," he roared. "What fuckin' practice!?"

"Yes, B., that's what I'm saying, a practice. We Irish are great practitioners of death, a something to dwell upon, but less seriously of course, a thing with no marked future in it, isn't that the answer? As the poet said, 'There is no cure for the hunchback except the grave.'"

His face froze into a prism of hurtful expressions. He threw himself down onto my bed and pouted like a scolded child.

"We're backwater people who are masters at hiding our conceit and madness, are we not, Brendan?"

"What class of an eegit am I," Brendan suddenly moaned, throwing up his arms.

"First-class, Brendan, a genuine first-class eegit."

"Well shur if I was in possession of your great sense of humor, I suppose I'd be able to see that."

"Practice, Brendan, practice, you'll get there, just practice."

At heart Brendan was a very serious man, but too ill-equipped to handle the true depths of his own seriousness.

"You're bent," I said in a whisper.

"B-bent!?"

"Bent, bent, look it up in the *Britannica* . . . I don't read it myself, its subjects change too rapidly. You're also a genius."

"A genius, me son."

"A sort of genius."

"A sort of genius, what in fuck's name is that? You have a strange fuckin' way of expressing yourself," he snapped in a slightly elevated octave.

"Fuck it Brendan, live your life, enjoy it. There's no turning back now, it's too late—"

"Too late!!!!"

"Oh Lord love a duck Bren, you've been in the wrong business. A job as clerk in a male whorehouse would be more up your alley. At least that way you'd get plenty of free arse and everyone would call you 'sir.' "

In an abyss of despair, tears welling up in his eyes, he began to recite poetry in his favorite language. Brendan was the greatest speaker of Gaelic that I had ever known. His language was impeccable. By comparison, I was a mere subnovice, yet I understood his meaning clearly. The harmonics of his recitations and actions brought joy to my heart. He had published his first words of Gaelic poetry at the age of twelve.

This was the first time that I succeeded in pulverizing him into going into one of these recitations. When he finished I asked him why he did not stick to writing poetry. He sat quiet for a time, then, "Well avick, it's like this, poets usually wind up being paupers." Another period of strained silence ensued. "Any man who puts pen to paper for the sheer love of writing is a fool," he spat, a look of greater despair thickening in the sag of his jowls.

The insincerity of his remark saddened me. After a lull, he continued to recite and quote himself. With a noticeable gleam creeping into his eyes and a sweeter lilt to his guttural voice, he recited from poems that he had once written about Oscar Wilde, about blackberries blooming on a wild bush, and about his second favorite topic: man's loneliness and quest for self-understanding.

Brendan detested himself for ever going commercial. For a considerable period of time, I had been aware that he loved and loathed Joan Littlewood. He lauded her genius and thanked her for his success as a writer. But in the same breath he blamed her for his abject failure as a man.

By early March, signs of impaired judgment and senile dementia were evident, but the lifelong indomitable will fought back with all of the tenacity of a bubonically diseased rodent. He needed to be immortalized as a renaissance man rather than remembered as an alcoholic clown took hold. For the next few days he sobered up and began to make plans for the long-range future. He went back to work on *Cork* and on a new novel that had emanated at the base of his boggled brain. In the cobwebs of his mind, he began to return to his past, but in the realization that childhood is gone. The time for personal assessment and true creativity is in the now. "People who make it a practice of keeping one foot in the past and the other foot in the future wind up pissing in the now," I had warned.

Brendan put away his whip. His penitential floggings desisted. His life took shape and form. Once again the little elf with the arsenal of incredible recuperatory powers was on the mend. He was asexual and ascetic, even taking command of his mind and his morals.

However, on Saturday, March the ninth, again he went back to the bottle and into a swift decline. Late in the evening he came to my room. The look of imminent death was on his face as I let him in and pushed him to the floor, then I pushed my pillow under his head, my two knees to his shoulders and the handle of my rigger's knife between his teeth to keep him from biting his tongue off. He was choking on his own vomit. "Peter, Peter, do yew think I'm mad," he muttered in a snatch of agonized whisper.

I phoned David Greggory. "Dave," I said pleadingly, "Can I take Brendan to your loft, he's in terrible shape, might even die, I need to have someone keep a close eye on him in the likely event that I have to run for a doctor!"

He instructed me to usher him on over to his studio on the second floor of a commercial building on Eighth Avenue and Forty-third Street. We managed to get some protein and tranquilizers into him, then put him to bed.

As usual, early in the morning he awoke and, much to his horror, found David and me in bed in the rear of the loft as he was en route to the bathroom. Suddenly his face became a stew of wickedness and disappointment. He stuttered, stammered, and quivered and began to flail his arms and kick and scream. Brendan was instantly imbued with the mistaken belief that Dave and I were involved in a homosexual relationship. He was desperately paranoid and still in love with me. In an instant he had his pants and his shoes on, and with the remainder of his clothes under his arm he fell on the landing and stumbled down the stairs and headed east on Forty-second Street.

On the corner of Forty-fifth and Broadway I caught up to him and pushed him into a pancake house where we ate stacks of pancakes and drank tea. In a fit of sullenness he threw handfuls of pancakes and syrup into my face. "What's wrong with you?" I roared. He refused to talk or to look at me.

"G-go on, go on. Look down that street," he suddenly shouted into my face, pointing to the marquees of the theaters. "I'm here, I'm not finished yet, it's not over yet. Yew still need me. I'm still alive."

Then he was on his feet and running east. I let him go.

Very late the same night a loud clatter of shrieks came to my door. I opened up.

"Peter, Peter, the dirty Mafia goons, they called me a dirty little pansy, a faggot, a queer," he lamented, throwing himself down on my bed. Tears ran down his cheeks as he unfolded his story of how he went to the home of a retired New Jersey police officer, where Valery's baby was being kept by the officer's wife. On the bus on the way back to New York a fight between Valery and Brendan broke out. The argument was over the provisions that would soon have to be made for the one-year-old boy's education and upbringing. Brendan bolted away from Valery and into a lavatory. There he was purportedly confronted by two burly men who observed his tears. "They referred to me as a fuckin' faggot, Peter."

"Don't worry, B.," I said strapping my fid and other nefarious-looking splicer's equipment to my waist, "we'll fuck off down to that depot and settle a score with those ginny thugs, leave it to me, B. Come on. When I get through cutting and carving, it's a load of stitches, plugs and brand new arseholes that those ferret-faced fucks will need."

Outside on Broadway, in the cold invigorating night air, the fantasy was soon a thing of the past. His face lit up. His tears ceased. "Let's cunt off down the road for a feed," he stuttered as he charged ahead of me. Suddenly he disappeared.

I did not see him again for the rest of the night or all the following day.

On Tuesday the twelfth, Bernie Geis called and asked me to take all of his belongings to the Chelsea Hotel on West Twenty-third Street. "Katherine Dunham is waiting for you." I discovered that on Sunday afternoon, in a state of exhaustion and despair, Brendan had gone to Geis's apartment.

I packed all of his personal belongings into a large manila envelope and taxied to the Chelsea. Mr. Bard, the owner of the hotel, instructed me to proceed to room 710.

"Hello, Mrs. Dunham, I'm Peter Arthurs, I'm here with Mr. Behan's rags and his—" The small birdlike white woman dashed back into the apartment without uttering a word. Seconds later a tall, attractive black woman came to the door.

"You must be Mrs. Dunham's maid," I said.

"*No,* I'm Miss Dunham," the lady explained, a hint of annoyance in her voice.

"I'm Peter Arthurs, I've come with Mr. Behan's rags."

"Oh yes, you're the boy that Mr. Geis spoke of. Come in."

I found Brendan sitting on a couch being fed and pampered by a young attractive black girl who was introduced to me as Lucille. Brendan did not look at me. He merely prattled, ate and told of his angst with publishers, Irish politics and the Irish Catholic Church. The girl seemed highly impressed and in happy spirits with her charge.

I was informed that on Monday afternoon he had gone to Geis's office and collapsed on the floor. Geis had been in the process of phoning me to suggest that we institutionalize him when Dunham arrived to discuss a previously proposed sequel to her autobiography *A Touch of Innocence.* Observing his advanced state of deterioration, the great lady of the dance had suggested to Geis that she bring him back to the dowager and home of the literati on Twenty-third Street. There, she and her temporarily unemployed entourage would get him together again.

She also believed that by working in close proximity to the famed author, she would naturally garner a few favored tips on the tedious craft of writing.

For the next few weeks under the aegis of the lady who was referred to by her entourage as Miss D., Brendan became a spartan disciplinarian, his deportment a model of everything good, gracious and charming. Ceal and Ural, two more members of Miss D.'s entourage, stood watch over him and saw to it that he ate, bathed and rose early in the morning and sat before his typewriter. Miss D. was a stalwart, no-nonsense lady whose rules and etiquette had to be properly and instantly obeyed. She instructed that no one was allowed to speak to Mr. B., without being carefully screened by Miss D. Mr. G.'s instructions were that Mr. B. could have all the food and ribbons and paper that his heart desired, but no booze and *"no pocket money!"*

Miss D.'s entourage began to compare Mr. B. with the former Chelsea drunk and Celtic poet in residence, Dylan Thomas, but they soon discovered that Brendan looked upon this comparison as invidious. Brendan did not appreciate being referred to as a "carbon copy" of anything. Brendan became a systematic performer, bumbling, shuffling, and appearing every inch the consumed, consummate, ambitious writer on the trail to doing great things. Greater things than he had previously done. His sudden temper tantrums, pill-popping, and alcoholism were nowhere in sight. During the first days of his rehabilitation, I was allowed two appointments per day, which consisted of no more than a few minutes each. Brendan was allowed a few minutes on each afternoon to sit in the lobby and talk to his well-wishers and new neighbors. When it became evident to Miss D. that I was a very close friend, I was welcomed to the fold.

In general, Brendan was comedic, nonmonopolizing and polite. In the eyes of his newfound friends he appeared every ounce the good natured Celtic sage who was steeped in the poetry of his people and the history of their land, and a man who had an assiduous concern for all. Sitting up in his chair, a chair that was carefully selected for him from the pile of antiques stored in the basement storeroom, in the warm ambience of a roaring fire in the grate, smoking a cigar, he was outgoing, anecdotal, hearty and congenial.

Katherine's friends and neighbors were cordially invited to participate in his talks. "I mean to say, I'm not only for mesself. I'm for everyone," he assured. His assurance was graciously accepted. Brendan was a master technician who proved that he had all of the tools to charm the cross off an ass on its way to Calvary.

Questions were quickly answered with complete clarity. If he did not have the correct information or answer, he graciously apologized and declined to comment. His chipper bearing was a charm to behold. By nightfall, after the dredgery and the drudgery of a creative day, he exuded all of the grace and charm of a frazzled clergyman entering retirement, proselytizing and hailing black mores and morals, values and virtues. "Shur if I was born a black chap mesself, wouldn't I have been a black muzzler, er, I mean a Black Muslim, wha."

Under the lording over and protective care of Miss D. and her concerned entourage, Brendan's health was quickly on the mend. The eloquent blacks catered to his every need and pandered to his childish delights and pontifications. "M-marvelous, s-s-smashing, great bit of grub," he muttered with boyish delight as he scraped his plate with the tips of his fingers and begged for second helpings. Like a shining white knight he referred to the ebony-colored, statuesque beauties as "me own darlin' daughters, me sweet children of love, me little rays of sunshine." He assured Ceal and Lucille, the principals of the group that, "If yew ever decide to become the mothers of the first technicolor bishop, or even a zebra-striped one, be sure to let your poor aul Irish father know." Here Brendan winked and concluded, "Yew get me meanin' don't yew?"

The well-constructed males of the entourage were spoken of as "outstanding specimens. Wouldn't I rather get a box of chocolates from them than a box in the mouth bejayzus." Miss D. was affectionately referred to as "herself," and "the great woman of the house." In all, his adopted family was publicly referred to as "The one and only family that I ever had. They found me just in time!"

His platitudes were usually accepted by Lucille and Ceal with "Oh Brendan Behan, you're so charming." Or, "Oh Brendan, you're such a typical Irish rascal."

"Did I ever tell yew, me daughter, that the only relations I care to encounter or to know are sexual relations." After making another round of aggrandizing remarks and witty comments Brendan then proceeded to pinch the girls on their ample bosoms and bottoms and compliment them on their perfect physical endowments.

Mrs. Gurley Flynn, the chairwoman of the American Communist Party, became a close friend and confidante. Communist meetings were held on a monthly basis on the fourth floor of the wrought-iron-railinged, ten-storied red brick building that once housed O'Neill, Flaherty, Wolfe, Moore, and many other great writers of bygone days. This was the hotel from where the thirty-nine-year-old Dylan Thomas had gone to drink thirty-nine shots of whiskey in the White Horse, then on to St. Vincent's Hospital to die.

Brendan was again in fine fettle, strutting in the wildly decorated lobby, drawing more attention than its sculpture and painting. "Did yew know that Judge James T. Comeford once barred me from participating in the St. Patrick's Day parade? 'Behan is disorderly,' says he, 'let him stay on his stage,' says he. Do yew know what I did?" Silence. "Well, I sent word to him to let him know that he was ill-informed about my occupation. 'I'm a writer, not an actor!' Not that I have anything against actors, or against dancers for that matter, for they too," he quickly emphasized, "like the rest of us have the legal and moral right to earn their kip." Miss D.'s entourage nodded in gratitude.

"Did yew know that I was given the option of taking me play, *The Hostage,* the one that I wrote in twelve days, to Moscow or New York! I'll take the Yankee dollars, says I, and against me wife's wishes and better judgment I flew to the Big Apple." The ingratiated eccentrics and people of no disapproving miens who lived in the hotel quickly developed a kinship for him. Intoxicated in the luxuriousness of his own loquacity he hammered ahead.

"Did I ever tell yew about the time that I locked up the two bobbies, that's Irish for cops, on the island of Carrareo. Then I threw the keys down a precipitous slope . . . wha! Another time this chap and mesself staggered out of a pub, drunk as judges, er, excuse me, I mean New York judges, well we decided to go looking for the grave of a friend. Mulcahy of the Coome was the name of the chap who resided in the oblong box. Before the poor aul keeper of the cemetery knew what was goin' on, there we were, staggerin' about in the fog, falling over headstones, drunk as whores at a high mass. Finally we found our grave. 'Terence Mulcahy,' says the other chap, who was spellin' out the name on the headstone. I was looking up at a statue of our Savior at the time. 'Not at all,' says I, 'that's not a resemblance of the man that *I* knew. Come on,' says I, 'we'll have to look elsewhere.'

"Now to be fully honest, even though I'll admit that I'm not a warlike man, I quite agree with my colleague, Mr. Shaw, that a perambulator hasn't much of a chance against a furniture van."

Brendan took to the stage like a pig to slop. His presence dominated the high-backed gilt ormolu chair that sat in the busy lobby, his tiny feet and legs swaying, never touching the floor, his face a phosphorescent glow, his voice booming to the level of raucousness as he again conjured tall stories and recounted his Borstal and Glasnevin days. His puzzling and opaque outbursts on the perils of pedophilia were once again being heard, the ancient agony returning and verifying the obvious. His old familiar bombast and his pompous declarations were again in full bloom. He complimented the Chelsea ladies, but in his heart of hearts Brendan sorely detested females as though they were a swarm of ugly worms gingerly awaiting his untimely demise.

On March the twentieth, I spotted Arthur Miller in the lobby and introduced myself to him. "Oh yes," Miller said, "I heard that he had moved in. I'm looking forward to meeting him." I went to room 707 and informed Brendan of my meeting with the great American dramatist.

"He's very anxious to meet you, B. Shall I arrange a meeting?"

"Miller . . . Miller . . . Miller . . . ?" Brendan said, scratching his scrotum with one hand, his rectum with the other. "Oh yes, isn't he the chap who was married to Marilyn Monroe?"

"Right again, Bren. He's also the ding-dong daddy of American dramatists."

Brendan threw me a wry look and shuddered at the thought of a confrontation with the master of American drama. "Now, what would a fella like that be wantin' from me?" he asked.

"Oh, I don't think he wants anything from you, B. He gives me the impression that he has a major interest in Irish dramatists. You're an Irish dramatist, aren't you?"

Later that evening, directly after Miss D. had fed us dinner, I arranged a meeting between the two world-renowned writers. Miller lived in room 614, one flight below Brendan and Katherine. "Be up right away, but I can only stay for a few minutes, have to drive to Connecticut," Miller said. I gave the message to Brendan and Miss D. Brendan immediately dashed across the hall to his room. Miller arrived punctually, but no Brendan was in sight. Five minutes went by. Six. Seven. Eight.

"Why don't we cross the hall?" I suggested.

Miller, with pipe in mouth, led the entourage. The door was ajar. Seconds later the tall, thin man shrieked and leaped back into my arms, his pipe tumbling from his mouth. I sped on past him into the studio apartment and found Brendan in bed on top of a young girl, each one as naked as the other.

"I'm Brendan Behan, I'm a writer," Brendan said bouncing out of bed and extending his hand to Miller. The girl screamed and dashed into the bathroom.

"Oh my God, oh Mr. Miller," she said, "I always wanted to meet you but I never thought that it would be like this."

"Please don't worry about it," Miller said.

"Shur isn't it a natural class of a thing, a natural body function, it's fuck all to get yur diddies in a didder over," Brendan roared at the girl as she continued to moan. Then he went to the refrigerator and extricated a bottle of Tuborg, opened it and pushed it against the chest of his visitor. Miller declined the offer. Brendan insisted. "Go ahead, divil a harm it will do yew!"

"Maybe the man doesn't drink," I said, taking the Tuborg from Brendan.

Brendan sat and talked incessantly, jumping from one topic to another. Miller smoked and listened. Then Brendan arose and extended his hand.

"What do you think of Peter here going down into those tanks and cleaning out all of that toxic muck," Miller said concernedly.

"He's young—he's young—he's young," Brendan snapped, again extending his hand. The interview was now unquestionably over. The girl emerged from the bathroom, wrapped in a plastic shower curtain.

The following day I phoned Miller, apologized for the embarrassment that I had gotten him into, then thoroughly assured him that it was "none of *my* doing."

""Don't worry about it," Miller intoned, "let's meet in the Oasis for lunch." I accepted his offer and met the author in the pub located in the middle of the block. The two of us subsequently became friends and ate together and talked a lot. Miller encouraged me to write (and to write this book). He commented and made invaluable suggestions concerning some short stories that I had been working on. He put his comments in writing. I showed his writings to Brendan. Brendan became enraged. "A load of gobshite and fuckin' aul ballox," he bellowed.

Miller did not think much of Brendan's writing. He reviewed *The*

Hostage as "chaotic." *The Quare Fellow* in his opinion was mere "gab on paper." *The Borstal Boy* "was a bore" he said with a dismissing sweep of his hand.

"Sure didn't I see the pair of yiz turning the corner this morning," Brendan said to me one day as he picked his nose and made another attempt to find out how burgeoning my friendship with Miller was.

"Oh yes, B., a great man, a great writer. He's doin' a lot for me, helping me to get my stuff into proper perspective, etcetera. Sure where would I be without him."

My remark shocked Brendan. Sulking and pouting, he charged into Katherine's apartment, slammed the door in my face and remained there the rest of the day.

Brendan continued to thrive. By the end of March he had regained ten pounds. His old bravura and braggadocio was once again reaching its zenith, but his insecurity among people whom he felt did not understand his fears and phobias began to gnaw on him.

One afternoon he called me up in a tizzy. "Listen avick, will yew for the love and honor of Christ, cumupcumup and get me out of this black fuckin' coffin that I'm nailed into."

"Be right up B., don't get your balls in a knot!"

"I'm Mr. A." I said to the tall pipe-smoking bespectacled black man who met me at the door. "I'm here to see Mr. B., but all for the love and honor of big C. Kindly do not inform Miss D."

Perplexed, the man who was obviously Brendan's present protector from himself, looked towards the ceiling. Vistas of smoke filled the air. The man's back was positioned towards Brendan, a position that I had managed to inveigle him into. Brendan, sensing the nature of my game quickly grabbed up an armful of clothes, tiptoed out of the room, then hid in a nearby vestibule.

"Oh, forget it mister, it's not important, I'll see him later," I said and hastily departed. The man went inside and closed the door. We went down to my room where Brendan remained in hiding. Miss D. was quickly informed of the sudden disappearance of Mr. B. A manhunt was quickly launched.

Brendan's whereabouts were soon discovered, but compromises were made. He would be given more freedom of movement, providing I tag along and keep an eye on his wanderings. Under no circumstances was I to give him spending money or to allow him to gargle!!

I gave him ten dollars per day. Enough to keep him half-drunk.

Sober, Brendan was a bore, the biggest bore of the century.

XV

One night while rambling around the East Village, Brendan suddenly decided to listen to a few sets of jazz at the Five Spot. Inside, he charged up on the stage and sang a pastiche of bawdy songs, rattled off a glint or two of prosaic poetry and a parody or two of self-criticisms, then he began to pound on the keys of the piano, and on to a little strumming on the strings of the bass fiddle, his roly-poly figure swaying to and fro in rhythm to his music. Two huge black men with glistening eyes and teeth to match ambled up onto the stage and told him to leave the instruments alone. Brendan became even more involved with his music. He twanged on the strings even harder. The men gave him another set of instructions, which Brendan refused to obey, waving them away with an annoyed brush of his hand.

A few seconds later the little elf was picking himself up from the rain-soaked sidewalk, spuming and referring to the men as "big fuckin' African bogmen."

"Come on, B.," I said as I pushed him into the back of a taxi. Our trip to the hotel was suddenly interrupted by a barking bulldog that was chomping at Brendan's trousers. The dog's owner claimed that he had hailed the taxi first and that we were trying to "swipe his ride." "Fuck off yew poxy-faced fuck," Brendan roared at the man. The dog bit Brendan. Brendan kicked the dog. I hit the man. Brendan hit me. The man hit me and the dog took a piece out of my leg. The driver of the taxi told us to get another cab and sped away. We went home in the rain.

Hours later when I was en route to a shipyard in Hoboken, New Jersey, to clean a tanker, I spotted Brendan in the rear of a burger shop talking up a storm and entertaining a conglomeration of local derelicts, winos and sex perverts. To satisfy my curiosity I went over, sat down in a booth behind him and overheard the gabfest.

By now the dog had taken on the physical dimensions of the hound of the Baskervilles. The owner was the reincarnation of King Kong, the battle had been one of fierce intensity.

I couldn't take it anymore. "Brendan," I said, "the fucking aul dog was nothing more than a broken-down, dilapidated bulldog, the guy who owned it was a cripple."

Brendan was crushed. Despondent. "You're a liar," he roared.

"No I isn't."

He insisted that we taxi to the Village and look for the pair.

"Are you fuckin' mad," I roared, "take a cab to the Village at this hour, why those two are unquestionably at home asleep by now. Besides I have to clean a supertanker in Hoboken in an hour. See you later."

Brendan came after me and demanded that I accompany him to the Village. I acquiesced and got into a cab. Our trip was in vain. The pair was nowhere to be seen. "We'll look some more," Brendan insisted.

"I have to be at work in an hour," I pleaded and changed cabs.

Keeping even a small amount of money in my pocket was next to impossible by virtue of the fact that I was subsidizing all of Brendan's outdoor activities.

One day I said to Letty Cottin, "Listen sweetheart, you better tell Geis that if he wants to get his money back, he better install a tape recorder in Brendan's room. Brendan will never write again. He's dondee."

Geis talked the matter over with Letty and the following day the tape recorder was installed in room 707. Letty asked me to introduce her to Arthur Miller. I made the arrangements.

"Peter Arthurs is a genius," Letty said to Miller.

"A genius?"

"It was *his* wonderful suggestion to get the recorder."

Friends of Geis's and Letty's came to the hotel and showed Katherine, her entourage and me how to operate the simple Japanese-made machine. For the next two weeks whenever Brendan felt like spinning a yarn or enunciating on any of his favorite topics, we simply switched on the machine. Brendan loved to hear himself talk.

As a pen-and-paper writer, Brendan was at the nadir of his days. His feelings about taping were mixed. Sometimes he felt like a phony and guffawed in the Oasis, "I'm on me way back to me shite machine." On other, more propitious occasions he claimed that his next opus would be a small masterpiece of mirthful malice. "I'd like to call me book, *me sufferings,* but since I'm not in charge of the thing it will be *The Confes-*

sions of an Irish Rebel. Who gives a ballox, it will never be regarded as the neoclassic thriller of the age!"

Eventually the tape recorder became to him a mechanical lump of misery and humiliation. But he was deeply in debt to a number of publishers. "Tomorrow will be another shite day," he whined, as each day finished.

The next few days of my life were spent cleaning the intestines of the S.T. *National Defender,* America's largest supership.

On or about April 11, I went to room 1026 on the tenth floor of the Chelsea, the room to which Brendan had been transplanted. I knocked on the door. My intentions were to give him some money. Brendan was flat broke. A bovine lady with a very proper English accent came to the vestibule. "Yes, what is it I can do for you?"

"Oh, my name is Peter Arthurs, I'm a very close friend of Brendan's. I just flew up from Baton Rouge. I want to see him."

"Mr. Behan is very busy at the moment," she said, "but if you care to leave your phone number, I'll see to it that he gets it, then when he has time he will grant you an interview."

"An interview," I chuckled, "No, no, you don't understand lady. You see I'm very close to the Behans. I once took them to Mexico; I'm a merchant seaman and I've been out of town for a time, I'm here to let B. know that I'm back."

"I'll see what can be done," the lady said in a tone of exasperation as she went back into the room and left the door ajar. ". . . yes he seems to know you, dear Brendan, he's blondish-looking, he has an Irish accent, a rather large sort of chap, a merchant marine . . . Peter Arthurs is his name, he claims he once took you to Mexico, just flew in from Baton Rouge . . ."

A familiar silence prevailed. Then Brendan's voice seeped through the crack of the door. "A merchant chap . . . hmm . . . blondish-looking and one of me own from the potato patch beyant . . . hmm . . . you say he's a rather large sort of a chap . . . Mexico . . . Baton Rouge . . . hmm . . . Peter Arthurs is his name . . . Peter who?"

The lady reappeared. "I'm frightfully sorry, but you see Mr. Beh—"

"Oh fuck!" I exclaimed as I pushed on past the elegant woman and burst into the room where I found Brendan sitting in a chair and having his hair and face toweled off by Miss D. A cadre of newsmen were photographing him and taping his talk. His face was excessively pallid, his eyes gelid but dancing with delight. His words were being recorded for posterity.

"Oh here's Peter Arthurs, a great friend of ours," Brendan sputtered. "He's a seaman and a damn good one; here write that down now," he instructed the newsmen.

A feeling of sheer disgust came over me. I darted out of the door with the English lady in pursuit of me, "But Mr. Arthurs, please do come back won't you, Mr. Behan is so anxious . . ."

Brendan's games and lordly pomposity were boring.

I discovered that during my absence, problems of a very niggling nature had been piling up. In the meantime Valery had moved her baby and crib into 1026. Geis was locked in a battle with the English lady over who had the legal rights to the tapes, once they were completed.

The English lady, I found out, was Rae Jeffs, a lady who had previously taped and edited Brendan's book, *Brendan Behan's Island.* She was the granddaughter of George Thompson Hutchinson, the man who founded Hutchinson publishing house in England. At the request of Geis she had flown to New York to take control of the taping operation. Paul Hogarth would do the sketches.

Brendan was now being sought out to be served with a lawsuit. He had, in *Brendan Behan's Island,* put his albino dog-doping story into print. A man claiming to be the albino filed the suit, claiming libelous damages. Brendan had also gone back on the bottle.

Brendan was mortally frightened of the court appearance. He confided in me "I don't stand a ghost of a chance, the chap that I libeled is the only albino dog trainer in Ireland. When I asked him what the consequences might entail, he said that he feared he might be forced to sell his home to ante up for court costs and fines, "worse, they might even trow me in jail," he moaned. Now for the first time in his life he feared the thought of being imprisoned.

One afternoon, Father Fox, a Catholic priest, Brendan and I went to the St. George. Brendan needed a swim and a sweat. As usual, he did a variety of wild and funny improvisations and impressions from the high board, dived and a full three minutes later resurfaced in the center of a lot of Hispanic youths. As usual his trunks were floating around in another part of the pool. The embarrassed man of the cloth ran to the locker room, rented another pair, and after a struggle got them onto Brendan's bare buttocks. On our way home on the subway, Brendan became quite an attraction as he made a series of funny faces for a gaggle of little black children who sat opposite us on the train.

He simulated a prisoner being executed by a firing squad by falling on the floor. The children laughed. However their laughter was short.

"Peter must be a genius," Father Fox suddenly said.

"G-genius . . . g-genius . . . why . . . what do you mean?" Brendan said gruffly.

"Well, look at his feet," the priest said, laughing. "He has no socks. In New York the word is that artists and writers who haven't the patience to don their socks and underwear are geniuses."

Brendan was furious. He got up, stood by the door and remained mute until we arrived at the Twenty-third Street stop, then dashed ahead of us and charged up to his room.

When we arrived he was elbow-deep in a drawer digging out all of the socks that he could find. "H-here avick," he said pushing a handful of socks into my chest. I very meticulously went through each pair of socks, then handed them back to him. "Gee, I'm really sorry, B., but none of these fuckers seems to match my clothes . . ."

Another furious rummage through the drawer, and another handful of socks were pushed into my chest. Again I carefully studied the socks' colors and gave them back. "Whew, but it sure doesn't seem to be our day, B." I said lugubriously. "You see, B., these little cunts are sorta semiconservative and a bit too Madison Avenue-ish in their style and color, and *you* know how *I* am about my frippery." I said, as I threw the armful of socks all over the room. His face went white and purple.

"Will yew fur the love and honor of dilapidated poor aul fuc—" I put my hand over his mouth and held it there for awhile.

"Brendan, for Pete's sake, control yourself. We're in the presence of a man of God," I said, releasing my grip. In his confusion Brendan did not realize that all of the socks were in fact mine. Even though I was much bigger than he in every physical way, Brendan for a considerable period of time had been borrowing my socks, ties, T-shirts and other clothing. Under no circumstances would he return them.

At his request I went to the liquor store, purchased a bottle of Jack Daniel's and brought it home. Drinks were guzzled. Suddenly Brendan and the man of God were locked in a verbal brawl. The argument was over the true definition of a professional writer. The priest contended that a professional writer is a person who earns money from his writings, irrespective of the amount. Brendan contended that a "true professional," is a man who makes his living solely from his work. The argument continued.

"You're a phony, Brendan Behan. You're strictly out for the dollar. What have you ever done for the Irish people, the working class in particular?" the priest asked.

"For Christ's sake, leave Brendan alone," I said to the priest.

"How dare you take the Lord's name in vain. Never again when in my presence shall you touch the hem of his garment," the priest shouted at me in a Moses-came-down-from-the-mount manner.

"Oh yeah! And who the fuck do you think *you* are? If you keep this up I won't buy you any more Jackie Dee's!" I warned.

The phone rang. I picked it up and heard the voice of Letty. "It's a message from Bernie. He wants you to take Brendan to a party tonight to honor the publication of Joey Adams's new book, *On the Road for Uncle Sam.*"

"A party, thanks. Can I bring a friend?" She assured me I could.

"Thanks, Let. See you later."

I gave the message to Brendan. "I'd love to attend," the priest toned in.

"He's the man to see," Brendan said pointing to me, "he's the bosun on this ship."

"I'd love to come along," the priest said dolefully.

"I'm sorry, but you see loudmouths and drunks are excluded. Brendan doesn't like drunks or loudmouths. Neither do I."

Brendan, Rae and I climbed into the rear of a taxi and alighted on the corner of Forty-ninth Street and Sixth Avenue. The party was in full swing. Celebrities from all strata were pouring into the double-tiered eatery. Brendan rushed up onto the podium and did a series of comic impressions. Adams approached Geis's table where Rae and I were sitting. "I'm sorry Bernie," Adams said in an emphatic tone, "but it's either he or I. I want him out, *right away.*"

"Will you take Brendan home," Geis said to me.

"Not on your left tit, Bernie. I'm having the time of my proletarian life. Ask Rae."

"Oh, O.K., I'll take the nuisance home," she said lugubriously. "I have a headache anyway." Just as she was about to depart in a huff she turned and said, "You Peter, not you, above all people in the world, for God's sake don't you go jumping on the bandwagon." Her remark was in reference to a discussion that was taking place between Bernie and me just as the chagrined Adams butted in. I was in the process of informing Geis that I had given Brendan a considerable amount of money. I itemized my lay out. He was in the process of assuring me my recompense when Adams approached.

The following early morning Brendan came to my room "to collect his dues." I awoke and found him rummaging through my pockets.

"I'll split whatever you find," I said, waking up and feeling as if an alley cat had shit in my mouth.

"What the fuck do yew think I'm looking for," he groaned in characteristic hangover anguish, "a crown of thorns and a handful of rusty nails?"

"Gee, Brendan," I said climbing out of bed, "too bad you got stoned to the balls last night. Whew! What a blowout it was, movie stars and heavies from all over. Gorgeous girls and even gorgeouser boys. But fuck it, B., next time. It's like you said, it's not over yet. Nirvana is around every corner."

"Will yew for cuntsake just give me me lolly," he roared as he put out his hand.

"I don't think I should give you any more lolly, Bren, it's bad for your partying habits, not to mention what it's doing to your liver."

Brendan threw himself into a corner, crossed his ankles and did a macabre imitation of the crucified Christ, while he moaned as if he were in agonizing pain. He twitched, coughed and salivated. His head dropped to his shoulder.

"Here, B.," I said handing him a bill, "it's a twenty, bring back thirteen. O.K. Now fuck off before I change my mind.

He saluted in stiff military fashion. "Praise be to the steeplejack jayzus on his crucifix," he muttered as he bumbled away.

I went back to sleep. Brendan, as usual, went down to the Oasis to get himself tanked up on his favorite suds, prior to engaging himself in his next "shite machine taping" session with Rae. One hour later, I was awakened. "Come up to 1026 right away," Katherine Dunham ordered me in a commanding tone.

When I arrived, I noticed that a chair was placed in the center of the floor. I was ordered to sit. Katherine and Rae circled me with looks of sheer annoyance. Brendan sat on the settee in the pose of a Sabu's monkey. Then he switched his pose to that of a Brahman priest, gesticulating and intoning mellifluous words and psalms and invoking his divine blessings over all of us.

"*You* have been giving Brendan drinking money," Katherine exploded. "If you continue to do so, a lawsuit will be brought against you."

"A lawsuit! By who?"

"By Letty and Bernie."

I burst out laughing.

"It's no joke, no laughing matter," Rae chimed in, moving a little closer. "There's a very important book being written here," she said. "You are holding up its production."

"But this is pure madness," I exclaimed. "Why I wouldn't dream of giving Brendan money and so early in the A.M. Would I, B.?" I said turning to Brendan.

Brendan's shenanigans came to an abrupt stop. Silence prevailed, then he jumped up to his feet and in his military style, with his hand to his forehead in salute, said, "Yes, yes. You are the guilty one, Peter Arthurs, you are the destructive force in this important machinery. You are hereby guilty of the crime of sharing your newfound riches, the money that you have stolen from the steamship company. I sentence you to—" (Brendan was referring to my settlement from Calmar Steamship Company for my injuries incurred on the S.S. *Marymar*).

"Why you fuckin' little weasel," I roared, as I jumped up and took hold of his throat and started to strangle him.

Katherine and Rae quickly jumped to the rescue and pulled me away.

"You're never to touch poor Brendan again," Rae shouted, as she pulled on my arms.

"Oh, fuck the lot of you," I said and departed.

Brendan came tearing down the hall after me. "Here, avick," he muttered as he pushed a wad of sweat-damp bills into the palm of my hand. I opened the bills and found a ten-dollar bill and three singles. "Good boy avick, keep up the good work. These taping sessions and these fuckin' women are driving me to drink. Your blood is worth bottling."

"Go away you little fuck-faced Judas Iscariot you," I roared into his face and trotted down the stairs.

No sooner had I entered my room than the phone rang. "Brendan wants you to come to 1026 right away," Rae said in a frayed voice.

"Tell him to fuck off," I said and hung up.

Again the phone rang, "But he refuses to tape if *you* are not here."

"Will I be sued if I don't come up?" I inquired. "Be right up," I said, and dashed up the stairs.

Harmony was restored and the session was underway. Brendan talked of his days at sea as a ship's painter, smuggler, pornographic writer, gunrunner and pimp in Paris. I burst out laughing. The talker and the taper eyed one another in suspicion. The machine was deactivated. I departed.

Brendan came each morning for his "Numismatic injection." Disharmony was restored.

What Geis, Letty, Rae and Katherine did not understand was that Brendan was an altruistic manchild who wanted no part of reality. The answer to the riddle was a simple one. No handouts, no booze. No booze, no fantasies. No fantasies, no bravura. No bravura, no talk. No talk, no tapes. No tapes, no books. Brendan's talk was the type of talk that was ideal for the making of salable books and plays.

I was having the time of my life. I was trapped in a vortex but was very much enjoying its vortical swirls and eddies.

Working at close quarters with the recalcitrant man, Rae quickly became disenchanted.

One morning when Brendan was behaving extremely brattish, Rae deactivated the machine right in the middle of a session, rewound the tape and charged down the hall. I followed her onto the elevator and chided her, "But Rae, you can't do this to the great man, you know from past experiences that on your next session, his tongue might not be so silvery!!"

"Oh, who gives a damn," she cried. "I have enough now," she said patting her coveted reel, "I can get a book out of what I have, if I have to. I'm exhausted, working with that bastard."

"Sue him," I shouted after her as she ran through the lobby, as she always did after each frantic session. "Isn't this the season for *suuuinggg.*"

One afternoon I went to the Seamen's Church Institute and dug out a pair of my old boxing gloves from the bottom of my storage trunk. I hung them on a nail in my room with the intentions of taking them to the McBurney Y, to do a workout. The following night I awoke in the wee hours of the A.M. to find Brendan naked, down on all fours, cursing and throwing punches at the legs of my furniture. His hands were wrapped in my gloves.

"I see you're really serious about making a big comeback," I chuckled as I got out of the bed. "However you're doing it all barseackwards. First you get your legs and your lungs in shape by running in Central Park, then you get into the sparring routine. Tomorrow we'll discuss a progressive resistance program. Later in the week I'll give you some pointers on nutritional guidance. In the meantime, why don't you fuck-off back upstairs to your own pigpen and let me get some sleep."

Brendan bobbed, weaved, spat, and fumed while he threw volley after volley of hooks and uppercuts.

"I'm telling you son, they're there, I saw the fuckin' little carbuncles," he snorted.

"Which carbuncles is that Bren?"

"The fuckin' little four-legged carbuncles."

I watched the playlet in motion and after a series of questions discovered that he was intent on "thumpin' the shit" out of mice that had prevented him from getting to sleep on my floor. He was once again suffering delirium tremens.

I went to the bathroom, filled a basin full of water, and splattered it all around the room. Some of the water hit him on the arse and genitalia. Then I opened the windows.

The chill air sent him into a paroxysm of shivers and shrieks.

"What the hell are you trying to do?" he bellowed. "Freeze me half to death, is it?"

"No, I'm not," I answered seriously, "I'm only trying to freeze the little fuck-pigs out while at the same time give *us* a chance to get some shut-eye."

Brendan raved and roared and ran from my room, his shriveling testicles cupped in the palms of my moldy boxing gloves. I closed the windows and went back to sleep.

In spite of his advanced deterioration, publicity remained his panacean pursuit. Brendan lived in constant fear of ever having his celebrity eclipsed by another man, or beast, for that matter.

One afternoon in the El Quijote, the Spanish restaurant located on the ground level of the hotel, George Kleinsinger, a famous Broadway composer, Chelsea-ite, eccentric and newly acquired friend of Brendan's, arrived with one of his pet pythons wrapped around his neck. An iguana's head peeped out from one of his pockets. Brendan barreled ahead as the reptiles grabbed much of the thunder. Kleinsinger took the pet iguana from his pocket and placed it on the bar. The frisky little nuisance ran back and forth and received a great deal of applause from the gathering. Brendan became enraged, picked up the monster and proceeded to clobber the composer about the face and neck with it. "Take that yew bloody eegit yew," he roared as he pummeled Kleinsinger. "Who in the name of jayzus do yew think yew are, what in fuck's name has the likes of *yew* ever contributed to the world of art and literature." Brendan then threw down the beast, dashed from the

El Q. and into the Oasis where another coterie of vassals awaited him.

R. E. L. Masters, the world-renowned expert and writer on the subject of sexual perversion was another Chelsea-ite whom Brendan had now befriended. The two writers developed a habit of sitting and talking for hours at a time. One day directly after Masters had parted, Brendan turned to me and said, "What do yew think Pete, do yew think yur man is some sort of a dodo, a wee bit the other way?"

"Maybe so, B. Hmm . . . I wonder what he thinks of you?"

One night at Rae's request, I took her and her daughter, Diana, to the famous Metropole. Diana dearly desired to hear the great Gene Krupa. Our pictures were taken. Between jazz sets I read a few excerpts from my latest vignette to Rae. The story was called *An Urchin in the Chain Locker.* It spoke of my 1948 flight from Dundalk to Liverpool in the chain locker of the S.S. *Black Sod.* "But that's nothing Pete, any hack could write that," she laughed.

"But Arthur Miller felt that it was viable and good, Rae."

The subject was quickly changed. I left Rae and Diana off at the Governor Clinton Hotel, where they were staying, then continued to the Chelsea.

I went up to Katherine's apartment, where I was greeted by a huge black man who held out his hand. His head was shaven and menacing to look at. "Hello, transparent man," he said shaking my hand with a great deal of exertion. Then letting go of it, he said, "You don't believe that you're a transparent man, do you. I'll bet, like all them other Irishers, you think that you're a white man! You're not *white*. You don't believe me? Well take a look at *that*. See what I mean," he said pointing to the depression on the back of my hand where his huge thumb had wedged itself seconds before. My blood rushed back to the surface. "If you were *white* that couldn't happen," he explained. "Hey man, I'll bet you dig sticking your dick into the pussies of them smooth black broads. Hmm . . . all you transparent dudes do."

"Pussy is pussy, mister, velvet or rusty, irrespective of what color of arse it's gleaned from. For my dough it's all up to the fucker who's doin' the fucking."

"Hey, man, you're my kind of transparent dude. You're O.K."

"Look, Miss D.," I said to Katherine, "I don't know who the black Yul Brynner is, but I just came by to see how B. is. Will you give me the key to 1026 and I'll go up."

"Don't take him seriously," Katherine said pulling me to the side, "he's a little difficult, he's an eccentric and doesn't mean what he says." Then she introduced us, "This is Charles Mingus and this is Peter Arthurs." We sat down, talked and drank a magnum of champagne.

As our conversation progressed, Mingus periodically leaned over, put his thumb on my forearm, depressed it and muttered, "See I told you you weren't *white!* You're *pink* baby, cool *pink.*"

Finally I made a depression on the back of his hand and watched the hue of his pigment return to its original color. "And you, sir," I interjected, "You're *black,* I bet you thought you were *brown.* Pure coal *black,"* I said softly, shaking my head and pointing an index finger at the gradually changing color. "Pure coal *black."* I later discovered that Mingus, who was a light-complected black man, was married to a white woman. Also he had a son whom he publicly referred to as "little nigger." I also discovered that he was a world-renowned jazz musician.

A short while later we all went up to 1026.

Mingus and Brendan instantly got into a verbal battle and I left in a maelstrom of heavy name-calling. "You're the Laurel and Hardy of Irish dramatists," Mingus declared as he left.

The following afternoon I was confronted in the lobby by a young man who introduced himself to me as Katherine's fiancé. He was extremely disturbed. "I love Katherine Dunham very much," the man said in a Danish accent, "and if you think that Brendan Behan is to continue referring to black people as a pile of niggers, you are mistaken!"

"Kindly take this matter up with Mr. Behan," I suggested, "he's the humanitarian around this camp."

That evening a compromise was tentatively reached. Brendan would desist from referring to black persons as "niggers" if Mingus would refrain from calling Irishmen "transparent men." Also, the Laurel and Hardy stuff would be deleted from Mingus's future dialogue.

The Danish gentleman, who was also a professional photographer, in a mood of reverie, did a major photo study of Brendan and me in Katherine's apartment.

The Silver Rail was an old run-down bar located on the corner of Seventh Avenue and Twenty-third Street. It catered primarily to black lesbians, whores, pimps and pushers. It became one of Brendan's favorite late-night hangouts. The bar was deep and dark. Brendan was not a favorite of the black three-hundred-pound platinum-wigged lesbian who ran the place and lorded it over her patrons.

One night as I was alighting from the IRT subway I caught sight of Brendan's back as he was clambering up the red brick steps to the bar. Split seconds later I caught another glimpse of him as he was in the middle of a somersault and landing on his back, followed by the mountainous publican. I approached with caution. A large white spot adjacent to the corpulent figure glistened. I moved closer. "Here, lady," I said picking up a platinum wig. "I believe you dropped this."

"Get that moddafugga outa hewe befow ah buss hees ass summow," she hollered as she pointed to the figure on the floor.

"Be glad to, lady," I said and picked up the quivering figure, flung it over my shoulder and carried it up to Dunham's apartment.

The following day, back at the "Rail," I was informed that the bold

Mr. B. had, upon entering the pub, wandered up to the lady, taken hold of the tips of her very ample bosom and in a cuddly manner asked, "Are these for real or for rubber?" The lady took to the remark with a smidgen of exception and threw a power-packed, lightning-quick roundhouse right.

Brendan's jaw absorbed the thunder.

Brendan was becoming a man of infinite vulgarity and evilness incarnate.

One night, in a predominantly black bar on Eighth Avenue, a young husky black man who was ultranegroid of feature approached Brendan, extended his hand and said, "Hello Mr. Behan, I recognize you, you're the famous Welsh fighter." The man then ordered three drinks, again extended his hand, and concluded, "I consider you my brother, drink up."

Brendan looked the man up and down with utter disgust.

"Listen mister," Brendan barked into the man's astonished face, "I already have a brother, a brother who I might add has a very different color of hide than yew have. Now sir, if it's all one and the fuckin' same to yew," he went on, his voice rising to a crescendo, "if there's anything I don't need in this zebra fuckin' zoo of yours, it's another brother, especially one with a thirty-three pound lower lip hanging from his face telling *me* what to do."

I turned to make a hasty departure. The incredulous man put a huge hand on my shoulder and said, "If you're leaving, don't you think you should take your friend along with you?"

"Why should I," I said, as I retreated. "I only met him for the first time a few minutes ago!" I quickened my retreat.

One afternoon as Katherine, Brendan and I were taxiing to Sardi's, purportedly to meet Anthony Quinn's agent to discuss the screen version of *Borstal Boy,* Brendan suddenly became frantic and started to shout, "I'm Brendan Behan, I'm no typical Broadway or Hollywood cunt, I don't give a fuck! If she doesn't leave me in peace I'll keep the book and give her nothing." At the Pennsylvania Railroad Station the car stopped for a red light. Brendan jumped out and ran east, shouting, "I'm no Broadway or Hollywood louse." Brendan was referring to the rights to the book that he was taping. He had agreed to allocate the subsidiary rights of it toward his child's future.

Katherine's phone and my phone were now receiving a steady bombardment of requests from the local publicans, priests and police. "Will you please come and take Brendan home?" was the usual hue and cry.

Katherine had by now come to the realization that she had opened her door to a monster-child. An ingrate. A hubristic brat. An absurdist nonpareil. A man whose ego knew no bounds. "Whew, you're really something. I sure wish you'd go over there with Peter and sit down," she said on a number of occasions as she tried in vain to shut him up while she was in the process of conducting business with her steady stream of business associates. "I'll be happy when Beatrice gets here and takes him off my hands," she confided to me.

Brendan's pontifical tone had reestablished itself.

The words *Nigs* and *Yids* were now added to Brendan's forever growing vocabulary. Brendan was upset with Bernard Geis for not advancing him more money. Geis is Jewish.

His feelings for Katherine Dunham were of a similar nature, but slightly more pronounced. Katherine had cultivated him, nurtured him back to health, restored him and prolonged his life.

The great lady's patience was being tapped. She sorely wanted out. She had proven herself a woman of rare magnitude, strength, charm and extraordinary personality. For the first two weeks under her care, Brendan vociferously condemned, repudiated and denigrated all whites as racists. He repeatedly referred to his own people—the Irish— as savages. The Black Muslims were in his humble opinion, "the real salts of the earth."

Katherine, or any of her entourage, never made mention of the Muslims. Brendan had originally carried himself off in a charming, penitent, contrite manner. His attitude had been that of the benign and the fatherly. His profile had been low, his need to rest and to recuperate awesome, his ebullient vibrations infectious. Now he was back to his normal pace, dragging derelicts home by the dozen and demanding that she feed them.

One morning Lucille called to inquire about what it was that titillated Brendan most in regards to "room furnishings."

"He's a pure lover of nature and things small in value," I said. We proceeded to Lamston's and purchased a load of artificial flowers and other plastic geegaws for room 1026. Brendan denounced the purchases as being "a pure waste of valuable drinking money."

Spending up to fifteen hours per day in the immediate company of the smooth-looking, svelte figures of the dancers, he became horny and continued to reach for fistfuls of well-muscled derrieres, but his attempts were now quickly rebuffed.

Slowly but surely he got back to his old familiar, feisty, ebullient and imperious self, behaving as though he were New York's latest premier of Irish politicians. His crude behavior shocked Katherine. His hostile, wisecracking sarcasm and demands were too much. The gaunt alcohol-ravaged look was gone, replaced by the bold, daring, glistening, pompous grin. A grin that she had not previously known.

Brendan's health was comparatively restored. He became the latest drunk in residence and the liar laureate of the Chelsea.

The management of the Chelsea begged him to cut back on his barefooted panhandling antics in the busy lobby.

Brendan danced, sang and told bawdy stories in his bare feet, then he held out his hand and assured his prospectives that "anything that you contribute will be for a worthy cause." Then he curtsied and introduced himself as "Worthy Cause."

One afternoon Letty Cottin called and asked me to stop Brendan from panhandling in front of the Chelsea. "Bernie says it's bad for his image and may hurt the sale of his books."

"But Letty, this is how he gets the material for his books. Let him be." My eardrum popped as I heard the receiver go down hard at the other end.

Gilbert Ortero and Manuel Muñoz ordered him out of the El Quijote. Brendan had loudly referred to them as "fuckin' Franco fascist cunts." To spice up the volley of insult, Brendan ran over to the table where Manuel was sitting eating and puked into his caldo de yago soup. The rare gold and silver hand-embroidered jacket that the publican was wearing absorbed the bulk of the vomitous matter. Brendan was again ordered to leave and never to return.

Each day I spent two to three hours rolling on the living room floor or crawling around on my hands and knees in the hallways while little Brendan sat on my back giggling hysterically. Brendan ignored his son. Seldom did he ever look at him. He loved and loathed me for paying so much attention to the boy.

Bernard Geis had flatly refused to give Brendan any more money. Brendan's word had not lived up to hopes. He averaged two to three drunks per day. His taping sessions decreased in number. He became maudlin and depressed to the point of incapacitation. Geis, Letty, Rae and Katherine begged me to sober him up and get him back to work. "Why should I?" I asked, "What's in it for me? Besides, he's enjoying himself."

Periodically a genuinely concerned AA member appeared and begged me to get him enrolled in the successfully proven fellowship. "Alcoholism is a rapidly progressive disease that can cause permanent madness," I was informed.

When I advised them that Brendan was a great deal madder and more of a menace to society when sober, they departed sadder but wiser than when they arrived.

Parties in his honor were canceled.

Our hourly contretemps increased.

Brendan had been alone all of his life. Alone, not in the literal sense but in the biochemical, physiological and psychological problematic sense. Disaster was inevitable.

He talked incessantly about boxing and boxers. For all of his life he had experienced great difficulty equating homosexuality with masculinity, strength and force, yet, he repeatedly insisted that all good boxers were "queens."

I wholeheartedly agreed that many were, but when I assured him that his theory could not rightfully be applied to all good fighters he became upset, insolent and dogmatic.

"Those that are worth their liniment rubs are," he insisted, "they'd have to be."

Picking back over the rile, the bile and the rubble of his life, Brendan was fast becoming aware that his great fortune in life could not change him. Quite the contrary. They merely served to unmask him. He was desperately groping for an exorcism. He realized that at the age of forty he was indeed ignorant of most social graces. He once confided in me that in a drunken rage he had charged into a dentist's office and demanded that the doctor extract half of his teeth. A bitter argument ensued until the astounded man finally agreed to his wish. Brendan felt that the gapped look would buttress his brawling womanizing image.

George Bernard Shaw once contended that the best way to hide a deep, dark personal secret was to proclaim it publicly as often as possible. Brendan was an avid reader of Irish writers. Brendan Behan had for years worked hard to hide his many deep, dark, personal secrets. He was not as bold as he was billed. He was happiest when in jail. It was there that he learned to orate and to hone his ability to write and to expound. In jail he had disciplined himself and become a prodigious reader. In jail he savored the camaraderie of strong men; the type of men that he could lean on. The type who would protect him from himself. He used his fellow convicts as his developmental models; a conglomeration of supermasculine identifications that he would publicly utilize in a later life-style. He had studied well the hard men's gestures, style of swagger and roll, and the rough mannerisms.

From the beginning, Brendan suffered from a deep sense of early-life arrest of his psychosexual development. Now, for the first time in his life, the little man who had successfully fooled the world into regarding him as the enfant terrible of Irish lettermen was trying hard to own up to the fact that he had never been a true gut penman. He was also learning that the deadly pursuit of immortality is a lonely man's game. At best, Brendan was a placebo writer. He was now attempting every trick in his prolific lexicon to get me to punch him out. Under no circumstances would I afford him this pseudovindication. He proselytized for homosexuality for the young, as though it were the only mind-broadener and new-horizon-creator available to them.

Brendan now wickedly condemned the IRA for their "mores, manners and murders," but on the occasion, when one of his famous-people-watchers chimed in and joined him in his villifications, he did a surprising quick hundred-eighty-degree turn and savagely belabored them for their "ill-advised mouthings."

Periodically a stunned viewer assured the fiery orator that "everything you have said is extremely interesting."

"Everything that I say usually is," Brendan quickly responded. "I just want to be scrupulously fair . . . eh, that is to myself, of course," he swiftly concluded with characteristic humor.

He lived in terror of process-servers. He smoked incessantly, stubbing out his cigarettes after one or two puffs. Smoking made him dizzy, nauseated and depressed, but the fear of not being able to smoke, fuck, fight or write sent him into pirouettes of deeper anxiety.

Often, when a knock came at my door, he would charge into my clothes closet or dive under my bed. I would open the door and allow in the chambermaid or the house handyman. After they had left I would coax him back into the room or into a perpendicular position. "Thank jayzus for that itself," he moaned.

On the transatlantic wire, Beatrice had always concluded, "For God's sake Peter, don't let him smoke cigarettes, make him smoke his cigars!" (She thought that this would cut in half the prospect of him falling to sleep and burning himself to death.)

In the ornate Victorian hotel Brendan felt like a perverted porgie in a tankful of white sharks. His panic and hysteria flourished. Charles Jackson, science fiction writer Arthur C. Clarke, Virgil Thomson and many more literary and cultural heavyweights lived there too. Frantic dashes back to the Intermission, his old lair where he once was king, were even more frequent.

One night I followed him there and from the vantage point of the dimlit vestibule I watched his fright-filled spoutings and gesticulations as he paraded about in the center of the filthy, cigarette-butt-strewn floor, talking twenty-six to the dozen on every topic that chanced across his mind. He talked for hours. When he had finished I walked over to him and said, "Come on home, B., we don't live in this neighborhood anymore." He dashed into the smelly bathroom and emerged clutching something in his hand. Then he walked up to Al, the bar's owner, and said, "Hey, yussir, give me a fuckin' pencil."

The easygoing man rummaged through the drawer and came up with a ballpoint pen, then handed it to him. Brendan looked at the pen with utter disdain. "Listen yew, critic, I asked yew for a fuckin' pencil, this is a fuckin' pen, if I wanted a fuckin' pen I would have asked yew for a fuckin' pen, I asked yew for a fuckin' pencil, so will yew be kind enough to give me a fuckin' pencil for fucksake, sir!" Another quick rummage through the drawer and Al came forward with a pencil. "Do yew see that," Brendan said to me, pointing out the window. I looked out onto the street, and in a white-hot flash felt a sharp pain in my solar plexis. I looked down on the floor and saw a cardboard tube that had been the tube of a roll of toilet paper. Inside of the tube was the long yellow pencil that Al had given to Brendan. "And that avick is how yew write," he said to me. "Write, write, for fucksake write. Paper and pencil is all it takes. Any kind of paper will do, even arse paper, but write, for I know only too fuckin' well that yew can write, and a damn sight better than I can." Brendan went up to the bar, stood on top of the elevated footrest and did a series of his most severe staring-down exercises into the face of the barman. Brendan highly regarded himself as a stalwart starer, the type that could put the heart crosswise in a marble statue or a rubber duck. Al had once remarked to me that in his profound opinion *The Hostage* was not a genuine Broadway vintage-type play. He further opined that had it not been for Brendan's cleverly timed antics, the play would never have made it further than Fourteenth Street.

Being a loyalist, I had informed my landsman of Al's opinions.

During the Cort's run of *The Hostage,* business at the usually comparatively quiet Intermission had boomed. Brendan hadn't forgotten. Neither would he ever.

One night at Bernie Geis's house, just as a cocktail party was about to get under way, a heavily bejeweled lady threw her arms around my neck and said, "Oh Mr. Behan, I simply adored your plays. I—"

"This is Mr. Behan," Geis gently interrupted, pointing to Brendan as he followed me in the door.

"Oh he looks so much like you, Mr. Behan. Then he must be your handsome son," the lady apologized, talking to Brendan and looking at me.

"Well not exactly," Brendan snapped, "you see in actuality, he's me Aunt Maggie, but don't worry, tomorrow I'm taking him to the doctor to have him fitted out with a pair of balls. The next time you see him, he'll be me uncle Joe."

The lady laughed in strained deference as Brendan buzzed about the apartment pinching her and her colleagues on their befrocked bottoms.

"Why don't you take Brendan home for a good night's sleep," Geis whispered to me, "then you can come back and enjoy the party."

Outside on Sutton Place Brendan muttered in despair "A right iggarint lot of fuckin' aul hypocrites."

Clumsy silence prevailed.

"I believe the word is ignorant Brendan. I-G-N-O-R-A-N-T."

Brendan, without uttering a word, flagged a taxi. Just as I was about to climb in behind him he slammed the door in my face, poked his thumbs into his ears and stuck his tongue out at me as he rolled up the glass.

One afternoon a very tense, petite, soft-spoken young lady showed up at the hotel to see Brendan. She was a freelance writer and photographer. She wanted to take him on a tour of the city and have him comment on various landmarks, monuments and institutions.

Brendan brusquely declined. "I'm busy, much too busy drinking myself to death. See me when I'm finished," he warmly suggested.

"Better do it now," I suggested. With an appreciable amount of reluctance he finally acquiesced. We hailed a taxi and headed for Central Park South.

Brendan was in good spirits, talking, telling jokes and holding the young lady's hands in his left hand. His right hand was placed between my thighs. The unsuspecting lady winced and chuckled with embarrassment. Suddenly he underwent a drastic change in personality, lambasting her with four-letter words and making gargoyle faces, ". . . and who the fuck do you think *you* are? I suppose you think *you* are better than me! Go on, go on and get your crumbling cunt and your twitching twat away from me," he demanded as he pushed her out the door of the cab.

I got out of the cab and took the whimpering girl to a coffee shop and ordered up some food. "Don't worry," I placated her, "Brendan is merely in one of his off moods, in a day or two he'll be happy to see you again." The girl thanked me, dried up her tears and went home.

Brendan was nuts. Delirious. Certifiably insane. He was also sober on that occasion.

XVI

On or about April 20, 1963, Beatrice phoned via the transatlantic line and announced that she was due to arrive on the Queen Elizabeth. Katherine sighed with delight. "Thank God," she said. Changes had to be quickly made. Who would carry the baby's crib to Katherine Dunham's dance studio on the top floor? No one volunteered. Valery took the boy and departed. I folded the crib and carried it upstairs. A short while later Rae Jeffs phoned me and said, "Brendan is out, hiding somewhere with Valery. She's demanding ten thousand dollars from Brendan. What should I do?"

"Give it to her," I said. "He's rich."

"If he doesn't straighten up before morning and meet Beatsie at the pier, I'm not going to be there," she said curtly and hung up.

At approximately seven-thirty A.M. I went up to 1026, put the key in the door, crept into the two-room apartment and found Brendan in bed. His two hands were clutching a half-full bottle of Jack Daniel's. I knelt down beside the bed, blew some hot breath into his quivering mouth and nostrils and awaited the response. No response came.

Brendan was snoring his easy rhythmical snores. He was slightly drunk but fully awake. "Wake up jolly Judas, let go your cock and grab your sock," I whispered into his mouth, "arise and shine it's crucifixion time." My little game was interrupted by the ring of the phone. "Hello Brendan I'm so happy you're—"

"I hate to be such a disappointment to you Rae but this is the other Irish author."

"Is he drunk? Is he still in bed?" Rae shouted into the phone.

"Oh dear, Rae," I whined in resignation and mock drunkenness. "You're getting yourself so unnecessarily upset. Do calm down, it's not like you atall atall."

"I might have known, I might have known," the lady went on, like an English Shakespearian actress stepping out of character.

"If you calm yourself down, Rae, I promise I'll take you ice-skating in Central Park," I said in a lilting voice, "but for heaven's sake let's wait until the weather gets warmer, what say."

I heard the phone go down hard, then I quickly taxied to pier 90. Dozens of people were milling about and shoving one another to get to the head of the queue that was eagerly awaiting the disembarking passengers. I spotted Rae at the top of the queue.

"Fancy meeting you here," I chuckled as I pushed ahead and confronted her face to face. The English lady reacted to my presence with utter disbelief.

"Oh, I couldn't think of having poor Beatsie arrive and be on her own," she blurted, "that half-mad animal, how could he be so cruel?"

"Thank God you're here," I said, "you've a heart of gold."

In a sea of anxiety-ridden faces, we suddenly spotted Beatrice. "Could Brendan not make it?" she asked, a look of disappointment growing on her face as she awaited our answer.

"He's not feeling too well this morning, Bea," I answered, "but not to worry." We kissed and embraced in the noisy din of the daze, then hailed a taxi and sped to the Governor Clinton where we deposited Rae. Then Beatrice and I taxied to the Chelsea.

In the lobby we were joined by Katherine. I made the formal introductions. "O.K., Beatsie," I said, "I'll leave you here. This way you can be alone with Bren."

"Oh no, no, no Peter," she exclaimed, a look of fear on her pale countenance, "you're coming up with me. Has he been drinking a lot?" she asked me on the elevator.

"Quite a sup, Bea, but thanks to Miss D., he's in good health."

"Miss D.?"

"That's Katherine Dunham. Around here, we call her Miss D."

We entered the eerie room with me in the lead. Beatrice put her bags down onto the hallway floor and timidly looked around the two-and-one-half-room apartment. "I won't wake him up if he's asleep," she said, a look of terror on her face.

"I'll get him up," I said ebulliently, moving towards the bed.

"It took yew a long fuckin' time to get here," Brendan shouted as he leapt out of bed. "Root me out a suit, the blue one, that's if yew had the mind to remember it," he exhorted.

The intimidated lady immediately set about opening her suitcases and extricated Brendan's dark blue silk mohair suit.

"It's full of fuckin' creases," he bawled at her as she handed it to him.

"That's because it's been in a suitcase," I interjected. "But don't fret, I doubt if the Chelsea-ites will mind."

Brendan hurriedly dressed. "Cum on for jayzus sake," he ordered us. "This place is drivin' me mad."

We went to the Oasis. Brendan guzzled eight to ten double J.D.'s and an equal number of T.B.'s, then sat glumly awaiting the hot lava to take hold in his veins. In the interim, I inquired of Beatrice about her father and mother and sister Celia.

"Oh she's been workin' in a new play," she said. "It's called *The Man in the Green Coat.*"

"Will yiz give over with yur talk about fuckin' plays, is that all yiz care about is fuckin' plays," Brendan roared at the two of us. Then he began stripping and reenacting his Glasnevin shoot-out.

"Will yew cum over here, Willie," he shouted at the owner of the Oasis. "Listen avick, there's something I want to ask yew since yur a man of the world," Brendan blurted to him, "What do yew think of me plans to divorce the one beside me here and marry the other cow, the cow with the calf, wha?"

"Oh my God, Brendan, how could you say a thing like that to the poor girl and her not even an hour in the country. Come on Brendan, get with it."

"Yes, that's right, B." I joined in, "give over with the fuckin' black puddin' talk and give the girl a chance." We breakfasted in sullen silence.

April 23, Brendan's fortieth birthday was celebrated in Fellini's restaurant in Greenwich Village. In three fast single draughts, Brendan guzzled three bottles of Italian red wine. In one single geyser the three bottles were splattered all over the attire of Rae, Beatrice and Bernie Pollack and Beulah Garrick, the couple who had thrown the surprise birthday party for him.

Outside on the sidewalk, he went into an emotional tizzy. While in the gentle process of putting him into a cab I touched his right arm, a little above the elbow.

One night, Charlie Young, a County Roscommon–born Brooklyn bar-owner friend of mine, showed up at the Chelsea to talk to Brendan. I had once introduced the pair in the Brooklyn–Long Island Railroad Station. Charlie had read *Borstal Boy* in the interim. "I loved your book, Mr. Behan," the six-foot-seven, two-hundred-eighty-pound midlander announced, looking down into Brendan's face, "but do I detect a drop of lavender in it?"

Brendan's beam of delight quickly turned to a vinegary sneer. In a huff he was up and on top of the booth and onto the floor, knocking over dishes of food as he went. Then he dashed out the door calling all midlanders a pack of illiterates who wouldn't know a book from a bog.

On or about April 28, in the Oasis I announced that I was off to Dublin.

"In that case you'll be in Dublin by this time tomorrow night!" Beatrice said.

"Not if the plane goes down in the middle of the Atlantic," Brendan butted in.

"Oh, for crying out loud, Brendan, that's no way to treat your good friend Pete," Willie Garfinkle said. "Are you going on a pleasure or a business trip?" he asked.

"Oh, it's a little of both you might say," I said casually. "I am very definitely looking forward to a renunion with a mutual friend of Brendan's and mine. She's there at the moment making a film. *Of Human Bondage* is its name. The friend's name is Novak. Kim Novak."

Brendan was clearly taken aback but did not deign to look up at me as he almost choked on his food.

The following day I flew to Dublin, deplaned, taxied to 43 Morehampton, informed Celia that Brendan insisted that I stay at his house, secured the key to Cuig and settled in.

My next order of business was to hurry down to 27 Anglesea Road, secure my hockshop tickets from Petro and redeem my valuables.

On or about May the first, I was hired as glorified extra and worked in the Gaiety Theatre, in a scene with Kim Novak.

The following day I dashed off a postcard to Brendan to inform him that I was having a gala time in Dublin, working in the film and living in his house. I mentioned that I was planning on throwing a supper party in his historical house and inviting some of the *Of Human Bondage* cast. "Kim Novak sends her regards" was my last line on the card.

Celia, Seamus Parker, who was her fiancé, and I developed a routine of chipping in, buying groceries and vegetables and dining together. One afternoon, just as we had finished our lunch and Celia was attending to the dishwashing chore, Seamus took me by surprise. "What do you think of Brendan's homosexual problem?" he asked.

"Homosexual problem? What homosexual problem?" The subject never came up again.

A few days later Celia, out of breath, came running to Cuig and blurted, "Oh Peter, Brendan just phoned, he's all upset, he wants you out of the house!!"

"But wasn't it Brendan who had always said 'A house is never a home until it is lived in by people," I reminded her. "Nothing to worry about, dear C., I was just in the process of moving. I'll drop B. a line. Ciao."

The following day, I moved into the Connagh Hill, an old but elegant guest house that was located in Bray and down the road from Ardmore Studios.

My next-door neighbor was Kim Novak. Desmond MacKey had utilized his influence to get me the suite. I was subsequently invited to the *Bondage* parties by Brian Smith, the wardrobe department manager. I dropped Brendan another card, apologizing for my change of address: "I wanted to get out in the country." I informed him of my new address and the identity of my glamorous next-door neighbor. I signed the card, "Your original flower of the flock secured the room for me. Thanks for the invaluable introduction." I posted the card on June the fifteenth. That date was exactly two years to the day after Ernie Kovacs's party in Hollywood.

Prior to returning to New York I dropped over at 71 Crumlin Road to say hello to the two elderly Behans.

"Isn't he a luvly boy," Mrs. Behan said to her pipe-smoking husband, who stood directly behind her in the doorway, a man she continuously referred to as "the Da."

"He's all right, leave the lad alone," the man demanded, peering over her shoulder.

"But will you look at his luvly coloring, his blue eyes, his rosy cheeks. I was just saying to mesself, if he married a Spanish señorita, well, wouldn't the children be luvly?"

"But mind you, he might be already married. Did you ask him? Better off never to get married," the Da said. "And where is the other fella," the Da inquired without affording his wife the opportunity to ask further questions, his pipe still in his teeth. "I mean to say, not that I care, of course, for it's none of me business, but is he in London or Paris or New York or where says you?"

"And there's the Da for you now, he's as quiet as a lamb, never had a cross word from him in forty years exceptin' I provoked it mesself, wha!" Mrs. Behan interrupted." Did you know that me brother, Peaner Kearney, wrote the lovely Irish national anthem?"

"Will you let the boy talk," the Da interjected sharply.

"He's presently staying at the Chelsea Hotel in New York," I said cheerfully.

"Must be a dirty aul dump," Mrs. Behan joined in. "Poor Brendan, if only Beatrice could bear him a child. He loves children!"

"Oh no, Mrs. Behan, it's a very old, quaint, famous hotel, filled with famous writers and gifted artists."

"Grand says you, grand," she said. "Nice to know that Brendan is amongst his own. He must be happy and enjoying himself. Brendan loves writers."

"Oh, very much so," I assured the lady.

"And you can call me Aunty Kathleen," she suddenly said. "Around here everyone refers to me as Aunty Kathleen, and here now son, here's a kiss on the cheek from the mother of the genius of Irish letters, Brendan Francis Behan," she said affectionately, kissing me on the cheek. The three of us stood in the doorway. Finally I hailed a cab and took the couple for a round of the local pubs.

In the Bailey, Davy Byrne's, and all of the other bars on Grafton Street that we visited, the elderly Behans graciously accepted accolades and drinks from the hordes of well-wishers. Prior to our departures Mr. Behan thanked his idolators and assured one and all that the plays he promised to write for them personally were "imminently forthcoming."

Along about closing time Aunty Kathleen turned to the Da and said, "There, now will you look at him, he's wilting, tired of the company of the auld folks and can't wait to get away from the pair of us, that's the way with the young of today." Then turning to me she said, "Shur I suppose you'd like to be a writer like Brendan Behan?"

"I'd like to be a writer, Aunty Kathleen. I would, I would!"

"Well, you're going to have to practice," she said emphatically. "Brendan never had to practice, Brendan had the aul genius born in him, it came into him with his mother's milk. But if *you* practice, you'll succeed. Practice, practice, practice, avick!"

"I will, Aunty Kathleen, I will, I will, I'll practice."

I left the Behans's home in a taxi. As the taxi was pulling away, Aunty Kathleen stood by the door of number 71 shouting after me, "Now you won't forget to practice will you not, remember what the mother of the genius Brendan Behan told you, practice, practice, practice. The practice is the thing, we can't all be geniuses, practice, practice, practice . . ."

Dublin's transportation system to Bray was shut down for the night. I taxied to Cuig, disliking the elder Behans. I found them to be gross, crass and pretentious. Mrs. Behan was the most mealy-mouthed woman that I had ever met.

I lay down in Brendan's bed and pulled the damp, musty blankets up over my face. I felt cold and lonely. I got up, clattered down the stairs and went in search of the cat. My idea was to take the warm, furry animal to bed with me.

Finally I spotted a pair of luminous eyes peering up at me from under the stairway. I reached down, heard a shriek and felt a claw ripping across the back of my hand. I washed the blood away, doused the scratches with iodine from a cabinet and went back to bed.

Sunday, June 16. Leopold Bloom's day in Dublin.

Early in the day I phoned Celia and Cecil to inform them that I was on to New York. "Give my regards to Brendan and Beatsie," Cecil said. As I was in the process of checking out, I lent a hand to Joe Reece, Kim Novak's chauffeur, and to Barbara Mellon, Miss Novak's stand-in, and stuffed the final threads of their personal belongings into their black Jaguar. On that day, Miss Novak was flying to London.

Bonzo Delimata, a cousin to James Joyce, picked me up and drove me to the airport. Along the route she drove me to Eccles Street, the street that was chosen by Joyce as the living site for his immortal Leopold and Molly Bloom. Next we drove to a rocky cliff in the suburb of Sandycove and viewed the nineteenth-century Martello Tower, where Joyce lived with Oliver Gogarty in 1904.

"Oh, you will give my regards to Arthur Miller, won't you, he's my favorite writer," Bonzo said as I boarded the plane.

I assured the lady that before the day was out I would make her sentiments known.

At approximately two P.M. I arrived at the Chelsea Hotel lobby. Just as I was checking in an anxious-looking entourage emerged from an elevator.

Brendan was strapped into a stretcher. His hands were joined. His hair was limp and wet with sweat. His eyes were closed. The condition of his face was blotchy, blue and pallid. I ran up to the side of the stretcher and focused in on his eyes and lips. For a few seconds his eyelids opened and quivered. Inaudible words seeped from his thin lips. His mouth curled.

The atmosphere in the lobby was straitjacketed. Beatrice was wan and on the verge of collapse.

Suddenly, a strange illumination swept over him! Had he died, I wondered.

"He's dead, the whore is dead," I suddenly blurted.

"Oh no, he's not dead," Beatrice moaned as she fell in behind the stretcher bearers, "he's just a little sick."

"Your mother says I should marry a luvly Spanish señorita," I shouted into the ambulance as two white-clad men pushed me away and drove off to University Hospital. The following morning Brendan awoke thoroughly convinced that Beatrice had institutionalized him in "the Grange," a well-known mental home in Ireland; he grabbed up his clothes and hastily departed. "They're not keepin' me in no fuckin' puzzle factory," he roared as he sat in his gilt ormolu chair in the Chelsea lobby. "They call themselves nurses and doctors. They're nothing but a pack of fuckin' turnip snaggers and low-life hillbillies." Brendan ranted, raved and struck up instant conversations with phantom listeners and his favorite ghosts that flickered across his addled mind.

On Monday, June the seventeenth, Warren Berry of the *Herald Tribune* came to the Oasis and interviewed Brendan, Kleinsinger, Agnes Boulten and me. Agnes was the widow of Eugene O'Neill and the mother-in-law of Charlie Chaplin. When the interview was over and Berry and the others had left, Agnes, Brendan and I remained. (Some months previously Agnes had given me a copy of *Long Day's Journey into Night,* O'Neill's autobiographical play, and inscribed it, "To Peter, a Norwegian seaman just like Gene. Take it all with a grain of salt." I showed it to Brendan and he threw the book to the floor, stomped on it yelling, "A load of shite." Brendan's insane hatred for Irish playwrights obviously included Irish-American playwrights.) I went to the bath-

room in the rear of the pub; when I returned I found Brendan screaming into her face and twisting her fingers.

"I'll tell yew who yur husband was," Brendan yelled into her frightened face, "he was given the name Gladstone after an aul English
ballox called William Ewart Gladstone, who was nothing but a fuckin'
hypocrite and a degenerate swine who in order to get the Irish vote in
the House of Commons in the year 1886, bullshitted and promised the
other actor, Parnell, all sorts of fuckin' reforms and other such shite,
then later helped to bring him down for having a love affair with
another codger's floozie, called Kitty O'Shea. Having love affairs with
other joker's Judies is in my opinion a natural class of a thing—fair field
and no favor, I do it mesself—but there is a fair crop of people who
refer to the same cunt Gladstone as the G.O.M., meaning the Grand
Old Man, but I'll tell yew this much and I'll tell yew no more, there is
also a wiser class of people who rightfully refer to him as the M.O.G.,
the Murderer of Gordon. Yur husband's father, who was a very patri-
otic but ill-informed Irishman, felt that callin' his son Gladstone would
be a good way of showin' his patriotism. A long-distance patriot would
be my way of classifyin' him . . ." When his spiel was finished, Brendan
leaned closer to the appalled lady and bent her fingers further backwards. She screamed with terror.

I grabbed hold of his wrist, inserted my thumb into the back of his
hand, my fingertips under the heel of his thumb and exuded the maximum amount of pressure.

"Ahhhh! What c-class of a f-f-fuckin' savage culshin' eegit thing was
that to do!" he yelled, as I let go.

"If you ever touch this lady again, I'll break every bone in your
dying body," I yelled into his face.

A few minutes later, upstairs in my room, Brendan sat sullenly,
counting the months of the year, "June, May, April, March, February . . ." Then, according to the distrustful, distrusting Brendan, Beatrice was four months pregnant. She had been in New York approximately four months! Niggling questions were again rattling his brain.
Prior to departing Brendan undressed and lay down on my bed. "I
won't fuck you, B., but I have a friend who will. Want to meet him?" I
received no answer.

On Monday, June the 24th, Berry's article appeared on the front
page of the *Herald Tribune.*

"BEHAN AND THE HILLBILLIES. A friend of *The Quare Fellow.*" Brendan detested the article. The bulk of the interview revolved
around me and my history as a seafarer. The name of my most recent
ship was also mentioned. The article referred to me as a part-time actor
and writer. My relationship with and the gist of my last meeting with
my father were also included.

Brendan was thrashing about like a demented porcupine in a forest on fire. Through the grapevine I heard that a chancrelike sore was discovered on his gum. Kleinsinger, Rae and Beatrice took him to a doctor for syphilis tests. I recalled a time in Hollywood when Brendan informed me that Oscar Wilde had died of syphilis. I phoned Rae Jeffs. "Listen Rae, I absolutely have to know the results of the test!?"

"What tests?" she said in a cold flat voice.

"You know what tests, the pox tests, that's what test."

"You better be careful," she said in a cold flat voice.

"*You* be careful," I said, "one of these days I'm going to call the DA's office and what I will have to say won't do a lot of people around here any good—"

She hung up. I went in search of Kleinsinger. I found him in his room. "The outcome of the test, George, don't fuck me about, what was it? If you don't ante up the answer," I said threateningly, "what Johnny Weissmuller didn't do to the jungle, I'll fuckin' well do to this glass menagerie of yours," I concluded, pointing to his vast array of snakes, turtles, monkeys, mynah birds, iguanas, piranhas, and rodents.

"To the best of my knowledge Pete, everything came out O.K.," he said as he proceeded to roll up a stick of marijuana and feed a mouse to one of his curled-up boa constrictors.

"It better be," I said hastily and departed.

I phoned Richard Brigham, the medical technologist at the SIU clinic and made an appointment. The blood test proved negative.

One day Katherine presented Beatrice with a bill for her grocery output. "Much too much," Brendan shouted, "shur she did fuck all for me!" A lawsuit was threatened. Feeling a personal obligation to Dunham for her care and concern for me, I let it be known that I would take her part in the suit.

As the days passed, Brendan became sorely exasperating and fractious. His talk centered on religion and the life hereafter. For centuries, Catholicism in Ireland was proclaimed "an addiction," "a life-style," rather than a religion. The journey to the life hereafter is the Irish Catholic's greatest dread. Brendan did not genuinely care about the immediate resolution of the church or its antievolutionist theme. He worried about his next orbit; that karmatic beyond that he had so wickedly japed.

One night a very elegantly dressed Katherine Dunham arrived in the El Q. accompanied by a tall silver-haired man. "This is James T. Farrell, and this is Peter Arthurs," she said, introducing us to each other. Then she scanned the packed restaurant in the hopes of spotting Brendan. "Oh, there he is," she said pointing to the threesome who sat huddled against a wall. Brendan was in a wicked mood, hissing, spitting and denigrating everyone in the restaurant and many who were not even aware of the restaurant's existence. He was a portrait of a cauldron of venomous vipers.

"Why don't you introduce Mr. Farrell to B.B.," I suggested warmly.

"Oh, do you think he'd mind?" the lady asked.

"I'm sure he'd be delighted," I said robustly.

The pair approached Brendan who was already on his feet awaiting their arrival. A look of welcoming delight was on his face.

"This is Mr. James T. Far—"

Brendan's look suddenly changed. "And who granted the likes of you permission to approach this table," Brendan roared at Dunham "Why don't you take yourself and all of your jungle bunnies and fuck off back to Africa where yiz belong, swingin' out of trees be yur tails—" Brendan never once looked at Farrell. Katherine was shocked. She quickly returned to where I sat.

"Your friend' is even sicker than I thought," Katherine said as the two hurried through the adjacent passageway.

Brendan did not particularly dislike Farrell. He merely hated what he stood for. Farrell was a very successful novelist who espoused in his writing the theory that man "is forever capable of creating himself anew." The name James T. Farrell was amongst the oodles of famous names that adorned the plaques on the front wall of the hotel. He was the only one still amongst the living. He was also regarded by many as the best living novelist in the land; the son of a wagon driver and an Irish domestic servant. His trilogy, *Young Lonigan, The Young Manhood of Studs Lonigan* and *Judgment Day* earned for him the reputation of being a bold, brazen realistic penman whose writing—albeit lacking in polish—was fast, tough and raw. He was a working-class writer. He had the reputation of penning up to five thousand words per day. He had written dozens of books. Farrell's fans numbered in the millions.

The following morning Katherine phoned me up, "Just who does that poor woman think she is married to? Does she think he's God? I presented them with a fair bill, everything was carefully itemized, what do they want?"

"Don't worry, Kat," I said, "pay no attention to him, his remarks are mere Behanesque doggerel, *you* know the hubris of the man. If anything comes up like I said, I'll take your side. *Slan leat.*"

One afternoon in Dunham's apartment, a socialite friend of hers pointed to me and said, "Look at him, he looks like Behan! Is he related to him?"

"No, he's not," Katherine intoned wearily, "but he talks just like him, he has the exact same personality."

The following day I phoned and advised her, "If a lawsuit is instigated, be sure that I will take Behan's side. I don't take to your brand of insult kindly."

Geis paid Dunham's bills. The proposed lawsuits were forgotten.

Brendan was now knee-deep doing playlet-inquests into the past, present and future. He was an accumulation of himself, complex, troubled, obsessed, detesting his primitive Catholicism and fearing the fork of the devil. However, in his own strange, junketing, effusive way the sporadic good humor that was once characteristic of him periodically returned to baffle us.

One night as Brendan and I were moseying down one of the halls of the hotel, we heard a great deal of screaming. We charged into the semiprivate bathroom where the calamitous clatter was coming from and discovered a three-hundred-pound woman sitting in a bathtub. "What's up," Brendan asked, "is the water too hot for yew or what?" Then he turned the cold water spigot on full blast.

"No, no, no," the bewildered woman yelled, "it's me, I'm stuck. I can't get out of this tub!"

I ran to my room and got a twenty foot piece of gantline that I had carried in my sea bag for years. (I had used this length of rope to hang up my punching bag on dozens of ships at sea.) I returned to the bathroom, draped one end of the rope over the top of the steel towel rack, made a bowling-on-a-bite with the same end, then dropped the makeshift bosun's chair down over the head and the half-acreage back of the damsel in distress. With the belly of the line now hanging at an approximate hundred-thirty-five-degree angle, I tied the bitter end of the line to the plumbing beneath the toilet water tank. My operation extrication was about to begin. "Come on, Brendan, let's jump on this with our hands," I said as I took hold of the belly of the semitaut line. "Hold on, lady, and we'll have you out in no time," I said, as we heaved frantically.

In split seconds, Brendan and I, the steel towel rack, along with some ancient rusted pipes, a load of plaster and the toilet tank were all in the bathtub. Finally we managed to get the weeping, quivering woman into her room and at ease with herself.

However, the lady's somnolence was of a short-lived duration. The next time that we saw her was later in the evening, and in the lobby. She was being patronized, spoken softly to and pandered to by two big white-coated men from a nearby clinic.

"But shur yur only goin' for a pause and any sensible man would tell yew that in these troublesome times, a pause is as good as a vacation," Brendan assured the unhappy lady as she was driven away.

Later, one of the Haitian housemaids explained to us that on that day when the fat woman awoke, she had instantly noticed that the bed had been moved some two feet from where it originally was. "There's the proof," the lady had shouted, pointing to an impression of cleaner rug adjacent to the feet of the bed, " the hotel is crawling with them."

The infamous Chelsea mice had once again been up to their niggling antics. "They picked up my bed and shook it violently," the lady charged.

The management and the local police wholeheartedly agreed and called for additional assistance.

Every so often, in the Chelsea Hotel, the cleaning department decides to move a bed or two and clean the rugs uunannounced.

Brendan was now once again in good spirits. For the next day or two I witnessed him, with Beatrice and Rae, going up and down Twenty-third Street waving his old familiar papal waves and good-naturedly stopping here and there to chat and to commiserate briefly on the vast uncertainties of life and to comment on his work in progress. "Great, great stuff—I'm tapin' a marvelous book, yew'll go mad for it, shur if the Mycenaean poets could have a go at it, well fuck it all, says I to mesself, so can I, wha! I'm only now gettin' in on their act of writing books by improvisin' them in talk," he told a Chelsea-ite.

Rae and Beatrice chuckled and accompanied him, holding both his arms below the elbows, always careful never to make a slip and take his spotlight from him as they commented briefly and praised his courage, steadfastness and dedication, their own Spartan discipline reasserting itself.

In due time the invaluable compilation of tapes would be flown to London, where Rae would extract, edit and carve books to be published under the name of Brendan Behan.

But as usual Brendan did not sustain himself for long.

One night, coming up to the end of June, as I walked north on Eighth Avenue, in the far-off distance I saw the emaciated, Gothic figure of Brendan shouting and running headlong into streams of fast-moving oncoming traffic. I quickened my pace, grabbed hold of him and dragged him to the curbstone, but he pushed me away and charged into the moving vehicles. He continued to shout at the top of his congested lungs, "I'm Brendan Behan, I'm Brendan Behan, I'm the author of two Broadway plays . . ."

Finally I managed to get him onto the side of the busy street, where we staggered into a moving bus. "Will yew for fucksake watch where yur goin,' yew culshie cunt yew," he roared at the driver while he kicked and pounded on the front fender. "You murdered yur mother and devoured your poor children." We struggled ahead and waded through a nest of feeding pigeons. Brendan kicked at the pigeons as they flew off and fluttered above his head. "Will yiz go away, yiz murderin' capitalists, are yiz trying to crucify me or what?" he screamed at the pigeons while flailing the air with his berserk hands.

Once again he was engaged in a never-ending losing battle between illusion and reality. He was totally debilitated and staggering precariously, a withering churl in a ghostly maze. His crapulous shabbiness was again rejected in the deluxe Spanish eatery. Once again he was asked to leave.

Through long arduous years of masterful manipulation and an adept ability to brag and to compete, with iconoclastic vigor and vehemence, Brendan had constructed an image of invincibility. Now the old self-esteem had finally faded, eroded. His behavior was alternating between that of a crazed blowfish and an old tightrope walker, attempting a last lark on a wind-whipped wire. The fire and the force were nowhere in evidence. The old greed, the gluttony and the gregariousness had quickly waned in exchange for sympathy and smidgens of compassion. The late night and early morning specter of Brendan sitting hunched up outside the Oasis or on the steps of the Silver Rail was commonplace. "Excuse me s-sir, b-but d-do yew honestly believe that I'm a p-phony?? Do yew regard me as a man? Do yew believe in the life hereafter?" he shouted into the faces of those who stopped and stared in disbelief.

Brendan's greed for life had known no restraint. He had put to use his every impulse, whim and incarnate evilry to garner notoriety and fame, almost always at the emotional expense of a friend or a wet-nurse. He had burned a lifetime, sharpening his tongue and whetting his appetite, only to be here now, in this sad and sorry state, totally consumed by the wicked machinations which he himself had feasted so voraciously upon.

The light of day had become his greatest enemy, a thing too much to deal with. Night. Its external, nocturnal and ubiquitous maze and measureless maw became the new theater of his life and the last bastion where he could work out his dreams and fantasies.

Eighth Avenue between Fourteenth and Forty-second streets, where he wandered, is for the faceless men, the wandering souls, the has-beens, the perverts, the pill poppers, the weed-heads, the winos, and the derelicts, their frozen landscape, an arena where they may wallow and eke out a mite of last-minute solace. This "boulevard of broken dreams," haunted souls, evaporated spirits and desiccated, living ghouls comes to life at night.

In a somnambulistic haze, when the darkly anonymous world of night began to deepen around the small frightened figure, Brendan, his right shoulder listing heavily to the starboard, could be seen wending his way west. Buttressed by a quick intake of fortifying liquids, the once proud, boastful gnome with the pen of fire in his hand was headed into the impending blackness to once again live out and to assuage the fantasies and the fears that had been the cathartic force of his evil genius and his rocketlike propulsion to fame and glory. "Excuse me s-sir, b-but could yew get a t-thrill out of w-watching a boy of s-six undress . . . ?" The cadaverous figure whom he had stopped to ask stumbled away in a wet-blanketlike haze to continue his panhandling pursuits without ever knowing of the identity of the man or the true terror in his soul.

The little pachyderm with the sad, sagging jowls and the squinting flatfish eyes stumbled ahead and continued in the pursuit of his assuagement. He bumbled ahead and told himself semibelievable yarns of his one-man cyclonic attacks on British armored vehicles that existed only in the far-out reaches of his fogged brain.

In a bar on Sixteenth Street, in the presence of a horde of malcontents, pushers, flesh peddlers, child molesters, nodders, muggers and murderers, rapists, anarchists, arsonists and other desirables, he did a final, partial strip, then improvised his Glasnevin gun by taking in hand an empty Coca-Cola bottle. Brendan once again reenacted his shoot-out: "Fire . . . fire . . . fire . . . what wuz I to do, I only murdered them because they were trying to murder me . . ."

He continued to rave, rant and blatter like a man with an advanced brain impairment. His glorious madness, his inimitable pomposity and his deep dark need to vent his white-hot venom was a virtuoso absurdity to behold. Here, and only here, in the pitch dark ubiquitousness could he consume himself so self-indulgently. Eighth Avenue was his cul-de-sac. Here in the purgatory of smut and flesh peddlers, during these walpurgisnachts of his great American dream, Brendan continued to stagger from one gaunt-faced zombie to another, his fraying ego still blazing like a kaleidoscope of neon tubes burning beyond their time. "Yussir . . . d-do yew believe . . . I mean d-do yew honestly think that there is something out there? Something bigger than ourselves . . . Do yew know me, sir, wha? . . . I mean do yew think that it was all a sham? A put-on? . . ."

During the final days at the Chelsea, the sounds of tapes being played and replayed were heard throughout the hallways. "My name is Brendan Behan. . . . If I am anything at all, I am an Irish man of letters. . . . It is said that the greatest honor that any man can have bestowed upon him is to have his work produced on Broadway. I am proud to be able to state that I am one such author. . . . I believe in equality for all people and that all men are created equal. . . . I have never seen myself as anything but a man of destiny and fairness. . . . If I have killed, I killed while in the commission of my duty as a soldier in the ranks of the Irish Republican movement. . . . America is a great and wonderful land. It is my newfound land, the land of my love. To those of yew who do not love America, I say to yew, yew must hate the whole human race." Brendan was back on the old battle turf playing the part of the puncher who could punch even harder than the mother superior.

A short time prior to the making of this recording, Brendan and I got into a heated argument in the Lido Bar on Seventh Avenue. The argument was over politics. Brendan wickedly slagged America and referred to it as being, "an imperial capitalistic state and the cause of me downfall."

I thoroughly assured him, "The cause of your downfall is the natural consequence of your own lifelong, unique brand of hedonistic imperial capitalism and piggishness. Insofar as my sentiments about the country are concerned, I regard it as my newfound land. Any son of a hate-mongering bitch who hates it, would have to hate the whole human race. Personally, I'm tired of ingrates and hate-mongers. As an Irish-born, American merchant marine, I am proud to say that I participated in two wars for the country. If need be, I will gladly participate in two more. *L'chaim.*"

Brendan referred to me as "a typical opportunist and capitalist," then he began to make a beeline for the door. I put my arms out and stopped him. "But Brendan how could you say such a thing to me. I, Peter Joseph Arthurs. I. Me. He. He, who has given alms. He who has eaten the Sultan's garbage. He who has worked so arduously in the house of the living dead." I burst out laughing into his face and let go of him. He barreled out the door in a huff, muttering and mumbling as he went.

Today a plaque is riveted to the facade of the Chelsea Hotel. It reads:

In Memory of
Brendan Behan
1923–1964

"To America
My New Found Land:
The Man That Hates You
Hates the Human Race."

Dedication from *Brendan Behan's New York* . . . written in The Hotel Chelsea in the spring of 1963.
Presented by:

Bernard Geis Associates
March 20, 1965

In actuality, the book was taped in Dublin just before his death.

XVII

From the beginning, Brendan had misconstrued my sexuality. Now he was painfully aware of his mistake. Our one-sided libidinal encounters and ersatz sex caused him enormous psychic trauma, fits of rage and repeated black voids.

He loved America and loathed Ireland. Beatrice detested New York and longed for Dublin. Under no circumstances did she want to have her baby in America. Brendan was adamant about hanging on in the Chelsea. The very thought of returning to the land that spawned him sent shivers up his spine. He was vividly aware of his rapid decline, his need for libation and his inability to keep his hands away from children, when drunk.

He had always referred to the Irish as a thankless, reviling, lambasting lot. I wholeheartedly agreed. He feared their taunting, their super-intuitiveness and need to destroy their most revered sons.

More than anything in the world I sorely wanted to batter the whey out of Brendan Behan. I felt that he had succeeded overwhelmingly in using, misusing, and abusing me. Now I wanted Brendan out of the country and home in Dublin amongst the people whom he feared the most. However, one major factor stood in the path of my plan—my economic status. I was broke and in need of a tank-cleaning paycheck. If I were to succeed in pushing him out of America, I would have to act swiftly.

Early in the morning of Thursday, June the twenty-eighth, I phoned the SIU, spoke to the port agent and informed him that my name could be put on the list for all immediate tank-cleaning operations. My rent was due at the Chelsea. Brendan's libations were becoming excessively expensive.

A few minutes later I found myself walking south on Eighth Avenue, on my way to a hardware store to purchase a can of lye and a bottle of ammonia. My intention was to mix the magic concoction and drop it into Brendan's much-used toilet bowl. Brendan had lost much of his control over his bladder and bowels. Calamitous dashes to the bathroom were commonplace.

Suddenly the chickens came home to roost. For years I had been living in Brendan's quagmire, a quagmire that had the consistency of quicksand. By my own immature, ill-conceived volition I was the protagonist in the muck. I deserved the consequence. I turned and walked back to the Chelsea.

Complacent in my decision to disengage myself further from his psychosexual sadomasochistic games, I called the Seaman's Church Institute, spoke to the chaplain in charge of the active Seaman's Credit Bureau and made arrangements to move into the "dog house" (Seaman's Institute). I packed up my life's belongings and began to move them into the lobby.

Sometime around noon, as I was placing a cardboad carton on the floor, I looked up and found a familiar fleecy hand tugging at my sleeve. "Listen avick, will yew cum and have a bite to eat and a sup to put in yur guts? The other cow is upstairs going mad lookin' for yew."

"I'd love to Bren, but I'm pushed for time. I've got to keep moving. I'm on my way to—"

"Will yew never mind that and just listen to yur elders, cumoncum-oncumoncum . . ." Brendan seemed excessively excited and anxious. My curiosity instantly burgeoned.

We sat down in the number one booth of the El Q. Beatrice joined us. "Oh, there's Peter," she said, as she sat down. "I've been looking high and low for you, where were you?"

Brendan clapped his hands for service. Carlos Hernandez, a Cuban-born waiter, rushed over with three menus. "Good afternoon, gentlemen," he said.

"We know what we want," Brendan said, waving the menus away. "Take care of this fella first," he said crisply, indicating me, "he's as hungry as a pack of wild dogs chewing on the arse of a mangy goat through a barbed wire fence."

"I just had my lunch at the Y, really I'm not up to it."

"Listen yew," he roared into my face, "I don't give a fiddler's fuck, where, what, or who, yew ate, yew are here now, and yur goin' to eat even if it fuckin' well chokes yew. Give him a sirloin steak and a lobster . . . and make it three bottles of yur best wine," he shouted at the waiter who stood poised with pencil and paper in hand. Then

Brendan ordered a concoction of steaks, chops, lobsters, octopus and wine for himself and his wife.

The next few minutes were spent in clumsy silence. Finally Brendan spoke, "Well Mrs. Behan," he barked into his wife's face, "yew'll soon be on yur own, then what will yew do, maby yew can write a book, why not call it *My Life with Brendan* . . . Of course yew can always remarry or go back to flogging tickets to the culshies in the museum where I met yew, huh?"

"Peter, will you be a good boy and tell Brendan that—"

"Shut yur fuckin' face, yew aul cow yew, before I shut it for yew," he bellowed into her tearstained face.

"Leave the poor girl be, will you for God's sake, Brendan."

The food arrived and we ate and drank voraciously. "We'll order some more," Brendan said with unusual exuberance.

"Brendan please, I can't eat another pick, I'm full to the—"

"Never mind, eat, eat, eat."

I arose, went to the bar, "Manuel," I said to the man who was bartender and half owner of the pub, "I wish you would tell me what is going on here today with Brendan?"

"Well," said the easygoing Spaniard, "you are aware that in the past we have had a great deal of trouble with your friend. We were forced to throw him out more than once. However we decided that today would be *Brendan Behan's Day*. Today is *his* day. We invited him and his friends. Food and drink is on the house. Eat up. It's our pleasure, dear boy. Go to your friend. He is looking at you," the bar man said as he kept an eye on Brendan. I returned to the booth a great deal wiser than when I had left it.

Obviously someone had informed the former seafarers who were now the owners of the bar that Behan was one of the world's greatest publicity machines. Business at the El Quijote was grim.

"What were yew talking to that fucking Franco lout about?" Brendan snapped.

"Why, is this some sort of confession box? Am I obligated to tell you everything I do?"

"Just shut up and eat your sirloin and lobsters," he growled. "Yew never got steak and lobsters when yew were a boy growin' up in Dundalk, did yew?" he said, leaning closer and barking into my face. Silence ensued.

"No, I didn't Brendan," I said in a subdued, supercontrolled voice, "and had I stayed at home in Dundalk, I would never have had the great privilege in life of meeting a first-class degenerate the likes of you, would I?" I said leaning even closer into his face.

Smatterings of wine and lobster shot from his salivating mouth onto our lapels and into the huge silver plateful of food that sat on the table.

Brendan flinched, winced and struggled to stifle his shock.

My uncompromising glare bore on. Suddenly Brendan looked like a man who had suffered from chronic trichinosis for all of his life. His head tilted and banged against the maroon-muraled wall. The flesh on the right side of his serrated face crumbled. I felt sad but satisfied. "I intend to finish my food," I said in a softer voice.

My assault had truncheoned his conscience, but Brendan was a one-upmanship craftsman and a sore loser. His face and eyes contorted in misery and disbelief. He sat pallid and impassive, as though the apex of his life had been swallowed up for all eternity in the brutal ring of my undeniable accusation. Here was Brendan the blatherskite, reduced to silence. His face was purplish with the hue of blue and wrath. It appeared as though a fit of convulsions or loss of equilibrium might overtake him.

In the course of the next few minutes he tried a number of times to venture a word in his own defense, but on each occasion, just as he was about to fight back, I filled my mouth with another goblet of the fine Spanish wine. Brendan's mouth continued to quiver while his features twitched and twisted. He struggled hard not to allow his pain to become evident, but the swift and sudden slap of my shocking abuse was indelibly there.

His head and shoulders drooped. Then the once fiery little elf mustered his ego and his equilibrium and again attempted to fight back. "Listen yew," he attempted in a somewhat controlled manner, "but if I'm to—"

"Just hold on for a fuckin' minute, sir," I said, "but didn't I just get through telling you that I intended to finish my dinner in peace. Now what are you anyway, some sort of reprehensible little faggot, a pig, a lemming! Who the fuck do you think you are to go about dictating the rights and the wrongs of life to anyone, huh! Do you think that you're talking to some twelve-year-old boy in some steam bath, huh? You fucking low-life living cesspool you."

His frame sank even deeper into the red upholstered depths of the booth. His chin hit his chest in resignation. His blood crawled scarlet up his face, a human montage of malignancy, pain, regret, guilt and humiliation.

An eerie silence pervaded the booth. Beatrice's face was in her quivering hands. For a flurry of moments I felt a twinge of remorse and regret. However the memory of that wretched day, June fifteenth, 1961, suddenly came to mind. My composure came back. I continued to stuff my mouth with the epicurean meal.

But the verbal battle was not over.

"Why don't yew sue me?" Brendan blurted. "If you feel that I used yew."

"Listen you," I roared into his face, "didn't I tell you that I intended to eat my dinner without anymore of *your* fuckin' gab, if you excrete out of your mouth one more sound, I'll be forced to pick up that plate,"

I said pointing to the shells and silverware, "and shove it down your yap." Just as I was in the process of picking up the plateful of bones, oyster shells, shrimp and lobster shells, Gilbert Ortero and Carlos came charging over and pulled me off him, then pleaded with me to go easy.

"Now Mr. Behan," I said, as I wiped my mouth with a red cloth napkin, "there are basically two kinds of people in this world, the listeners and the nonlisteners. Needless to say, the listeners eventually become learners. You sir, are of the legion of the latter, and on that note, sir, I'll thank you for the luvly dinner and bid you adieu." I arose and said to Beatrice who was blocking my exit, "Excuse me B., but I must go, I have a number of important things to take care of." I again turned to Brendan. "Now sir, in regards to the lawsuit which you have mentioned, no fuckin' way will I contribute further to your bullshit fame, if you want someone to sue you for publicity stunts, get someone else. Not on the strength of my good name will you get any more of your trumped-up publicity." I departed feeling like a man; a whole, totally vindicated person who for the first time in his life was navigating under his own steam. His own oxygen. As I was entering the adjoining corridor, I looked back and saw Brendan clawing the air, and trying to speak but unable to do so. It was as if he had swallowed a giant squid as opposed to a couple of lobsters and a few octupus.

I went to my room, took down a sheaf of yellow papers on which I had previously written a number of personal anecdotes and sat on my bed. I left the door ajar.

The little man, who for so long had prided himself for being a tried and true champion in the one-upmanship sweepstakes, would in his quiet desperation underestimate my Celtic psyche and make a final stand to even the score. Underestimating the intelligence and the intestinal fortitude of the Irish proletariat is an age-old failing of the Irish upper-middle class, the pompous and the successful. The Irish are cultivators of contenders as opposed to champions. I was morally determined to keep this victory intact, come hell or high water.

Fifteen minutes went by. Half an hour. One full hour. Finally, a familiar knock came to the door, "Is it yurself me aul scholeara? Are yew there? Are yew busy or what are yew up to?" Brendan was an effective predator.

"Yes, yes, I'm in. Is it B.? Come in, man, come in, be with you in a min."

His face was aflutter with false cordiality and an ingratiating grin. The reason for his visit was evident in the corners of his mouth, the curl of his lip and in the recess of his squinting eyes.

"What are yew up to avick?"

"Oh nothing of any major significance. Just jotting down a word or two here and there," I said, matter-of-factly.

Silence prevailed while I continued to delete and jot.

"Listen avick, but I was just wondering if yew'd like to . . . Well what

I mean is . . . bejayzus me aul son, but yew didn't have to eat the fuckin' face off me in front of the other aul cow below, but shur I suppose yew had every right to do so . . . Shur then again, shur I suppose that that's the way it is in this ipso facto mad fuckin' business that we're in, wha! Great man avick, great man."

Feeling thoroughly assured that his footing was now solid, he moved about with the grace of a starved cat eyeing a juicy bird. I continued to sigh, delete and add. The tension in the room became straitjacket.

"And shur what are yew working on atall atall, me aul son," Brendan started, "I hope it's not me yur writin' about." Silence prevailed.

"Listen Brendan," I said crisply, raising my head from the sheets, "but you will have to excuse me. I'm working extra hard on these personal anecdotes, unlike the ones I wrote in California. Arthur Miller has promised to read and edit them for me. I'm pressed for time, call me later . . ."

I raised my manuscript and hid my face.

"Listen yew," Brendan roared through my manuscript, "yew better not be writing about me. Go home to yur ships where yew belong and leave the writing to the writers."

Calmly I put the sheaf of papers on my bed, put my feet on the floor, looked Brendan in the eye and said in a soft voice, "No Brendan, I'm not writing about *you,* I'm writing about people, people who were and still are the real meaning of my existence."

His face swelled with rage. His body shook from head to toe. Suddenly in a fit of uncontrolled fury he made a desperate grab for my papers. I grabbed him by the arms, above the elbows, "Now you listen to me, you rat-faced chicken-fucker," I said as I shook him, "if it wasn't for the commercial genius of Joan Littlewood, your 'Quare Fucker,' your 'Hostage Hooligan' and your 'Borstal Ballox' would never have been heard of. You sir are in no position to tell anyone what to write about or whom to write of."

His face dropped to his chest. I let go of him.

Brendan was incredulous; a puny cry of agony stifled in his throat; the stunned elf became immobilized. Then his body shuddered spasmodically. For a brief few moments he struggled to hold on determinedly. As he attempted to recover his equilibrium, his face grew even more cyanotic. Another spasm sent the canted little wreck spinning against a wall, his original sense of mission apparently abandoned as his slitty eyes dilated and tried to assess the meaning of what was taking place. A wave of hysteria and hopelessness washed over him, evident in the twitch of his quivering lips and the look in his glazed eyes. A plaintive scream escaped from his mouth. His breath came in protracted heaves. He lunged for the door, but his left foot crossed his right and sent him pirouetting against the door frame. Watching the desperate, ghostly little figure go through these pathetic perambulations, I felt a sudden feeling of elation and euphoria well up in me.

Pawing and staggering, he finally made it out the door and down the winding hallway. I ran after him. "Oh excuse me for an important moment, Brendan," I said, "but there is a thing or two I want you to help me with before you vanish!" I said exuberantly while I stood in front of him with pen and paper in hand and blocking his exit to the stairway. "First of all B., was it Thursday the fourteenth or Friday the fifteenth of June 1961 that you went to the big blowout at Ernie Kovacs'?" He cringed and sighed. "Also, how many, in your opinion, a rough opinion will suffice, clarion calls for the passage of laws to imprison the pedophiles of the world did you make since I met you?"

The solipsistic man grabbed hold of his chest, retched and staggered down the marble steps. I returned to my room and did some more self-inventory taking, then phoned the SIU hall and announced that something very urgent had come up and I would very definitely not be able to accept a tank-cleaning offer for a while. Then I phoned the dog-house and canceled my reservations. Also, I left strict instructions with the switchboard, "under no circumstances, are you to put through any A.M. calls from the Behans."

One thing was now clear in my mind, beyond the shadow of a doubt: Brendan Behan was wandering in the antechambers of his imminent demise. If I were to cauterize old hurts! if I were to gain a fair margin of victory and with a comfortable edge to boot, I would have to act swiftly. I blessed myself, prayed to God, asked for his guidance then asked Him to forgive me if I was going astray and doing wrong. Next I phoned my attorney, Thomas Gordon, at his office in Brooklyn, "Thomas, Peter Arthurs. Listen, you always said that you wanted to meet my famous buddy, Brendan. Well, I believe that he's just about due to fly the coop to Dublin, better come to the Chelsea right away, O.K.? See you."

Later that evening in the El Q. I introduced the Behans to my attorney. The three talked for awhile, then Gordon purchased a round of drinks, excused himself and left. Prior to his departure, Gordon asked me not to let it be known to his mother that he had drunk with Brendan. The Gordons were strict Irish Catholics.

"He seems like a nice chap," Beatrice blurted out, "what does he do?"

"Oh, he's an attorney, Bea, my attorney. I just retained him to sue some dirty rotten son of a bitch that has been taking advantage of my strength of mind and body . . . It will be a dirty fight, but I expect to win. The public will love it." The Behans eyed one another in horror, then sped through the glass door as though the bar were on fire.

Prior to his departure, I had gotten a personal loan of fifty dollars from Gordon. Half of the money was to pay my rent for the following week at the Chelsea. The other half was to eat on.

While cleaning the bowels of the S.T. *National Defender,* I had informed the port captain and other steamship executives who were aboard during the operation, that through an unpatentable but proven new rigging invention of mine I could guarantee a cleaner ship and a faster job, but for a sizable bonus at the end of the trip.

"Impossible," they said.

"Not so," said I, "I have made it work on a flotilla of other tankers." My invention had proven itself to be very viable and valuable in its time- and money-saving advantages. My reputation as a meticulous tank-cleaner was becoming known far and wide. My special formula for deep-tank rigging, then put into operation, prevented the pump men from having to cut off the sludge discharging pumps, thus stopping the entire butterworthing operation in progress in a given set of tanks. Thus, invaluable "blowing-out," rebutterworthing, rerigging, and chemicalizing time was saved.

My method was designed to shift butterworth machines in the bottom compartment by manipulating and tripping gantlines, leading from the bottom to the upper main deck, through the tank trunks and butterworthing plates. It was designed specifically for use in very deep superships, that is, ships whose tanks are heavily fortified by steel bulkheads and bays, and excessively complicated to reach by normal procedure. The tanker corporation owners had finally adhered to my advice, and promised me a bonus.

The S.T. *National Defender* had arrived in the port of Baton Rouge on the day that I had guaranteed it would. I picked up my discharge and my two hundred fifty dollars per day for my employment. However, I was informed that I would have to pick up my bonus money at the office, 10 Columbus Circle, in New York.

On three different occasions, the staff at the office advised me that my problem was "shipboard business" and had nothing to do with the office. I was also informed that if I returned to the office, the police would be called. I retained Thomas Gordon and instigated a suit for breach of promise.

My reason for retaining Gordon was never explained to the Behans.

My name-calling had a visceral impact on Brendan. The glass of red wine that he was guzzling at the time of my initial outburst was the last that he would ever soak up in America. In the days to come, albeit he was now on the dry, Brendan sank deeper and deeper into the winter of his discontent. His attitude became one of desultory menace, sarcasm, and scorn. His chill sense of status was like that of an ancient hobbyhorse groaning and creaking towards its final jaunt. The literalness of life overshadowed his every other thought as he entered a deep dark realm of change and unusual personal inventory taking; that terrible territory of petrification and penance when all men gaze hopelessly into their pasts when their futures are no longer a thing to be weighed.

On a number of occasions I came upon him perched in his ormolu lobby chair, staring off, pointing, muttering, fantasizing and behaving as though he were making a last desperate grapple and grope for a spark of equanimity. His features sagging, his eyes staring glassily and accusingly, the crinkle of a smile intermittently seeping into his sadsack face. Brendan's reminiscences were surly, dull, and disdainful. The panoply of his impending second parenthood, the transitoriness of his days past and the Dublin albino dog trainer libel suit weighed heavily upon him. He watched me like a hawk eyeing an edible lizard, never looking me square in the eye, when he passed me in the lobby or on the street.

Brendan was now discovering how fleeting fame could be.

He needed his death like an old plow horse needed to be put to rest. Now with death as the inescapable final aspect of life to be dealt with, Brendan for the first time in his life was fully aware of the undeniable affirmation of life itself. No longer were the sounds of his sweet, maudlin, bombing, shooting mantras reverberating through Chelsea town. His Quijote meetings with R. E. L. Masters became like that of the bad boy and the forgiving priest.

On Saturday afternoon, after I had finished a workout at the Y, I suggested to Pedro, a new friend, a coffee-colored Puerto Rican, to come back to the hotel with me for a cup of coffee. We traveled by way of the El Q.

Brendan was sitting at the bar with Masters. At my suggestion Pedro and I stopped for a lemonade. Brendan became hysterical as he ogled the exceptionally good-looking boy in the mirror that adorned the rear of the bar. To exacerbate his misery, I put my arm around the boy's shoulder, ruffled his hair, stood up and said aloud, "Come on Pedro, you and I have some very important things to do." I paid the bill and departed through the adjoining corridor, stopping short at the door to look back.

Brendan was standing at the end of the bar watching my every move, hysteria in his face. Then he dashed back to where Masters was sitting. Pedro and I then went up to my room to sit down and discuss the topic that we had planned to discuss from the moment of our first meeting: the prospect of his becoming a professional merchant seaman through my sponsorship in the SIU.

For the next day or two I kept up my pursuit of Brendan, but in the lobby, in the El Q. and in the Oasis, whenever he saw me approach, he ran like a frightened puppy dog with Beatrice in hot pursuit. A pang of guilt reverberated through me at the painful sight of the dying Brendan and the pregnant Beatrice scurrying for cover. However, the sudden recollection of one of many bitter, bilious memories enabled me to carry on with my odious mission, a mission that had to be accomplished at all costs.

I was almost broke. In a matter of a few short days I would be forced for economic reasons to catch a berth. I wanted Brendan out of the country before I would have to work hard to achieve my goal. I left.

His wife's baby was due in November. The female menses of child-bearing would be most intolerable and viewed as a horrible impingement by him. I was also aware that a comfortable time margin would be mapped out by him to return to America from Ireland. If he were still alive he would venture back to America no later than the end of September or early October. However, the chances were that he would meet his maker or become too hopeless to make another transatlantic crossing. For both of us, time was running out.

Sunday, June the thirtieth, in the Oasis Bar, I caught up to a bottlenecked Brendan. He was hemmed in, sitting in a corner booth. Rae sat adjacent to him. Beatrice sat opposite him. A clog of minions and vassals pandered to him and sat in a semicircle. At the time I had entered the bar, Brendan was bragging about how great he was treated by the French press and French critics over his dramatic success with their production of *The Hostage*. He was speaking in English but his intonations were French.

"In Paris, I was quite a bigshot, the Martini Company, the biggest brewery in the business, made me the guest of honor at a party for me play. The party was held in their headquarters in the Champs-Elysées. Did yew know that Jean-Louis Barrault is a great admirer of mine, trew another big going-away shindig for me, and why not, wasn't *The Hostage* the best thing that happened to Paris in years?"

I listened for a while, then moved over to his booth and sat down. Brendan instantly switched his talk to a time when he had purportedly done battle with "two big fuckin' cabbage-headed cunts on the island of Carrareo." I patiently awaited the opportune moment. Brendan eyed me coldly and with trepidation. Finally I moved and engaged him in a forced question-and-answer conversation. He flinched, winced, stuttered and stammered.

"Wha! Must have been some punch-up, Brendan . . . hmmm," I said dreamily.

Brendan's face twisted in agony. "F-fuckin jayzus, is this to be another crucifixion Sunday?"

"Oh, come on Mr. Behan," I retorted in an exasperated tone. "I am merely attempting to get this thing into its proper perspective," I said dramatically, as I reached over and took hold of his tiny quivering hand, then I began to examine its back and palm. "Hmm, could be, could be," I said, questioning the genuineness of the story that he was telling. Brendan quickly pulled his hand away, clenched a fist and banged it into the palm of the other hand to create a mite of visual sound effects. He continued his story. He looked pitifully puny and crazed. His face was blue and yellow. His eyes bulged. His head seemed swollen out of proportion and pushed down between his hunched shoulders.

Sitting there coldly observing the tiny manchild desperately attempting to put himself across as a worldly, one-punch, KO artist, I burst out laughing into his face. "Oh dear God, Brendan, is there no end?" I chuckled. "Whew! Are you stating in effect that you pivoted the total weight of your body from the ball of one foot to the other, then at the precise moment of impact, that this is the hand that broke the culshie camel's back when you—"

Brendan quickly pulled his sleeves down over his hands, leaped up onto the table, knocked over several glasses, jumped to the floor, fell, rolled over onto his side, screamed in pain, got up, and darted out the door. Rae ran after him.

"Oh my God, Peter, you, you above all people in the world, you are a man, how could you, surely you realize that Brendan is desperately ill and nowhere near the same Brendan that you knew in Hollywood two years ago!" Beatrice said, tears welling up in her face as she followed Rae and Brendan.

"The Brendan that I knew two years ago in Hollywood, huh! Was the carnivorous little swine any different then?" I shouted after her.

Halfway down the block I overtook Arthur Miller, who was moving at a slower pace. His fourteen-year-old brown-and-white basset hound was sniffing the ground and dawdling behind him.

The sad procession of humanity wended its way into the hotel lobby. Miller and I leaned on the fender of a furniture truck that was parked at the curbstone. Miller shook his head in compassion. "It's a shame Peter. Is there nothing you can do? What a waste!" Brendan's tortured face appeared at the window. He eyed us coldly.

"No Arthur, there is nothing I can do. This is the end . . ."

Brendan suddenly appeared on the sidewalk. He ran halfway out to where Miller and I were standing, shaking our heads. He tucked his thumbs up under his suspenders, snapped them, winced, and spewed a mouthful of saliva over the dog, then looked at Miller with malignancy in his face.

To avoid another unnecessary painful face-to-face encounter with Brendan, Miller walked west on Twenty-third Street.

I now held a four-point lead over the dying elf.

July first, late in the evening I again caught up to him in the lobby as he was sitting pondering his past and picking his nose. "Listen, B.," I said in a serious, very personally concerned, clear voice, "for the last couple of weeks around here, you have been doing a great deal of guffawing and with much eloquence on the subject of death and the life hereafter. Now I was just thinking to myself, hmm, death and all of its irrevocabilities et cetera, et cetera, hmm, who gives a fuck wha? I mean to say, sure the worms will get what's goin', but so what, why begrudge the poor little fuck faces a bit to eat? I mean, wasn't it yourself who always said 'Fuck the begrudgers and so forth?' Hmm . . . now what about that! Just think of those poor little cunts down there fuckin' about, blind as a bat, groping in the miasma, looking for a fig to keep their slimy bodies and souls together from the beginning of one dark night to the other wha! Well B., I have a friend, a nice chap, you'd love him, he earns his kip be workin' in a downtown morgue, now he claims that times are so tough that the cargoes of cadavers that they are getting lately are empty, vague, unworthy of burial. Now in regards to the life hereafter, ah! Well now, that's a worm of a different color and physical dimension. Now in my opinion, that is if I may be permitted to venture an opinion, for indeed I'm sure you will agree, dear B., that even I too, have a right to opine—"

Brendan screamed in misery and hurried to the elevator, his two slitty little eyes fusing into a single horror-stricken slash in the middle of his furrowing forehead. I ran after him and blessed him. *"Ego vos absolvo ab omnibus peccatis vestris in nomine Patri et Filii et Spiritu Sancti."* I blessed him again, *"In nomine Patri.* Now go with God, sir, the nonbegrudging jayzus will see you right. And remember, that the twenty-fifth of this month is the feast of St. Christopher, the patron of weary travelers." Brendan forsook the use of the crowded elevator and charged up the adjacent stairway.

Wednesday, July 3. Out of dire necessity I subwayed to the SIU hall and on the eleven o'clock call I "threw in" and got an able seaman's berth aboard the supership S.T. *Montpelier Victory.* Then I subwayed back to the Chelsea to pack my rags.

Outside of the Chelsea entrance I came across a very weary Beatrice. I was fully prepared to keep moving, but much to my surprise she walked over to me, extended her hand and said, "Good-bye, Peter, we're leaving today."

"Leaving today, Beatrice? I don't understand! Leaving to where?"

"We're going home on the Queen Elizabeth."

Her message somewhat surprised me, but sent waves of relief surging through me.

"Brendan is in the barbershop getting his hair cut," she intoned, pointing to the barbershop across the street.

"I'm leaving today also," I said, "I got a berth on a supertanker."

The news that I was shipping took her by surprise. She looked at me in terror as I began to cross the street, "Oh I'll just make it a short good-bye," I said reassuringly.

I stepped into the shop and found Brendan talking up a storm. He caught my reflection in the mirror. He winced, squirmed and closed his eyes. "I hear you're out today, B.," I said with great concern. "Your baby is due in November. I'll expect to see you in September, or October. With the help of God and of course the wonderful Arthur Miller, I will by then have a few well-polished stories finished. Maybe I will let you read them, I'll see!"

I held out my hand. Brendan's eyes remained shut and as tight as a fish's arsehole. His hand remained under the white barber's sheet. Finally one eye opened, a hand begrudgingly crept out, and took hold of mine as though it were an ancient mackerel. "Good-bye, B.," I said. "Maybe when you get back I will let you read the play that I'm work-ing on, but I won't promise. By then you'll almost be a father." He flinched and tried to pull his hand away. I tightened my grip. "If it's a boy calf, perhaps you will name him after me, wha?" With my free hand I scratched my scrotum. I let go of his hand, turned, opened the door and departed. I crossed the heavily trafficked thoroughfare. I walked up onto the Chelsea sidewalk, took in a deep breath and felt like a man walking in space. I had opted for a full house, but by sheer dint of fate had dealt myself a royal flush. In my heart of hearts I felt thoroughly sure that I would never again see Brendan Behan.

Had I informed him that we would both be heading out to sea at the same time, he would have boarded the *Queen Elizabeth* with the two women, planted them safely in their cabins, conjured up a quick excuse to see someone of importance in a smoking lounge, then darted down the gangway and back to the Chelsea neighborhood, where he would have remained in hiding until the ship had sailed.

On Wednesday, July 3, the *Queen Elizabeth* sailed for Ireland.

On Thursday, July 4, the *Montpelier Victory* sailed for Texas.

On Monday, July 8, the two ships reached their destinations.

XVIII

October 8, 1963, sitting in the huge mess hall of the supership *Montpelier Victory,* and in the process of finishing up a snack prior to going to the helm, I was set upon by my former watch partner Doyle Boyette, for no reason known to me. Boyette wound up with a broken nose and a mild concussion. I received chip fractures on the fourth and fifth fingers of my right hand.

On October 9, the orthopedic surgeon at the Houston Street Clinic placed my hand in a cast and declared me not fit for sea duty. I checked into the Chelsea. From the Garfinkles, I learned of Brendan's hospitalizations and steeper decline. He was spending little or no time in his home. Sometime during the first week of November, George Kleinsinger informed me that Brendan was preparing to return to New York.

On Friday November 22, President John F. Kennedy was shot dead in Dallas. Now I knew for sure that Brendan would never return. Such a brutal episode would surely cauterize his desires to return in any immediate future. He was the most easily frightened man that I had ever known.

Two days later, Beatrice's baby was born. Brendan promptly showed up for the televised party in the hospital. I also heard that later, at another celebration party in the Dolphin Hotel, Brendan arrived in the lobby pantless. He claimed that he had stopped off in the hotel bathroom but couldn't find any toilet paper and refused to put his pants back on. A roll of paper was quickly found.

Sometime around Christmas Willie Garfinkle's son had had a letter from Beatrice. Her prediction, according to the boy, was that Brendan was on his last legs. Later, none to my surprise, I heard that he had had himself circumcised. In another tabloid I read that he had been found unconscious near his mother's house, a huge gash on his forehead.

One night in the El Q. when I was staggering around drunk and in the throes of getting into another fisticuff, Ingeborg Morath, Arthur Miller's wife, came over to me, put her hand on my shoulder and said, "Come over to the booth, Peter, Arthur wants to talk to you!"

"I can't Inge, I'm too drunk, I'm ashamed of myself."

"That's O.K., come anyway, Arthur wants to talk to you."

I followed the gracious lady to the booth where Miller was, then sat down. They gave me a lecture on the perils of alcoholism. Later, in room 604, Inge cooked a meal for me and lectured to me some more. In the process of making his point clear, Arthur showed me the somewhat limited flexibility in his right wrist, an injury he had incurred in a fight on a T.2 tanker when he was a pipe fitter in the Brooklyn shipyard.

On March, 1, 1964, I received a fit-for-duty slip from the USPHS (United States Public Health Service) and a settlement from the Montpelier Tankship Corporation for the injury to my hand.

On March 4, I shipped as tank rigger and chemical sprayer aboard the S.T. *National Defender.* On St. Patrick's Day I was discharged in the port of Baton Rouge. I taxied to New Orleans, checked into the Roosevelt Hotel and made the rounds of my old Bourbon Street haunts.

A short while later I took the night coach to New York, checked into the Chelsea and left strict instructions with the clerk that I was not to be awakened under any circumstances until at least the P.M. hours of Saturday the twenty-first. I took a couple of downers, five fingers of whiskey and got into bed. Major tank-cleaning operations call for a minimum of eighteen to twenty hours work per day by the extra carefully selected personnel. I was beat.

At approximately five-thirty P.M. on the evening of Friday, March 20, Mr. Apple, the manager of the Chelsea phoned me. "Mr. Arthurs, there's a number of reporters here to talk to you about Brendan Behan. They want to interview you."

"But didn't I leave word that under no circumstances was I to be awakened. Just tell the shower that besides being a two-fisted battler and a literary genius, Brendan is a terrific guy, one of the great humanitarians of the century. Now is it O.K. if I go back to sleep?"

"Apparently you don't know Mr. Arthurs, your pal is dead—"

"*Dead!!!*"

"That's right, Mr. Arthurs, he died a few hours ago."

"*O.K.* Apple," I said, "you can send them up."

A twinge of sadness and guilt flickered in my brain. For a fleeting moment I felt that I had dismally failed in life, not only had I failed, I hastened the inevitable. Then a strange sense of relief came over me. Split seconds later a coterie of reporters headed by Dick Schaap of the *Herald Tribune* came to my room.

The next couple of hours were spent by me recounting and reminiscing and telling of Hollywood, the Kilmainham milk story and Brendan's fall down the stairs in Cuig.

On the night of the twentieth, and early in the A.M. of the twenty-first, New York's newspapers loudly announced the passing of Brendan.

The *New York Times:* "A REBEL HE LIVED, A REBEL HE DIED."

The *Herald Tribune:* "ON BEHAN'S BLOCK IN NEW YORK AS THE WORD SPREAD." (The reference was to the south side of Twenty-third Street.)

The *Daily News:* "GARGLE GETS BORSTAL BOY AT FORTY-ONE."

Being a life-long fantasist and ardent follower of funerals, I spent the weekend in the Oasis drinking, reading newspapers and watching TV bulletins concerning Brendan's death from jaundice, kidney complications, diabetes and alcohol. Patrons of the bar and Chelsea residents came by my booth to offer words of sympathy and bring me up to date with bits and pieces of news they had heard or read about his funeral.

Late that Sunday evening, alone and deep into my cups, I returned to my room exhausted, lay down and permitted the events of the past few days to come to focus in my mind's eye.

On March 21, Brendan's remains were removed from the Meath Hospital where he had died, to Donnybrook Church. The following day a mass was read and an honor guard, consisting of eight IRA officers, escorted the coffin from the church. The funeral procession wended its way past Cuig.

As the dirge moved on towards the desolate ground of Glasnevin Cemetery the crowd thickened, police officers saluted the coffin draped with the flag of the Irish Republic. A major turnout of his old comrades in the Republican movement marched on either side of his coffin in strict military phalanx. The politicians of Ireland, in solemn tribute to one of the most controversial Irishmen of the ages, agreed that no interference would come to the outlawed movement during their trek. They had gathered from far and wide to participate in this funeral, a funeral which was to go down in history as one of the biggest in the nation's history.

Commandant R. MacIonnraic and Deputy Prime Minister Mr. Lean MacEntee were present, representing Eamon De Valera, president of Ireland.

A fourteen-year-old boy, a bugler from the old Fianna, the organization that Brendan had joined when he was only six years old, sounded the Last Post.

Former IRA colleagues gave graveside orations. Priests, playwrights, poets, puncers, rebel patriots, pimps, prostitutes, bombers, dynamiters and gunfighters attended. A flock of women who were the mothers, the grannies, the great-grannies, the whores, wives and fishmongers of Dublin City collected and sprinkled a few twigs down upon the burnished lid. Lilting whispers wafted through rustling leaves and around the headstones. "He's gone now." "We won't see the likes of him again for many a moon." "He was one of a kind." "A marvelous man." "A genius. Too bad he was so innocent." "He loved life." "He adored children."

Later when the crowds had gone, the IRA guard of honor drew their revolvers and fired a last salute to their fallen blood brother.

Fire! Fire! Fire! The crackle of their shots reverberated across the high stone walls and throughout the somber city. Brendan had gone back to his Banba for the last time.

Suddenly I found myself laughing aloud. "B., you schemy little bastard yew. You won, didn't you—even in death, wha!"

I felt lonely, sad and empty, like a man dissected.